MW01389562

Foreign Policy
Decision-Making
in Nigeria

*This book is dedicated to my father,
Bassey Nda Inamete.*

Contents

List of Figures	9
Preface	11
Acknowledgments	13
1. Introduction	17
2. In the Beginning: The Balewa Era	20
3. The Ironsi Government Interlude	42
4. The Gowon Era	44
5. The Robust Years: The Muhammed/Obasanjo Period	62
6. The Shagari Government	104
7. Love the Nation: The Buhari Era	122
8. Economic and Security Components Do Also Matter: The Babangida Years	136
9. The Shonekan Government Interlude	237
10. The Abacha Government	240
11. Opening a New Chapter: The Abubakar Era	281
12. The Obasanjo Government: The Second Episode	285
13. An Overview of Nigeria's Foreign Policy Decision-Making System	289
Bibliography	296
Index	311

Figures

Foreign Policy Decision-Making Structures during the Balewa Government	26
Foreign Policy Decision-Making Structures during the Gowon Government	47
Foreign Policy Decision-Making Structures during the Muhammed/Obasanjo Government	63
Main Decision-Making Structures Involved in Nigeria's International Relations during the Shagari Government	107
Main Foreign Policy Decision-Making Structures during the Buhari	124
Foreign Policy Decision-Making Structures during the First Phase of the Babangida Government, August 1985 to October 1988	141
Foreign Policy Decision-Making System during the Second Phase of the Babangida Government, November 1988 to Early August 1990	142
Foreign Policy Decision-Making System during the Third Phase of the Babangida Government, Late August 1990 to December 1992	143
Foreign Policy Decision-Making System during the Fourth Phase (the Transitional Government Phase) of the Babangida Government, January 1993 to August 1993	144

Preface

THE DYNAMICS OF FOREIGN POLICY DECISION-MAKING OFTEN PRESENT US with the essence of that foreign policy. Though numerous other factors impact on a country's foreign policy, the structures and processes of the decision-making system allow us to examine how foreign policy decisions of countries were, are, and will be forged, as numerous studies of foreign policy have shown. This text seeks to add to the body of knowledge relating to foreign policy decision-making by examining and analyzing the nature, profile, frameworks, and dynamics of foreign policy decision-making in Nigeria.

I am grateful to all my colleagues at Florida A and M University for their encouragement. Thus, I thank Professor Larry E. Rivers, who was the chairman of our department when I joined the faculty of the university. I also thank Professors Brown, Cohen, Cotton, Eaton, Eidahl, Gaston, Hemmingway, Jackson, Jones, Malik, Paul, Simmonds, and Wright (all of the Department of History and Political Science).

Acknowledgments

THE CHAPTER ENTITLED "LOVE THE NATION: THE BUHARI ERA" WAS previously published as "Foreign Policy Decision-Making System and Nigerian Foreign Policy during the Buhari Era" in *The Round Table* (no. 314): 198–212. Thus, I thank Carfax Publishing, a member of the Taylor and Francis Group P.O. Box 25, Abingdon, Oxfordshire, OX14 34E, England, The United Kingdom, the publisher of *The Round Table,* for the permission to use the above article in this book.

Foreign Policy Decision-Making in Nigeria

1
Introduction

THERE ARE MANY FACTORS THAT IMPACT ON FOREIGN POLICIES OF COUNtries. Some of these factors are the personalities of political leaders who are involved in the foreign policy milieu, the nature of the foreign policy decision-making system, the nature of the political system, the nature of the national attributes, and the nature of the international system (East, Salmore, and Hermann 1978). The impact of each of these factors varies in relation to a particular foreign policy issue—one or more of the factors may be prominent, while others may be of modest or negligible significance. In order to completely understand, explain, or predict the foreign policy of a given country, the relative impact of these factors must be analyzed and evaluated.

The dynamics and frameworks of foreign policy decision-making system have been subjected to vigorous analyses by numerous scholars (for example, Allison 1971; Anderson 1987; Halperin 1974; Hermann 1978; Hermann, Hermann, and Hagan 1987; Hilsman 1987, 1–203; Janis 1972; Kegley 1987; Powell, Purkitt, and Dyson 1987; Wiarda 1990, 154–321).

Although all the above-mentioned factors that affect foreign policy are important, the nature of the foreign policy decision-making system occupies an interesting position. As Margaret G. Hermann, Charles F. Hermann, and Joe D. Hagan (1987, 309) note: "[A]lthough we recognize that numerous domestic and international factors can and do influence foreign policy behavior, these influences must be channeled through the political apparatus of a government which identifies, decides and implements foreign policy." This political apparatus of a government is the foreign policy decision-making system. Thus, by studying the foreign policy decision-making system we gain interesting knowledge about the nature of foreign policy dynamics.

Charles F. Hermann (1978) postulates that the nature of the decision structures affects the nature of the decision process, which in turn affects foreign policy conclusions. The decision structure can be comprised of a predominant leader with a small subordinate and pliable staff; an authoritative leader with individuals who have some autonomy and independence (although the leader may be able to remove any of them—but at a significant cost to the leader); an authoritative leader with individuals who represent the views of some bureaus or groups; a small group of individuals who can act on their own and who are fairly (though not exactly) equal in power; a small group of individuals who represent the views of some outside entities to which they belong, and who are fairly equal in power; a large group of individuals who can act on their own and who are fairly equal in power; or a large group of individuals who are representatives of outside entities, and who are fairly equal in power (Hermann 1978; Hermann, Hermann, and Hagan 1987). Each of these different decision structures results in different decision processes. For example, a decision structure consisting of a predominant leader with a subordinate and pliable staff gives rise to a decision process in which the staff serve mainly to reinforce the view of the strong leader and to quickly give the leader the information which he or she needs in order to reach the decision. Thus, such a decision process is faster and more efficient than others (Hermann 1978) and often results in a sharp-edged policy output. On the other hand, a decision structure consisting of a large group of individuals who are representatives of outside entities, and who are fairly equal in power, results in a very slow and cumbersome decision process that involves competition and bargaining among the members (Hermann 1978). This sort of decision process results in a decision output that has a compromise profile.

Many theorists have made efforts to provide conceptual models of decision-making. For example, Graham T. Allison's study (1971) provides lucid models. He delineates the rational actor model, organization process model, and bureaucratic politics model. The rational actor model sees the decision-making process as being based on goals being prioritized, and actions being taken, based on rational, logical, and unified dynamics (Wiarda 1990, 22–25). The organization process model is seen as a decision-making process that follows the standard operating procedures of organizations (Wiarda 1990, 28–29). The bureaucratic politics model describes the decision-making process that involves several bureaucracies representing their separate interests. These bureaucracies compete and then bargain among themselves, giving rise to a compromised decision output (Halperin 1974; Wiarda 1990, 25–28).

Some, like Irving L. Janis (1972), analyze the decision-making model of small groups. According to Janis, small group decision-making dynamics tend to foster excessive concurrence of views and avoidance of disagreements that lead to poor quality of decision outputs. Janis sees these sort of decision structures, processes, and outputs as exhibiting what he calls the group-think syndrome.

The foreign policy decision-making system can also be viewed as consisting of stages. These are the information collection and interpretation stage, options formation stage, choice stage, and implementation stage (Hermann 1978, 71–73).

The decision structures vary in different countries. Additionally, in a particular country, the decision structure also changes in relation to issue and time. Thus foreign policy decision structures may be "prime ministers, presidents, politburos, juntas, cabinets, interagency groups, coalitions and parliaments" (Hermann, Hermann, and Hagan 1987, 309).

Within the foreign policy decision-making system we also have the ultimate decision unit. The ultimate decision units are often "at the apex of foreign policy decision making in all governments or ruling parties" and these groups of individuals, "if they agree, have both the ability to commit the resources of the government in foreign affairs and the power and authority to prevent other entities within the government from overtly reversing their position" (Hermann, Hermann, and Hagan 1987, 311). For vital foreign policy issues the ultimate decision unit will be at the apex of the foreign policy decision-making system, while for routine foreign policy issues "the ultimate decision unit may be at a much lower level." Additionally, in some countries, technical foreign policy issues (for example, economic, military, and scientific issues) may have different ultimate decision units (Hermann, Hermann, and Hagan 1987, 311).

As shown above, scholarship in the area of foreign policy decision-making is rich in conceptual and theoretical frameworks, and these frameworks inform this study of foreign policy decision-making in Nigeria. This study analyzes and evaluates the Nigerian foreign policy decision-making structures and processes and relates them to Nigerian foreign policy from 1960 (when Nigeria became an independent country) to 1999. This period covers the Balewa, Ironsi, Gowon, Muhammed/Obasanjo, Shagari, Buhari, Babangida, Shonekan, Abacha, Abubakar, and Obasanjo Governments. For analytic ease and convenience, the foreign policy decision-making system and Nigerian foreign policy for each of these governments is analyzed separately, starting with the Balewa Government.

2
In the Beginning: The Balewa Era

THE BALEWA GOVERNMENT LASTED FROM 1960 TO 1966. EVEN THOUGH Tafawa Balewa became the prime minister in 1957, for the purpose of this book, the Balewa era (in terms of its own foreign policy) is seen as starting in 1960 when Nigeria started handling its own foreign policy after gaining independence. The fact that it was the first government for an independent Nigeria meant that the Balewa Government had the privilege of shaping the foreign policy decision-making structures and processes of a newly independent country.

The parliamentary system was in operation in the country during the Balewa era. Thus, the prime minister, Tafawa Balewa, and all the other ministers were also members of Parliament. (Additionally, the prime minister was the head of government, while the president was the ceremonial head of state.) The nature of the foreign policy decision-making system reflected this parliamentary system. Some, like Akinyemi (1974 and 1979a), have noted that the country's federal system, like other federal systems, impacted on the conduct of foreign relations during the Balewa era.

The major foreign policy structures during this era were the Office of the Prime Minister, the Cabinet, the Ministry of External Affairs, the Ministry of Defense, Federal Ministry of Finance, the Federal Ministry of Economic Development, the Federal Ministry of Commerce and Industry, the Federal Ministry of Industry, the Federal Ministry of Information, the Federal Ministry of Education, and Parliament.

THE OFFICE OF THE PRIME MINISTER

Many scholars of Nigerian foreign policy during the Balewa era have noted the pivotal role of the Office of Prime Minister (for example, Aluko 1983, 82–84; Idang 1973, 6, 48–49, 92–96, 108, 113, 152; Ofoegbu 1990, 99–100; Ojo 1980, 574–75; Olusanya and Akindele 1986a, 26). Throughout his tenure, Balewa was much interested in being in control of foreign policy formulation and he did achieve this goal. Idang has noted the several factors that enabled Balewa to be in full grip of the foreign policy formulation. The conciliatory, moderate, calm, placating attitudes of Balewa (which enabled other members of the foreign policy elite to allow him to dominate the foreign policy formulation dynamics), the pragmatism and personal goals of the political leaders of the various political parties, and the nature of the relationship among the political parties are seen as the factors that enabled Balewa to be so firmly in control of the foreign policy framework (Idang 1973, 48–49).

From October 1960 to July 1961 and from December 1964 to January 1966, Balewa, the prime minister, also had the portfolio of external affairs ministership (Idang 1973, 6). This situation further strengthened the role the Office of the Prime Minister played in foreign affairs.

Despite the fact that until its independence in 1960 Nigeria had no formal power over its foreign affairs, "an external affairs division was established in the Prime Minister's office in 1957"; and it was this external affairs division that "was later transformed into a self-contained unit with a distinct cadre of External Affairs Officers, and in October 1960 was reconstituted into the Ministry of Foreign Affairs and Commonwealth Relations" (Idang 1973, 109). That the Office of the Prime Minister had an external affairs unit before 1960 might have helped Balewa to continue to control foreign affairs after Nigeria became independent in 1960. The Ministry of Foreign Affairs and Commonwealth Relations was renamed the Ministry of External Affairs in 1963 (Idang 1973, 101, 107n.), and it maintained this name during most of the period covered by this study.

The Office of the prime minister, as a foreign policy decision structure, consisted of the prime minister and a relatively small number of career civil servants. This sort of decision structure roughly corresponded to the model of predominant leader with a small subordinate and pliable staff as conceptualized by Charles Hermann (1978) and Charles Hermann, Margaret Hermann, and Joe Hagan (1987). Such a foreign policy decision structure often results in a decision process in which the staff provide the leader with the information he needs to reach a decision, and then mainly reinforce his views. As also earlier noted by Charles Hermann (1978), this sort of foreign policy decision-making process is often faster and efficient. However, this process is prone to not having all the possible ranges of information, policy analyses, and policy options, and therefore sometimes results in inadequate decisions.

For a very brief period, from 1961 to 1962, the Office of the Prime Minister had a prime minister's personal adviser on African Affairs (Idang 1973, 48, 48n). K. O. Mbadiwe, who occupied this position, seemed to have been given this role until he could find a more adequate political position (Idang 1973, 48n). Thus, Mbadiwe as a personal adviser on African Affairs had an insignificant role in foreign policy formulation.

Olusanya and Akindele (1986a, 27) have noted that "[T]he extent the Prime Minister relied upon him is unknown," and Idang (1973, 48) has also noted that "Mbadiwe as a person did not participate actively in the formulation of foreign policy."

The visibility of the Office of the Prime Minister, in terms of foreign policy framework, was highlighted by its organization of the 1961 All-Nigeria Peoples' Conference. The conference provided "an adequate picture of the foreign policy attitudes, perceptions and priorities of a national cross section of the Nigerian intelligentsia" (Idang 1973, 92), thus providing the Office of the Prime Minister with an adequate and broad base of public opinion to guide its foreign policy formulation. To further underscore the inadequate role that K. O. Mbadiwe might have played in terms of foreign affairs, Idang (1973, 92) has noted "that one of Dr. Mbadiwe's first (and perhaps the last) official actions as the Prime Minister's Personal Adviser on African Affairs was the convening of" this conference.

The nature of the structure and processes of the Office of the Prime Minister, as noted above, enabled Balewa to have a full grip on the formulation of foreign policy. Thus his views on major foreign policy issues were often easily and adequately translated into foreign policy. For example, Balewa's more favorable view of the West than the East resulted in Nigeria, during his era, being more friendly with the West. This resulted in Balewa's Nigeria having diplomatic relationships with Eastern bloc countries that were clearly not as robust as Nigeria's relationships with Western bloc countries, especially in terms of the economic components of international relations (Ogunbadejo 1978, 806–9; Ogunbadejo 1988, 84–88). Balewa also tried to give Africa a significant place in the Nigerian foreign policy framework (Igweonwu 1985, 113). On the whole, though Balewa's foreign policy activities in the African region were significant, they were perceived as moderate in comparison with the foreign policy activities in Africa effected by the more radical African countries (Idang 1973, 117–29). Balewa was particularly interested in economic integration efforts in the West Africa subregion and in the African continent as a whole (Ojo 1980, 575). He was not very enthusiastic about the immediate continental political integration of the whole Africa espoused by more visionary African leaders like Kwame Nkrumah.

Swiftly and decisively, Nigeria broke diplomatic relations with France in 1961 due to the latter's atomic tests in the Sahara (*African Concord* 10 June 1991, 33; Anglin 1964, 261; Idang 1973, 41). This showed that the moderate Balewa could sometimes be assertive. It also showed that the foreign decision structure and processes of the Office of the Prime Minister do easily lead to swift and sharp-edged decisions.

Other organizations worked with the Office of the Prime Minister on the French atomic tests issue. According to Akinterinwa (1990, 283–90), the

Office of the Prime Minister, the Cabinet, and the Ministry of External Affairs were significantly involved in the decision to terminate diplomatic relations, while the Office of the Prime Minister, the Ministry of External Affairs, and the Ministry of Justice were the major units involved in the decision to reestablish diplomatic relations with France in 1965. Nonetheless, the Office of the Prime Minister was the main force in the decision processes for both the termination and the renewal of relations with France.

The Anglo-Nigerian Defense Pact was another major foreign policy issue during the Balewa Government in which the Office of the Prime Minister was again at center stage, although other decision units— prominent political leaders, the political parties, and interest groups— were also involved. According to Ojo (1990a, 255–74), the making and the later termination of the Anglo-Nigerian Defense Pact involved the Office of the Prime Minister (in a leading role), the political leadership of the Ministry of Defense (as personified by Muhammadu Ribadu, the deputy prime minister and the federal minister of Defense), other federal ministers (Maitama Sule, Waziri Ibrahim, and Okotie Eboh), the major political parties, and Ahmadu Bello (the premier of the Northern Region) playing important roles, while the Parliament, the Cabinet, the Ministry of External Affairs, the career senior civil servants and the senior military officers of the Ministry of Defense, interest groups, and protest groups played very insignificant roles. However, according to other scholars like Idang (1973, 39 n, 41, 56 n, 57, 76 n, 82, 88), the Anglo-Nigerian Defense Pact (which was created in 1960) was abrogated in 1962 mostly because of the actions of interest groups and protest groups. Maybe the reality lies somewhere midway between the above views of Ojo and Idang.

As noted earlier, during significant portions of the Balewa era, the prime minister also held the portfolio of the external affairs ministry. This meant that, for those portions of the Balewa era, the Office of the Prime Minister effectively superimposed itself over the Ministry of External Affairs. During such periods, the already prominent role of the Office of the Prime Minister, in terms of foreign affairs, was even further enlarged and made more robust.

It is important to note that the Office of the Prime Minister was able to play a prominent role in foreign policy (as well as domestic policy) due to the guidance and support that Tafawa Balewa got from Ahmadu Bello (the premier of the Northern Region). Nigeria of the Balewa era had an interesting political situation: Ahmadu Bello, a premier of one of the regional governments of the federation, had more real political power and influence (though not necessarily formal power and formal authority) than Tafawa Balewa, the prime minister of the federal government (who, constitutionally, was supposed to have the most formal *and* real political authority and power in the country). Ahmadu Bello, who was the leader of Northern Peoples' Congress (NPC) (the party that had the highest number of seats in the Parliament), preferred to remain in his political base in Kaduna as the premier of the Northern Region, while he sent Tafawa Balewa (an NPC leader junior to Bello) to Lagos as the prime minister of the Federation. It was commonly perceived that Balewa followed Bello's advice on policies (Ojo 1990a, 259). A strong-willed Bello easily influenced a calm, placating, and moderate Balewa. Bello, possibly, preferred a very active Office of the Prime Minister, since such a body enabled him to influence the domestic and foreign policies of the federal government through Balewa.

The Cabinet

As in all parliamentary systems, the Cabinet was the body responsible for the formulation of all governmental policies, including foreign policies for possible enactment by the Parliament. However, as noted above, the Office of the Prime Minister was often in full control of the foreign policy formulation framework. Thus, in reality, the Cabinet (which was the national decision structure consisting of the prime minister and all other cabinet-level ministers, and serving as a collective decision structure made up of all its members) was not a significant structure in the foreign policy formulation milieu. According to John Mackintosh (quoted in Idang 1973, 6), "within the government, foreign policy was originally formulated almost entirely by the Prime Minister. There has been no Cabinet Committee on this subject and the Cabinet appears to have been told rather than consulted on major points." Idang (1973, 113) also adds "that the Cabinet was largely excluded from the foreign-policy process."

Thus, during the Balewa era the Office of the Prime Minister was in actual control of foreign policy formulation, while the Cabinet was mostly simply informed of the country's foreign policy decisions. Additionally, while "the Cabinet was totally excluded from the formulation of foreign policy," the Cabinet Secretariat (which mostly consisted of career bureaucrats) worked with the Office of the Prime Minister to formulate foreign policies (Ofoegbu 1990, 100). However, though the Cabinet was insignificant in terms of foreign policy formulation, there is a strong probability that it was not totally excluded from the process. For example, Akinterinwa (1990, 284) has noted that the Cabinet was involved in the decision to sever relations with France due to the atomic tests.

The Ministry of External Affairs

The Ministry of External Affairs manages Nigeria's international relations. As noted earlier, during the early phase of the Balewa era this ministry was named the Ministry of Foreign Affairs and Commonwealth Relations; it was renamed the Ministry of External Affairs in 1963 (Idang 1973, 107, 107n.), and it maintained this name throughout most of the period covered by this study.

In terms of organizational structure, during the Balewa era the ministry was headed by the minister of External Affairs (who was the political head of the ministry). Next below the minister were two ministers of state, with Cabinet ranks, and a parliamentary secretary (Idang 1973, 108). The minister, the ministers of state and the parliamentary secretary together constituted the political leadership of the ministry. The permanent secretary, a career civil servant, was at the head of the administrative machinery of the ministry. The permanent secretary coordinated all the functions of the ministry and also served as the main adviser to the minister; and, assisted by a deputy permanent secretary, he supervised the heads of divisions (who had a direct access to the permanent secretary) (Idang 1973, 108). The ministry had divisions as its basic units (these were both geographical and functional units). During the Balewa era the divisions were Accounts; Administrative and Establishment; African; Asian; Consular and Treaties; Economic; Euro-Western; Information; International; Protocol; and Research Divisions (Idang 1973, 108). It was through these eleven divisions (three of which were regional geographical divisions) that the ministry carried out its functions. All the Nigerian foreign missions came under one of the above three regional geographical divisions or the international division. The country (and, more specifically, the region of the world) in which the Nigerian foreign mission was located determined which of the above three regional geographical divisions it came under. Nigerian foreign missions accredited to international organizations came under the international division. (Through a series of administrative reforms the divisions within the Ministry of External Affairs are now differently arranged.)

In terms of its functioning, the Ministry of External Affairs had the authority to formulate and implement foreign policies. However, as noted earlier, the Office of the Prime Minister had a virtual monopoly on foreign policy formulation. Thus, most of the time the ministry handled the function of mainly implementing foreign policies that had been formulated by the Office of the Prime Minister. The fact that the prime minister, for significant portions of his tenure, held the portfolio of external affairs minister (the Balewa era lasted from 1960 to 1966; the prime minister held the external affairs portfolio from 1960 to July 1961 and from 1964 to 1966) (Idang 1973, 6), meant that the full grip of Tafawa Balewa on foreign policy formulation was very strong. During these periods, even though he "was usually assisted by two or more Ministers of State in the External Affairs Ministry," these ministers of state "were only useful during parliamentary debates and on state visits, but hardly relevant to foreign policy formulation" (Idang 1973, 6). The fact that Balewa did not even involve the ministers of state (who were there to assist him) in foreign policy formulation, meant that he really ensured that the ministry did not compete with him. One could conceptualize that, during the periods Balewa held the external affairs ministry portfolio, the Office of the Prime Minister was superimposed on the Ministry of External Affairs in terms of the foreign policy formulation framework.

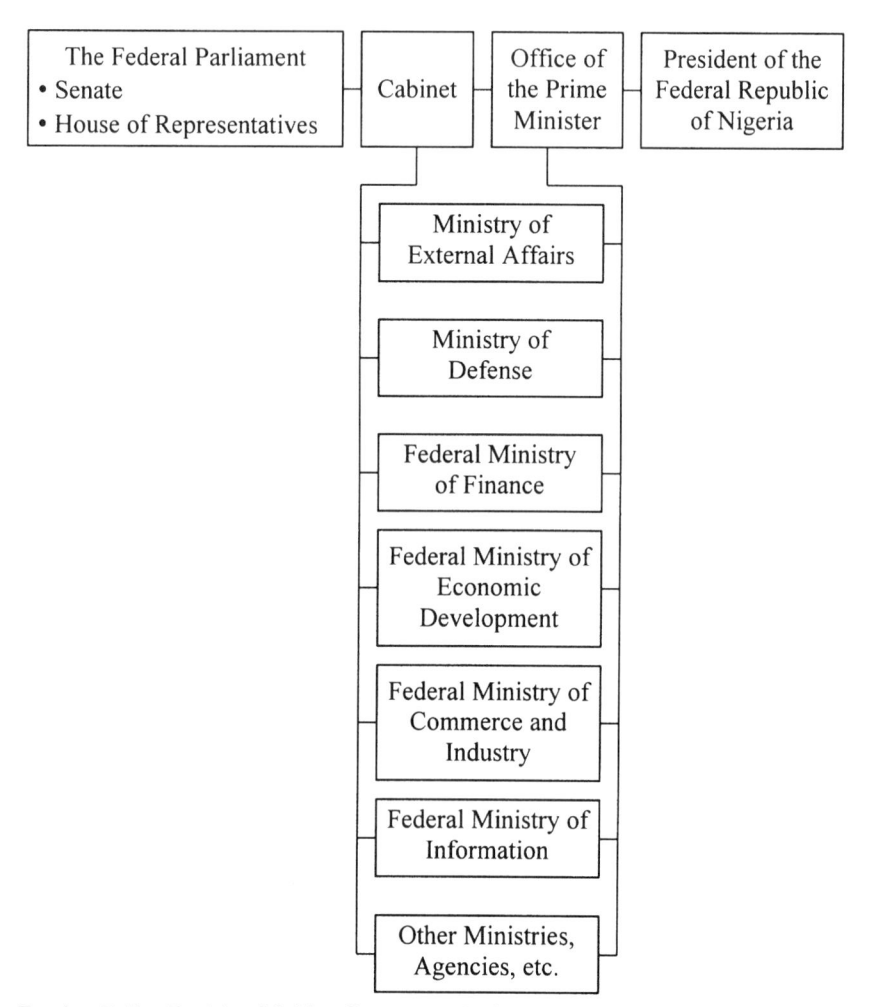

```
┌─────────────────────┐   ┌────────┐   ┌──────────┐   ┌─────────────────┐
│ The Federal Parliament │   │        │   │ Office of │   │ President of the │
│ • Senate            │───│ Cabinet │───│ the Prime │───│ Federal Republic │
│ • House of Representatives │   │        │   │ Minister  │   │ of Nigeria       │
└─────────────────────┘   └────────┘   └──────────┘   └─────────────────┘
                              │             │
                              │   ┌─────────────────┐
                              ├───│ Ministry of     │
                              │   │ External Affairs│
                              │   └─────────────────┘
                              │   ┌─────────────────┐
                              ├───│ Ministry of     │
                              │   │ Defense         │
                              │   └─────────────────┘
                              │   ┌─────────────────┐
                              ├───│ Federal Ministry│
                              │   │ of Finance      │
                              │   └─────────────────┘
                              │   ┌─────────────────┐
                              ├───│ Federal Ministry of │
                              │   │ Economic        │
                              │   │ Development     │
                              │   └─────────────────┘
                              │   ┌─────────────────┐
                              ├───│ Federal Ministry of │
                              │   │ Commerce and    │
                              │   │ Industry        │
                              │   └─────────────────┘
                              │   ┌─────────────────┐
                              ├───│ Federal Ministry of │
                              │   │ Information     │
                              │   └─────────────────┘
                              │   ┌─────────────────┐
                              └───│ Other Ministries, │
                                  │ Agencies, etc.  │
                                  └─────────────────┘
```

Foreign Policy Decision-Making Structures during the Balewa Government

The ministers of state and the top career diplomats in the ministry mostly shared Balewa's worldview. Thus, they mostly concurred with his decisions and presented him policy position papers that reinforced his own views: for example, in the case of Balewa's decision not to break diplomatic relations with Britain (as demanded by the unanimous decision of the Organization of African Unity Special Ministerial Council in 1965) since Zimbabwe's (then called Rhodesia) unilateral declaration of independence was not crushed by Britain (Aluko 1983, 82–84).

From 1961 to 1964, Jaja Wachuku was the minister of External Affairs. Though this meant that Balewa formally relinquished the external affairs ministry portfolio during this period, he was actually still in control of foreign policy formulation. By also giving the ministers of state ranks in the Cabinet, Balewa was able to control foreign policy through them. One of the ministers of state in the ministry, Nuhu Bamali, was particularly useful to Balewa. Since Bamali had a cabinet rank, just like Wachuku, Balewa was able to use Bamali to perform significant foreign policy activities for him (Olusanya and Akindele 1986a, 21). This prominence of Bamali was a source of significant conflict and competition between Wachuku and Bamali. For example, Bamali once openly fumed: "Jaja thinks I am so naive to be gagged, he can't gag me. . . . Jaja is not superior to me, we are all both Cabinet Ministers" (quoted in Olusanya and Akindele 1986a, 21). This sort of public statement by Bamali clearly shows that Wachuku, in reality, did not have adequate control over the ministry (even though he was formally its political boss). Balewa was able to use this deep cleavage within the political leadership of the ministry to maintain control over foreign policy during this period. Additionally, the fact that "despite the great difference in their political background and experience," Balewa and Wachuku "were always in complete agreement as to what the fundamental and procedural assumptions of Nigerian foreign policy should be," meant that "the appointment of Jaja Wachuku as External Affairs Minister did not drastically change the situation" (Idang 1973, 6). Thus, Balewa was still effectively in full grip of the foreign policy formulation framework during the period Wachuku was the minister of External Affairs. As Idang (1973, 133) has noted, "[E]ven after Mr. Wachuku had been appointed External Affairs Minister, the Prime Minister still continued to remain a "super-Foreign Minister," exercising full and constant control over foreign affairs." Though in some instances, like the Nigerian "decision to reject associate status in the EEC," the ministry played a vital part, "it is still difficult for anyone to say that the Ministry of External Affairs during the Balewa period played a creative role in foreign policy formulation" (Idang 1973, 113).

Though the Ministry of External Affairs manages the country's international relations, there are many other ministries that have some functions relating to that aspect of government, including the Ministries of Defense, Finance, Economic Development, Trade, Industry, Information, Labor, Justice and Internal Affairs. Their role during the Balewa era will also be analyzed.

THE MINISTRY OF DEFENSE

Since the Balewa Government was the first government for an independent Nigeria, during this period Nigeria was building and developing a military organization that would adequately meet the national security needs of a medium-sized country.

The minister of Defense was the political head of this ministry. Next to the minister were one or two ministers of state, and after the latter was a parliamentary secretary. The minister, ministers of state, and parliamentary secretary constituted the political leadership for the Ministry as a whole and also served as the direct civilian control over the armed forces. The ultimate civilian control over the armed forces was exercised by the president of the federal republic of Nigeria (through the advice of the prime minister, who was the head of the government of the federal republic of Nigeria). The president, who performed the ceremonial role of the head of state, was also (acting under the advice of the prime minister) the commander in chief of the armed forces. The parliamentary secretary, a career civil servant, served as the administrative head of the ministry.

The chief of the defense staff was the highest military officer in terms of authority. Thus, this person served as the military adviser to the minister of defense and the prime minister. Through the prime minister, the chief of the defense staff also provided military advice to the president who was, as noted above, the commander in chief of the armed forces.

The military organization was divided into the Nigerian army, the Nigerian air force, and the Nigerian navy. Each of these armed services units was headed by a chief of staff. During the Balewa era, each of these armed services units also had an immediate direct civilian control in the person of a minister of state. For an example, M. T. Mbu was the minister of state in the Ministry of Defense in charge of the Nigerian navy (Idang 1973, 93; *West Africa* 29 March–4 April 1993, 500).

The very fact that the Ministry of Defense was the organization of the government that managed the national defense and security needs of the country (in terms of protecting the country against external and internal threats to the country's sovereignty, sociopolitical stability, and territorial integrity) made the functioning of the ministry intertwined with the international affairs of the country. Specifically, it was the ministry that articulated, developed, implemented, and managed the security components of Nigerian foreign policy.

The 1960s was a period in which many African countries emerged from colonialism after gaining their independence. Thus, maintaining the independence and sovereignty of all African countries was vital to every African country, including Nigeria, for if any newly independent country was being threatened or compromised, it was perceived as an indication that the same fate might also befall the others. It was therefore in their self-interest to mutually help protect other African countries. Thus, Nigeria was much involved in the efforts to restore stability to Zaire (then known as Congo Leopoldville and later as Congo Kinshasha). This crisis had meant that the independence, the sovereignty, and the territorial integrity of Zaire was seriously compromised. Apart from "participating in the UN Advisory Committee on the Congo," serving "on the Secretary-General's Congo Club," and providing the "Chairman of the Congo Conciliation Commission," Nigeria also "contributed 1,796 soldiers and policemen to Operation des Nations Unies au Congo (ONUC)" (Peters and Aminu 1986, 94). Thus, Nigeria made significant contributions to the United Nations' efforts to resolve the political and security problems in Zaire. It was the Ministry of Defense, through the Nigerian soldiers sent to Zaire, that helped to implement this security component of Nigerian foreign policy. The fact that Nigeria also "acceded to the request of President Nyerere for assistance to help put down a mutiny within his armed forces" (Peters and Aminu 1986, 93) also shows another instance wherein the Ministry of Defense, through the Nigerian soldiers sent out to end the mutiny in Tanzania, helped implement a security component of Nigerian foreign policy.

The fact that there was a military under-secretary that was attached to the Ministry of External Affairs (Idang 1973, 109) shows there were significant formalized routine interactions between that ministry and the Ministry of Defense. Thus, to some extent, the Ministry of Defense was able to adequately articulate, develop, communicate, implement, and manage the security components of foreign policy.

The fact that the Ministry of Defense has always been one of the prominent ministries gives it a lot of visibility and credibility (which enables it to always adequately participate in the foreign policy milieu).

The Ministry of Defense also engages in liaison with the "armed forces of adjacent territories, clearance of foreign military aircrafts and warships; visits of foreign service chiefs; and visits of defense and war colleges" (Idang 1973, 115). These activities significantly enhance the role of the ministry in the security dimension of foreign policy.

As shown by the details given above about the structure and functioning of the ministry, it played a significant role in Nigeria's international affairs during the Balewa era.

OTHER MINISTRIES AND AGENCIES

Apart from the Ministries of External Affairs and Defense, there were many other ministries with activities that related to Nigeria's international affairs, although only in part. These ministries were the Federal Ministries of Finance, Economic Development, Trade, Industry, Information, Labor, Justice, and Internal Affairs. Apart from these ministries, in reality, all other ministries, departments, and agencies of the federal government of Nigeria had some activities that related to the country's international affairs (but for some of these others, their international activities were relatively insignificant and invisible).

The Federal Ministries of Finance, Economic Development, and Commerce and Industry were the organizations of government that were mainly in charge of the economic components of Nigerian foreign policy. The Federal Ministry of Finance, in terms of its international activities, focused on Nigeria's international financial relations, including relations with international financial institutions; while the Federal Ministry of Economic Development focused on Nigeria's relations with international economic development bodies and Nigeria's efforts to avail itself of international technical and economic assistance; and the Federal Ministry of Commerce and Industry focused on Nigeria's international trade relations (Idang 1973, 115; Olusanya and Akindele 1986a, 23–24). The federal minister of Finance, in many parliamentary systems, is often the senior minister who is next in rank to the prime minister. Thus, the federal minister of Finance was often in a prominent and visible position to articulate and push his ideas about the country's international financial relations and the country's international economic relations in general. Adding to his prominent and visible position in the Balewa Government, the federal minister of Finance, Festus Okotie-Eboh, was a flamboyant politician who often spoke his mind on a lot of issues, including how Nigeria's international economic and financial relations should be shaped (Ojo 1981, 34, 35). The changes (though small) that occurred in Nigeria's international economic and financial relations might have been due to the input of Okotie-Eboh.

Nigeria in the Balewa era, as a newly independent country, was much in need of international economic and technical assistance. Thus, the Federal Ministry of Economic Development, which was in charge of this policy, became a key player in determining the sort and magnitude of assistance that Nigeria was able to obtain. Since such assistance was vital to Nigerian development plans at that stage of the country's nationhood, the role of the

Federal Ministry of Economic Development was highly important to the Balewa government, and thus the Federal Ministry of Economic Development was a significant factor in foreign economic policy decision-making.

The role of the Federal Ministry of Commerce and Industry, in terms of its international trade relations functions, had a formalized and routinized relationship with the Ministry of External Affairs. Officials of the Federal Ministry of Commerce and Industry were seconded to the Ministry of External Affairs to serve as commercial attachés in Nigerian embassies abroad, with these commercial attachés mainly coming under the policy control of the Ministry of External Affairs during the period of their secondment duties (Ojo 1976, 51–53; Olusanya and Akindele 1986a, 25–26). This arrangement was never satisfactory to both the Federal Ministry of Commerce and Industry and the Ministry of External Affairs, since the commercial attachés often felt slighted by the foreign service officers of the Ministry of External Affairs. The commercial attachés (even though under the policy control of the Ministry of External Affairs) were often loyal to their own federal Ministry of Commerce and Industry; they felt that their career prospects were poor relative to the foreign service officers, while the Ministry of External Affairs often felt that the commercial attachés were performing duties that should have been done by the Ministry of External Affairs officials (Ojo 1976, 50–66; Olusanya and Akindele 1986a, 25–26). (These are problems that seem to still persist to the present.)

Idang (1973, 138) notes that Tafawa Balewa was mainly interested in formulating the political components of foreign policy (with the Ministry of External Affairs doing the job of implementing this policy), while allowing ministries like the Federal Ministries of Finance, Economic Development, and Commerce and Industry to take charge of the economic components. Idang (1973, 138) also notes that, though an Economic Division was established in the Ministry of External Affairs in 1963, this division was not adequately staffed; and thus, even after 1963, the Ministry of External Affairs was not able to be a major factor in Nigerian foreign economic policy decision-making.

Thus, throughout the Balewa era, the Federal Ministries of Finance, Economic Development, and Commerce and Industry were the major organizations involved in the formulation, implementation, and evaluation of the economic components of Nigerian foreign policy, even though the Ministry of External Affairs was also significant in this policy area.

The Federal Ministry of Information was another ministry that had an impact on foreign policy. Though it was a ministry with a major focus on the domestic scene, it was also the ministry that was entrusted with important international functions. It had the function of handling Nigeria's external publicity activities (Idang 1973, 115; Olusanya and Akindele 1986a,

23). This involved the provision of information both about Nigeria as a country and about the country's foreign policy positions and actions, and the projection of the cultural heritage of the country.

At the beginning of the Balewa era (which was also the period just after Nigeria's independence), there was "jurisdictional dispute . . . between the Ministry of External Affairs and the Ministry of Information as to which of the two agencies of government should be in control of the country's external publicity" (Olusanya and Akindele 1986a, 23) before it was finally decided that the Federal Ministry of Information should be in charge of this foreign policy area. However, the decision was a compromise (and it was not unlike the situation in the international trade relations policy area between the Ministry of External Affairs and the Federal Ministry of Commerce and Industry, where the two ministries had a more or less shared responsibility, as noted earlier). The decision was "that the Ministry of External Affairs draws its information officers, where possible, from the Ministry of Information if they can provide the people; and once such officers get into the Ministry of External Affairs they cease to be adjuncts of the Ministry of Information. . . . The Ministry of Information has no authority to interfere with the officers while they are with us" (Jaja Wachuku, quoted in Olusanya and Akindele 1986a, 23).

This sort of arrangement was never satisfactory to both the Ministry of External Affairs and the Federal Ministry of Information, since the situation intensified bureaucratic turf battles between the two ministries over the control of external publicity activities. In fact, problems created by this arrangement were similar to those noted earlier between the Ministry of External Affairs and the Federal Ministry of Commerce and Trade over their struggle for control over international trade relations activities.

The Federal Ministry of Justice was one unexpected ministry that managed to have some visibility in terms of international issues during the Balewa era. This was largely due to the fact that Taslim Olawale Elias (a world-renowned professor of law who later was a justice of the International Court of Justice, from 1976 to 1991, and the president of the International Court of Justice, from 1983 to 1986) was the federal attorney-general and the federal minister of Justice. The international reputation of the federal attorney-general as a luminary in the areas of international law and comparative law enabled him, personally, to play significant roles in international affairs. For example, "a government motion withdrawing Commonwealth privileges from South African nationals tabled by the Attorney-General and Minister of Justice, Dr. T. O. Elias, in the House of Representatives, was carried unanimously" (Idang 1973, 123). Additionally, "The United Nations recognized this man's qualities by appointing him chairman of the committee that drafted and gave to Congo its constitution. By the same token, he was invited by the African Community as the Attorney-General of the Nigerian Federation to participate not only as a member, but as chairman of the committee that drafted the constitution of the Organization of African Unity" (*West Africa* 31 August–6 September 1992, 1486). Aluko (1986, 89) has also added that Taslim O. Elias's committee, which drafted that Charter of the Organization of African Unity, produced a "Charter which contained about 90 per cent of all the provisions of the Charter of the Monrovia Group of States of 1961 of which Nigeria was a leading member." Clearly indicating that the federal attorney-general was often consulted by the prime minister on some foreign policy issues, Asobie (1986, 147) notes that the federal attorney-general, together with Tafawa Balewa and Jaja Wachuku (who was later to become the minister for External Affairs), prepared the "first foreign policy statement issued by the Federal Government" just less than two months before Nigeria became formally independent.

All the above activities, in the realm of international affairs, show that the federal attorney-general was a key member of the foreign policy elite during the Balewa era.

Other ministries, like the Federal Ministries of Labor and Internal Affairs, also on occasion played some role in international affairs (especially relating to the problems in South Africa). For example, the federal minister of Labor "at the Geneva meeting of the International Labor Organization (ILO), moved a resolution to the effect that South Africa should be asked to quit the organization. The motion was carried by 163 to nil, with 89 abstentions. When South Africa refused to quit, the Nigerian delegates, backed by the other African delegates, walked out of the next ILO meeting in 1963" (Idang 1973, 123). Also, Usman Sarki, the federal minister of Internal Affairs, expelled "the South African Dutch Reformed Church from Nigeria" (Idang 1973, 123).

As shown above, so many ministries were involved in foreign policy issues. Obviously, this meant there was much need for adequate coordination of foreign policy activities, in order to ensure that all the ministries were harmoniously engaged.

Foreign Policy Coordination

Despite the obvious need for foreign policy coordination, the Balewa Government did not seem to carry out this function very well. As Idang notes (1973, 115–16), "No attempt was made to devise an organizational arrangement for inter-ministerial co-ordination and cooperation. The Cabinet which could have performed this co-ordination function was rendered powerless by the great dominance" of the prime minister, Tafawa

Balewa, "in the process of making foreign policy and by the widespread deference paid to his ability in foreign affairs." This situation resulted in the "overlapping of jurisdictional lines of demarcation and responsibility among the ministries concerned with various aspects of foreign policy formulation and execution" (Idang 1973, 116).

Focusing on the foreign economic policy decision-making system, Anglin (1964, 260) also notes that

> in general, little formal coordination of policy exists between the Ministry of External Affairs and the economic ministries . . . except at the highest political level, the Council of Ministers. There is an interdepartmental committee of permanent secretaries as well as considerable *ad hoc* and informal consultation among senior civil servants . . ., but in practice liaison is often far from satisfactory. Part of the explanation is that officials in External Affairs tend to assume that their own economic division, staffed by regular foreign service officers, is normally fully competent to advise on economic aspects of policy, a conviction that is not universally shared by other ministries.

Focusing on the Cabinet, Akindele (1990b, 246) sees it as a body that mostly met only for stamp approval of policies. Thus, the Cabinet was not in a position to provide real coordination of policies (including foreign policies). On the other hand, the real major player in foreign affairs was the Office of the Prime Minister (Akindele 1990b, 246–47).

On the whole, the very dominant role of Tafawa Balewa in foreign affairs meant that on those major foreign policy issues (about which the Office of the Prime Minister became the ultimate decision structure), there was little need for coordination, since the Office of the Prime Minister easily made the decisions and also easily made the Cabinet and the Parliament go along with these decisions. The areas where coordination presented big problems were those routine foreign policy issues and activities wherein the various ministries were the ultimate decision structures: for example, many international trade issues and activities (which caused a lot of friction between the Ministry of External Affairs and the Federal Ministry of Commerce and Industry) and external publicity issues and activities (which caused a lot of friction between the Ministry of External Affairs and the Federal Ministry of Information).

Apart from the Office of the Prime Minister, the Cabinet, and the various ministries (which were all part of the executive branch of government), the legislative branch of government, as represented by the Parliament, was also a vital part of the federal government of Nigeria during the Balewa era. To some extent, the Parliament had a role to play in Nigerian foreign policy.

The Parliament

Though the Parliament (which consisted of the Senate and the House of Representatives) had the formal power to be a vital partner in the shaping and making of Nigerian foreign policy during the Balewa era, many people were not satisfied by the actual role the Parliament played in foreign policy.

The fact that the Parliament was the law making part of the government meant that, at least formally and conceptually, it could impact on foreign policy activities in a wide-ranging way. In terms of foreign policy, specifically, the Parliament was empowered to "make laws for Nigeria or any part thereof for the purpose of implementing a treaty, a convention or an agreement between the Federation and any other country" (The 1963 Constitution of the Federal Republic of Nigeria, quoted in Idang 1973, 56). However, the Constitution did not give the Parliament the power "to approve the appointment of ambassadors, or force the recognition of a régime" (Idang 1973, 56). On the whole, with the power to approve treaties, conventions, and agreements, the Parliament (if it was assertive enough) could still have had a significant impact in the foreign policy arena.

In reality, certain factors caused the Parliament not to be one of the important decision-making structures in foreign policy. The way the parliamentary system of government operated during the Balewa era was one of these factors. As is normal in parliamentary systems, the party (or the coalition of parties) that has the majority of members of the Parliament forms the government; and thus has its senior members of Parliament become the ministers that make up the Cabinet. The member of Parliament who is the leader of the party, or coalition of parties, with the most seats in the Parliament serves as the prime minister. Thus, there is a partial fusion between the executive and legislative branches of the government. The reality of this situation is that if the prime minister and/or the Cabinet have a strong control over the members of parliament from the majority party, or coalition of parties, the prime minister and/or the Cabinet can always have their decisions approved by the Parliament (without much significant input from even members of parliament who belong to the majority party or coalition of parties) by having the majority whip easily line up the votes to approve a policy that was mainly formulated by the prime minister and/or the Cabinet. During the Balewa era such dynamics were in operation, with foreign policy being mainly formulated by the Office of the Prime Minister. As noted earlier, even the Ministry of External Affairs was never much involved in the formulation of foreign policy (only with its implementation). The dominant role of the Prime Minister meant that he formulated foreign policies, which were then easily supported by the Cabinet, and easily approved by the Parliament (since members of Parliament that belong to a majority coalition of parties always readily supported the decisions of their senior members of Parliament, who are also the prime minister and other Cabinet ministers).

The nature of the coalition government during most of the Balewa era enhanced the prime minister's ability to control much of the foreign policy arena. From 1960 to 1964 the Balewa government was a coalition of the Northern Peoples' Congress (NPC) and the National Council of Nigerian Citizens (NCNC); and from 1964 to 1966, the Balewa Government was a coalition of NPC, NCNC, and the Nigerian National Democratic Party (NNDP) (Idang 1973, 39). In these two coalition governments, the NPC was the clear senior political party. Tafawa Balewa belonged to the NPC. The NPC mainly represented the interests of the northern part of the country. Reflecting the ethnic/religious tensions between the northern and southern parts of the country, NPC's mistrust of NCNC (Idang 1973, 53–54), and the ideological differences between the NPC and NCNC (NPC was a relatively conservative party, while the NCNC was a moderate party with some militant and radical elements within it) (Idang 1973, 65–76), the NPC was keen in ensuring that it had its full grip on major policy areas like foreign policy. NPC saw the prime minister as the person who could help the party control this policy area. The fact that Tafawa Balewa was only the second-ranking leader of the NPC (the leader of the NPC, as noted earlier, was Ahmadu Bello, the premier of the Northern Region) (Idang 1973, 15) might have put Balewa in a situation where he had to please the NPC leadership by closely keeping watch over, and controlling, the foreign policy formulation process. Idang (1973, 54) notes that it is "a plausible guess" that Balewa's "unwillingness to relinquish his personal control of the Ministry of External Affairs derived largely from this feeling of insecurity on the part of the Northern elite."

Some, like Gambari (1975, 158), hold the view that the dynamics of coalition governments during the Balewa era contributed to the country not having an effective leadership. (Interestingly, the NCNC, which formed an alliance with Northern Elements Progressive Union (NEPU), a northern party that was often at odds with NPC, was able to form the coalition governments of 1960 to 1964 and 1964 to 1966 with NPC.)

By 1961 NPC had a majority of the seats in the federal House of Representatives (Idang 1973, 75); thus it could have its policies approved by the House even without the members of Parliament from its coalition partner parties. This reality made NPC, through Balewa, much more comfortable with that party's control over foreign policy issues.

A major weakness in the Parliament was the fact that, throughout the Balewa era, there was no parliamentary committee on foreign affairs, and when a parliamentary motion was made for the establishment of such a committee, the government opposed it, and a majority of the members of

Parliament agreed with the government to vote to kill such an idea (Akindele 1990d, 160–63; Olusanya and Akindele 1986a, 26). The very fact that the majority of the members of the Parliament easily agreed with the government not to have a parliamentary committee on foreign affairs clearly shows that the prime minister effectively controlled the Parliament in foreign policy issues. However, there were adequate pressure points in the general public that helped to sensitize the Balewa Government to public views about foreign policy issues. As Olusanya and Akindele (1986a, 26) note: "During the Balewa regime, there was a reasonably good amount of press comments and public debates on foreign policy issues, particularly among the foreign policy elites in the labor unions, the universities and the political parties. Perhaps the best example of such public discussion and criticism of government policy which led to a historic result was the successful public campaign against the Anglo-Nigerian Defence Pact."

Despite the fact that the Parliament had no committee on foreign affairs, it was still able to deal with and debate foreign policy issues, and some government officials informed the Parliament about some foreign policy issues. For example, the parliamentary secretary in the Ministry of Commerce and Industry told the Parliament about efforts to improve intra-African trade relations and lay foundations for African economic integration (Ojo 1980, 573). Additionally, the Parliament was one of the decision structures that was involved in the effort in the 1960s to determine the sort of relations that Nigeria should have with the European Economic Community (Anglin 1964, 260; Ojo 1980, 574).

However, on the whole, the Parliament was never a significant decision structure in terms of helping to shape and make foreign policy. As shown earlier, the Office of the Prime Minister formulated foreign policies and the Parliament mostly easily approved such policies.

An Overview

The profile, functioning, and impact of the foreign policy decision-making system during the Balewa Government (the first government of an independent Nigeria) reflected the fact that the institutions involved were having their first experiences as foreign policy-making organizations. All the Balewa era foreign policy decision-making structures were laying the foundations for a foreign policy decision-making system that was going to become stronger with each successive government. The Balewa era foreign policy decision structures gave birth to foreign policy processes, values, and traditions that have become more sophisticated with the years. Successive governments, due to new realities, have also added and/or changed some foreign policy decision structures, processes, values and traditions.

As shown in this analysis of the nature of the foreign policy decision structures, processes, and output, during the Balewa era, the Office of the Prime Minister clearly controlled the formulation of major foreign policies. The prime minister often merely informed the Cabinet about these already formulated policies and the latter mainly agreed with him. Then the Parliament, which was very pliable in the area of foreign policy, often approved these policies. Some of the factors that enabled the Office of the Prime Minister to wield such an influence were (1) the tension between the northern and southern parts of the country; (2) ethnic and religious frictions; (3) NPC's mistrust of NCNC (a junior partner in the coalition governments); (4) the fact that by 1961 NPC (the senior party in the coalition governments) had the majority of the seats in the federal House of Representatives (and thus could have its policies passed in the House without the votes of the members of Parliament that belonged to other parties in the coalition governments); (5) the conservative and somehow feudal tendencies of the NPC; (6) the fear of the northern elites of a possible future domination of the country by the southern part of the country; (7) Ahmadu Bello (the leader of the NPC and the premier of the Northern Region) plausibly having significant control over Tafawa Balewa (the prime minister but only second-ranking leader of NPC) and Balewa plausibly attempting to meet the desires of Ahmadu Bello and the other members of the northern elite (that southern political leaders did not have undue influence in a government that was clearly headed by NPC) by personally having a full grip of some important policy areas (like foreign policy) and, thus, showing his northern elites (and especially Ahmadu Bello) that he was adequately protecting the interest of the Northern Region.

Balewa's desire to have control over foreign policy meant that, from 1960 to 1961 and from 1964 to 1966, he retained the external affairs ministry portfolio. Even from 1961 to 1964, when Jaja Wachuku was the minister of External Affairs, Balewa still controlled the formulation of foreign policy. Thus, throughout the Balewa era the Office of the Prime Minister was clearly in charge of foreign policy formulation while the Ministry of External Affairs mainly was left with the implementation of foreign policy.

As a foreign policy decision-making structure, the Office of the Prime Minister consisted of a predominant political leader and a small number of mostly subordinate career bureaucrats who were a pliable staff group. This decision structure gave rise to a decision process in which the staff mainly reinforced the views of Tafawa Balewa, instead of the staff mainly providing him with alternative policy options or challenging his views if he was pursuing inappropriate policy options or holding faulty assumptions. Thus, these pliable staff members mostly found Balewa the information that would help him to reach the decision he wanted to reach, instead of finding him the information that would have dissuaded him from pursuing his policy options (when such options were perceived as inadequate). This sort of decision process was often relatively fast and efficient, since everyone seemed to have been following the decision direction they perceived from the prime minister. Such a decision process (unlike one that is the result of bureaucratic compromise) often leads to sharp-edged decision output, as in the Nigerian decision to break diplomatic ties with France due to the latter's atomic bomb test in the Sahara Desert. This kind of decision-making situation sometimes might have also exhibited the group-think syndrome (Janis 1972) analyzed earlier.

Additionally, the logic and dynamics of the Office of the Prime Minister allowed the personality of Tafawa Balewa to significantly permeate the decision processes and output. He was a devout Muslim with a kind and trusting personality and sincere love for the well-being of all peoples. As noted earlier, Balewa was also a calm, humble, and dignified person who liked to placate other people. He was also a person from a very traditional background with a moderate view of the world. All these personality traits made him careful not to use his power recklessly. In fact, most of the time he tried to fashion policies that would respect the views of the many divergent groups in the country. Thus, during the Balewa era, Nigeria pursued moderate foreign policies in terms of East-West relations (though the country leaned more in favor of the Western bloc), African issues, and relations with neighboring countries. In fact, Balewa seemed to have been caught in between the pressures exerted by the more conservative forces in his party, the NPC (and represented by his northern elites, especially Ahmadu Bello), and the more radical and militant forces represented by labor unions, the intellectual class, youth groups, NEPU (which represented the views of common persons, grass root politics, and egalitarian forces in the north), and the radical wing of the NCNC. Being a placating person, Balewa followed moderate policies that sought to find the middle ground among these divergent forces. Thus, Balewa's policies mostly were not conservative and rigid nor radical and militant.

During the Balewa era, the regional governments established some offices in some countries to foster the interests of their respective regions in these foreign countries. (These offices were similar to the type of offices that the Quebec Province in Canada has in some foreign countries.) These sorts of arrangements tended to make the federal government of Nigeria feel that the regional governments were complicating the country's foreign policies in those countries in which these regions had their offices (by presenting more than one point of official contact with Nigeria). Due to the unsatisfactory situation of this sort of arrangement, after the Balewa era the regions were prohibited from having offices in foreign countries. Thus from the end of the Balewa era until the present, the state governments (which is the nomenclature that in 1967 replaced regional governments) do not have offices in foreign countries.

It seems that the Balewa Government also realized there was a need to lay foundations for structures that would provide intellectual standards for foreign policy decision-making. Thus, during the Balewa era the Nigerian Institute of International Affairs (NIIA) was created (Banjo 1986, 1–16). This body fit Balewa's penchant for nonreckless use of power and his love for balanced, calm, and objective views of issues and events; he often defended the need for NIIA, as a premier foreign policy think tank, to be independent, even though NIIA was created and funded by his government (Banjo 1986, 16). Interestingly, Tafawa Balewa even had to fight against his own government in order to maintain the independence of the NIIA and enable the think tank not to be directly controlled by the government. According to Banjo (1986, 16), Balewa "defended" the NIIA "against the expressed preferences of his Minister of External Affairs and the foreign service establishment." Thus, this was a situation in which Balewa, who concentrated much of the foreign policy formulation in the Office of the Prime Minister (at the expense of the Ministry of External Affairs), sought to ensure that his government had no direct control over the NIIA. Maybe he wanted independent, objective intellectual input to exist within the foreign policy milieu in order to broaden the intellectual horizon of the foreign policy elites and foreign policy makers and also make available numerous foreign policy options that the foreign policy makers might utilize when they were groping for foreign policy directions.

The above analysis of the foreign policy decision-making system during the Balewa era shows that the Office of the Prime Minister tended to be the ultimate decision-making structure in those foreign policy issues with political dimensions. The Ministries of Finance, Economic Development, Commerce and Industry, and External Affairs were mostly in charge of the economic components of foreign policy, with the first three ministries playing the major roles. Though the Ministry of External Affairs had its own Economic Division, it was never able to play a major role in terms of international economic relations relative to the three other ministries. Specifically, the Federal Ministry of Finance was in charge of international financial relations while the Federal Ministry of Economic Development was in charge of international economic and technical assistance and cooperation. The Federal Ministry of Commerce and Industry and the Ministry of External Affairs shared the responsibility for international trade relations, and this joint responsibility caused a lot of friction between the two ministries.

External publicity and international cultural relations were jointly managed by the Federal Ministry of Information and the Ministry of External Affairs, and similarly there was a lot of friction between these two ministries.

Generally, coordination of foreign policy activities were inadequate. However, coordination was unnecessary for major foreign policy issues with political dimensions, since such issues were completely controlled by the Office of the Prime Minister. In the areas of international economic relations, external publicity, international cultural relations, and routine diplomatic activities, there was need for adequate coordination.

This situation resulted in the functioning and output of the Office of the Prime Minister, in terms of foreign affairs, reflecting the rational model of decision-making. This office being in complete control of foreign policy formulation for issues of political dimension meant that it was more able to prioritize foreign policy problems, search for various policy options, calmly calculate the merit and demerits of all these options, and then choose the option that best suited the foreign policy problem. The Office of the Prime Minister was able to afford the luxury of the rational model of decision-making due to internal and external factors. The internal factors were the fact that the Office of the Prime Minister consisted of a relatively small number of people, and the fact that it consisted of a predominant political leader being surrounded by subordinate and pliable staff members. The small number of people meant less red tape and the members easily agreeing about the nature of the problems, possible solutions, and choice of solutions. The external factors were the fact that the Office of the Prime Minister did not have to compete with, bargain with, or reach a compromise with the Cabinet, Parliament, or the ministries. Thus, the foreign policy formulation framework was unitary and efficient, maximizing policy output.

On the other hand, as shown above, the areas of international economic relations, external publicity, and international cultural relations involved many ministries who mostly sought to advance the interests of their respective ministries, instead of focusing on the interests of the country. These ministries usually competed with each other, bargained, and reached compromises with each other. The policy output therefore was the product of compromise rather than that of the best-available policy option. Thus, foreign policy decision-making in these policy areas mostly reflected the bureaucratic politics model of decision-making.

In the areas where routine diplomatic activities were involved, officials mainly relied on the written and formal standard operating procedures that were created for such routine activities. Thus, in these areas the decision-making reflected the organizational process model of decision-making.

3
The Ironsi Government Interlude

THE IRONSI GOVERNMENT WAS VERY BRIEF. IT LASTED FROM JANUARY 1966 to July 1966. This government ushered in the first era of military governments. J. T. U. Aguiyi-Ironsi was the head of state and the leader of this government. Notably, the Ironsi era was a period of severe political tension and instability due to ethnic and religious cleavages and conflicts. Thus, the Ironsi Government, throughout its very brief tenure, was almost totally occupied with domestic issues: the very survival of the nation as one country was at stake.

Therefore, there was no significant change in terms of foreign policy approach. It is also important to note that the Supreme Military Council replaced the Parliament as the highest decision-making and law-making body of the country. This government also attempted to replace the federal system of government with a unitary system of government; but the Ironsi era was brought to end before the unitary system became operational. After the Ironsi era, the country reaffirmed its federal nature. Thus, from 1960 to the present, Nigeria has been a federation.

Despite its brief duration and focus on domestic problems, the Ironsi Government was able to affect the Nigerian foreign policy decision-making system in a significant way; and this action was "an important step which had far-reaching impact on the conduct of foreign policy. The 'independence' of the regions in foreign policy, which allowed Nigerians to sound many contradictory tunes on foreign policy was abolished. Their various regional 'mini-embassies' abroad were closed down. And only Federal Government authorized agents could make foreign policy initiatives or even speak on foreign policy" (Ojo 1986, 438).

This was a major change in the foreign policy decision-making system. However, this change was very much tied to the domestic situation. By formally abolishing the federal system and replacing it with the unitary system (though this change was never operational and the change itself formally reverted back to the federal system after the Ironsi era, as noted above), the Ironsi Government had to abolish a foreign policy feature that strongly reflected the federal system of government (the regional governments establishing offices in some foreign countries). Though the federal system continued after the Ironsi era up till today, successive governments have loved the tidiness and wisdom of not allowing the state governments to compete with the federal government in foreign affairs. Thus, all these successive governments, up till the present, continue to uphold the policy of the Ironsi Government of not allowing state governments to have offices in foreign countries.

4
The Gowon Era

LIKE THE IRONSI GOVERNMENT, THE GOWON GOVERNMENT WAS A MILItary government. From 1966 to 1975, Yakubu Gowon was the head of state and head of government of Nigeria. This period covers important events in the history of the country. From 1966 to 1967 the country experienced extreme societal cleavages, instability, and violence, and the threat of secession from the now-defunct Eastern Region. In 1967, the Eastern Region declared itself the independent Republic of Biafra, but the federal government was determined to stop the secession from being realized; and thus, the Civil War began just after the declaration of secession. Additionally, just after the secession was declared the federal government turned the four-region federal system into a twelve-state federal system. This move corrected a major fault in the federal system, the fact that the then Northern Region, as one of the component regional units in the federal system, was politically more powerful than all the other three regions combined. More importantly for the federal government's goal of keeping the country together, the new system created states for the significant minority groups in the southern part of the country (including the then Eastern Region) and the northern part of the country, and thereby engendered broad national support and sociopolitical forces that were to be vital in helping the federal government to win the Civil War. The Civil War ended in 1970, and the Republic of Biafra ceased to exist. The end of the war was followed by a period of successful national reconciliation and reconstruction programs. After this phase, the country experienced a robust growth in the economy, due mainly to significant increases in the price of petroleum (the main export product of the country) as a result of the activities of the Organization of Petroleum Exporting Countries (OPEC).

All the above events, during the Gowon era, had profound impacts on the nature of the country's international relations. The Civil War was a period during which Nigeria bought many weapon systems for the Nigerian army, air force, and navy from foreign countries. This resulted in Nigeria establishing stronger international security and military relations with some countries. This was also a period in which Nigeria had to marshal its diplomatic resources in various international organizations (like the Organization of African Unity and the United Nations) and in many foreign countries, to assure world opinion that it was prosecuting the Civil War without flagrant abuse of international law and human rights. Nigeria also had to work hard diplomatically to minimize the number of countries that extended diplomatic recognition and/or military and economic support to Biafra. The end of the Civil War (which also meant the end of Biafra) saw Nigeria trying to repair diplomatic relations with these countries. With Nigeria emerging from the Civil War stronger and also being blessed with economic boom due to rising petroleum prices in international markets, the country began to focus on regional integration efforts in West Africa, the strengthening of the Organization of African Unity, the relations between the industrialized countries and the less industrialized countries, the struggle for national liberations (in African countries that were then still under colonial rule or racial oppression), and the Middle East issue.

Thus, throughout the Gowon era, the country's foreign policy and diplomatic activities were constantly and consistently in full gear. The way foreign policy decision structures and processes related to these foreign policy and diplomatic activities is examined in this section.

During the Gowon era, the decision-making structures that significantly had something to do with foreign affairs, either partially or wholly, were the Supreme Military Council; Dodan Barracks (which encompassed the Head of State's Office and the Supreme Military Headquarters); the Federal Executive Council; the Cabinet Office; the Ministries of External Affairs, Defense, Finance, Economic Development, Trade, Industries, Information, and Petroleum Resources; the Nigerian Institute of International Affairs; and the Nigerian National Petroleum Corporation. The profiles, functioning, and roles of these decision structures, in terms of Nigeria's international relations during the Gowon era, are analyzed below.

THE SUPREME MILITARY COUNCIL

The Supreme Military Council was the highest national policy and decision-making body during the Gowon era. The head of state and government was the chairman of this body. (The Gowon Government being a military government meant that most members of the Supreme Military Council were military officers.) Other major members of the Supreme Military Council were the chief of staff of the Supreme Military Headquarters; the chiefs of staff of the Nigerian army, navy, air force; other senior military officers; the military governors of the states; and the administrator of the former East Central State (this last member was a civilian).

Though the Supreme Military Council was the highest policy body, it seems it was sparingly involved directly and intimately with foreign policy issues. It seems that it mainly served as a body to which foreign policy decisions, made by lower bodies, were merely reported. According to Olajide Aluko (1976, 412), "under the administration of General Gowon major decisions on foreign policy were taken by the Federal Executive Council . . . and later reported to the Supreme Military Council . . . merely for information." Thus, it can be concluded that though the Supreme Military Council was the highest and most important policy and decision-making body, its impact was more in terms of domestic policy and less in terms of foreign policy, since it was not much directly involved with foreign policy issues.

Dodan Barracks

During the Gowon era, Dodan Barracks was a military barracks that also served as the office and official residence of the head of the Federal Military Government of Nigeria. Also located within the Dodan Barracks was the Supreme Military Headquarters, which encompassed the office of the chief of staff of the Supreme Military Headquarters. (The complex of buildings that served as the office and official residence for the head of the Federal Military Government and the offices for the Supreme Military Headquarters was just a portion of Dodan Barracks; also housed there was a sizeable group of buildings for the lodgings of the rank and file of a military unit and for other military uses.) Because of the location of the office and residence of the head of the Federal Military Government and the offices for the Supreme Military Headquarters within the Dodan Barracks, that name itself (Dodan Barracks) connoted the center of the federal government of Nigeria during the Gowon era.

It is also important to note that all the military governments in Nigeria, up till the Babangida Government, made Dodan Barracks the center of the federal government of Nigeria. Interestingly, the Shagari Government (the civilian government that separated the first era of military governments from the second era of military governments) also located the office and residence of the president within the Dodan Barracks. Thus, from 1966 to 1991, Dodan Barracks served as the center of the federal government of Nigeria. In December 1991 Abuja replaced Lagos as the capital of Nigeria (*West Africa* 23 December 1991 - 5 January 1992, 2162; *West Africa* 6–12 January 1992, 35). Thus, Dodan Barracks, which is located in Lagos, from December 1991 ceased to serve as the center of the federal government of Nigeria.

In this section of this study Dodan Barracks as a decision-making struc-

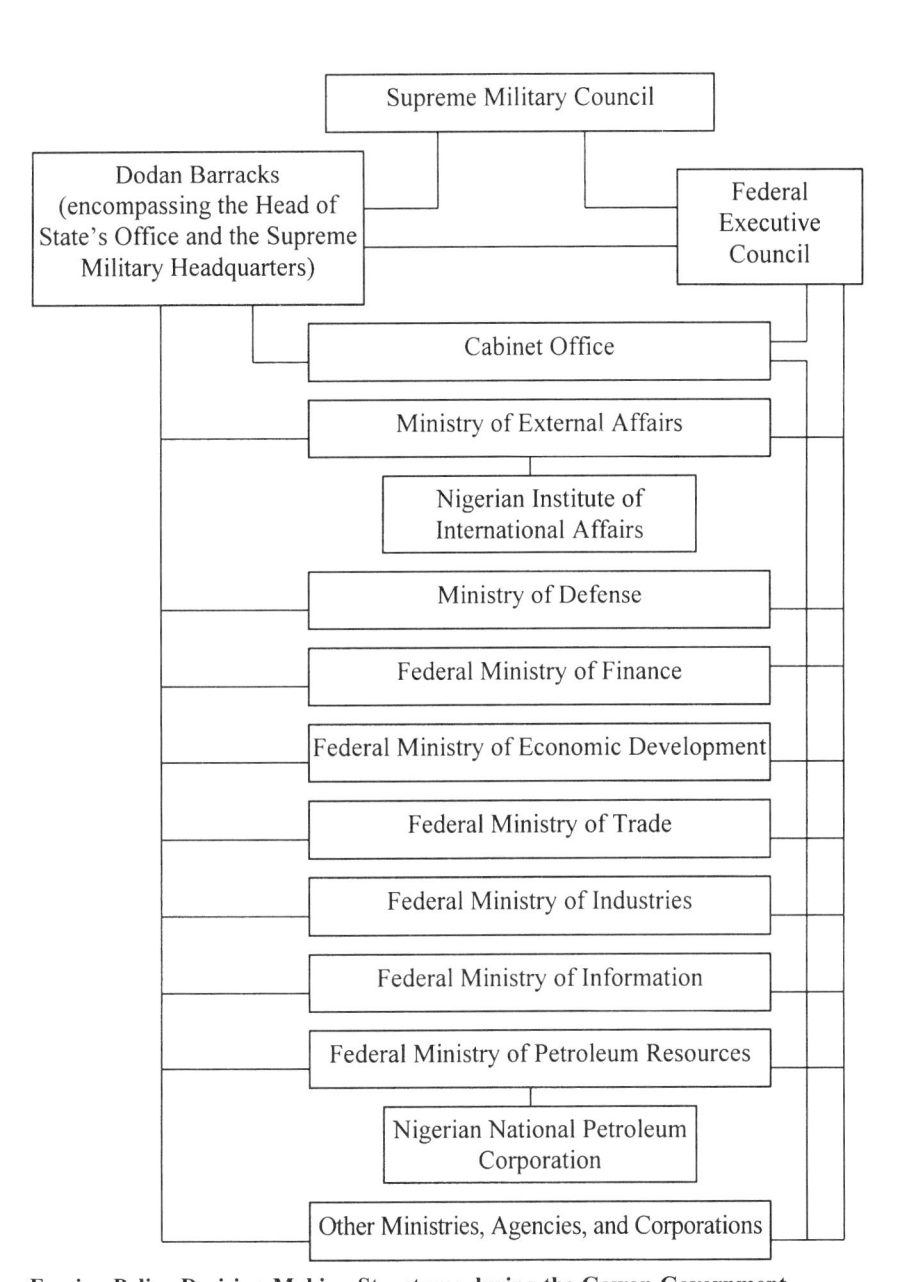

```
                    ┌─────────────────────────┐
                    │ Supreme Military Council │
                    └─────────────────────────┘
┌──────────────────────┐          ┌──────────────┐
│ Dodan Barracks       │          │   Federal    │
│ (encompassing the    │          │  Executive   │
│ Head of State's      │          │   Council    │
│ Office and the       │          │              │
│ Supreme Military     │          └──────────────┘
│ Headquarters)        │
└──────────────────────┘
                ┌──────────────────────────────┐
                │        Cabinet Office         │
                └──────────────────────────────┘
                ┌──────────────────────────────┐
                │  Ministry of External Affairs │
                └──────────────────────────────┘
                    ┌──────────────────────┐
                    │ Nigerian Institute of│
                    │ International Affairs│
                    └──────────────────────┘
                ┌──────────────────────────────┐
                │      Ministry of Defense      │
                └──────────────────────────────┘
                ┌──────────────────────────────┐
                │  Federal Ministry of Finance  │
                └──────────────────────────────┘
                ┌──────────────────────────────────┐
                │ Federal Ministry of Economic      │
                │         Development               │
                └──────────────────────────────────┘
                ┌──────────────────────────────┐
                │   Federal Ministry of Trade   │
                └──────────────────────────────┘
                ┌──────────────────────────────┐
                │ Federal Ministry of Industries│
                └──────────────────────────────┘
                ┌──────────────────────────────┐
                │Federal Ministry of Information│
                └──────────────────────────────┘
                ┌──────────────────────────────────┐
                │Federal Ministry of Petroleum      │
                │          Resources                │
                └──────────────────────────────────┘
                    ┌──────────────────────┐
                    │ Nigerian National    │
                    │ Petroleum Corporation│
                    └──────────────────────┘
                ┌──────────────────────────────────┐
                │Other Ministries, Agencies, and    │
                │         Corporations              │
                └──────────────────────────────────┘
```

Foreign Policy Decision-Making Structures during the Gowon Government

ture will be examined in terms of its impact on foreign policy decision-making systems during the Gowon era.

The Supreme Military Headquarters was a decision unit that was mostly concerned with domestic issues. It served as the focal point of the military role in national governance. Since the Gowon Government was a military government, the Supreme Military Headquarters was a vital decision-making unit. Thus, it was the main immediate military body that served the head of the Federal Military Government and the Supreme Military Council.

The Supreme Military Headquarters also served as the nexus between the Federal Military Government and the purely military bodies (the Ministry of Defense and its component units of the Nigerian army, navy, and air force). During the Gowon era, the portfolio of the commissioner of defense was retained by the head of the Federal Military Government. The Supreme Military Headquarters thus provided the support staff that helped the head of the Federal Military Government (General Yakubu Gowon) to provide political and policy leadership to the Ministry of Defense. Thus, though the Supreme Military Headquarters was not very visible in terms of general foreign affairs, it was well placed to have impact on Nigeria's international security and military relations (though in a quiet way). Specifically, its staff was in position to advise Yakubu Gowon on decisions concerning the buying of major military weapon systems from abroad, to which foreign countries Nigerian military officials would go for some of their training needs, and with which foreign countries Nigeria would forge strong, moderate, or weak security and military relations. Thus, during the Civil War era (when Nigeria made a lot of changes in terms of its procurements of its major weapons from abroad, military training programs in foreign countries, and general international security and military links), the Supreme Military Headquarters, together with the Ministry of Defense, were vital in the collection, analysis, and interpretation of the information that Gowon and the Supreme Military Council needed in order to make their decisions. The Supreme Military Headquarters played this role throughout the Gowon era, though such a role must have been much more pronounced during the Civil War era.

Yakubu Gowon, though allowing the Ministry of External Affairs to be in adequate control of foreign affairs, had certain foreign issues he was passionately involved with. Gowon's strong desire to achieve speedy national reconciliation among all Nigerians after the Civil War also had its international counterpart: Gowon's desire to achieve reconciliation with African countries that backed the unsuccessful attempt of the former Eastern Region to secede as the Republic of Biafra (see Gambari 1989, 7). Gowon was also interested in ensuring that Nigerians had adequate control over the commanding heights of the Nigerian economy. Through his economic policy, the roles of foreign firms were lessened in some sectors of the economy (Akinsanya 1986, 226). This policy also had international ramifications, reshaping the nature of Nigeria's international economic relations. Gowon was also interested in the problems in southern Africa and other parts of Africa where people were then struggling for their freedom (Ajala 1986, 201); in the problems facing people of African ancestry all over the world (Olusanya and Akindele 1986a, 7); in the economic situation of the developing countries in relation to the industrialized countries (Aluko 1986, 90; Gambari 1989, 8); and in the Middle East issue (Akindele 1985, 55). Gowon was the chairman of the Organization of African Unity (OAU) in 1973 (Ojo 1986, 440); in this position he advanced some initiatives that would impact on the above issues. However, one foreign policy issue almost constantly captured the interest of Gowon, and that was the economic and political integration of West African countries. Through his persistence and leadership, the foundations were laid for the emergence of the Economic Community of West African States (ECOWAS) (Ede 1986, 187; Gambari 1989, 8; Ofoegbu 1979, 129–33).

The Dodan Barracks was able to help fashion Nigeria's foreign policy in a certain way. However, the impact of Dodan Barracks was mainly in terms of broad policy outlines for those foreign policy issues that interested Gowon. Thus, the Ministry of External Affairs was firmly in control of the foreign policy machinery, in terms of the most policy processes. As Aluko notes (1976, 413), during the Gowon era "it was the Ministry that formed the lynch-pin of the country's foreign policy." Thus, Dodan Barracks was mainly giving broad foreign policy initiatives and guidelines, while the Ministry of External Affairs remained the nerve center of Nigeria's foreign policy. In reality, Dodan Barracks was never interested in moving the control of foreign policy away from the Ministry of External Affairs to itself. Dodan Barracks seems to have been mainly interested in providing political leadership, in terms of providing broad policy outlines and initiatives in relation to some key foreign policy issues. Thus, there was never any effort to create an in-house foreign policy unit within the Dodan Barracks, with the staff and material resources that could enable it to compete with the Ministry of External Affairs in foreign policy decision-making processes and output).

THE FEDERAL EXECUTIVE COUNCIL

The Federal Executive Council was the forum for the political heads of the various federal ministries (called Commissioners during the Gowon era).

In effect, the Federal Executive Council was the Cabinet. Some permanent secretaries (the most senior career civil servants in the ministries and other bureaucracies) were also members of the Federal Executive Council (Aluko 1976, 413); and this reflected the prominent and visible role of career civil servants in the policy process during the Gowon era. Since the Gowon Government was a military government and not a parliamentary democracy, formally the Federal Executive Council was an advisory body (rather than a collective decision-making body) for the Federal Military Government and the head of the Federal Military Government. The head of the Federal Military Government was the chairman of the Federal Executive Council. However, in reality the Federal Executive Council was a significant national decision-making body, during the Gowon era, since during that period, the Federal Military Government very much depended on the various federal ministries (especially their senior career civil servants) for guidelines for policy formulations. The Federal Executive Council was the body through which the Federal Military Government collectively met with the political heads of the various federal ministries (who were often assisted in this forum by the senior civil servants from the respective ministries). The civil servants played a major role in almost all policy formulations during this era (Aluko 1983, 77), and the Federal Executive Council was the body through which the civil servants collectively directly impacted on national policies. Thus, the Federal Executive Council was a major policy-making body of the Federal Military Government during the Gowon era.

However, the impact of the Federal Executive Council was more significant in the domestic policy arena. According to Aluko (1983, 80), most decisions "were made by the head of State Government and the Ministry of External Affairs," and were "later referred to the executive council for formal ratification." The fact that the Federal Executive Council formally adopted the major foreign policy decisions (though the decisions were actually made by the head of the Federal Military Government and/or the Ministry of External Affairs) still made the Federal Executive Council a significant foreign policy decision-making structure. In this sense, the Federal Executive Council was in reality more significant than the Supreme Military Council (which was the highest national policy-making body) during the Gowon era. According to Aluko (1976, 412), as noted earlier, during the Gowon era, "major decisions on foreign policy were taken by the Federal Executive Council . . . and later reported to the Supreme Military Council . . . merely for information." Thus, during the Gowon era, the Federal Executive Council was an important foreign policy decision-making structure, though it was not as important as Dodan Barracks or the Ministry of External Affairs.

The Cabinet Office

The Cabinet Office was the structure that effected the administrative coordination of all the federal ministries and agencies of the government. Additionally, the Cabinet Office functioned as the administrative fulcrum for the Federal Executive Council.

The fact that the Gowon Government allowed career civil servants to be very prominent and visible in the policy-making process (Aluko 1976, 412–13; Aluko 1983, 80), as already noted earlier, meant that the Cabinet Office was a significant factor in the national policy-making milieu, since it was an administrative organ in the federal bureaucratic system, wherein senior career civil servants effected the national administration and administrative coordination of the various federal ministries and agencies.

Though mainly important in domestic policy and administrative affairs, the role of the Cabinet Office was such that it also had an impact on foreign affairs issues where and when there was need for coordination among various federal ministries and agencies: for example, external information and cultural relations, international security relations, international trade relations, international financial relations, and international economic integration efforts. For example, in 1970 the Cabinet Office participated in the coordination of policy review of the impacts of European integration on Nigeria (Aluko 1990b, 206). The Political and the Economic Divisions of the Cabinet Office, in addition to their dominant domestic policy agenda, handled many of the foreign affairs issues that merited the attention of the Cabinet Office.

On the whole, the role of the Cabinet Office in foreign affairs issues was mostly low-key and bureaucratic in nature. Comparatively, Dodan Barracks and the Ministry of External Affairs were the visible, prominent, and dominant foreign policy decision-making organs.

The Ministry of External Affairs

Though Dodan Barracks was more visible in foreign affairs than the Ministry of External Affairs, the latter was clearly in charge of the management of Nigeria's international relations during the Gowon era. Dodan Barracks, as noted earlier, was mainly visible in terms of providing broad foreign policy guidelines in relation to those foreign policy issues that interested Yakubu Gowon.

The organizational structure of the Ministry of External Affairs during the Gowon era was not much different from that of other eras. At the apex of the ministry was the commissioner of External Affairs (Aluko 1983,

80–81). A political appointee, the commissioner constituted the political leadership of the ministry. Immediately below this position was the permanent secretary of the ministry. He served as the administrative head of ministry. He coordinated the various units of the ministry, oversaw the general administration of this ministry, and also served as an adviser to the commissioner. The position of the permanent secretary was always held by a very senior career civil servant.

The component units of the ministry were geographically oriented departments, functionally oriented departments, and some special units (Aluko 1983, 81). Each geographical department was split into divisions, and the division broken into sections, and the sections in turn divided into country(ies) desks (Aluko 1983, 81).

In terms of the functioning of the ministry, the decision-making processes linked the country(ies) desks, sections, divisions, departments, the permanent secretary, and the Commissioner of External Affairs. The decision processes consisted of drafts done by desk officers, based on all the information available (including diplomatic dispatches), and passed on to heads of sections, divisions, and departments (for their modifications, support, or recommendations of the policy proposals contained in the drafts), and then to the permanent secretary or the commissioner for an action to be taken (Aluko 1983, 81).

Aluko (1983, 81) also notes that the main functions of the ministry often consisted of "the collection and interpretation of information on developments in foreign countries. This is the source of advice and policy proposals tendered to the Minister/Commissioner for External Affairs, and to the Head of State/Government. Such information is used for briefing other ministries; for ministries preparing for visits abroad; for discussions with foreign visitors; for drafts of questions in the national Assembly; and for preparing speeches." Thus, the functioning of the ministry often had direct impact on other ministries and the national leadership, as regards the country's international relations.

During the Gowon Administration, career civil servants became very influential in the political system. This might have been due to military leaders not having adequate political and administrative backgrounds, and thus becoming very dependent on their experienced senior career civil servants. Additionally, the military leaders might have perceived the senior career civil servants as being more loyal and reliable (and also being less of a political threat) in comparison to the political appointees who served as commissioners (and thus political heads) of the ministries. Like other ministries, the Ministry of External Affairs, during the Gowon era, had career diplomats and career civil servants exercising tremendous influence. Aluko (1976, 413) notes that "the Permanent Secretary, who was then Mr. Joe Iyalla, was a member of the Federal Executive Council." The fact that Iyalla, a career civil servant, was made a member of the Federal Executive Council shows the prominent role of career civil servants during the Gowon Government. It meant that, as a member of the Federal Executive Council, Iyalla was helping the political leaders to formulate policies. Thus, during the Gowon era career civil servants were not limited to their traditional role of merely providing information to the political leaders (who make policies) and implementing the policies (which the political leaders have made). Career civil servants of the Gowon era were thus perceived as part of both the policy formulation and policy implementation processes. Aluko (1983, 77) believes that the Gowon era saw the bureaucrats rise to their highest prominence.

Another important feature of the foreign policy decision-making system during the Gowon era was that the Ministry of External Affairs clearly dominated this arena. This was most likely caused by the great confidence the Gowon Government had in career civil servants. Thus, the career diplomats and career civil servants of the Ministry of External Affairs might have been perceived by the government as being very competent to manage the country's foreign affairs without close supervision by the national leadership represented by Dodan Barracks. Dodan Barracks, as noted earlier, mainly provided broad foreign policy guidelines and directions.

The dominance of the Ministry of External Affairs and the career diplomats over the foreign policy decision-making system resulted, predictably, in mostly cautious foreign policy outputs (since career diplomats are often cautious and moderate diplomats). For example, during the Gowon era "Nigeria was one of the last African countries to break diplomatic ties with Israel following the Yom Kippur War of October 1973" (Aluko 1976, 412).

The pivotal role that the Ministry of External Affairs was able to play in the foreign policy decision-making system was also due to the sort of leadership that the commissioner for external affairs was able to provide. Dr. Okoi Arikpo, who was the commissioner, was a respected politician and an able administrator. His steady and competent leadership earned the respect and support of the career diplomats who dominated the Ministry of External Affairs. Arikpo's ability to work effectively with the career diplomats was also enhanced by his cautious and moderate foreign policy decision-making approach, shared by the career diplomats.

The effective and competent manner in which Arikpo, and the Ministry of External Affairs that he headed, managed Nigeria's international relations during the Civil War period and the immediate post-war period, showed that the Gowon Government was correct in allowing the ministry to have clear primacy in the foreign policy decision-making system. During the Civil War, the ministry was able to help Nigeria to develop new and vital relationships with Eastern Europe (military weapons from the Soviet Union and other East European countries were very important in helping Nigeria militarily extinguish the secession of Biafra), while still maintaining adequate relationships with the traditional friendly countries of the West. The ability to pursue that sort of active nonaligned foreign policy during the Cold War era, without causing significant conflict with either the Western bloc or the Eastern bloc, was another testimony to the seasoned and accomplished diplomatic skills of the officials of the Ministry of External Affairs. However, the ministry was not able to match the effective and innovative Biafran external publicity skills. Arikpo mainly used the traditional diplomatic approach of explaining the facts of the Civil War to the world media and audience. Arikpo's focus on the sources of foreign military assistance to Biafra (Ajala 1986, 200) illustrates such an approach.

Though the ministry was not adequately effective in terms of external publicity, it was very effective in using diplomatic channels to convince key world powers and major international organizations to understand Nigeria's actions and intentions in its effort to end the Biafran secession. Thus, apart from France, key major Western countries, like the United States, Britain, and Germany, did not prominently oppose the way Nigeria was trying to end the Civil War. Though the Biafran external publicity efforts caused worries in the United States, Britain, and other countries about the possibility of violation of human rights in Nigeria, the governments of these countries did not forcefully try to obstruct the way in which Nigeria was bent on stopping the Biafran secession militarily.

The diplomatic skills of the Ministry of External Affairs were also very effective in dissuading the United Nations and the Organization of African Unity from actively intervening in the Civil War with peacekeeping operations. Thus, instead of peacekeeping efforts, the United Nations mainly sent ad hoc observer teams to Nigeria to monitor human rights situations in the war zones. The Organization of African Unity, instead of sending its own peacekeeping force, organized peace talks between Nigerian and Biafran delegations in other African countries. By keeping important foreign countries, and major international organizations, from being intimately involved in the Civil War, the Ministry of External Affairs helped the Gowon Government to militarily defeat Biafra and end the secession (and thus reintegrate the country on its own terms).

After the Civil War, the Ministry of External Affairs also helped Nigeria to reinforce its links with the Western world, repair relations with countries that had supported Biafra, and build a strong position in Africa. Thus, Nigeria quickly established adequate relations with countries like Cote d'Ivoire, Tanzania, China, and France that had supported Biafra. Arikpo, in particular, through visits to China (Owoeye 1986, 300), France (Nwokedi 1986, 288), and other countries, laid the foundations for the resumption of these adequate diplomatic ties. Additionally, "Gowon assisted by his able Commissioner for External Affairs, Dr. Okoi Arikpo, as well as bright career diplomats in the African Department of the Ministry of External Affairs, Lagos, succeeded not only in promoting unity and solidarity among African states but also in making the OAU to serve as an instrument of Nigerian foreign policy" (Aluko 1986, 90).

Thus, Nigeria emerged from the Civil War to play a vital role in Africa through the Organization of African Unity (OAU). The Economic Community of West African States (ECOWAS) was another foreign policy focus of the Gowon Government. Yakubu Gowon, with the diplomatic role of the Ministry of External Affairs, in addition to the more prominent and positive role of the Federal Ministry of Economic Development, was able to convince West African countries to create ECOWAS as a regional integration framework.

On the whole, the Ministry of External Affairs, as the major organ of foreign policy decision-making, served the Gowon Government adequately.

OTHER MINISTRIES AND AGENCIES

Although the Ministry of External Affairs was the major organ involved in the management of Nigeria's international relations, other federal ministries and agencies, as usual, were also involved.

In terms of the security/military component of Nigeria's international relations, the Ministry of Defense was the major organ, its profile raised by the Civil War. The Ministry of Defense worked together with the Ministry of External Affairs to establish new and vital security and military relations with the former Soviet Union, the now defunct Czechoslovakia, and other East European countries in order to procure the weapon systems that were crucial to Nigeria's ability to stop the Biafran secession. (Orobator [1983, 212–13] notes that the role that the former Czechoslovakia played in transferring weapons to Nigeria even impacted on the former Czechoslovakia's domestic politics and relations between it and the former Soviet Union.

The huge amount, and numerous types, of weapons that a country like the former Soviet Union supplied to Nigeria meant that the Ministry of Defense had to be closely involved in giving the former Soviet Union adequate technical information about the sort of weapons that Nigeria needed. According to Ogunbadejo (1986, 256–57), "the Soviets, for the first two years of the war, supplied only air weapons: MIGs and Ilyushins. In 1969, however, ground weapons were added; these included heavy (122-mm) guns, a considerable number of Kalshnikovs, and 107-mm recoilless rifles. . . . Ironically, it was the 122-mm guns, supplied in the last phase of the war, that played a crucial part in the final determination of the conflict." Thus, Soviet weapons were vital in helping Nigeria to militarily stop the Biafran secession. Appropriately, "Nigeria's ambassador in Moscow, George Kurubo, insisted that, in the final analysis, Soviet aid was 'responsible for the federal victory more than any other simple thing, more than all other things put together'" (Ogunbadejo 1986, 257). To further underscore the prominence of the security/military component of Nigeria's relations with the former Soviet Union, during the Civil War (and the resultant visible and important role of the Ministry of Defense), George Kurubo, who was Nigeria's ambassador to the former Soviet Union during the period of the Civil War, was an officer in the Nigerian military with the rank of a brigadier-general.

Nigeria also got some military supplies from Western countries during the Civil War. The Ministry of Defense also worked with the Ministry of External Affairs to manage these security/military contacts.

Even during peace time, the Ministry of Defense is an important organ in Nigeria's international security/military relations. The end of the Civil War meant accelerated security/military relations between Nigeria and Western countries like the United Kingdom and the United States, and continued military ties with the former Soviet Union. Most of these security/military ties involved Nigeria's procurement of weapon systems from these countries and also the utilization of military training facilities in those foreign countries. These activities meant that the Ministry of Defense, and its defense attachés stationed in some Nigerian foreign missions, played vital roles in Nigeria's international security/military relations on a continual and consistent basis.

The profile of the leadership of the Ministry of Defense also helped the ministry to have a high visibility in the country's policy milieu. Throughout the Gowon era, the portfolio of commissioner (or minister) of Defense was held by the head of state. The fact that Gowon held this ministerial portfolio and was thus the direct political head of the Ministry of Defense undoubtedly enhanced the ministry's visibility and the foreign policy milieu. Additionally, the fact that the Gowon Government was a military government also meant more prominence for the Ministry of Defense in the national policy milieu (including the foreign policy decision-making arena), since the ministry represented and embodied the military establishment.

Various decision structures were involved in the economic component of the Nigerian foreign policy. The major decision structures in this policy arena were the Ministry of External Affairs (mainly through its International Economic Department), the Federal Ministry of Finance, Federal Ministry of Trade, Federal Ministry of Economic Development, Federal

Ministry of Industries, Federal Ministry of Petroleum Resources, and the Nigerian National Petroleum Corporation.

The International Economic Departments of the Ministry of External Affairs often liaised with these other decision structures involved in international economic relations. As usual, conflicts between the Ministry of External Affairs and some of these other decision structures, over the issue of which of them should play the primary role in some particular matter of international economic policy was always common during the Gowon period (just as in other periods).

The role of the Federal Ministry of Finance, as noted in an earlier part of this work, has always been in the area of international financial and fiscal relations. Additionally, the Central Bank of Nigeria always has significant links with the central banking systems of other countries.

International trade issues logically always concern the Federal Ministry of Trade, while the Federal Ministry of Economic Development is often concerned with international regional economic integration policies and international economic assistance activities. Thus, during the Gowon era, the Ministry of External Affairs together with the Federal Ministries of Trade and Economic Development were the major decision structures involved in formulating and managing Nigeria's role in the Economic Community of West African States and Lome Convention One (Aluko 1983, 84–86). The international visibility of the Federal Ministry of Trade was shown by the fact that the federal commissioner of trade served as the spokesperson for African countries in the international trade negotiations between African, Caribbean, and Pacific countries and European Community countries (Nweke 1983, 26–27).

The role of the Federal Ministry of Industries related to the international ramifications of Nigeria's industrialization policies and activities: for example, the policies on foreign investments in Nigerian industries. Additionally, the Gowon Government instituted the "Nigerianization" policy, which sought to give visible roles to Nigerians in certain economic enterprises (Akinsanya 1986, 226). The aspects of this policy that related to foreign investments in some Nigerian industries, for example, gave the Federal Ministry of Industries some role in Nigeria's international economic relations.

During the Gowon era, petroleum became even more important as Nigeria's biggest and dominant foreign income earner. The Federal Ministry of Petroleum Resources managed Nigeria's international activities relating to petroleum resources. Most importantly, this ministry was in charge of Nigeria's relations with the Organization of Petroleum Exporting Countries (OPEC). (Nigeria became a member of OPEC in 1971 [Olusanya and Akindele 1986a, 17].) The Federal Ministry of Petroleum Resources might have been as important as the Ministry of External Affairs in terms of Nigeria's relations with countries whose main ties with Nigeria, during the Gowon era, were in terms of their role as OPEC member-countries. For example, in the 1970s Venezuela was a visible member of OPEC (Ogwu 1986, 114). Nigeria's major link with Venezuela, during the Gowon era, seemed to have been mainly in terms of OPEC membership and international political economy of petroleum. Thus, there is a very high possibility that the Federal Ministry of Petroleum Resources played as important a role as the Ministry of External Affairs in terms of Nigeria's relations with Venezuela. The Nigerian National Petroleum Corporation (NNPC) was the umbrella organization that, through foreign and local contractors or the corporation's direct activities, engaged in all facets of the petroleum industry (exploration, development, drilling, refining, transportation, storage, and marketing of petroleum products and resources). The fact that the workings of the petroleum industry involved the use of a large amount of foreign technological components, and the fact that a large portion of the petroleum resources had to be sold to other countries, made the NNPC an important organ in Nigeria's international economic relations.

The Gowon Government was also much involved in efforts to solidify the foundations for a future iron and steel sector in the economy. The former Soviet Union was the major foreign technical partner of the Gowon Government in nurturing the steel industry (Alli-Balogun 1988; Ogunbadejo 1986, 258). This made the Nigerian Steel Development Authority another organ that played a role in international economic relations.

The cultural component of Nigeria's international relations had the Federal Ministry of Information (FMOI) as an important organ. The ministry handled external publicity in the broadcast media (mainly through the Voice of Nigeria—an international broadcasting service) and print media. The ministry also sent some of its officials to serve in some Nigerian foreign missions as information attaches. The ministry, in conjunction with the state ministries of information and with private arts and cultural organizations, also organized and sponsored visual arts and performing arts groups that toured foreign countries to project Nigeria's cultural values and heritage. During the 1970s, the Ministry of External Affairs (MEA) was also given "additional responsibilities" in the area of external publicity (Aluko 1983, 80). As usual, there were conflicts between FMOI and MEA over the control of external publicity activities. The Federal Ministry of Education was also always involved in some aspects of international cultural relations, for example, international student exchange programs, international educational cooperations, and relations with the United Nations Educational, Cultural, and Scientific Organization.

The Nigerian Institute of International Affairs (NIIA), as noted in an earlier section, is a government owned foreign policy think tank. During the Gowon era, the head of the Ministry of External Affairs had "ministerial responsibility" for the NIIA, and this situation often caused some conflicts between the ministry and the NIIA (Banjo 1986, 20). The fact is that the NIIA, through its publication activities, seminars, and conferences, does influence the views of the foreign policy elites. Thus, the NIIA does always have impact on foreign policy design and formulation. However, due to the conflicts mentioned above, NIIA did not seem to perform at its full potential during the Gowon era. Nevertheless, the importance of the NIIA was fully appreciated by the Gowon era foreign policy-makers. For example, Okoi Arikpo, the commissioner of External Affairs, noted that the NIIA "is an instrument of public policy. It should not therefore indulge in idle pursuits unrelated to our national policies and pre-occupation" (Arikpo, quoted in Banjo 1986, 17).

COORDINATION

With so many ministries and agencies involved in Nigeria's international relations, there was an obvious need for coordination. Sometimes the coordination caused conflicts among the ministries and agencies and, at other times, the coordination went on smoothly. Thus, for example, despite some separate visions, the Federal Ministries of Economic Development, Trade, and External Affairs were able to work together on the Lome Convention One and on the formation of ECOWAS (Aluko 1983, 84–86).

As Aluko (1983, 80) notes, "Constant inter-departmental consultation is necessary to offset the difficulties that arise, because in practice given issues can rarely be broken down into purely military, economic, political or other component parts." The strong and visible position the Ministry of External Affairs had in the foreign policy decision-making milieu during the Gowon era helped the ministry to coordinate the other ministries and agencies involved in the foreign policy arena. Thus, though there were some "skirmishes with some home ministries" on the issue of "information, and international economic and financial cooperation . . . the foreign service . . . [had] to act as a single actor in Nigerian decision-making. Therefore the rational policy model will be more suitable" (Aluko 1983, 81). The fact that the Gowon Government was a military government (and thus a governmental system that discouraged open and strong dissensions by, and among, government agencies and ministries) might have also helped to foster the rational actor model of foreign policy decision-making.

An inter-ministerial council set up in 1970 provides another case for the analysis of foreign policy coordination during the Gowon Government. The Gowon Government "set up an inter-ministerial council consisting of the heads of the economic divisions of the Ministry of External Affairs and the Cabinet Office and the top officials of the Ministries of Trade, Industry, Economic Development and Reconstruction and Finance to study and report on the implications for Nigeria of Britain's accession to the Rome Treaty" (Aluko 1990b, 206). According to Aluko, this inter-ministerial council produced a report that was possibly the basis of Nigeria's policy toward the then European Economic Community (EEC) in the early 1970s. Thus, this inter-ministerial council was very adequate as foreign policy coordination machinery.

The issue of the sort of relationship Nigeria was to have with OPEC also involved a lot of policy coordination. The Federal Executive Council was said to have handled the issue (and thus served as the coordinating body for the various ministries and agencies); and, though they were divided on the issue, the members of the Federal Executive Council who favored Nigeria joining OPEC prevailed, due to the input of civil servants who had a powerful presence in the Federal Executive Council during the Gowon Government (Soremekun 1990, 296). The members of the Federal Executive Council who opposed Nigeria joining OPEC were of the view that Nigeria's membership in that body would drag Nigeria into the problems of Middle East, while the members who supported the move prevailed by successfully arguing that such would not be the case (Soremekun 1990, 296). During the Gowon era, the Petroleum Advisory Board (PAB) (consisting of the permanent secretaries of the Federal Ministries of Economic Development, Finance, Industries, Petroleum Resources, and Trade and representative of the Supreme Military Headquarters) also played an important role in coordinating petroleum policies (including OPEC affairs). A senior career civil servant, Phillip Chinedo Asiodu (who was the permanent secretary of the Ministry of Petroleum Resources, the chairman of PAB, and the exofficio chairman and general manager of the then Nigerian National Oil Corporation [now named Nigerian National Petroleum Corporation] exerted a very powerful influence in the country's petroleum affairs and policies (Soremekun 1990, 296–97).

Concerning the foreign policy decision-making processes that led to Nigeria resuming diplomatic ties with African countries that had recognized the Republic of Biafra during the Civil War (Cote d'Ivoire, Gabon, Tanzania, and Zambia), Amuwo (1990, 316–17) notes that the key participants in that decision-making were the Supreme Military Council, the Ministry of External Affairs, key members of the government, and some interest groups.

The decision-making processes that led to Nigeria championing the formation of the Economic Community of West African States (ECOWAS) also presented a very interesting scenario. The office of the Head of State, the Federal Ministry of Economic Development, and the Federal Ministry of Defense were strongly for the creation of ECOWAS (due to the economic benefits of regional integration and greater regional and national security they saw ECOWAS as engendering), with the extra-governmental enthusiastic support of Nigeria Chamber of Commerce, Industry, Mines, and Agriculture (which hoped to benefit from the larger ECOWAS market); while those opposing the creation of ECOWAS were the Federal Ministries of Trade and Industries (which thought that ECOWAS would mean the economic drain of Nigeria by poorer members of ECOWAS and that the Nigerian economy was strong enough to develop and industrialize without the help of regional economic integration) and the Federal Ministry of External Affairs (which saw movements into Nigeria of citizens of the ECOWAS countries that were former French colonies as posing national security risks for Nigeria) (Ojo 1990b, 346–63). The greater power and influence of those ministries and groups that supported Nigeria championing the creation of ECOWAS led to Nigeria deciding to lead and initiate that creation.

On the whole, as shown above, the Gowon Government was a period during which coordination of foreign policy decision-making was mostly adequately handled, as shown by the above examples of the EEC, OPEC, renewal of diplomatic ties (with Cote d'Ivoire, Gabon, Tanzania, and Zambia) and the creation of ECOWAS.

5
The Robust Years:
The Muhammed/Obasanjo Period

THE MUHAMMED/OBASANJO GOVERNMENT SPANNED THE YEARS 1975 TO 1979. General Murtala Muhammed was the head of state from July 1975 to February 1976, and General Olusegun Obasanjo served as the head of state from 1976 to 1979. Obasanjo, who was the chief of staff of the Supreme Military Headquarters when Muhammed was head of state, became the head of state when the latter was assassinated in a coup attempt. Despite the assassination, the coup was unsuccessful, since those who led it were subdued, tried, and convicted. Obasanjo (who was the second in command to Muhammed) succeeding the latter, and carrying on most of the policies of the Muhammed era, meant that the Obasanjo era was a direct and credible continuation of the Muhammed era. Thus, the period from 1975 to 1979 has been perceived as, and called, the Muhammed/Obasanjo era.

The Muhammed/Obasanjo Government era is often perceived as a period during which there were significant changes in foreign policy dynamics and output, including changes in the foreign policy decision-making structures and processes.

The major decision-making structures that were involved in foreign policy decision-making during this era were the Supreme Military Council, the Head of State's Office, the Supreme Military Headquarters, the National Council of States, the Federal Executive Council, the Cabinet Office, the Federal Ministry of External Affairs, the Federal Ministry of Defense, the Nigerian Institute of International Affairs, and many other federal ministries and agencies that had significant roles in foreign affairs. The profile, role, and impact of each of these decision-making units in the foreign policy milieu are analyzed below.

THE SUPREME MILITARY COUNCIL

As in the Gowon era, the Supreme Military Council (SMC) was the highest national policy-making body during the Muhammed/Obasanjo Govern-

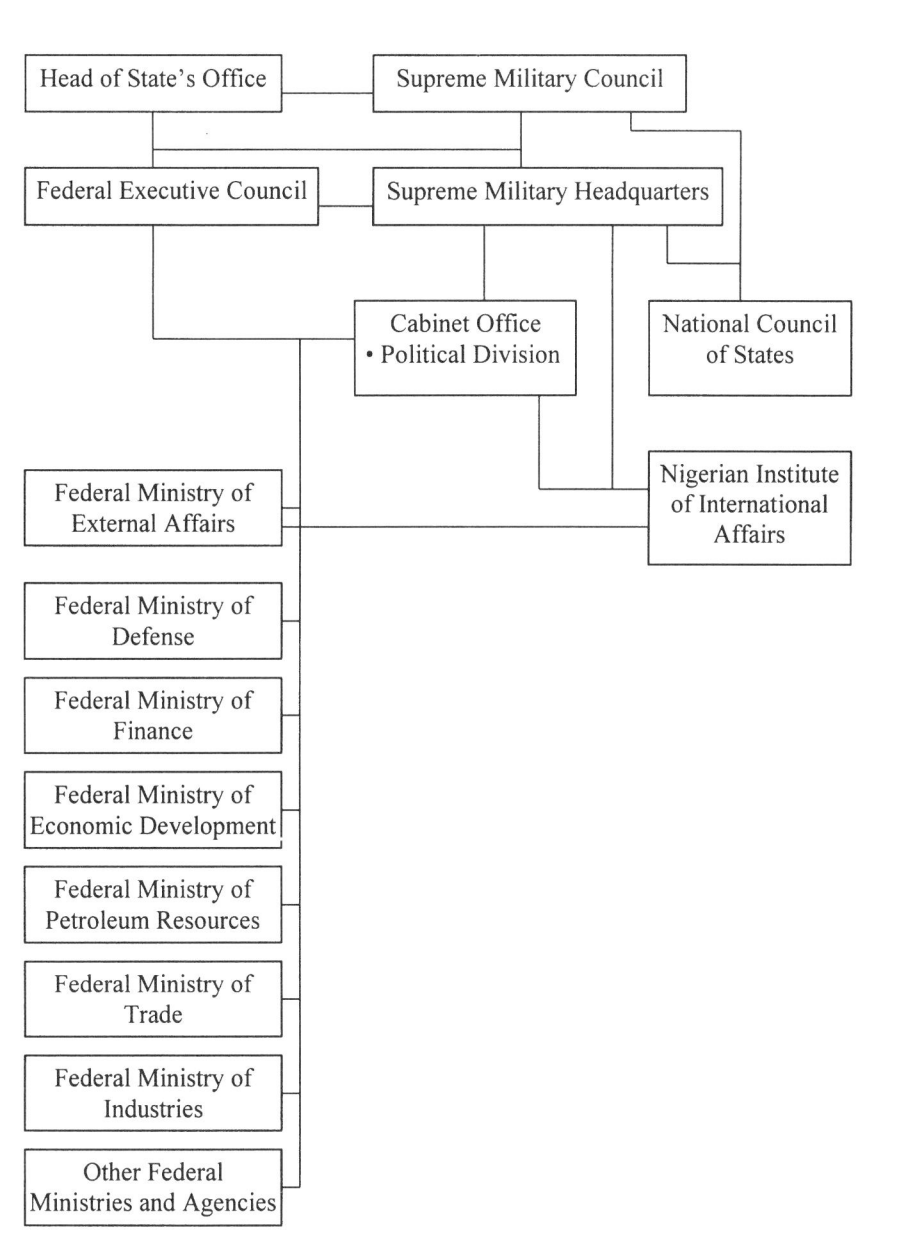

```
┌─────────────────────┐  ┌─────────────────────┐
│ Head of State's Office │──│ Supreme Military Council │
└─────────────────────┘  └─────────────────────┘
         │         │              │
┌─────────────────────┐  ┌─────────────────────────┐
│ Federal Executive Council │──│ Supreme Military Headquarters │
└─────────────────────┘  └─────────────────────────┘
                    │              │
                ┌──────────────────┐  ┌──────────────────┐
                │ Cabinet Office   │  │ National Council │
                │ • Political Division │  │ of States        │
                └──────────────────┘  └──────────────────┘
                                │
                        ┌──────────────────┐
                        │ Nigerian Institute │
                        │ of International │
                        │ Affairs          │
                        └──────────────────┘
```

- Federal Ministry of External Affairs
- Federal Ministry of Defense
- Federal Ministry of Finance
- Federal Ministry of Economic Development
- Federal Ministry of Petroleum Resources
- Federal Ministry of Trade
- Federal Ministry of Industries
- Other Federal Ministries and Agencies

Foreign Policy Decision-Making Structures during the Muhammed/Obasanjo Government

ment period. However, unlike in the Gowon era, the SMC during the Muhammed/Obasanjo era was clearly and effectively the highest and most dominant national policy-making body. According to Aluko (1976, 412), while "under the administration of General Gowon major decisions on foreign policy were taken by the Federal Executive Council (FEC) and later reported to the Supreme Military Council (SMC) merely for information, this position" was "reversed," during the Muhammed/Obasanjo era. He thus notes that the SMC of the Mohammed/Obasanjo era took "decisions on major foreign (and domestic) policy matters and simply" informed "the FEC about its decisions" (Aluko 1976, 412). Sotunmbi's analysis (1981, 3–4) reinforces that of Aluko. During the Gowon era, though the SMC was formally recognized as "the supreme policy-making body . . ., in practice, the civilian-dominated Federal Executive body was the real decision-making body." (The Gowon era FEC "was made up of the Head of State as Chairman, the Chief of Staff Supreme Headquarters, the Inspector General of Police and Civilian Commissioners" [Sotunmbi 1981, 3].) On the other hand, in the Muhammed/Obasanjo era, the SMC was effectively and clearly the dominant national policy-making body, as noted above. It was the SMC and not the FEC, or the National Council of States (NCS), that was "competent to take major domestic and foreign policy decisions" (Sotunmbi 1981, 4), during the Muhammed/Obasanjo era. Thus, for an example, the 1979 decision to nationalize the British Petroleum (BP) Company operations in Nigeria (in order to change the British policy concerning Zimbabwe—which was then under a white minority rule—toward a direction Nigeria hoped would lead to a genuine black Zimbabwean majority rule) "was taken by the Supreme Military Council and not the FEC" (Aluko 1990a, 385). Even more importantly, during the Muhammed/Obasanjo Government, the SMC was given the power "to supervise the other decision-making bodies" (Sotunmbi 1981, 4), which were the FEC and NCS.

In the Muhammed/Obasanjo era, the SMC consisted of 22 members with the head of state serving as the chairman (Sotunmbi 1981, 3). Other members of the SMC were the chief of state of the Supreme Military Headquarters, the chiefs of staff of the Nigerian army, navy, and air force, the inspector general of the police force, commanders of army divisions, heads of major units of the navy and the air force, and representatives of the senior officers of the army, navy, air force, and police force (Sotunmbi 1981, 3). Very significantly, unlike the Gowon era SMC, the Muhammed/Obasanjo era SMC membership did not include the military governors of the states (Sotunmbi 1981, 3). This exclusion of the state military governors from SMC membership made them clearly subordinate to the national leadership as represented by the SMC, the head of state and the chief of staff of the Supreme Military Headquarters. The governors of the states

5: THE ROBUST YEARS: THE MUHAMMED/OBASANJO PERIOD

were made members of the NCS. The NCS, as noted earlier, was a policy-making body that was subordinate to the SMC and the latter had the power to supervise its work. Thus, this subordination of NCS to SMC further deepened the subordination of state governors to the national leadership.

Simply put, an "analysis of Nigeria's decision-making organs" during the Muhammed/Obasanjo era shows "the supremacy of the SMC over all other organs" (Sotunmbi 1981, 5). The Muhammed/Obasanjo Government was a government that was eagerly committed to a lot of changes in the country's domestic and foreign policies. Thus, the SMC of that era was involved in a lot of new domestic and foreign policy initiatives. Implementation of new ideas and actions, according to Gboyega (1985, 41), "requires sacrifices and personal adjustments." Since the Muhammed/Obasanjo Government initiated a lot of new ideas and policies, in both domestic and foreign affairs, the government was also somewhat involved in mobilizing the populace to understand and support these changes. Luckily for the government, its foreign policy initiatives were very popular with the citizenry. Its foreign policy being anchored on Pan-African interests, goals, and sentiments, together with the general assertiveness and robustness of its foreign policy initiatives may have accounted for this mass public support. In terms of domestic policies, some of the major initiatives were local government reforms (see Onajide 1989, 33; Olowu 1988, 80), increase in agricultural productivity, land-use reforms, expansion of educational facilities, increase in industrialization, and transition from military government to a democratic civilian polity.

The SMC "was expected to meet at least four times a year" (Sotunmbi 1981, 4, 5). In between these SMC meetings, committees and/or informal groups worked on policies that were given to the SMC during its meetings for consideration and possible approval. Though some scholars, like Tawari (1985, 71–73), have noted that committees can be less effective decision-making instruments, the SMC seemed to have designed and operated committees and informal groups in such a way that they were very efficient. In fact, an informal group within the SMC that Sotunmbi (1981, 5; 1990, 368) refers to as the "Committee of Five" seemed to have been the vital force of the SMC itself. All the members of the "Committee of Five" were also members of the SMC (Sotunmbi 1981, 31 n), and they were Murtala Muhammed, Olusegun Obasanjo, Shehu Yar'adua (who succeeded Obasanjo as the chief of staff of the Supreme Military Headquarters), Theophilus Danjuma (chief of staff of the Nigerian army), and Ibrahim Babangida (a senior and important military officer in the Muhammed/Obasanjo Government; Babangida himself was later to become president of the third government that followed the Muhammed/Obasanjo Government) (Sotunmbi 1981, 13n). "While the SMC was expected to meet at least once in three months the Committee met weekly during which it took far-reaching decisions. It is believed that such decisions were generally adopted by the SMC" (Sotunmbi 1981, 5).

Aluko (1990a, 385) buttresses the view that the decisions of the "Committee of Five" were mostly "ratified with little or no questions from the other members of the SMC." Additionally, Aluko states that the arrangement of having the "Committee of Five" as the inner core of the SMC resulted in speedy decisions "and a measure of secrecy that could hardly find a place in any democracy." The above facts show that the "Committee of Five" was the real power within the SMC. The fact that the most important SMC members (the head of state and the chief of staff of the Supreme Military Headquarters) belonged to this informal committee most likely accounted for the committee being the source of power within the SMC. After the death of Muhammed, the "Committee of Five" inevitably turned into the "Committee of Four."

The SMC also had formal committees. One of these was set up to coordinate Nigerian assistance for Angola (Sotunmbi 1981, 27). The SMC also had some committees that consisted of and were headed by non-SMC members. The most prominent of these was the Adedeji Committee. This committee was headed by Professor Adebayo Adedeji and its members were "drawn from the universities, the mass media and the military" (Akinyemi 1979b, 154–55). This committee was "to provide an in-depth overhaul of the foreign policy system, substance and apparatus" (Akinyemi 1979b, 154–55). Outside committees of this sort provided the SMC with very vital intellectual advisory policy input. However, none of these formal outside committees or formal in-house SMC committees was as important as the informal "Committee of Five."

The Adedeji Committee produced the Adedeji Report of 1976. The Adedeji Report recommended, among other things, "the establishment of the national Advisory Council of Foreign Policy under the chairmanship of the Chief of Staff of the Supreme Headquarters and with the Commissioner for External Affairs as the deputy chairman" (Aluko 1990a, 385). This recommendation was accepted by the Federal Government (Aluko 1990a, 385). This action strengthened and expanded the role of the SMC in foreign policy decision-making.

Apart from the roles of the informal and formal committees, the functioning of the SMC was also much affected by the roles of individual SMC members. Agenda setting, policy discussions, and efforts to formulate and enact policies involved members negotiating with each other. For example, M. D. Yusuf, inspector general of the police force and a member of the SMC, was very much interested in Nigeria's impact on events in Angola, due to the contacts that an Angolan, who was a member of the MPLA (the Portuguese acronym for the Popular Movement for the Liberation of Angola) had with him. Basically, "in November 1975, an MPLA functionary arrived in Lagos with the objective of persuading Nigerian Leaders to recognize his government. He met the Inspector General of Police and asked him to use his influence in favor of his party" (Sotunmbi 1981, 20). It is important to note that at the time of this contact the Nigerian government "was still basically interested in a national government which, the policy-makers believed, had the best chance of uniting all the ethnic groups" (Sotunmbi 1981, 22) in Angola. The concept of a national government was seen by Nigeria as a sort of government that should be formed through MPLA sharing power with other significant political groups, movements, and parties. At the time of contacts between Yusuf and the Angolan, MPLA alone governed Angola and did not wish to share power with other political groups. With Yusuf's role, Nigeria's policy toward Angola had added dynamics.

On the basis of Yusuf's contacts with the MPLA official, the former decided to talk with Muhammed "on behalf of the Angolan government and then campaigned for its recognition. He appeared to have argued that the South African military intervention was ultimately a threat to Nigeria's external security" (Sotunmbi 1981, 20).

It seemed that Yusuf's efforts in persuading Mohammed to support the MPLA Government in Angola had significant impact. Soon after Yusuf's contact with Muhammed, the SMC sent two secret missions to Angola. The fact that two secret missions were sent (instead of one) is an indication that the policy-making body wanted to get as much objective information as possible.

> The delegations consisted of military officers, some of whom were flown down by Captain Paul Thahal then of the Nigerian Air Force. The first group landed in Luanda on the eve of independence. The second followed a few days after. Both groups visited the battlefronts and established the presence of South African military units within 100 kilometres of the capital. Their report, apart from confirming the deep penetration of the invading army, also indicated that the MPLA was firmly established in and around Luanda.
>
> Since members of the two missions were not known to have any preference for the MPLA, their report was accepted as authentic and unbiased. (Sotunmbi 1981, 21)

Muhammed was very angry when this report revealed South African invasion of Angola; thus, as soon as the extent of this intervention was known, the Nigerian recognition of the MPLA Government in Angola "become a foregone conclusion" (Sotunmbi 1981, 21). Thus, the role of one member of the SMC (Yusuf) who was not even a member of the Nigerian army, navy, or air force was crucial in helping to shape a decision that came to define the assertive foreign policies of the Muhammed/Obasanjo era. Yusuf, the inspector general of police, was a highly respected professional police officer who was seen as a very dedicated and patriotic Nigerian by many members of the SMC (who were mostly military officers) including Muhammed, who was a general in the Nigerian army.

As a decision-making body, the SMC was diverse. Some members had different views on various subjects. Some of them even opposed Nigeria's recognition of the MPLA Government in Angola. Surprisingly, one of those who opposed the MPLA governing Angola alone was Joseph Garba, the commissioner of External Affairs. Even though he was in charge of Nigeria's foreign affairs, a general in the Nigerian army, and a member of the SMC, the SMC took the decision to recognize the MPLA Government in Angola. Even after this Nigerian decision, Garba was still urging other Angolan political groups to join the MPLA in governing Angola (Sotunmbi 1981, 22). Garba was not defying the SMC. He implemented the SMC policy of the Nigerian recognition of the MPLA Government in Angola, and was only later hoping to help Angola readjust its political configuration to a more balanced state in the future. Garba, despite not having his view on this issue win in the SMC, did later triumph in other foreign policy issues. A loyal and dedicated army general, Garba served in the government (and, later, as the commandant of the Nigerian Defense Academy [see *Newswatch Who's Who in Nigeria* 1990, 339]) throughout the Muhammed/Obasanjo Government.

Because the SMC operated under a military government and had military officers as most of its members, it was not significantly encumbered by factors such as the opinions of the public and interest groups, which democratic governing bodies have to seriously take into account. Thus, the SMC was able to act with more speed and decisiveness than is possible in a democratic governing organ (Sotunmbi 1981, 32). Under Muhammed's leadership, the SMC was firmly controlled by him (Sotunmbi 1981, 32), but under Obasanjo's leadership, the SMC was "more than a mere rubber stamp." Most issues were thoroughly debated and decisions arrived at by consensus (Sotunmbi 1981, 13n).

THE HEAD OF STATE'S OFFICE

During the Muhammed/Obasanjo Government, there was no decision-making body formally and distinctively recognized as the Head of State's Office. Thus, by referring to such we do not mean a separate and formal decision-making body by that name, but rather the head of state and the senior career bureaucrats and military officers who worked directly for him on a daily basis in his office. In his official capacity the Head of State was seen as part and parcel of the SMC and the Supreme Military Headquarters. However, as noted earlier, the SMC was mandated to meet at least four times in a year and the informal group called the "Committee of Five (Four)" met weekly. When the SMC or "Committee of Five (Four)" were not in session, the head of state mostly worked in his office: thus we refer to the impact of the head of state with his office staff members as the impact of the Head of State's Office.

It must be noted that the Head of State's office was not a relatively very large office with a lot of its own staff. The Supreme Military Headquarters was the formal and larger staff organization that provided the policy and administrative support for the head of state and the general administration of the country. The chief of staff of the Supreme Military Headquarters administered the Supreme Military Headquarters for the head of state, and thus was the person who assisted the head of state in performing his duties. Thus, the chief of staff of the Supreme Military Headquarters was a visible national figure who was perceived as the number two person in the country. The roles of the Supreme Military Headquarters in the foreign policy decision-making system will be analyzed in a separate section below.

The office and official residence of the head of state and the Supreme Military Headquarters were located in the Dodan Barracks. The SMC meetings and the meetings of the powerful "Committee of Five (Four)" also took place within the Dodan Barracks. Thus, in the Muhammed/Obasanjo era Dodan Barracks served as the powerful place where the most important policy and administrative decisions of the federal government occurred. The general public also perceived Dodan Barracks as the place where most important decisions affecting the country emanated from. Dodan Barracks served a similar role during the Ironsi, Gowon, and Buhari eras.

Since the Muhammed/Obasanjo era had first Muhammed and then Obasanjo as the head of state, the Head of State's Office will be analyzed for both Muhammed's and Obasanjo's periods. The two periods will be analyzed separately.

Heads of state often had a few number of senior career bureaucrats as policy and administrative assistants and some military officers as military aides. The career bureaucrats who served the head of state were often very highly skilled officials: experts in policy and/or administrative affairs. However, these were efficient technocrats with no significant political bases. Also, like all career bureaucrats, they were steeped in the culture and tradition of career bureaucracy. Thus, they offered their advice to their political leader(s) and deferred to that (those) leader(s) to make the policy. Whatever their personal view about the policy adopted by the political leader(s), the career bureaucrats had to implement the policy—even when they strongly disagreed with the policy, they did their best not to openly and publicly defy or disobey the policy, though they might have been implementing the policy only lackadaisically. Additionally, career bureaucrats were also known for not risking their careers by not being insubordinate, controversial, or partisan.

The military officers who served as personal military aides to the head of state were often middle-level rank officers, and thus far below the head of state, who held the rank of a general in the military. In true military tradition these military aides always obeyed the very senior military officer.

These career bureaucrats and military aides, due to the factors noted above, mainly collected and analyzed data and information for the head of state in the form of policy position papers and official memoranda, and thus gave the head of state necessary information and papers he needed for SMC and "Committee of Five (Four)" meetings. Therefore, these career bureaucrats and military aides mainly helped Muhammed (and later Obasanjo) to pursue the sort of policy options that these heads of state were favoring. This was particularly true in the case of Muhammed, with his strong views, aggressive personality, and penchant for fast, energetic, and decisive actions. These career bureaucrats and military aides also handled routine tasks, such as schedules and appointments management, speech writing, and trip planning and management for the head of state.

Muhammed was seen as "a devout Muslim from an aristocratic family in Kano" who "was tough, inflexible, strong-minded and aggressively intolerant" (Aluko 1976, 412). Additionally, he was seen as "a visionary who believed in taking risks, calculated or otherwise" (Akinyemi 1979b, 161). Muhammed was also a person who had strong interests in international relations in both academic and policy contexts. He was an active member of the Nigerian Society of International Affairs who attended the society's annual meetings (Akinyemi 1979b, 153–54; Sotunmbi 1981, 18). The Nigerian Society of International Affairs is the premier professional body in the country for those involved with international relations in academic and/or policy contexts. Akinyemi (1979b, 153) also notes that "the 1972 annual conference of the society witnessed . . . a lively exchange of views" in which Muhammed was a key participant. Thus, as a military officer (even before he was a head of state) Muhammed was very interested in international relations in both academic and policy contexts. Therefore, he assumed the Office of the Head of State with a lot of interest in international affairs and with significant knowledge about international dynamics.

An aggressive, intense, and action-oriented posture, in addition to interest and knowledge of international affairs, made Muhammed eager and able to effect a lot of fast, dramatic, and significant changes in the foreign policy arena. These fast and dramatic changes also affected the domestic policy arena, as noted earlier, in the areas of local government reforms, educational policies, and industrial policies. He pushed for policies that acutely linked the domestic and foreign policy arenas. For example, he "achieved the feat of unifying the trade unions" in Nigeria, while in the same time period also "banning foreign trade union organizations and secretariats from operating in Nigeria" (Ogunbadejo 1986, 258).

Muhammed's strong personality also made him very direct in dealing with other countries. For example, when President Gerald Ford of the United States sent a letter to African leaders, including Muhammed, trying to influence their views on Angola, Muhammed was openly displeased and made public his negative reply to that letter (Eze 1986, 170; Ofoegbu 1979, 136; Sotunmbi 1981, 28). On the same issue of Angola, Muhammed was very uncompromising at the special OAU summit held in January 1976 at Addis Ababa, Ethiopia (Aluko 1986, 91).

Muhammed's strong views on foreign policy also made him very uncomfortable with the country's main foreign relations organ, the Ministry of External Affairs. He "resisted well-articulated opinion from the Ministry of External Affairs" (Ofoegbu 1979, 145). Instead, he used "Dodan Barracks, State House and Cabinet Office (political division) as a mini-Foreign Office," and "was thus able to receive unorthodox and non-bureaucratic advice and policy analysis on Angola, the liberation movements and Southern Africa" (Ofoegbu 1979, 145).

Obasanjo, who succeeded Muhammed as head of state, mostly followed the domestic and foreign policies frameworks of Muhammed, as noted earlier, though in a relatively calmer posture. Obasanjo was a close friend of Muhammed. However, they were different in their personalities and styles of governance. While "Muhammed was open, Obasanjo was secretive" (Akinyemi 1979b, 161). Obasanjo was also "the administrator *par excellence,* cautious and calculating" (Akinyemi 1979b, 161).

Like Muhammed, Obasanjo was a very active member of the Nigerian Society of International Affairs (Akinyemi 1979b, 153–54; Sotunmbi 1981, 18). At the 1972 annual conference of the society, held in Zaria, Obasanjo presented a paper that elicited a lot of discussion from others, especially Muhammed (Akinyemi 1979b, 153–54; Sotunmbi 1981, 24, n. 2). Thus, like Muhammed, before becoming the head of state, Obasanjo had developed an understanding of international relations in both academic and policy contexts. This prior interest and knowledge of international relations also made Obasanjo eager and able to be very involved in foreign affairs when he became a head of state.

Like Muhammed, Obasanjo had a group of career bureaucrats who served directly under him as his policy and administrative assistants, and also a group of military officers who served as his military aides. Though the positions of these career bureaucrats and military assistants made them clear subordinates who were there to provide Obasanjo with the data, information, and policy analyses he needed to pursue the policies he favored, and to be well briefed for SMC meetings, due to the cautious and deliberative ways Obasanjo made decisions, these career bureaucrats' and military officers' policy advice possibly was solicited, and used, by Obasanjo in reaching his decisions.

His decision-making style also impacted on the SMC. The SMC, during Obasanjo's leadership, was a true deliberative body. In the majority of cases "issues were thoroughly debated and decisions arrived at by consensus" (Sotunmbi 1981, 13, n. 15). During the Obasanjo era, the power behind the SMC configured in the form of a triumvirate made up of Obasanjo, Yar' Adua (the chief of staff of the Supreme Military Headquarters) and Danjuma (the chief of staff of the Nigerian army) (Ofoegbu 1979, 145). Obasanjo, unlike Muhammed, seemed not to be very keen in keeping the foreign policy decision-making machinery directly under him (Ofoegbu 1979, 145). "Gradually, the Ministry of External Affairs recovered its erstwhile position in the realms of foreign policy, and either working along or in conjunction with, or guided and directed by the triumvirate" of Obasanjo, Yar'Adua, and Danjuma (Ofoegbu 1979, 145). This improved working relationship between Dodan Barracks and the Ministry of External Affairs was exemplified by the decision-making processes involved in the decision to temporarily close the Nigerian foreign mission in Kampala, Uganda, in 1979, due to domestic political upheaval in Uganda. Obasanjo and the key officials of the Ministry of External Affairs shared similar views in this matter (Aluko 1983, 87–88).

Obasanjo's deliberate and thoughtful approach to decision-making extended to domestic policy. For an example, he worked hard to ensure that an ombudsman system was enshrined into the Constitution (Ayeni 1986, 140–41).

The cautious and calmer foreign policy posture of Obasanjo did not mean lesser foreign policy initiatives. Rather it meant more careful foreign initiatives. Obasanjo's keen interest in foreign affairs also meant his involvement in significant foreign policy issues. For example, he went "to Jamaica for a mini summit of some world leaders on plans for restructuring the world economic order" (Ede 1986, 189). Ojo (1986, 441) even notes that "Obasanjo is known to have followed the South African situation with more than keen interest even before" the Muhammed/Obasanjo era. With such strong interests in foreign affairs, it is not then surprising that he was acutely involved in foreign policy-making when he became the head of state. Thus, for example, he paid good attention to Israeli-South African relations in the late 1970s (Ojo 1986, 441). Additionally,

> following the Soweto rioting of June 1976, the Obasanjo government went ahead to bring some of the leaders of that riot to Nigeria to form the South

African Revolutionary Youth Council (SARYCO). Some of the boys who were brought to Lagos were sent to various educational and military institutions in Nigeria.

Given all the interests, the involvement in and the concern of Nigeria for the liberation struggle in Southern Africa from late 1976, Nigeria began to be invited to the meetings of the frontline states. At such meeting the Obasanjo government was able to provide more moral, diplomatic, financial and military assistance to both the freedom fighters and to some of the frontline states such as Zambia, Botswana and Mozambique. (Aluko 1986, 93)

Obasanjo was closely involved in the formulation of Nigeria's foreign policy towards Zimbabwe. A wide-ranging and sustained diplomatic effort had to be mounted by Nigeria in order to effect changes inside Zimbabwe—and in the international system—that helped lead to the independence of Zimbabwe. Obasanjo achieved this by coordinating a foreign policy offensive that involved "nationalizing Shell BP, recognizing ZANU [Zimbabwe African National Union] as the legitimate representative of the Zimbabwean people, drawing large African support and precipitating the Independence of Zimbabwe" (Eze 1986, 170). (Action relating to the Shell BP Company in Nigeria was aimed at influencing British policy toward the Zimbabwe issue.)

During an official visit to the United States (Asobie 1986, 164 n. 39), Obasanjo articulated a major Nigerian foreign policy principle. He noted that Nigeria has "chosen the path of non-alignment as a philosophy in the conduct of our foreign policy, which means in essence that we welcome the friendship and cooperation of all the nations, on the basis of mutual respect and complete sovereign equality" (Obasanjo, quoted in Asobie 1986, 157). Expanding on this theme, and reflecting the Cold War global atmosphere of the late 1970s, at the Khartoum Summit of the OAU in July 1978 Obasanjo noted that, in terms of

> the context of foreign intervention in Africa, there are three parties involved. These are the Soviets and other socialist countries, the Western Powers and we, the Africans. If the interests of Africa are to be safeguarded, there are certain considerations which each of the parties must constantly bear in mind. To the Soviets and their friends, I should like to say that having been invited to Africa in order to assist in the liberation struggle and the consolidation of national independence, they should not overstay their welcome. Africa is not about to throw off one colonial yoke for another. Rather, they should hasten the political economic and military capability of their African friends to stand on their own. . . . The Soviets should, therefore, see to it to be in their interest not to seek to perpetually maintain their presence in Africa, even after the purpose for which they were invited has been achieved. This way they run the risk of being dubbed a new imperial Power as indeed they are already being called, even by

those with whom they have had long association. Let the Soviets and their collaborators heed this timely counsel!

To the Western Powers I say that they should act in such a way that we are not led to believe that they have different concepts of independence and sovereignty for Africa and Europe. A new Berlin-type conference is not the appropriate response to the kind of issues thrown up by the recent unfortunate Kolwezi episode. Paratroops drops in the twentieth century are no more acceptable to us than the gunboats of the last century were to our ancestors. . . . The detente which the Western nations seek with the Soviets in Europe cannot be effective without extending it to include Africa as well. The Western nations' primary interest in Africa is our raw materials. But they should begin to see the market Africa offers to their manufactured goods as even more important since they can develop substitutes for raw materials, but not for markets. If they saw Africa primarily as market rather than a source of raw materials, they would realize the importance of ensuring that they do not disturb our peace and stability. . . .

We African leaders must also realize that we cannot ask outside Powers to leave us alone while, in most cases, it is our own actions which provide them with the excuse to interfere with our affairs. . . . There is no better defence against external forces than the government which endeavors to carry the majority of the population along with it and treats its people fairly decently. We must not allow the East and the West to divide us and set us against ourselves under any guise. (Obasanjo, quoted in Olusanya and Akindele 1986a, 6–7)

In this speech, Obasanjo provided an impressive, clear, and direct articulation of Nigeria's view of the world in relation to Africa. Due to the straightforward tone and absence of bland, language, there is a probability that the Ministry of External Affairs' input into that speech was not prominent: Obasanjo himself, with possibly the officials in the Dodan Barracks and/or the Cabinet Office, probably wrote this speech). Thus, this speech possibly further indicates the strong role of Obasanjo in the foreign policy decision-making milieu.

On the whole, the strong interest and knowledge of international affairs by Muhammed and Obasanjo resulted in their being very involved in foreign policy decision-making. This reality also led to assertive and effective foreign policy initiatives, as shown above, by the Muhammed/Obasanjo Government. Nigeria's policy towards Angola, South Africa, and Zimbabwe preoccupied the attention of this government. As also noted above, these southern African issues also impacted on Nigeria's relation with Western and Eastern countries. One other indication of this assertive foreign policy was the fact that Nigeria "cancelled a scheduled visit to Lagos by the American Secretary of State, Dr. Kissinger" (Ofoegbu 1979, 136). Essentially, all the foreign policy initiatives of the Muhammed/

Obasanjo Government led "to the characterization of this period as the 'dynamic' phase of Nigeria's foreign policy" (Aribisala 1986b, 114).

The Supreme Military Headquarters and Its Chief of Staff

The Supreme Military Headquarters represented the military apparatus that was mainly focused on the governance and administration of the country during most eras of military government. (The body existed only in military eras, not during civilian government periods.) As noted earlier, the Supreme Military Headquarters, the office and the official residence of the head of state, and the Supreme Military Council were located within the Dodan Barracks, making that term synonymous with the seat of sovereign power during eras of military governments, when Lagos was the capital of the country.

The Supreme Military Headquarters, generally and collectively, as a decision-making system, was often perceived as consisting of the head of state, the chief of staff, other senior military officers, and other military officers seconded to the Supreme Military Headquarters. All the military officials of the Supreme Military Headquarters were primarily engaged in the governance and administration of the country during the eras of military governments. In contrast, most other military officers and personnel were engaged in purely military duties in combat or noncombat units of the army, navy, and air force, or working as staff officers in the Ministry of Defense. For example, the military officers attached to the office chief of defense staff in the Ministry of Defense primarily focused on the military task of coordinating the armed forces. The officers who were seconded to the Supreme Military Headquarters, though primarily involved in the governance and administration of the country during this tour of duty, still belonged to their respective service branches, and after their tour of duty with the Supreme Military Headquarters, returned to these (though some of the most senior officers retire after their tour of duty with the Supreme Military Headquarters).

The chief of staff of the Supreme Military Headquarters was the senior military officer who directly supervised the Supreme Military Headquarters for the head of state. In the preceding Gowon Government, the chief of staff of the Supreme Military Headquarters was an important senior military officer who helped to run the center of the military government. In the Muhammed/Obasanjo Government, the position of the chief of staff was greatly strengthened and enlarged, the military officer occupying this position enjoying unprecedented national visibility and power.

It is important to note that these new powers that the chief of staff held during the Muhammed/Obasanjo Government were the result of the head of state simply assigning more visible and important national political and administrative duties to the chief of staff. In reality, before the Babangida Government (which lasted from 1985 to 1993), the chief of staff only "oversaw the running of Supreme Military Headquarters and had to wait for specific job assignments from" the Head of State (*Thisweek* 20 October 1986, 18). It was only in 1986 that the Babangida Government, in an official gazette of the federal government, specifically listed all the official duties of the person who held the post of the chief of general staff (as the title was renamed). During the Muhammed/Obasanjo Government, in addition to his official duty of running the Supreme Military Headquarters, the chief of staff was also given more duties by the head of state. The head of state simply transferred some of his important national policy and administrative duties to the chief of staff—thus the latter's prominent national role. For example, the state governors were then dealing directly with the chief of staff, unlike in the Gowon era, when they were dealing directly with the head of state.

The new powers and visibility of the chief of staff resulted in making his roles and duties in the national policy and administrative milieus more distinct from that of the head of state. In the Gowon era, the chief of staff was perceived by the public as merely supervising the Supreme Military Headquarters and, thus, having relatively lower national visibility.

In the Muhammed/Obasanjo era, the first chief of staff of the Supreme Military Headquarters was Olusegun Obasanjo. The fact that Muhammed and Obasanjo had a good working rapport might have contributed to Muhammed making the role of chief of staff a more visible one. Obasanjo's personal attributes might have also contributed to more powers being given to his position. "He was a respected and popular figure both within the armed forces and among the civilians. His popularity derived largely from his success as Commander of the Third Infantry Division" (Sotunmbi 1981, 17) of the Nigerian army, which was successful in the final military actions that led to the end of the Civil War in 1970.

After the death of Muhammed, Obasanjo became the head of state. Shehu Yar'Adua then succeeded Obasanjo as the chief of staff of the Supreme Military Headquarters.

As noted earlier, the chief of staff of the Supreme Military Headquarters was the chairman of the National Advisory Council of Foreign Policy. Thus, the Supreme Military Headquarters, through its chief of staff, was positioned to play a vital role in the foreign policy decision-making system. Throughout the Muhammed/Obasanjo era, the visible role of the chief of staff meant that he was clearly the second most important person in the country after the head of state.

5: THE ROBUST YEARS: THE MUHAMMED/OBASANJO PERIOD

When Muhammed was the head of state, the Ministry of External Affairs was not trusted to handle foreign policy issues the way the government desired. Thus, Dodan Barracks constituted one of the bodies that was relied on to take on some of the load of the Ministry of External Affairs. As noted earlier, Muhammed used "Dodan Barracks, State House and Cabinet Office (political division) as a mini-Foreign Office" (Ofoegbu 1979, 145). This shows that the Supreme Military Headquarters (Dodan Barracks) became one of the important foreign policy decision-making bodies. The very active role of the Supreme Military Headquarters in foreign policy can be further indicated by the fact that Obasanjo (when he was the chief of staff) led a Nigerian delegation to Angola to find out the sort of assistance the new government in Angola would need from Nigeria (Sotunmbi 1981, 27).

When Obasanjo succeeded Muhammed, as noted earlier, the Ministry of External Affairs recovered its prominent role in the foreign policy decision-making milieu (Ofoegbu 1979, 145). A military triumvirate consisting of Obasanjo (head of state), Yar'Adua (chief of staff of the Supreme Military Headquarters), and T. Y. Danjuma (chief of staff of the Nigerian army) mainly provided foreign policy guidance and direction to the Ministry of External Affairs (Ofoegbu 1979, 145). The fact that Yar'Adua was a member of this triumvirate shows that the Supreme Military Headquarters continued to be a significant foreign policy decision-making structure. In 1978, the federal government of Nigeria took actions against Barclays Bank in Nigeria (due to the bank's investment policy, which seemed to be giving economic comfort to the apartheid government in South Africa), and in 1979, the federal government nationalized the British Petroleum Company in Nigeria in order to influence British policy toward Zimbabwe and South Africa (Sotunmbi 1981, 35–36, 37 n. 6(b). The actions against Barclays Bank and British Petroleum were very high-profile and assertive, and thus do not seem to be the sort of policies or actions that could have originally emanated from the Ministry of External Affairs (which is often dominated by cautious, careful, and nonassertive career diplomats). Thus, it is likely these actions originated from the Supreme Military Headquarters, and more specifically the triumvirate of Obasanjo, Yar'Adua, and Danjuma (and this further indicated the prominent role of the Supreme Military Headquarters in foreign policy).

In March 1979, Yar'Adua chaired the First Kano Conference, which was convened to bring delegations from various African countries, including Chad, to chart a solution to the internal strife that was taking place in Chad (*Newswatch* 1 December 1986, 25). Yar'Adua also paid a visit to Saudi Arabia and made categorical pronouncements about Nigeria's view of the Middle East issues (Ojo 1986, 442). He also visited the former Yugoslavia to help arrange for more economic and technological cooperation between that country and Nigeria (Alli-Balogun 1986, 349). In a visit to the Federal Republic of Germany, he sought to foster technological cooperation between Nigeria and Germany (Arisbisala 1986a, 313). He also visited China, where his focus to address the issue of trade imbalance between Nigeria and China (Owoeye 1986, 303). In 1979, Yar'Adua also paid a four-day official visit to the former Soviet Union in order to evaluate and strengthen economic, trade, scientific, technological, cultural, and foreign policies between the two countries (Ogunbadejo 1986, 260–61). All these numerous visits to foreign countries to discuss substantive foreign policy issues further show that the chief of staff and the Supreme Military Headquarters machinery per se, played a significant role in the foreign policy decision-making milieu. Thus, throughout the Muhammed/Obasanjo era, the Supreme Military Headquarters remained a vital factor in the foreign policy decision-making system.

NATIONAL COUNCIL OF STATES

The National Council of States (NCS) was created by the Muhammed/Obasanjo Government. The NCS consisted of the head of state, the chiefs of staff of the Nigerian army, navy, and air force, the inspector general of the police force, and the military governors of the states (Sotunmbi 1981, 4, 13 n. 9). (The head of state was the chairman of the NCS.) The NSC was the only formal national body that included state governors. Additionally, as noted earlier, the NCS was under the complete control of the Supreme Military Council. The fact that the head of state and other senior members of the Supreme Military Council were also members of the NCS helped to ensure that the NCS was completely under the control of the Supreme Military Council.

The NCS functions were "limited to matters affecting the States" (Sotunmbi 1981, 5). Thus, the NCS was mainly a forum for the management of the relationship between the federal government and the state governments and the interstate relationships. The NCS was therefore the premier intergovernmental body for the functioning of federalism in the country.

The NCS was, therefore, mainly focused on domestic political, economic, and social issues. However, the fact that many of the states share boundaries with one or more of the following foreign countries—Cameroun, Chad, Republic of Niger, Republic of Benin, and Equatorial Guinea (its Bioko Island portion in the Atlantic Ocean)—meant that the relevant states are inevitably linked internationally. Issues of border demarcation conflicts, movement of undocumented aliens across the borders, smuggling of goods, international exchange of currencies, sharing of natural resources like water in the border areas, and the handling of extradition cases have impacts on the states with international borders. Border conflict issues are often the major problem affecting these states. The governments of the relevant states depend on the federal government (which has the function of managing foreign relations) to handle and alleviate these problems. Though each state government can, and does, individually work with the federal government to manage problems that may arise with foreign countries, the creation of the NCS by the Muhammed/Obasanjo Government meant that the NCS became an additional avenue for the management of international issues. Through the NCS, the federal government can work with the affected states as a group to fashion solutions for border issues. Thus, though the NCS mainly focuses on domestic issues, the international issues that impact on states that have borders with foreign countries give the NCS some role in foreign affairs (though such a role is often relatively smaller, and less nationally and publicly visible, compared with other governmental organs whose primary focus is on foreign affairs).

The Federal Executive Council

The Federal Executive Council (FEC) was the federal cabinet. It consisted of the head of state, the inspector general of police, the federal attorney general, and the commissioners of the federal ministries (Sotunmbi 1981, 5). Chaired by the head of state, the FEC served as a body that helped to shape policy and also to execute policies of the federal government under the general direction of the Supreme Military Council (Sotunmbi 1981, 5). As was common during this era, the Supreme Military Council exercised supremacy over all other national organs, including the FEC (Sotunmbi 1981, 5), both in terms of domestic and foreign policies. Compared with the FEC of the Gowon Government, the FEC of the Muhammed/Obasanjo Government was a relatively less powerful body. According to Aluko (1976, 412), while during the Gowon Government, "major decisions on foreign policy were taken by the Federal Executive Council (FEC) and later reported to the Supreme Military Council (SMC) merely for information," during the Muhammed/Obasanjo Government, it was the SMC that took "decisions on major foreign (and domestic) policy matters and simply informs the FEC about its decisions." Thus, though the FEC was involved in the formulation and execution of foreign policy, its role was relatively subordinated to that of that SMC during the Muhammed/Obasanjo Government era. For example, as noted above, the SMC formulated the major foreign policies and simply notified FEC about these foreign policies.

The Federal Cabinet Office

The Federal Cabinet Office serves as that organ of mostly senior career civil servants that provides the political leaders of the federal government with the staff for the coordination and direction of national policy formulation and administration. Much of the work of the Cabinet Office involved that of policy design, planning, development, implementation, and evaluation. In fashioning new policies the policy design and policy planning roles of the Cabinet Office are more visible. Some, like Ikporukpo (1984, 29), have noted that the interest of governments in effecting certain sorts of developments have often made governments interested in planning.

The Cabinet Office is often divided into various divisions—for example, political and economic. The fact that the Cabinet Office deals with all national policy and administrative issues means that foreign policy is just one of the policy areas that the office handles. However, due to the fact that the national political leadership, during the period that Murtala Muhammed was the head of state, did not adequately involve the Ministry of External Affairs in the formulation of foreign policy, the Cabinet Office became a very prominent organ in foreign affairs. As mentioned earlier, Ofoegbu (1979, 145) notes that Murtala Muhammed's leadership used the "Dodan Barracks, State House and Cabinet Office (political division) as a mini-foreign office." Major General Joseph Garba (1987, 21–24), who was the first commissioner for External Affairs during the Muhammed/Obasanjo Government, also notes how the Cabinet Office was a vital foreign policy decision-making organ in relation to the Nigerian foreign policy toward Angola during this era. Other observations of Garba also illustrate the roles the Cabinet Office played in the Nigerian foreign policy decision-making system. In noting the influence of the Cabinet Office and other organs over even personnel matters in the Ministry of External Affairs, Garba (1987, 23–24) noted that "in such a hurry were the Chief of Staff and those in the Cabinet Office's Political Division that they caused me to elevate to Ambassador, a young foreign service officer, who because of his knowledge of Portuguese had been sent to open our legation in Luanda. This, of course, created displeasure among his superiors and contemporaries, and was to cause me continuing difficulty in the Ministry."

In matters of substantive foreign policy, the roles of the Cabinet Office (and the Supreme Military Headquarters) were even more significant. Even though he was the commissioner of External Affairs, Garba (1987, 21) explained, "I had yet to fully understand where our government's Angola policy was being developed, but I could now begin to sense the nature of the process, orchestrated (I would later learn) by the Chief of

Staff, Supreme Headquarters, Brigadier Olusegun Obasanjo, working through the Political Division of the Cabinet Office." Garba also noted that the role of the Cabinet Office and other organs in foreign policy decision-making extended beyond Nigerian foreign policy toward Angola. According to him, "What took somewhat longer for me to understand, was that Nigeria's policy towards Angola and all the liberation movements of southern Africa was run, not by the Ministry of External Affairs, but mysteriously from other corners of the government: the Cabinet Office, the Office of the Inspector-General of Police (formerly that of the Assistant Inspector General, Special Branch and others)."

Though the Ministry of External Affairs, as noted earlier, did recover some of its traditional role in foreign affairs when Olusegun Obasanjo became the head of state (Ofoegbu 1979, 145), other organs, like the Cabinet Office, continued to play a visible role in foreign affairs. The fact that a very senior career diplomat, Oladapo Olusola Fafowora, was seconded from the Ministry of External Affairs to serve in the Cabinet Office as principal secretary (political) and as secretary of the National Foreign Policy Council of the Cabinet Office, from 1976 to 1978 (*Newswatch Who's Who* 1990, 316), shows that the Muhammed/Obasanjo Government adequately staffed the relevant units of the Cabinet Office, in order for the Cabinet Office to be able to perform prominent roles in foreign affairs. By staffing the relevant units of the Cabinet Office with excellent career officers like Fafowora, the Muhammed/Obasanjo Government clearly made the Cabinet Office able to perform some of the roles that the Ministry of External Affairs traditionally performed.

The Ministry of External Affairs

The above discusion notwithstanding, the Ministry of External Affairs was still a very important foreign affairs organ. As noted above, the Muhammed/Obasanjo Government used "Dodan Barracks, State House and Cabinet Office (political division) as a mini-Foreign Office" (Ofocgbu 1979, 145). However, the Ministry of External Affairs could not be made totally insignificant in foreign affairs. Though Dodan Barracks, the State House, and the Cabinet Office might have become increasingly prominent in terms of major foreign policy formulation, the formulation of foreign policy in routine matters and the implementation of most foreign policies (both major and minor) was mostly done by the Ministry of External Affairs (MEA). Thus the MEA was still an important foreign affairs organ during this era, though its prominence in foreign affairs was relatively lower in comparison with other governmental periods. Additionally, as also noted earlier, when Obasanjo became the head of state, the MEA regained some of its roles and visibility in the foreign policy decision-making arena.

Nevertheless, it was intensely and glaringly obvious that the Muhammed/Obasanjo Government significantly lowered the profile and importance of the MEA in the foreign policy decision-making milieu. According to Aluko (1976, 413) a vital change that was introduced was "the demotion of the Ministry of External Affairs in the making of the country's foreign policy." When comparing the importance of the MEA during the Gowon Government period and the Muhammed/Obasanjo Government period, the difference is very glaring. As noted in an earlier part of this study, during "the Gowon Government it was the Ministry that formed the lynch-pin of the country's foreign policy. Its views and recommendations were given great weight in taking decisions under the Gowon Administration. Its administrative head, the Permanent Secretary, who was then Mr. Joe Iyalla, was a member of the Federal Executive Council" (Aluko 1976, 413). Conversely, during the Muhammed/Obasanjo Government period, "the Permanent Secretary of the Ministry" was "excluded, as were other permanent secretaries, from the Federal Executive Council," and, additionally, "only scant attention" was paid "to the views and recommendations of the Ministry in the making of foreign policy decisions" (Aluko 1976, 413). This situation was largely due to the fact that the major political leaders of the Muhammed/Obasanjo Government "thought that most of the senior officers in the Ministry of External Affairs were conservative, if not reactionary and routine-bound," and, thus, these political leaders "were somehow suspicious" of these senior career diplomats (Aluko 1976, 413). Additionally, the national political leadership also consulted "some organizations and individuals outside the Foreign Service, especially those in the University and the press" (Aluko 1976, 413).

When Olusegun Obasanjo succeeded Murtala Muhammed as head of state, the MEA recovered some (though not all) of its former powers, as noted earlier. However, at the early phase of his leadership of the country, Obasanjo himself was still uncomfortable with the MEA. In 1976, he "told a meeting of all Nigerian ambassadors in Africa that his government was unhappy with their performance and that they should be more imaginative and positive rather than spending their time in their posts 'wining and dining'" (Aluko 1983, 78). Nevertheless, soon after Obasanjo made the above expressions to the ambassadors, his government "became increasingly dependent on the same foreign service. Indeed his government came so to respect the advice, views and judgment of the Ministry of External Affairs and its overseas missions that some responsibilities hitherto performed by home ministries—for example, external publicity, and international economic and financial matters and institutions, and the implementation abroad of decided policy on behalf of some home ministries, both federal and states—were given to External Affairs" (Aluko 1983, 78). As noted above, the MEA undoubtedly became more important when Obasanjo was head of state, in comparison to the MEA's very low profile and importance during the period that Muhammed was the head of state. Nevertheless, even during the Obasanjo era, the MEA never enjoyed the sort of national profile and visibility that it had during the Gowon Government.

During the Muhammed/Obasanjo period, the MEA had its usual structure of commissioner as its political head, the permanent secretary as its administrative head, and the various regional and functional departments, divisions, sections, branches, desks, and other units as the configuration of the ministry. The work of these various units constitute the functioning and processes of the MEA. The commissioner and some ambassadors were usually the only political appointees. Thus, the career diplomats mostly dominated the functioning of the MEA. Since most career diplomats are often cautious and moderate in their behavior, the MEA mostly exhibited cautious and moderate functioning and outputs. It was this reality that made the Muhammed/Obasanjo Government (which was eager to make major radical changes in foreign policies) use Dodan Barracks, the State House, and the Cabinet Office to formulate major foreign policies (and thus exclude the MEA from participating). This resulted in the assertive foreign policies that were the hallmark of the Muhammed/Obasanjo Government.

The cautious policy and administrative behavior of the MEA also resulted in too much secrecy in its functioning and mode of operation, and thus, very inadequate information was often given to the public to explain how and why certain foreign policies were being implemented (Akinyemi 1979b, 161). The Muhammed/Obasanjo Government recognized this problem and tried its best to ameliorate it, since the government knew "that a wider section of the public" had become interested in foreign affairs (Sotunmbi 1981, 37 n. 5). For example, in 1978, the commissioner of External Affairs had a dialogue with a group of Nigerians who had academic interests and general influence in international affairs (Sotunmbi 1981, 37 n. 5).

The assertive and wide-ranging foreign policies that were formulated by the Muhammed/Obasanjo meant that the MEA was involved in implementing many foreign policies. For example, the MEA was involved in efforts to massively revamp and reshape the World Black and African Festival of Arts and Culture (FESTAC) that Nigeria had agreed, before the Muhammed/Obasanjo Government period, to host. Nigeria "undertook diplomatic action inside and outside Africa to explain its FESTAC policy, revive world interest in it, reconstitute FESTAC's world committees, and fix firm dates for the festival" (Ofoegbu 1979, 142). In the process of accomplishing these tasks:

> Nigeria encountered considerable differences and disagreements with Senegal. These centered first around whether non-Black Africa should participate in the intellectual aspects (the colloquium) of the festival. The second was the wisdom of spending on the festival alone an amount which was more than the national budget of some member states of the OAU. The third was Nigeria's national control, through its national ministries and departments, of the festival's international secretariat, funds and activities. These concerns led Senegal to allege that Nigeria intended to use its wealth in order to impose its opinion on Africa. (Ofoegbu 1979, 142)

The fact that FESTAC took place, with all the invited countries fully participating, meant that the MEA deployed a significant amount of its human and material diplomatic resources to successfully manage and reduce the diplomatic problems (including the Nigeria-Senegal issues noted above).

Nigeria also encountered some other diplomatic problems, due to its manner of securing a nonpermanent position at the Security Council of the United Nations. Sometime

> in 1977, after the OAU Heads of States meeting in Libreville had unanimously supported the candidate of the Republic of Niger as the African representative to fill the non-permanent seat at the UN Security Council, the Nigerian government went ahead to canvass for the same post, even though its representative did not object to the OAU's choice at Libreville. For some obscure reason, Nigeria with its oil wealth then, and potential political and military weight, was able to get enough countries in Europe, North America, Latin American and Asia to vote for its candidate to defeat the OAU's choice for that non-permanent seat at the Security Council from 1977 to 1979. Although Nigeria won the seat, it was a pyrrhic victory. For only five African countries out of 49 voted for Lagos at the UN. The overall effect of this was to make African countries suspicious of the Nigerian Government. (Aluko 1986, 91)

This significant diplomatic problem meant that the MEA had to again deploy its diplomatic resources to manage the issue and regain the confidence of many African countries. The fact that Nigeria, during the Muhammed/Obasanjo Government, was able to work with African countries to fashion common policies toward many issues, for example, the Zimbabwe, South Africa, Angola, Mozambique and Middle East issues, meant that the MEA was able to manage and reduce this diplomatic problem.

The fact that the Nigerian relationship with the former Soviet Union involved a lot of expansion of areas of technical cooperation (for example, in the areas of cooperating to construct iron and steel complex and petroleum pipelines in Nigeria), and some ups and downs in the political dimensions of their relationship (Ogunbadejo 1986, 258–61; Ofoegbu 1979, 138–39, 146–48) also meant that the MEA had to deploy a lot of diplomatic resources for the monitoring and managing of Nigeria's relationship with the former Soviet Union during the Muhammed/Obasanjo era.

Chad was another issue that absorbed a lot of Nigeria's diplomatic attention. Through a series of conferences Nigeria arranged in Kano and Lagos for all Chadian parties and foreign countries that were involved in Chad, and through Nigeria's peacekeeping efforts in Chad, the Muhammed/Obasanjo Government sought to stabilize the Chadian political system, which was in the process of fragmentation (Akinyemi 1981, 7–13; Haley 1984, 102–300; *Newswatch* 1 December 1986, 18, 25). This expansive series of conferences on Chad and the peacekeeping efforts also meant another significant portion of human and material diplomatic resources of the MEA being used for the Chadian issue.

Angola was another major foreign policy area that the Muhammed/Obasanjo Government focused on. The MEA did not agree with Nigerian foreign policy toward Angola, which was formulated by the national political leadership without involving the MEA (Sotunmbi 1981, 9–10 and 22–23). This disagreement that the MEA had with the national political leadership was a vital factor that helped to reduce the profile and importance of the MEA in the foreign policy decision-making milieu during the Muhammed/Obasanjo era. Particularly, the MEA position on Angolan policy glaringly showed the cautious and moderate postures of the MEA, which contrasted with the assertive, energetic, and fast-paced foreign policies that the national political leadership of the Muhammed/Obasanjo Government formulated and made the MEA implement.

Despite the problems the MEA had with the national political leadership over Angola and other issues, there were some areas where the MEA and the national political leadership shared the same visions. One such issue related to temporary closure of the Nigerian foreign mission in Kampala, Uganda in 1979, due to Uganda's extreme political instability and the violent overthrow of the Ugandan government. The major decision-makers involved in this issue were the head of state (Obasanjo), the commissioner of External Affairs (Henry Adefope), "the Director of African Department in the Ministry of External Affairs, Ambassador L. S. Osobase, and the then Nigerian High Commissioner to Tanzania, Ambassador S. U. Yolah" (Aluko 1983, 87). Thus, unlike in the Angolan issue, the head of state involved the MEA in policy formulation. Additionally, all the decision-makers involved shared the same views, and thus, decided to temporarily close the Nigerian foreign mission in Kampala (Aluko 1983, 87–88). In fact, the

MEA officials, rather than the national political leadership, seemed to have been the vital factors in determining the policy. For example: "[T]he dispatches that were sent by Ambassador Yolah from Dar es Salaam in late 1978 and during the first half of 1979 were critical to the decision process. In one of his dispatches in January 1979 Yolah argued eloquently that if the situation were to deteriorate in Uganda the Nigerian Government (1) should put an end to its mediatory role between Amin and Nyerere which the latter had openly criticized; and (2) should take urgent action to evacuate Nigerian diplomats in Kampala and close down the mission there" (Aluko 1983, 88). The fact is that all the major decision-makers, including the head of state, closely followed and accepted the above recommendations of Ambassador Yolah. Thus, in essence, the MEA was the vital factor in the decision to temporarily close the Nigerian foreign mission in Kampala. Additionally, after the decision had been taken, "the Ministry of External Affairs put out a press statement late in April 1979, that given prevailing circumstances in Uganda, it was unsafe to keep Nigerian diplomats there. Therefore the government decided to close down its mission in Kampala until such a time as the situation in that country returned to normal" (Aluko 1983, 88). The fact that this statement emanated from the MEA, instead of Dodan Barracks, further shows that the MEA was the major element in the decision to close the mission in Kampala.

During the Muhammed/Obasanjo Government, Joseph Garba was the first commissioner for External Affairs. He was later succeeded by Henry Adefope during the latter phase of the Muhammed/Obasanjo Government. As noted earlier, Garba was a military officer with an excellent career background. According to Aluko (1976, 412), Garba was a "thorough soldier with a strong determination to get things done quickly and efficiently." His attributes of favoring speed and efficiency might have helped ensure that the assertive and fast-paced foreign policies of the Muhammed/Obasanjo Government succeeded. However, his independent thinking and strong personality also brought him into conflict with the SMC. Particularly, Garba as the political head of the MEA seemed to have been influenced by the cautious and moderate postures of the career diplomats in connection with the policy toward Angola, to the discomfort of his colleagues in the SMC (Akinyemi 1979b, 155; Sotunmbi 1981, 10, 22, 31, 33). However, as noted earlier, as an active and loyal military officer, he made sure that the MEA implemented all the foreign policies that the SMC formulated (including those he disagreed with). The fact that he played a significant part in ushering in the Muhammed/Obasanjo Government, and the fact that he was also a member of the SMC, made Garba an effective political head of the MEA who was respected both by his colleagues in the national political leadership located at Dodan Barracks and by the career diplomats at the MEA.

Garba was particularly adept and forceful in articulating to international audiences Nigeria's positions on many foreign policy issues. For example, before and after the 1977 Afro-Arab summit in Cairo, he noted his lack of agreement with the policies of Arab countries toward economic development and liberation efforts in Africa (Ojo 1986, 441). Also, when the French foreign minister visited Nigeria, Garba told him that Nigeria would not allow a "situation in which the fortune and benefits accruing from the development of our country are simply and condescendingly drained to enrich others" (Garba, quoted in Nwokedi 1986, 290). On another occasion, Garba informed the international community about some of the strands of the nonalignment conceptualization that helped gird Nigeria's foreign policy. He noted that Nigeria wanted "to take independent stand on major issues and we don't want to sit on the fence. . . . What I think we want to do is to be neutral. When you are neutral you tend to be in a better position to assess issues objectively" (Garba, quoted in Asobie 1986, 157). As these examples show, Garba seemed to have been always ready and able to articulate his views on foreign policy issues.

Henry Adefope, who succeeded Garba as the commissioner of External Affairs, was also an active duty military officer. Adefope was a general in the army who seemed to be absorbed more with professional military life than with national policy and political issues. While his predecessor was a member of both the SMC and the FEC, Adefope belonged only to the FEC (Aluko 1990a, 385). Thus, obviously, the role of Adefope in national policy circles was not as strong as Garba's. Adefope was also rather a reserved man who made few public pronouncements. He neither sought nor attained national visibility, even when he was serving as the commissioner of external affairs. He seemed to be a person who enjoyed listening to others more than talking. He did seek to broaden public support for foreign policy initiatives. For example, as noted earlier, he invited a group of Nigerians with academic interests and influence in foreign affairs for a dialogue in 1978 (Sotunmbi 1981, 37 n. 5]).

On the whole, the assertive, energetic, and fast-paced nature of foreign policies during the Muhammed/Obasanjo era often meant that the MEA functioned in a very high gear. Nigeria's involvement in numerous African issues and the fact that, for example, in 1978 alone about 10 important international figures visited Nigeria (among them President Jimmy Carter of the United States, Chancellor Helmut Schmidt of the Federal Republic of Germany, President Mengistu Haile Mariam of Ethiopia, President Sekou Toure of Guinea, Prime Minister Michael Manley of Jamaica, the United States chief of army staff, the commander in chief of the air Force of the former Soviet Union, and one of the vice premiers of the People's Republic of China)(Akinyemi 1979b, 168) meant that human and material diplomatic resources of the MEA were often at optimum utilization level.

The Ministry of Defense

The profile structure and functioning of the Ministry of Defense during the Muhammed/Obasanjo Government placed the ministry in a position to contribute to the attainment of Nigerian foreign policy goals, especially in the area of international security/military relations.

During the Muhammed/Obasanjo Government period, the Nigerian economy was very robust, due to the significant amount of money the country earned from the export of petroleum. This good national revenue profile enabled the military to be equipped with more hardware and more training facilities. The Muhammed/Obasanjo Government also prepared the military to revert to purely military life, since a civilian democratic government was to succeed the Muhammed/Obasanjo Government. (After a thorough governmental transition program, the Muhammed/Obasanjo Government handed the government to an elected civilian government in late 1979.) A major plank in the plan to prepare the military for purely military life (after many years of military governments in the country) was an effort to produce greater professionalism in the military rank and file. (Efforts were also made to foster a more apolitical military.) Thus, with more military weapon systems, increased training facilities for all the branches of the military, and more military professionalism, the armed forces were more able to handle the security/military components of the country's foreign policy.

Muhammed, and later Obasanjo, as heads of state of a military government, were both able and willing to utilize the military in achieving the country's foreign policy goals.

Nigeria's policy toward Angola clearly showed the significant role of the armed forces in foreign policy. For example, as noted earlier, in order to verify "information about the activities of the South African intervention force in Angola," the government "decided to send secret missions" to Angola (Sotunmbi 1981, 20). These "delegations consisted of military officers, some of whom were flown" to Angola by "the Nigerian Air Force" (Sotunmbi 1981, 20–21). The fact that the Ministry of External Affairs had a very insignificant role in these delegations to Angola, while the various branches of the armed forces were very prominent, shows the important role the Ministry of Defense was playing in foreign affairs. When Muhammed was head of state, the government, according to Sotunmbi (1981, 33), "preferred to treat foreign policy largely as an affair for the military. The decision to recognize the MPLA government reflects this position—it was the affair of the military. The public was not consulted and the civilian professionals in the Ministry of External Affairs, who opposed recognition, had their views set aside."

After hearing from the delegations, Nigeria decided to give assistance to Angola. This assistance was mainly in the form of military equipment for the MPLA to use in defeating the South African intervention force and Angolan liberation groups opposed to the MPLA (Sotunmbi 1981, 27). The Nigerian air force planes flew these military materials to Angola (Sotunmbi 1981, 30, n. 5). That Nigeria's assistance to Angola had very visible military content further made the role of the Ministry of Defense more prominent, in terms of the country's foreign policy toward Angola.

When Obasanjo became the head of state, as noted earlier, the Ministry of External Affairs was able to play a more visible role in the foreign policy decision-making milieu. However, the resurgence of the Ministry of External Affairs did not mean the eclipse of Ministry of Defense. Since other major foreign policy issues, like Chad and Zimbabwe, had very high security/military dimensions, both the Ministry of External Affairs and the Ministry of Defense played visible roles in foreign affairs (with the Ministry of Defense focusing on the security/military components of these foreign policies).

The very prominent and visible security/military components of Nigeria's foreign policies have always been due to how the foreign policy elites conceptualize the country's foreign policy interests and goals. Nigeria often believes that weak and unstable African countries (especially neighboring countries) often mean those countries are very dependent on non-African countries, and therefore constitute threats to Nigeria's national and security interests. Thus, one major foreign policy goal of Nigeria has often been a continual and consistent policy of helping neighboring countries, and other African countries, that are experiencing serious instability and weak national foundations to become more stable and strong (and thus also become less dependent on non-African countries). In turn, Nigeria itself becomes more secure, stable, and strong. This sort of conceptualization, design, planning, and operation of Nigeria's foreign policy has been analyzed by many Nigerian foreign policy scholars. Fawole (1981–1983, 96), for example, notes that "as Professor Aluko further argued, Nigeria had been interested in avoiding being surrounded by a string of weak states whose political, economic and military survival heavily depended on western powers. This is understandable because her security cannot be readily assured with the presence of foreign troops close to her borders." Nigeria sees more stable, strong African countries as being made possible by developing more viable and less dependent economic systems. Additionally, Nigeria also sees this development of healthier and less dependent economic systems in African countries as being made possible through regional economic integration efforts. It is this sort of logic that has informed Nigeria's longstanding and prominent role in creating, fostering, and accelerating economic integration among west African countries through the ECOWAS. Thus, it is within the context of the "furtherance of political and territorial security" of Nigeria (Fawole 1981–1983, 96) and other countries in the region, that Nigeria's interests in cooperation among west African countries, and Nigeria's "keener interests in developments in neighboring states" (Aluko, quoted in Fawole 1981–1983, 96) can be understood.

Nevertheless, Nigeria sees the strengthening of countries through economic growth as a long-term project. For countries that are currently seriously weak and unstable, the short-term goal is the application of security/military components of Nigeria's foreign policy and/or the political components of Nigeria's foreign policy (rather than an emphasis on the economic components of Nigeria's foreign policy alone) to stabilize these countries. This task of helping to stabilize countries that are experiencing serious political instability and societal cleavages is often done by utilizing the human and material resources of the Ministry of Defense (as represented by the various branches of the armed forces) in providing peacekeeping roles, peacemaking roles, military logistical support roles, military hardware and/or other forms of military assistance to these countries; and/or by utilizing the political/diplomatic resources of the Ministry of External Affairs to help promote peace and stability.

During the Muhammed/Obasanjo Government, the problems facing the Republic of Chad best demonstrated Nigeria's application of the security/military components of its foreign policy, together with the political/diplomatic components, for the purpose of helping to stabilize neighboring countries. The Ministry of Defense managed and operated the security/military components of Nigeria's foreign policy towards Chad, while the Ministry of External Affairs managed and operated the political/diplomatic components. On the whole, the Chadian issue became a task that consumed a lot of Nigeria's security/military and political/diplomatic resources (Agbakoba 1982, 33–34; Ede 1986, 186–87; Fawole 1981–1983, 95–96; Peters and Aminu 1986, 93–94; *Newswatch* 1 December 1986, 18, 25).

"Under Nigeria's diplomatic initiatives, President Felix Malloum" of Chad "agreed to step down and was granted asylum in Nigeria" (Ede 1986, 186). Additionally, "in March 1978 1,000 Nigerian peace-keeping troops led by then Colonel Mohammadu Magoro moved into Ndjamena," the capital of Chad, "as a buffer force between warring Frolinat troops and Chadian National Army. It was Colonel Magoro who swore in the provisional government" in Chad (Ede 1986, 186).

> Nigeria went into Chad twice, alone in 1978 at the invitation of the Chadian government. . . . In the 1978 operations, Nigeria was both a peace-keeper and a peace-maker. It had to, among other functions, supervise the demilitarization

of N'Djamena and the surrounding district up to 100 km; control the Chadian Air-Force; provide security for all important Chadian personalities; enforce a "ceasefire" agreement; ensure free movement of civilian population throughout Chad; establish a buffer zone between the troops of the two adversaries—Hobre and Malloum, and provide a forum for the parties to negotiate and discuss through daily conferences under Colonel Magoro, the Force Commander. (Peters and Aminu 1986, 94).

As shown above, the Nigerian military forces were involved in so many tasks in Chad that it appears that apart from purely security and military functions, they were also involved in the task of nation-building in Chad. Thus, clearly the task of stabilizing Chad was heavily on the shoulders of Nigeria's Ministry of Defense. The series of Kano Conferences and Lagos Conferences organized by Nigeria, in Nigeria, for Chad, represented the main thrust of the political/diplomatic dimension of the Nigerian policy toward Chad. These conferences brought together all Chadian political groups and observers from other countries that had very strong interests in Chad (for example, Libya and France), under the auspices of the federal government of Nigeria, to search for lasting solutions to the Chadian problem. However, due to both internal Chadian factors and international factors, lasting solutions to the Chadian problem were not possible, and Nigerian efforts to stabilize Chad did not yield positive results. Nevertheless, the Chadian peacekeeping and peacemaking roles for the Nigerian armed forces provided excellent opportunity for the Nigerian military to enhance its peacekeeping and peacemaking capabilities. According to Peters and Aminu (1986, 95), the Chadian and other peacekeeping, peacemaking, and military logistical support "operations have allowed the armed forces, especially the Army and the Air-Force, to acquire much needed exposure and experience." These prior experiences and exposures greatly aided the Nigerian armed forces in the peacekeeping and peacemaking operations that they were later to engage in: for example, in Liberia.

In the Chadian situation, other countries that were seriously involved in the issue were Libya and France. Fawole (1981–1983, 95–98) is of the view that Nigeria always has had a very narrow interest in Chad: of seeking to safeguard its national security by working for a stable political system (no matter which political group controls the government, as long as that group maintains and fosters stability in Chad), while some other countries have had wider interests in Chad. Specifically, he notes that "unlike Libya and France, Nigeria possesses neither economic nor strategic interests in Chad. Her foreign policy since independence is devoid of territorial ambitions. Her concern for peace in the country is a strategy to ensure her own territorial security. The imperatives of national security is therefore the premise on which Nigeria's involvement in the conflict will be analyzed" (Fawole 1981–1983, 95). Fawole (1981–1983, 98) also adds that "[T]here is no doubt however that Nigeria is not particularly interested in whoever is in power in N'djamena so long as her own security would be reasonably assured and the spectre of external subversion removed." This viewpoint resulted in Nigeria shifting its support from one leader or group to another, according to which leader or group Nigeria perceives, at a particular time, as capable of stabilizing Chad and also capable of maintaing independence from either Libya or France for military, economic, and/or political support (Fawole 1981–1983, 95–98). (Nigeria often perceives the presence of Libya and France in Chad as a serious national security problem for Nigeria.) The fact that Nigeria often chose to support one leader or group against another means that "Nigeria cannot be judged strictly as an impartial regional arbiter. The exigencies of national security has [sic] forced her into the position of an overtly partisan mediator in Chad" (Fawole 1981–1983, 98). This acutely partisan role in Chad undoubtedly made it very difficult for Nigeria to successfully play the role of a mediator. On the whole, Fawole sees Nigeria's role in Chad as being completely soaked in realism without any pretense of being guided by any lofty set of ideals. According to him, "Nigeria's repeated mediatory involvements in Chad have been dictated by the imperatives of national security rather than any pan-African ideals" (Fawole 1981–1983, 97).

During the Muhammed/Obasanjo Government, Angolan and Chadian issues were two of the most important foreign policies issues. As shown above, the Ministry of Defense played a very important part in these two issues, by managing and operating the security/military components of Nigeria's foreign policy. Therefore, the ministry was a visible and important factor in the Nigerian foreign policy decision-making system during the Muhammed/Obasanjo Government.

Additionally, some Nigerian foreign missions do have defense attachés. These defense attachés (who are officers of the Nigerian armed forces) play the role of helping to manage the security/military relationship between Nigeria and the respective host countries. Thus, the defense attaches provide an avenue through which the Ministry of Defense is continually and routinely involved in the management and operation of the security/military components of Nigeria's foreign policy.

THE NIGERIAN INSTITUTE OF INTERNATIONAL AFFAIRS

The Nigerian Institute of International Affairs (NIIA), as a premier think tank that focuses on international affairs, is often in a position to be a significant factor in the foreign policy decision-making system.

The NIIA, organizationally, is divided into Research, Library, and Documentation Services and Administration Departments (Banjo 1986,

19). The Research Department is responsible for the various research activities and programs that provide foreign policy analysis, advice, and recommendations. The Research Department is subdivided into various divisions (Banjo 1986, 21). Research officials are assigned to each of these divisions, and each research official "has a primary project within" the subject area of each of the divisions, "as well as a geographic area of specialization which is generally aimed at reflecting the foreign policy priorities of Nigeria" (Banjo 1986, 21). One of the duties of the research officials is the preparation of "policy papers for government on request" (Banjo 1986, 21). This particular aspect of the duties of the research officials helps the NIIA to be a very significant factor in the foreign policy decision-making milieu. Although the NIIA is a relatively independent government owned think tank, which is formally not mandated to be involved in foreign policy formulation and implementation (but mainly mandated to engage in the scientific study of international affairs and to provide the public, including government officials, with information on the nature and dynamics of international issues and events), in reality the NIIA sometimes does play a part in foreign policy decision-making.

The additional fact that NIIA research officials are "increasingly consulted by various newspapers, radio and television stations for views and commentaries on current international issues" (Banjo 1986, 21) also further increases the impact of the NIIA in the general foreign policy decision-making milieu.

Apart from their roles in the preparation of foreign policy position papers for government officials and the presentation of their views through the print and electronic media, NIIA officials are also responsible for many other formal activities and programs. These include public enlightenment lecture programs, conferences, seminars, Round Table meetings, special briefings, enlightenment and training programs, dialogue sessions with foreign policy think tanks of other countries, Patrons Dinner (which is a public event that enables the President of the Federal Republic of Nigeria, who is also the patron of the NIIA, "to give an address reviewing the state of the world and stating Nigeria's view on key world issues"), and publication of numerous journals, monographs, and books (Banjo 1986, 21–24).

These numerous activities and programs of the NIIA have a significant impact on the foreign policy decision-making milieu. As noted by Professor Akindele (1986, 66), "in the field of foreign policy, as in other fields, the quality of decisions made is not unrelated to the amount of information at the disposal of policy makers." The NIIA provides foreign policy makers with a lot of relevant foreign policy information, thus enhancing the quality of foreign policy decisions in Nigeria.

The Muhammed/Obasanjo Government, which was very interested in robust and assertive foreign policy initiatives and actions, and which at the same time was not comfortable with the Ministry of External Affairs (normally the main machinery for foreign relations), right from the beginning was very aware of the enormous capabilities of the NIIA in foreign affairs. The NIIA was, thus, utilized very visibly by the Muhammed/Obasanjo Government in its various assertive foreign policy initiatives and actions. The role of the NIIA in the foreign policy decision-making milieu was so important and visible that the Muhammed/Obasanjo era can be considered as the golden age of the NIIA.

The importance of the NIIA to the Muhammed/Obasanjo Government is also indicated by the fact that one of the first official duties of this government was the appointment of the head of the NIIA. Thus, the position of the director-general of the NIIA, "which had been vacant for over a year, was filled within three weeks of the" inception of the Muhammed/Obasanjo Government (Akinyemi 1979b, 154).

One of the first things the Muhammed/Obasanjo Government wanted the new director-general of the NIIA to do was formulate "new guidelines for Nigerian foreign policy, with the directive that it should be submitted within a week" (Akinyemi 1979b, 154). As directed, these new guidelines were submitted and they were approved by the head of state (Akinyemi 1979b, 154). The fact that it was the NIIA, and not the Ministry of External Affairs, that formulated the new guidelines further demonstrates the importance and visibility of the NIIA during the Muhammed/Obasanjo Government.

Professors Olusanya and Akindele (1986a, 27) note also that the use of "NIIA for policy advice did not become pronounced until the" era of Muhammed/Obasanjo. During this era, the "NIIA's Director-General was very much involved in foreign policy," and the NIIA itself "emerged as an influential foreign policy 'think-tank' for the nation" (Olusanya and Akindele 1986a, 27).

Apart from giving foreign policy advice and being involved in foreign policy formulation through its guidelines, the NIIA was also involved in foreign policy implementation. For example, in order "to find out the actual needs of Angola," the government sent a "delegation led by Dr. A. Bolaji Akinyemi, Director-General of the Nigerian Institute of International Affairs" to Angola (Sotunmbi 1981, 27). Additionally, during this visit to Angola, the delegation led by Akinyemi held a "series of meetings" with Angolan officials (including the president), and also discussed the possible future acquisition of a building for the Nigerian Embassy in Luanda, Angola and the urgent need for a Nigerian ambassador to Angola to be appointed (Akinyemi circa 1983, 7). The fact that the director-general of the NIIA headed this delegation, which was involved in very substantive issues in Nigerian-Angolan bilateral relations, clearly shows that the director-general was involved in foreign policy implementation.

5: THE ROBUST YEARS: THE MUHAMMED/OBASANJO PERIOD

Thus, on the whole, during the Muhammed/Obasanjo era, the NIIA performed foreign policy advisory, foreign policy formulation, and foreign policy implementation roles. This almost comprehensive participation in the foreign policy decision-making processes made the NIIA a tremendous contributor to the foreign policy decision-making frameworks.

However, not surprisingly, this very visible role of the NIIA also brought it into a lot of conflict with the Ministry of External Affairs (Akinyemi circa 1983, 6–8; Banjo 1986, 20–21; Olusanya and Akindele 1986a, 27). Professor Akinyemi, who was the director-general of the NIIA throughout the Muhammed/Obasanja era, might have found the conflicts between the NIIA and the Ministry of External Affairs to be inappropriate. He (Akinyemi circa 1983, 6) observes that

> in my naivety, I had always assumed that that cherished concept called national interest will always dictate that it is not really who does what that counts, as long as the decision is in the national interest. How wrong I was, I was soon to find out that bureaucratic in-fighting for the power to make decisions and to fight against any encroachment on that power was more important than whether the decision is actually taken or not. Incidentally, this is not unique to Nigeria. I believe it is a world-wide phenomenon. However, it is unhealthy and it should be treated as a disease to be cured, and not just tolerated.

Clearly, Akinyemi was not happy with the conflicts the NIIA had with the Ministry of External Affairs. However, due to the fact that the national political leadership wanted the NIIA to play an important and visible role in the foreign policy decision-making milieu, despite the conflicts the NIIA was still able to fulfill a very crucial role in foreign affairs. Additionally, even though the Ministry of External Affairs was formally the supervising ministry for the NIIA (Banjo 1986, 21), due to support from the SMC and the Supreme Military Headquarters, the Ministry of External Affairs was not able to relegate the NIIA to a low-profile role. (The Ministry of External Affairs often seems to hold the view that the roles of foreign policy formulation and implementation solely belong to it, while it sees the NIIA as being entitled only to engage in scientific study of international affairs and the sharing of its research with the general public.) Interestingly, in 1981, the Shagari Government made a change that resulted in the NIIA being supervised by the Executive Office of the President (Banjo 1986, 21). Surprisingly, the Shagari Government (which succeeded the Muhammed/Obasanjo Government) did not utilize the NIIA as much as the Muhammed/Obasanjo Government had. Still, the change made by the Shagari Government freed the NIIA from the strings of the Ministry of External Affairs, and also formally linked it to the highest levels of government.

The ability of the NIIA to play a very effective role, during the Muhammed/Obasanjo era, was also due to the leadership provided by Professor Akinyemi. As Ofoegbu noted (1979, 144), "no management of the NIIA has associated scholars of foreign policy and international relations with work of the institute in research and policy planning, as did the management of Director-General Bolaji Akinyemi. Dr. Akinyemi's management of the institute has included the bringing of Nigerian intellectuals in the various fields of international relations and senior policy decision-makers from the universities, the press, the Foreign Office, Defence, Cabinet Office, the institute and some research establishments" to analyze major foreign policy issues. Due to these initiatives and activities, the NIIA, under Akinyemi's management, "was able to do for the country and its foreign policy more than all the past administrations of the institute had done between 1963 and 1975" (Ofoegbu 1979, 144).

OTHER MINISTRIES AND AGENCIES

Apart from those evaluated above, many other ministries, agencies, and organs also played significant roles in Nigeria's international relations during the Muhammed/Obasanjo era. For example, though the NIIA is the premier foreign policy think tank, the Nigerian Institute for Policy and Strategic Studies (NIPSS) and the Nigerian Institute of Social and Economic Research (NISER) also provide policy research outputs that can inform foreign policy decision-making frameworks. The fact that the NIIA "carries out joint research projects with" NIPSS and NISER (*International Research Centers Directory 1994–1995* 1994, 858) often helps the latter two bodies to have some significant role in foreign policy research activities. Nevertheless, during the Muhammed/Obasanjo era, NIPSS and NISER were never able to play the crucial and visible roles in foreign affairs that the NIIA did; the NIPSS and NISER had more impact on the domestic policy milieu.

The role that the NIIA and other think tanks played during the Muhammed/Obasanjo Government might have been due to that government's general strong emphasis on research and development activities in all fields of knowledge, especially science and engineering. Compared to previous governments, this government provided more funds for research and development activities (Eleazu circa 1979, 4). In making an input in relation to the *Public Service Review Commission (Udoji) Report Main Report,* Professor Iya Abubakar has been quoted as observing that "the man in the field has a problem, but does not know that an answer 'exists'; the man in the university has the answer, but does not know that the problem exists" (Abubakar, quoted in Eleazu circa 1979, 5). In order to

5: THE ROBUST YEARS: THE MUHAMMED/OBASANJO PERIOD

solve this problem, Professor Abubakar "therefore suggested that it is the duty of the university to see that these two—the man with the problem and the man with the answer are brought together" (Eleazu circa 1979, 5). *The Udoji Report* (which was produced during the Gowon Government) aimed at making the civil service and, indeed, the entire governmental process, function more efficiently. The Muhammed/Obasanjo Government came to power in a policy environment in which there were serious awareness, discussions, and debates about how to increase efficiency in both the public and private factors. One aspect of this focused on the generation and utilization of new and improved ideas. The Muhammed/Obasanjo Government, which came to the political scene with the zeal and enthusiasm to improve the quality of both domestic and foreign policies, logically perceived the think tanks (rather than the government ministries and departments) as being more able to help the government to generate and utilize new and improved ideas. This factor resulted in the NIIA and other think tanks having more visibility in the policy decision-making milieu.

Nevertheless, it is important to note that the visibility of some think tanks like the NIIA did not mean the Muhammed/Obasanjo Government relied solely on think tanks. The true picture is that, while previous governments relied almost exclusively on the government ministries and departments for the formulation, implementation, and evaluation of policies (scarcely utilizing the research outputs of the public policy think tanks), the Muhammed/Obasanjo Government decided, where appropriate, to adequately utilize the think tanks in order to formulate new and improved policies, and also in order to increase the general quality of public policies, (while at the same time still depending on government ministries and departments to formulate and implement policies in those policy areas wherein they were performing adequately. In reality, the Muhammed/Obasanjo Government utilized think tanks (mainly the NIIA) mostly in the foreign policy area (due to the fact that it perceived the Ministry of External Affairs as being unready for the robust, assertive, and bold changes in foreign policies that the government were embarking on), while the ministries and departments still dominated the domestic policy arena. Even in the foreign policy arena, the NIIA was very visible and important only in some aspects: specifically, in the political/diplomatic and security/military dimensions (particularly the former) of foreign policy, while various ministries and agencies dominated the cultural and economic dimensions of foreign policy. The NIIA was able to be visible and active in the political/diplomatic dimension of foreign policy due to the Government's dissatisfaction with the Ministry of External Affairs. Though the NIIA was to some degree significant in the security/military dimension of foreign policy, the immense stature of the Ministry of Defense in the policy milieu made the ministry the senior policy organ in this dimension of foreign policy. Additionally, the mostly technical and routine nature of the dynamics in the cultural and economic dimensions of foreign policy made the ministries and agencies the major policy organs in these dimensions of foreign policy.

The Federal Ministry of Information was the major player in the cultural dimension of foreign policy. As usual, the information attachés in Nigerian foreign missions were officials of the Ministry of Information who were on secondment to the Ministry of External Affairs. The information attachés were in charge of managing the media relations and cultural activities of Nigerian foreign missions in the host countries. The Nigerian international broadcasting activities done by the Voice of Nigeria radio services also come under the ministerial supervision of the Federal Ministry of Information. Voice of Nigeria broadcasting services were a very vital and effective part of Nigeria's foreign policy toward Angola and other countries in southern Africa during the Muhammed/Obasanjo era (Sotunmbi 1981, 37 n. 7).

A major international cultural event that occurred during the Muhammed/Obasanjo Government was the World Festival of Black and African Arts and Culture (FESTAC), which was hosted by Nigeria in 1977. The Ministry of Information (the main organ charged by the government to organize the FESTAC event), the Ministry of External Affairs, the state governments, and others all played significant roles in organizing the FESTAC. However, some, like Balogun (1986, 5–6), believe that the FESTAC could have been organized with more emphasis on the cultural heritage of Nigeria.

In the economic components of foreign policy, as usual, many ministries and agencies were involved, though the Ministry of External Affairs (through its international economic relations unit) sometimes shared some functions (as assisting or junior partners) with these ministries and agencies. For example, Nigeria's international financial relations (especially relations with international financial institutions) were primarily managed by the Federal Ministry of Finance and the Central Bank of Nigeria. On the other hand, the Federal Ministry of Trade was the primary organ that managed and regulated Nigeria's international trade relations.

Though the preceding Gowon Government laid the foundations for ECOWAS, the Muhammed/Obasanjo Government helped to nurture it. During the late 1970s, ECOWAS was still going through a lot of growing pains (Ezenwa 1981, 205). The Federal Ministry of Economic Development was the primary ministry that managed Nigeria's relationship with ECOWAS (with the Ministry of External Affairs also being actively involved). With the head office of ECOWAS being located in Nigeria, that organization being fairly new, and Nigeria being the country that led the creation and nurturing of the organization, both the Ministry of Economic

5: THE ROBUST YEARS: THE MUHAMMED/OBASANJO PERIOD

Development and the Ministry of External Affairs devoted a significant amount of their human and materials resources and time to ECOWAS.

The Muhammed/Obasanjo era was also a period during which Nigeria, through bilateral participation with other west African countries, created and operated some economic enterprises, offered economic assistance, and/or provided economic infrastructures. For example, Nigeria participated "in the cement and sugar factories in Benin Republic, in the bauxite and iron ore projects in the Republic of Guinea; roads were wholly financed linking Nigeria and Niger; and the two-lane Birni Nkonni bridge in the Republic of Niger was built by the Nigerian government for N 668000. Oil was sold at deferred payment schedules to Ivory Coast and Ghana among other states" (Akinyemi 1979b, 166). These bilateral economic activities covered many areas, as shown above. This meant, in turn, that those ministries and agencies that focused on economic matters (for example, the Federal Ministries of Industries, Works, Trade, Economic Development, and Petroleum Resources and the Nigerian National Petroleum Corporation) were involved in creating and/or operating the above economic cooperation activities, with the Ministry of External Affairs assisting with diplomatic resources when and where such resources were needed.

The development of the Nigerian iron and steel industry was also one of the major economic policies of the Muhammed/Obasanjo Government. The centerpiece of the iron and steel industry is the Ajaokuta iron and steel complex. Other major components of the steel industry are the steel rolling mills sector of the industry. The Muhammed/Obasanjo Government developed the steel rolling mills at Aladja, Jos, and Katsina. These three steel rolling mills were constructed with loans from Japan (Halliru 1988, 108). On the other hand, the Ajaokuta iron and steel complex was built with the technical assistance of the former Soviet Union. The former Soviet Union, which had a long-standing role in the Nigerian iron and steel industry (Ofoegbu 1979, 138), became even more prominent once the industry became one of the priority sectors of the economic policy of the Muhammed/Obasanjo Government. For example, "in June 1976, a formal cooperation agreement was finally signed between Lagos and Moscow for the establishment of the iron and steel complex" at Ajaokuta (Ogunba-dejo 1986, 258). The Muhammed/Obasanjo Government's

> determination to build on the foundation established by previous administrations on iron and steel complex was further demonstrated in June 1977 [*sic*], when the Permanent Secretary of the Federal Ministry of Industries, Mallam Ahmed Joda, led a delegation to Moscow to discuss the issue. The delegation, which included the project manager of the Nigerian Steel Development Authority, Dr. Adegboye, familiarized itself with the design of the iron and steel complex and with the method and organization of production in the USSR's

own iron and steel plants, thus resolving some of the preliminary difficulties connected with establishing the complex in Nigeria. (Ogunbadejo 1986, 258)

As shown above, the development of the steel rolling mills, and the Ajaokuta iron and steel complex, involved extensive international scientific and technological relations (as well as general international economic relations) between Nigeria and other countries. As also shown above, the Federal Ministry of Industries and the Nigerian Steel Development Authority were the major organs involved in managing Nigeria's international scientific and technological relations in this area.

The petroleum industry, which is the backbone of the Nigerian economy, by its very nature has an international profile. The exploration, development, drilling, refining, storage, transportation, and marketing of petroleum resources involve complex Nigerian international scientific and technological relations with multinational corporations and governments in other countries. The fact that petroleum is the dominant Nigerian economic export further deepens the international profile of the petroleum industry. The Nigerian National Petroleum Corporation (NNPC) and the Ministry of Petroleum Resources, as in previous periods, continued to be the major organs that managed Nigeria's international scientific, technological, and trade relations in the area of petroleum resources during the Muhammed/Obasanjo era. The Ministry of Petroleum Resources (with some possible technical assistance from the NNPC) also continued to manage Nigeria's relationship with the Organization of Petroleum Exporting Countries (an organization in which Nigeria holds membership) during the Muhammed/Obasanjo Government. The decision-making processes that led to the Muhammed/Obasanjo Government's "nationalization of British Petroleum company BP in July 1979," in order to influence Britain's behavior in a direction to help end minority governments in Zimbabwe and South Africa (Sotunmbi 1981, 36, 37 n. 6), most likely involved significant technical input (about the takeover of BP by Nigerian petroleum technicians, engineers, and managers) from the NNPC and the Ministry of Petroleum Resources, while organs like the SMC, the Supreme Military Headquarters, the Cabinet Office, the NIIA and the Ministry of External Affairs focused on the foreign policy and diplomatic issues that related to the takeover of BP. (The successful takeover of BP resulted in the company being renamed African Petroleum (AP) Company.)

The Muhammed/Obasanjo Government was also responsible for creating a body charged with the promotion and development of nuclear energy resources in Nigeria, and also designated Ahmadu Bello University and Obafemi Awolowo University as places were nuclear research centers were to be created (Henderson 1981, 412; Ogunbadejo 1984, 37). The fact that nuclear research and development involve significant international interactions and, additionally, nuclear resources and energy are often regulated by international agencies, gives the nuclear resources and energy sector an international profile. These Nigerian international scientific and technical relations, in the area of nuclear resources and energy issues, likely mainly involved the Nigerian Atomic Energy Commission, with the SMC, the Supreme Military Headquarters, and the Ministry of Defense likely supervising the policies and actions of the commission. (The Nigerian Atomic Energy Commission was established by the Muhammed/Obasanjo Government in 1979 [Henderson 1981, 412].)

One other important organ in the foreign policy decision-making milieu was the Nigerian Security Organization (NSO). It was created by the Muhammed/Obasanjo Government in 1976. According to Peters (1986, 152), Nigerian "[I]ntelligence activity, prior to 1976, was limited to the activities of the various armed forces intelligence units, the police special branch and the intelligence unit of the Ministry of External Affairs." The NSO was charged "with the following functions: the prevention and detection of any crime against the security of Nigeria, the protection and preservation of all classified matter concerning or relating to the security of Nigeria and such other purposes the Head of the Federal Military Government may consider necessary with a view to securing the maintenance of the security of Nigeria. The NSO was therefore expected to combine the functions of . . . counter-intelligence activities . . . with foreign positive intelligence" (Peters 1986, 152). The NSO clearly had a very important role to play in the foreign policy decision-making milieu. One of its functions was the supply of an adequate base of information about other countries that would enable the foreign policy decision makers to formulate high-quality foreign policy decisions, which would, in turn, enhance the national security interests of Nigeria. The fact that the NSO was a newly created organization meant that it was still in the process of laying solid organizational foundations during the Muhammed/Obasanjo era. Obviously, this fact also meant that the NSO, during that era, was not yet ready, and able, to perform its roles at full capacity. Additionally, the fact that the NSO was "resented by the other agencies, especially the military and police" (Peters 1986, 153) also added to its growing pains. In fact, this resentment (prompted by the fear of the military and the police that the NSO was encroaching into their fields) persisted far beyond the Muhammed/Obasanjo era. For example, Peters (1986, 154) has noted that "a feeling within the military establishment to have a military counterweight to the civilian NSO, especially because of the way the NSO had been used by the political leadership" led to the creation of the Defense Intelligence Agency (DIA) in 1984. The intensity of the friction between the military and the NSO finally led to the latter being disbanded and its functions being parcelled out to two new organizations (the National Intelligence Agency [NIA], and the State Security Service [SSS]) and the DIA. The dissolution of the NSO and the creation of the two new intelligence organizations was done in 1986, by the Babangida Government, as a result of the implementation of the report of the Shinkafi Panel, which was set up to recommend ways to reorganize the intelligence community (Peters 1986, 157–58). The NIA is charged with foreign intelligence activities, the SSS with domestic intelligence activities, and the DIA serves as the umbrella body for the Directorate of Military Intelligence (DMI) of the army, the Directorate of Naval Intelligence (DNI) of the navy, and the Directorate of Air Intelligence (DAI) of the air force (though the DMI, DNI, and DAI remain as relatively autonomous intelligence bodies that are still under their respective branches of the armed forces).

Until it was disbanded by the Babangida Government, the NSO remained intact during the Muhammed/Obasanjo Government, the Shagari Government, and the Buhari Government. While it was in existence, despite its conflicts with the military and police, the NSO was "first among equals in the Nigerian intelligence community" due to the fact that the "NSO's position as the first among equals was backed by the government" (Peters 1986, 152–53). Thus, during the Muhammed/Obasanjo Government, the NSO was able to contribute to the national security components of Nigerian foreign policy.

Conclusion

As shown above, numerous ministries, agencies, and organizations were involved in the foreign policy decision-making milieu. One of the key features of the Muhammed/Obasanjo Government was its way of coordinating and managing foreign policy and the national security system. During this era, as analyzed earlier, and as Aluko (1976, 412) and Ofoegbu (1979, 145) note, the Supreme Military Council and the Supreme Military Headquarters (both at Dodan Barracks) and the Cabinet Office tightly managed and dominated the foreign policy formulation system, and closely supervised the foreign policy implementation processes. Thus, the traditional heavyweight in the foreign policy decision-making system (the Ministry of External Affairs with its career diplomats who often have cautious and moderate foreign policy positions) was not the dominant force during the Muhammed/Obasanjo era. The national political leadership at Dodan Barracks, with inputs from the NIIA, the MEA, and other ministries and agencies, mainly formulated the major foreign policies. Prior strong interests of the key people of Dodan Barracks (Muhammed and Obasanjo were both very active members of the Nigerian Society of International Affairs [Akinyemi 1979b, 153–54]) made them very interested in foreign policy, and also relatively well prepared to be strongly involved in foreign policy decision-making. The relatively shared worldviews of the leaders at Dodan Barracks; the strong perception of national interests and goals, and the sense of urgency in advancing those interests and goals by the leaders at Dodan Barracks; the reduced role for the cautious career diplomats of the MEA; and the tight coordination, management, control, and domination of the foreign policy decision-making system by Dodan Barracks led to very rigorous, vigorous, robust, and assertive foreign policies and actions during the Muhammed/Obasanjo Government. Thus, the foreign policy arena had a fast, robust, energetic, and bold profile during this era. Most view this era as the golden age of Nigerian foreign policy.

The domination of the foreign policy formulation processes, close supervision of the foreign policy implementation processes, and the general efficient management of the foreign policy decision-making system by Dodan Barracks, expectedly made the foreign policy decision-making profile, during the Muhammed/Obasanjo era, to mostly conform to the rational-actor model of decision-making.

6
The Shagari Government

THE SHAGARI GOVERNMENT BEGAN IN 1979 AND ENDED IN 1983. In order to facilitate an adequate analysis of the foreign policy decision-making system in relation to Nigerian foreign policy during this era, the various government organs, ministries, agencies, and units are examined separately, in terms of their decision-making structures and processes. The coordinating structures and processes in the foreign policy milieu are also evaluated. The impact of these various structures and processes on Nigerian foreign policy is also analyzed.

When Shehu Shagari became the president of Nigeria in 1979, his government also marked the first government in Nigeria that had a formal presidential system of government. Thus, while the Balewa Government, which was the first civilian government of an independent Nigeria, had a parliamentary system of government, the Shagari Government, which was the second civilian government, had a presidential system of government. (In between the Balewa and Shagari Governments was the first era of military governments.) The first term of the Shagari Government started from 1979 and ended at the end of the third quarter of 1983. The second term of this government was extremely brief, lasting just about the last three months of 1983. Thus, this study focuses mostly on the nature of the foreign policy decision-making dynamics and Nigerian foreign policy during the first term of the Shagari Government. (The Shagari Government was brought to an end by the advent of the second era of military governments.)

The major decision-making structures during the Shagari Government that were positioned to play significant roles in the foreign policy decision-making milieu were the Executive Office of the President, the Federal Executive Council, the National Security Council, the National Defense Council, the National Council of States, the Cabinet Office, the Ministry of External Affairs, and the Ministry of Defense. Apart from these major decision-making structures, other governmental organs, ministries, agencies, and units were involved (though to a lesser extent) in activities that had impact on Nigeria's international relations. These include the Federal Ministry of Finance, the Federal Ministry of Internal Affairs, the Ministry of National Planning, the Federal Ministry of Information, the Central Bank of Nigeria, the Nigerian Institute of International Affairs, the National Institute of Policy and Strategic Studies, and the National Assembly (in particular, the Foreign Relations Committees of the House of Representatives and the Senate). The above major decision-making structures (and to some extent, some of the decision-making structures that had lesser roles in Nigeria's international relations) are evaluated in this study in terms of their structures, decision processes, and role in the foreign policy decision-making milieu.

THE EXECUTIVE OFFICE OF THE PRESIDENT

The Executive Office of the President (EOP) was designed in such a way that, if adequately staffed and operated, it could help the president to efficiently and effectively perform his job as the chief foreign policy maker. Within the EOP were the vice president, the secretary to the Federal Government, the advisers to the president on Political Affairs, the adviser on National Security, and the adviser on Economic Affairs. Thus the president had high-level officials within the EOP, who, if they were assigned the duties, could have helped in the collection, analysis, and interpretation of information relevant to foreign policy issues. These same individuals were also capable of providing the president (on the basis of the information they had) with an array of various possible foreign policy options when he was about to make a foreign policy decision. These same officials also possessed the knowledge, work experience, and stature in the national policy-making machinery to help the president to coordinate the various ministries, agencies, and units that were involved in Nigeria's international relations. Additionally, these same officials were also in the position to help the president to monitor implementation of various foreign policy decisions and the evaluation of ongoing or past foreign policy initiatives and actions. However, in examining the role the EOP played in the foreign policy-making milieu, it appears that President Shehu Shagari was not able, or willing, to make the EOP the hub or the nerve center for foreign policy-making dynamics.

Possibly President Shehu Shagari felt that the relevant ministries should be the focus of activities in terms of foreign affairs. There is also the fact that the prior parliamentary system of government in Nigeria meant that the first experience of a presidential system of government, which started with the Shagari Government, was practiced with some parliamentary system overlay. Thus, there was not a significant tendency to centralize foreign policy decision-making dynamics within the chief executive's office. Gambari (1989, 10) notes that the Shagari Government's management of national political affairs in the country showed that "Nigeria was operating a presidential system with a parliamentary system mentality." Thus, it can also be safe to posit that the foreign policy decision-making structures and processes of the EOP, in the presidential system of the Shagari era, were operated with a parliamentary system mentality. In a parliamentary system the prime minister, though leading in terms of foreign affairs, often allows the minister in charge of foreign affairs to be the day-to-day manager of the country's foreign relations.

The less active nature of Shehu Shagari also accounted for the EOP not serving as the nerve center for foreign policy decision-making dynamics. During the early period of the Shagari Government, Stanley Macebuh (1979) observed that Shagari was operating a "minimum" government, in terms of both domestic and foreign policy. Throughout the Shagari era, some scholars, like Olajide Aluko (1983, 90), had hoped that "President Shagari could come to grips with foreign policy and provide effective direction, leading the foreign service from the front rather than from behind," and thus "have considerable impact on the decision-making process." However, the "minimum" government that Macebuh observed in the early period of the Shagari Government seemed to have covered the lifespan of that government, particularly in terms of foreign policy. Almost less than three months to the end of the Shagari Government, it was noted that negative comments were made about "the low-key style of quiet diplomacy" of the government, which was attributed to the administration's policy of "omission and avoidance of taking positive and clear stances" in the foreign policy arena (*West Africa* 10 October 1983, 2350) Thus, to some, the foreign-policy decision-making system of the Shagari Government lacked any trace of dynamism (Johnson 1990, 512).

As noted earlier, the EOP was well staffed with high-level political leaders and presidential advisers, who could have enabled the president to play a more dynamic role in terms of foreign policy, if they had been given adequate foreign policy roles. One of these was the Vice President. Alex Ekwueme was a highly experienced political leader, a lawyer, and an architect who had operated a very successful architectural firm before becoming the vice president. Ekwueme did do what most vice presidents often do in presidential systems (in terms of foreign affairs), which was to travel to meetings and events in foreign countries that the president was unable to attend. Apart from this role, Ekwueme did not seem to play a major role in terms of foreign policy decision-making.

The secretary to the Federal Government was another important official with the EOP, whose role it was to help the president in his task of national policy-making and administration. In terms of domestic policy, the secretary to the Federal Government played a key role in policy-making and

```
┌─────────────────────────────────────────────┬──────────────────────────┐
│ Executive Office of the President           │ The National Assembly    │
│ • President and Commander-in-Chief of the   │ • Senate                 │
│   Armed Forces                              │ • House of               │
│ • Vice President                            │   Representatives        │
│ • Secretary to the Federal Government       │ • Foreign Relations      │
│ • Advisers to the President on Political    │   Committees of the      │
│   Affairs                                   │   Senate and the House   │
│ • Adviser on National Security              │   of Representatives     │
│ • Adviser on Economic Affairs               │                          │
│ • Other Advisers                            │                          │
└─────────────────────────────────────────────┴──────────────────────────┘
```

	Federal Executive Council	National Security Council
Nigerian Institute of International Affairs	Federal Cabinet Office	National Defense Council
	Ministry of External Affairs	
National Institute for Policy and Strategic Studies	Ministry of Defense	National Council of States
	Federal Ministry of Finance	Central Bank of Nigeria
	Federal Ministry of Internal Affairs	
	Ministry of National Planning	
	Federal Ministry of Information	
	Other Ministries, Agencies, and Corporations	

Main Decision-Making Structures in Nigeria's International Relations during the Shagari Government

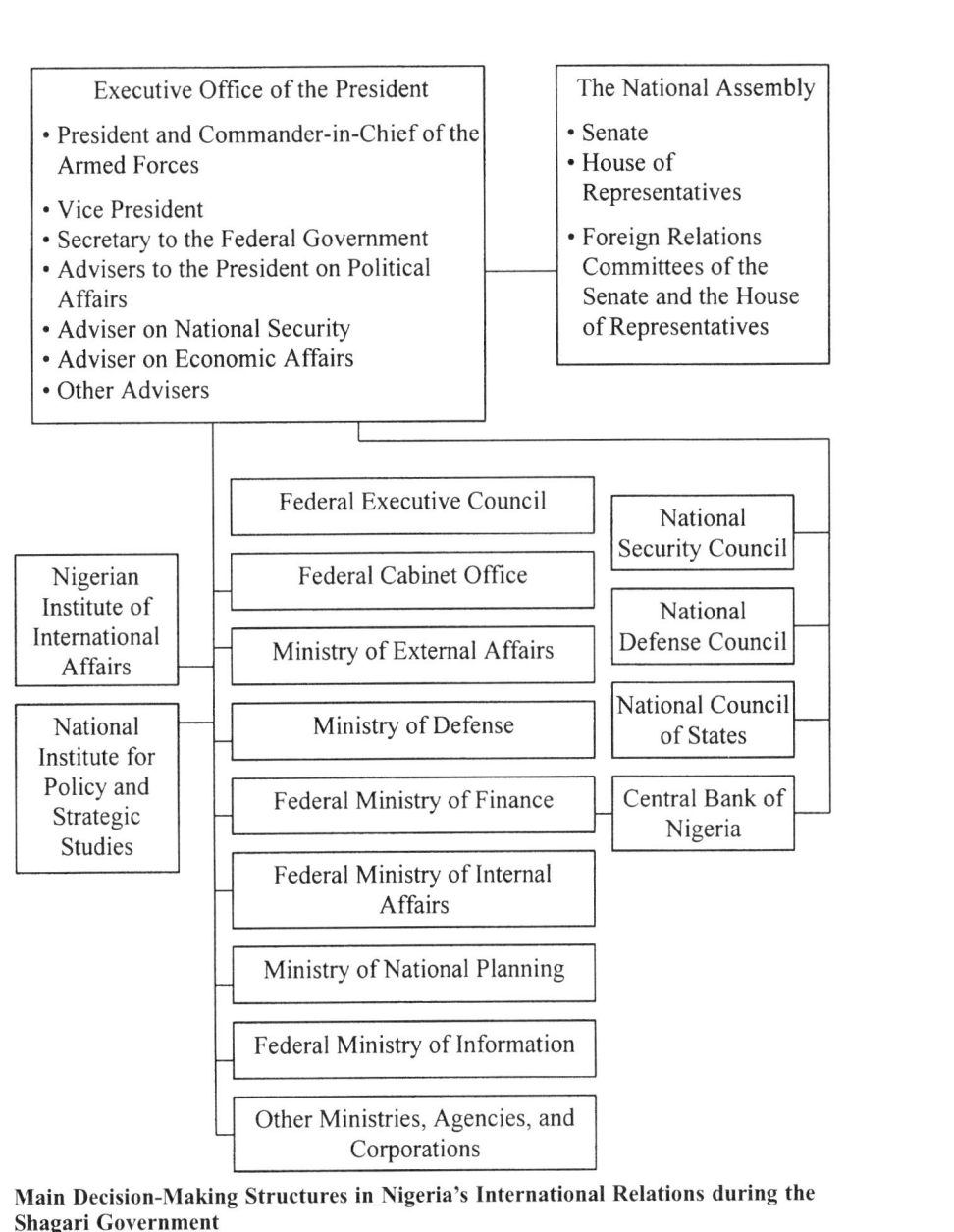

administration. However, since the EOP was not made the nerve center of foreign policy decision-making by the president, the secretary to the Federal Government did not play a major role in foreign policy decision-making. The other important aides in the EOP that could have helped the EOP to be the hub of foreign policy decision-making dynamics (if the president had wanted the EOP to play that role) were the advisers to the president on Political Affairs, the Adviser on National Security, and the adviser on Economic Affairs. Ogunbadejo (1980, 401, 407) notes that Chuba Okadigbo, who served as an adviser to the president on Political Affairs, concentrated mostly on domestic political affairs. The person who later was appointed as an additional adviser to the president on Political Affairs did the same. Similarly, the adviser on Economic Affairs mostly focused on domestic economic issues. It has also been noted that the person who served as the adviser on National Security either did not have the adequate experience for the job, or was unable to adequately understand the role he was supposed to play (Peters 1986, 156–57). Thus, on the whole, key advisers in the EOP (advisers to the president on Political Affairs, adviser on Economic Affairs, and adviser on National Security), who could have been important players in turning the EOP into the hub of foreign policy decision-making, did not play these roles.

The deteriorating internal security situation, during the Shagari era, made the president (who was already the commander in chief of the armed forces) later take on the portfolio of the minister of Defense (he did not have this portfolio in the early phase of his government) (*Europa Year Book 1982, Volume Two* 1982, 1127; *Europa Year Book 1983: A World Survey: Volume Two* 1983, 1150). This sort of decisive action showed that, if the president did desire it, the EOP could have easily been the center of foreign policy decision-making dynamics.

When the search for the solution to the problem of undocumented aliens in Nigeria came up, the Shagari Government accepted the recommendation of the Aniagolu Tribunal of Inquiry, which probed the problems caused by these aliens (Aluko 1985, 554). In order to implement the recommendations of the Aniagolu Tribunal, the Shagari Government noted that it directed the EOP, together with the Ministry of Defense, the Federal Ministry of Finance, the Federal Ministry of Internal Affairs, and the Nigerian police force to form an inter-ministerial committee (Aluko 1985, 554) to implement the recommendations of the tribunal. Thus, though the EOP, generally, was not very prominent in the foreign policy decision-making arena, when the president was preoccupied with the problem of millions of undocumented foreign nationals in Nigeria, he made the EOP play a vital role in the issue. If the president had paid the same attention to other foreign policy issues, maybe the EOP could have been the hub or nerve center of foreign policy decision-making dynamics.

The Federal Executive Council

The Federal Executive Council (FEC) was the council of the ministers, and, thus, the cabinet body at the federal level. The membership included the president (as chairman), the vice president, and the ministers. The 1979 Constitution specifically gave a formal foreign policy role to the FEC. The constitutional "provisions on the foreign policy institutions, section 136(2) states, *inter alia,* that, in order to determine the general direction of the country's foreign policy, the President shall hold regular meetings with the Vice-President and all the ministers in his government" (Ogunbadejo 1980, 403). However, it is also important to note that though the FEC is given a formal role in the country's foreign policy decision-making milieu by the Constitution, that role is basically advisory. Since the presidential system was operating in the country during the Shagari era, the FEC served only as an advisory body for the president. For example, a major decision to suddenly expel about three million undocumented aliens from Nigeria in early 1983 (which subjected Nigeria to a lot of criticism in the international media) was made by the president on the recommendations of one minister (Aluko 1985, 539, 550–51). It wasn't until two days after the minister who had recommended the decision had publicly announced it that the FEC met to discuss the issue and the decision (Aluko 1985, 551). It has also been noted that most ministers were not even notified before the announcement; thus, most of them heard about the adoption of the alien expulsion decision through the radio or television (Aluko 1985, 551). In the light of the almost insignificant role that the FEC played in this major decision, which had a tremendous impact on Nigeria internationally, one can understand Professor Olajide Aluko (1985, 550, 551) seeing the status of the ministers as being "hardly higher than that of servants of the President," and the role of a cabinet body like the FEC as being "hardly more than advisory."

Thus, on the whole, the role of this council of ministers, in terms of foreign policy decision-making dynamics, was that of a deliberative body that could have played a significant advisory role for the president, exposing him to a broad array of views, information, opinions, and possible foreign policy options from a group of seasoned political leaders who were heading the major units (the ministries) of the executive branch of government. But as the above shows, sometimes the FEC was not even allowed or enabled to play an adequate advisory role.

The National Security Council, the National Defense Council, and the National Council of States

Apart from the FEC, the 1979 Constitution provided other advisory bodies for the national leadership: the National Security Council (NSC), the National Defense Council (NDC), and the National Council of States (NCS). The NCS had a primarily domestic policy role. As noted in an earlier section of this study, it is the body that plays a key role in the federal system of government in Nigeria, since it serves as a formal forum for the national leadership to meet with leaders of the various state governments. During the Shagari Government, the NCS membership included the president, the vice president, and the state governors. Though primarily focused on domestic policy issues, the NCS was in a position to help the president think through some foreign policy issues that had much impact on the states. The state governors could also help the president implement certain actions. Nigeria constantly has border problems with neighboring countries. The governors of the many states who share common borders with neighboring countries often directly bear the brunt of public anger about land encroachments, border area violence that involve civilians, and/or security forces encroaching from neighboring countries. During the Shagari era, these border incidents were significant, especially for the states that bordered Chad, Niger, and Camerouns (Peters and Aminu 1986, 88–89). States bordering Benin Republic also had border problems. During the NCS meetings, the governors of the affected states had the opportunity to influence the president's actions in dealing with these international border problems. The president also had the opportunity to use the NCS to elicit the help of the affected governors in containing, or solving, the international border problems (in terms of support for Nigerian security forces in the border areas, and the enhancement of good neighbor policies and initiatives by communities living near the border areas). For example, during the 1981 Nigerian-Cameroun border crisis, Clement Isong, the governor of Cross River State of Nigeria, visited the Ikang area where the border crisis specifically started in order to assess the situation, and he was briefed by Lieutenant Colonel F. Ehigiator of the 13th Infantry Brigade of the Nigerian army based in Calabar (Nweke 1990, 399).

The other two advisory bodies (the NSC and NDC) were even more directly involved in foreign policy matters (if, or when, they were adequately utilized). The NSC was given the power "to advise the President on matters relating to public security including matters relating to any organization or agency established by law for ensuring the security of the Federation" (the 1979 Constitution, quoted by Ogunbadejo 1980, 403). The NDC, on the other hand, had "the functions of advising the President on matters relating to the defense of Nigeria's sovereignty and territorial integrity" (Ogunbadejo 1980, 403). However, despite these significant roles that the NSC and the NDC were designed to play in the foreign policy decision-making milieu, the Shagari Government did not provide them with adequate staff support, energetic and experienced political leaders, and the encouragement that would have enabled them to play significant foreign policy roles (see Peters 1986, 156–57). Thus, though entrusted by the Constitution to serve as significant advisory bodies to the president, in terms of foreign policy matters, the NSC and NDC were never able to adequately play these roles.

The Cabinet Office

As noted in an earlier section of this study, the Cabinet Office was an organization composed of senior career civil servants, and served as a machinery that helped in the national policy process and administration frameworks. The Cabinet Office was significant during the Shagari Government. Quite possibly, the fact that the Shagari Government allowed the Cabinet Office to play visible roles can be attributed to Nigeria's parliamentary heritage. A Cabinet Office is more relevant in a parliamentary system, where it serves as the main national policy and administration machinery for the prime minister and his or her Cabinet. In the true presidential fashion, the Shagari Government should have absorbed the Cabinet Office functions completely within the EOP. But this did not happen. Soon after assuming office, Shehu Shagari included high level appointments of top career civil servants (then referred to as permanent secretaries and now renamed director-generals) for the Cabinet Office in his first appointment of top career civil servants to various positions. Shagari posted the following as permanent secretaries to the respective units within the Cabinet Office: Alfa Wali, Political Department; E. E. Nsefik, council secretariat; J. E. Uduehi, Special Services; S. B. Agodo, Police Affairs; and F. I. Oduah, Economic Department (*West Africa* 22 October 1979, 1963). By including such visible appointments in one of his first major presidential acts, Shagari signaled that he was going to use the Cabinet Office in a very visible manner. This actually became a reality. For example, it was a Cabinet Office announcement that notified the public that the Ministry of National Planning would be handling the functions that the Ministry of Economic Development used to perform (*West Africa* 15 October 1979, 1905). The visible roles that the top career civil servants were performing made Macebuh (1979, 2077) observe that the president was "placing an unfair burden on the career officers in the Cabinet Office." Macebuh added that Shagari was relying "far more heavily on civil servants than is consistent with the presidential system," and that he would have preferred to see political appointees in the EOP, rather than career civil servants in the Cabinet Office, playing these visible roles.

Though serving as one of the major machines of national policy and administration, and thus having its primary focus on the domestic arena, some departments of the Cabinet Office do have significant roles in foreign policy matters. The Political Department, the Economic Department, and Special Services are some of the units of the Cabinet Office that do have some interests and activities relating to foreign affairs. One good example of the Cabinet Office's interests in foreign affairs is that the Nigerian Institute of International Affairs (NIIA), during the succeeding Buhari era, first had the Cabinet Office as its supervising government body, before the NIIA came under the supervision of the Supreme Military Headquarters (Banjo 1986, 21).

By allowing the Cabinet Office to play a visible role in the national policy milieu, the Shagari Government made it possible for the office to have some impact in foreign policy matters.

THE MINISTRY OF EXTERNAL AFFAIRS

The Ministry of External Affairs (MEA) continued its usual role as the main governmental body with the duty of managing Nigeria's relations with other countries, international organizations, and other significant international actors during the Shagari era. At that time the minister of External Affairs was Professor Ishaya Audu. As the former vice chancellor of Ahmadu Bello University, he possessed a strong background of administrative ability and academic leadership. As the minister, he was the political head of the MEA. The MEA also had two ministers of state: Patrick Bokolor, and Abubakar Usman. Audu, Bokolor and Usman together constituted the political leadership of the MEA. However, Audu was clearly the leader among the three, since he was the only minister with cabinet status, while Bokolor and Usman, as the ministers of state (junior ministers), were not members of the FEC (Olusanya and Akindele 1986a, 21). During the very brief second term of the Shagari Government, Emeka Anyaoku (who later became the secretary-general of the Commonwealth of Nations) was the minister of External Affairs.

The MEA, as usual, was divided into geographical and functional units during the Shagari era. Through these units (which also have further subunits), the MEA performed its main tasks of collecting, analyzing, interpreting, and reporting information relating to foreign policy matters; and on the basis of this information helped the president, and the entire national leadership, to make adequate foreign policy decisions, by helping to provide various foreign policy options that could be adopted. The task of implementing foreign policy decision-making also mostly falls on the MEA, as well as the handling of international negotiations.

The MEA, during the Shagari Government, abolished the position of the permanent secretary (the highest career officer who administratively coordinated a ministry), and had in its place five director-generals in order to decentralize the ministry, but the over-decentralization brought about by this action resulted in the succeeding Buhari Government reestablishing the position of the permanent secretary in the MEA (Ofoegbu 1990, 90–94).

As shown earlier, the EOP did not serve as the nerve center of foreign policy. This fact meant that, in many cases, the MEA had a relatively free hand in foreign policy. However, though the MEA had enough freedom to handle foreign policy issues that had mostly political and diplomatic contents, foreign policy issues that had sociocultural, economic, or security ramifications tended to be primarily handled by various other governmental ministries, agencies, or units that were most relevant in terms of their technical or professional functions. Structural and legal frameworks even helped to reinforce this tendency. While the minister of External Affairs was a member of the NSC, he was not a member of the NDC (Ogunbadejo 1980, 403). Thus it meant that, in terms of defense issues that had international implications, the minister of External Affairs was not able to be present in that council to present his input. The exclusion of the minister of External Affairs in the NDC might have stemmed from an inadequate reasoning that defense issues should remain with those in the defense organizations.

This tendency not to involve the MEA in some policy issues that had international ramifications (but were not concerned with political or diplomatic issues primarily and directly) was also reflected in Shagari's management of the problem of millions of undocumented aliens in Nigeria, mentioned ealier. Shagari made the aliens expulsion decision based on the recommendation of the federal minister of Internal Affairs (Aluko 1985, 551). Professor Ishaya Audu, the minister of External Affairs, first heard about the decision to expel these aliens through the radio and television (Aluko 1985, 551).

This case indicated that though the MEA was prominent in terms of foreign policy that primarily focused on political and diplomatic issues, the ministry was sometimes not involved with policy issues that had international ramifications (but were not directly and primarily focused on political and diplomatic issues). Nevertheless, the MEA was the most prominent body that had control over most foreign policy issues, since most such issues do primarily focus on political and diplomatic aspects. Audu, Bokolor, and Usman provided able political leadership for the MEA. The fact that about 50 percent of the Nigerian ambassadors, during the Shagari Government, were political appointees (Ogunbambi 1986, 163) meant that the political leadership of the MEA had a good number of ambassadors who were more likely to share the policy goals, visions, and ethos of the political leadership. Since the tone of the Shagari Government's foreign policy was rather moderate, the MEA was also moderate in its actions and initiatives. The moderate tone set at the EOP affected all decision-making bodies, including the MEA.

THE MINISTRY OF DEFENSE

Though the MEA has primacy over foreign affairs, as noted earlier, other ministries, agencies, and units are also involved in activities that have significant international ramifications. One such organization is the Ministry of Defense (MOD). The MOD provides Nigerian foreign policy with the human and material resources for modifying the behavior of other international actors through the threat (or use) of military actions. The MOD (with its three service units the Nigerian army [NA], the Nigerian air force [NAF], and the Nigerian navy [NN]) was capable of playing its role in Nigerian foreign policy because ofi ts previous experience in the Nigerian Civil War and various peacekeeping operations in foreign countries; furthermore, it possessed adequate military hardware well-trained professional military officers and nonofficers.

For example, in January 1980 the NAF assisted the Organization of African Unity (OAU) in airlifting the troops Benin, Congo, and Guinea had contributed to the OAU's peacekeeping force in Chad (Ogunbadejo 1980, 406). The MOD also engaged in the creation of new bilateral relations with other countries in a very visible way. For example, the minister of Defense, Akanbi Oniyangi, "while presenting a Fokker 27 aircraft to the Republic of Sao Tome and Principe in July 1981," expressed the view that Nigeria and that country "should enter into a strategic arrangement for a 'mutual air and sea logistical support'" (Nwokedi 1985, 206–7).

The external operations of the intelligence arms of the NA, the NN, and the NAF also play an important part in enhancing Nigeria's ability to modify the behavior of other international actors through the use (or threat) of military actions. The Directorate of Military Intelligence (DMI), the Directorate of Naval Intelligence (DNI), and the Directorate of Air Intelligence (DAI) enables the NA, the NN, and the NAF to more accurately evaluate the military strengths and capabilities of countries that could pose a threat to Nigeria (Peters 1986, 153–54). The information and evaluations that the DMI, DNI, and DAI often possess enable the MOD to provide vital policy inputs into the foreign policy decision-making milieu, especially during periods of international crisis.

Nigeria does often have border problems with neighboring countries, and during the Shagari era it had a significant number of these, as noted earlier. Though the border problems are not often primarily, solved through military means, the MOD does play a key role in the handling of most border problems with other countries, in terms of information, physical military presence near the borders, and occasionally actual military actions. In 1981, Nigeria had a serious border problem with Cameroun (Aminu 1986, 82; Peters and Aminu 1986, 88–89). Fortunately, this problem was resolved diplomatically (Aminu 1986, 82). There was also a border problem with the Republic of Niger, and this was also resolved diplomatically (Peters and Aminu 1986, 89). Chad was another country that had a border problem with Nigeria. In this particular case, Nigeria resolved the problem militarily (Peters and Aminu 1986, 89, 96). In December 1983, when Chadian soldiers moved into some parts of Borno State in Nigeria, "[T]he Third Armoured Division commanded by Major-General Muhammadu Buhari was sent in to dispel" the Chadians (Peters and Aminu 1986, 96).

The continuing internal crisis in Chad also occupied the attention of Nigeria during the Shagari era, and the MOD was a vital element in Nigeria's actions and initiatives toward Chad (see Agbakoba 1982; Peters and Aminu 1986, 93–95). The visible role of Nigeria in Chad was indicated by the fact that "Major-General Ejiga of Nigeria commanded the OAU Forces in Chad," which included troops from Nigeria, Senegal, and Zaire (Peters and Aminu 1986, 94).

The professional training of Nigerian military officers also continually facilitate the MOD's ability to play a vital role in the foreign policy decision-making milieu. Peters and Aminu (1986, 95) note that "the training process for military officers through the Nigerian Defense Academy (NDA), Command and Staff College (CSC) and the National Institute for Policy and Strategic Studies (NIPSS) emphasizes the learning of not only military subjects but also an understanding of international and domestic issues." Thus, the officers of the NA, NN, and NAF are very adept in articulating, analyzing, and implementing the defense components of Nigerian foreign policy. The fact that some of these military officers also serve as defense attachés in some Nigerian embassies abroad further enhances the role of the MOD.

Other Governmental Organs, Ministries, Agencies and Units

Foreign policy can be viewed as having about four main components: political, military/security, economic, and cultural. In terms of Nigerian foreign policy, the MEA, as shown earlier, can be seen as focusing on the political component of foreign policy, and thus, also having the primacy in Nigerian political diplomatic activities. The MOD, as also shown earlier, handles the military/security components.

Though the MEA does have subunits within its organization that focus on the security, economic, and cultural components of Nigeria's foreign policy, there are other governmental organizations that deal with (and maybe even have primary roles in) these components of foreign policy. For an example, as shown earlier, the MOD has primacy in terms of the military/security components of Nigeria's foreign policy. In practice, the MEA shares its functions with other organizations, especially in international activities that do not primarily involve international political and diplomatic relations.

In terms of the economic components of Nigeria's foreign relations, the Federal Ministry of Commerce (FMC) mainly handles government policies relating to Nigeria's foreign trade relations. The worsening economic situation, particularly Nigeria's international debt, made the economic components of Nigeria's foreign relations become more important during the latter period of the Shagari Government (*West Africa* 26 September 1983, 2246; *West Africa* 5 December 1983, 2832). In order to prudently manage Nigeria's international debts, the Federal Ministry of Finance (FMF) was involved in wide-ranging negotiations with major international financial institutions (*West Africa* 26 September 1983, 2246). The FMC together with the Central Bank of Nigeria (CBN) were the major organizations involved in the management of the financial aspects of Nigeria's international economic relations (*West Africa* 26 September 1983, 2246).

Petroleum is the main economic product of Nigeria. The Nigerian National Petroleum Corporation (NNPC) was the conglomerate that dominated this industry during the Shagari era. The NNPC (a government-owned commercial corporation) seemed to have been allowed to play a visible role in terms of the handling Nigeria's relations with OPEC, according to Macebuh (1979, 2077). Shagari did have a position for a special adviser for Petroleum and Energy in the EOP (Soremekun 1990, 305 n; *West Africa* 22 October 1979, 1963). The fact that NNPC was handling Nigeria's relations with OPEC shows that this adviser's office in the EOP was not adequately staffed, and that the fact that the Shagari Government did not have a ministry for petroleum affairs might have left a gap in the president's petroleum policy circles. Additionally, Soremekun (1990, 300) notes that the relationship between the NNPC and presidential assistants in the EOP was marked "more by conflict than cooperation, since both groups were engaged in a perennial struggle for the President's attention." This further complicated the situation.

The development of the steel industry in Nigeria was a major policy area for the Shagari Government. The fact that the industry was being developed with the help of foreign countries, especially the former Soviet Union, meant that the Ministry of Steel Development (MSD) was another significant organization in terms of Nigeria's international economic relations. In fact, during the Shagari era the steel industry formed the main focus of Nigeria's relationship with the former Soviet Union (Ogunbadejo 1988, 96–97). However, Nigeria and the former Soviet Union had to work out a lot of details in order to move the steel industry forward (Alli-Balogun 1988, 632–33).

During the Shagari era, ECOWAS continued to be important to Nigeria. The fact that the Ministry of National Planning (MNP) liaised with the MEA to manage Nigeria's relations with ECOWAS also enabled the MNP (which was mainly focused on domestic affairs) to have some activities in the international arena. The MNP had the primary responsibility for Nigeria's relations with ECOWAS; and thus, the ministry, had a vital international role.

The Federal Ministry of Information (FMI), the Federal Ministry of Sports (FMS), and the Federal Ministry of Social Development, Youth, and Culture (FMSDYC) were the major governmental bodies that liaised with the MEA to manage Nigeria's international sociocultural relations. For example, the FMI, during the Shagari era, established offices in some foreign countries to provide information about Nigeria.

Apart from the MOD, the Federal Ministry of Internal Affairs (FMIA) featured prominently in terms of the security components of foreign policy. The FMIA had the Immigration Department as one of its subunits. Since, as noted earlier, international border problems were common during the Shagari era, the FMIA had to liaise with the MOD and MEA in order to handle this issue. However, as shown earlier, it was the problem of millions of undocumented aliens in Nigeria that helped the FMIA become very visible in the policy milieu. It was the FMIA that chiefly handled the policy formulation and implementation of the expulsion of the aliens (though it liaised with other organizations at some later stages in order to grapple with this problem) (see Aluko 1985).

The Nigerian Security Organization (NSO), as the umbrella intelligence body, continued in its role during the Shagari era. Its international activities gave the NSO a visible role in the foreign policy milieu (Gambari 1989, 25; Peters 1986). Thus, the NSO was another significant body in terms of the security components of the Nigerian foreign policy.

The Nigerian Institute of International Affairs (NIIA) and the National Institute for Strategic and Policy Studies (NIPSS) continued as policy studies organizations that play unique roles in the foreign policy decision-making milieu. Both of these think tanks, especially the NIIA, continued to provide intellectual input into the foreign policy process (and thus, broaden and increase the policy options that were available to the foreign policy makers). Nweke (1986, 46) notes that the NIIA "plays a vital role in the foreign policy-making process," and that it "has become so central to the policy-making framework that its inputs have become part of the most useful technical inputs in the entire process." As noted earlier, through its research, seminars, dialogues, conferences, special briefings for officials, publications, and public enlightenment programs, the NIIA is able to have a lot of impact on foreign policy decisions (Banjo 1986, 21–24; Nweke 1986, 46–47). The operation of these programs has prompted Nweke (1986, 46) to posit that the "NIIA has succeeded in introducing and institutionalizing mechanisms and procedures for generating information and knowledge required to support national decision-making." During the Shagari era, the MEA ceased to supervise the NIIA; the EOP did (Banjo 1986, 21). This meant that the NIIA had a more direct access to the President. In a speech he gave in 1980, President Shagari himself specifically noted the vital role that NIIA plays in the foreign policy milieu (Akindele 1981, 29–30).

Evaluations of the dialogue programs the NIIA had with its counterparts in other countries, by Ogunbambi (1981), Ogwu (1981), and Vogt (1981), also show that the NIIA was vital in the foreign policy process during the Shagari era. (The institutionalized position of the NIIA in the foreign policy process is underscored by the fact that it was even more visible and important during the preceding Muhammed/Obasanjo Government.)

The role of the NIIA during the Shagari Government was significantly due to its able leaders. Professor Bolaji Akinyemi, who was the director-general of the NIIA during most of the Shagari era, made the think tank grow in both size and efficiency. Professor Ibrahim A. Gambari, who succeeded Akinyemi as the director-general, also provided able leadership. The fact that these two scholars later headed the MEA for succeeding governments (Gambari was the minister for External Affairs during the Buhari Government and Akinyemi served as the minister for External Affairs during a portion of the Babangida Government) shows that the NIIA was a vital force in the foreign policy milieu. However, on the whole, NIIA was more visible and powerful during the Muhammed/Obasanjo Government than during the Shagari Government.

Another major organ of the government that had an impact on Nigeria's foreign policy during the Shagari era was the National Assembly (a bicameral legislature, consisting of the House of Representatives and the Senate). The 1979 Constitution gave the National Assembly some powers it could use to play a significant role in foreign policy matters. The National Assembly had the power to approve any treaty Nigeria negotiated with other countries, and the Senate had to approve the appointment of high government officials such as, for example, the ministers in charge of the MEA and MOD (*The Europa World Year Book 1983: A World Survey, Volume Two* 1983, 1150). The National Assembly also had significant war powers. The two houses of the National Assembly had to consent before the president could declare war, and the Senate had to give prior approval before any member of the armed forces could engage in a combat activity outside the country (see Ogunbadejo 1980, 402–3; *Europa World Year Book 1983: A World Survey, Volume Two* 1983, 1150).

The Foreign Relations Committees, in both the House and Senate, were the major units in the National Assembly that focused on foreign policy matters. These committees seemed to play credible roles in the foreign policy milieu. For example, the Foreign Relations Committee of the Senate "under the Chairmanship of Senator Jalo Waziri . . . conducted many hearings on foreign policy issues" (Ogunbadejo 1980, 405). Waziri, who was a prominent and flamboyant politician, used his stature to give the committee a lot of visibility and impact. His committee both championed and defended Nigeria's decision to participate in the 1980 Moscow Olympic Games (Ogunbadejo 1980, 405). The National Assembly played a significant role in the foreign policy milieu.

Foreign Policy Decision-making Coordination

This study shows that numerous organs, ministries, agencies, and units were involved in foreign policy matters during the Shagari Government. Apart from the National Assembly, all these other bodies belonged to the executive branch of government. Thus, logically, the EOP, as the apex of national leadership, was in the right position to coordinate all these various executive branch bodies that were involved in foreign policy decision-making. The fact that, as also shown earlier, the EOP had no specific official who was given the power to focus primarily on foreign policy (though there were many EOP officials with positions that could have easily enabled them to play this role: for example, the advisers on Political Affairs and the Adviser on National Security) meant that the EOP was not equipped to coordinate foreign policy matters on a regular and consistent basis. The EOP mainly coordinated (or played a significant role in) the foreign policy milieu during periods of crises such as the persistent problems of undocumented aliens in the country (Aluko 1985, 554, 555).

As shown earlier, the Cabinet Office did sometimes try to coordinate foreign policy matters. Also, inter-ministerial committees often served as coordinating machineries on a regular or consistent basis. As expected in any governmental setting, such committees are often weak and slow to formulate and/or implement a decision. It was only a body like the EOP (which was at the apex of the national policy process, and which personally represented the president), if it was energized for the purpose, that could have been able to provide adequate foreign policy-making coordination.

The EOP's failure to adequately coordinate (except in crisis situations), resulted in each of the various organizations that were involved in foreign policy matters having primary control over certain aspects of the foreign policy that coincided with the primary functions of each of these organizations. Thus the MEA, as shown earlier, had control over foreign policy issues that mostly had political and diplomatic ramifications. On the other hand, the FMIA controlled the decision processes (which almost totally excluded the MEA) that resulted in the decision to expel about three million undocumented aliens from Nigeria, as also shown earlier, since the Immigration Department was a subunit within the FMIA. In the same fashion, the FMF had the leading role in terms of Nigeria's international financial relations, while the MOD had primacy in the area of international security/military relations.

Thus, on the whole, foreign policy coordination was handled by the EOP during crisis periods, while particular ministries dominated certain aspects of foreign policy decision-making (with inter-ministerial committees only serving as weak chains in the policy circle) during the Shagari Government.

Conclusion

This study shows that most of the decision-making structures at its disposal were not adequately utilized by the Shagari Government. Starting from the top, the EOP did not adequately coordinate foreign policy making or provide adequate foreign policy guidelines and directions. Key advisers within the EOP, for example, the advisers on Political Affairs and the adviser on National Security, did not play significant and visible roles in the foreign policy milieu. Advisory bodies like the NSC and NDC, likewise, played no significant role in the foreign policy process. While the FEC was another advisory body that was not adequately utilized, the Cabinet Office was sometimes significant (though only moderately so) in the foreign policy process.

This situation gave rise to each of the various ministries, agencies, and units controlling certain aspects of Nigerian foreign policy. The MEA was clearly in charge of foreign policy issues that were primarily political and diplomatic in character. This made the MEA, unfettered by bodies like the EOP, clearly the main machinery for Shagari era diplomacy.

Foreign policy issues that primarily had security dimensions were mainly handled by the MOD, FMIA, and NSO. For example, the decision to expel the aliens was primarily handled by the FMIA with the MEA not even tangentially consulted. Likewise, the MOD was the primary body that handled Nigeria's action in the border problem with Chad in 1981. As also noted earlier, the Third Armored Division of the Nigerian army, headed by the Major General Muhammadu Buhari, quickly pushed out the Chadian troops from the portions of Nigeria they had moved into.

The cultural components of the foreign policy were controlled by FMI, FMS, and FMSDYC, while the FMI, FMC, CBN, NNPC, MSD, and MNP controlled the economic components of the foreign policy.

There were liaisons between or among these various decision-making structures. However, these liaisons were weak due to the lack of strong control and direction from the EOP. Each of the various ministries, agencies, or units thus were able to dominate some particular aspects of Nigerian foreign affairs. The "minimum government" from the top (as Macebuh [1979, 2077] described Shehu Shagari's style of government) gave rise to this situation. The under-utilization of the units within the EOP that were to help the president to manage Nigeria's foreign relations, and the consequent compartmentalization and control of various aspects of Nigeria's foreign affairs by the various government organizations, greatly accounted for the Shagari Government being perceived as having had a low-profile posture, in terms of foreign policy behavior. Thus some have commented that the Shagari Government did not have clear foreign policy positions or take positive actions (*West Africa* 10 October 1983, 2350), and that the that Government "turned the inherited activist foreign policy" of the Muhammed/Obasanjo Government "into a reactive, pacifist one" (*African Concord* 10 June 1991, 31–42).

Despite the inadequate utilization of the officials within the EOP (who were to provide foreign policy directions to help the president), there were a lot of intellectual outputs from the NIIA and NIPSS that the President could have utilized to energize his foreign policy actions and initiatives. Interestingly, the inadequate utilization of officials within the EOP (for example, the adviser on National Security and the advisers on Political Affairs) seems to have resulted in the president lacking officials who could have digested and more attractively packaged the intellectual outputs from the NIIA and NIPSS for the easier and faster consumption and utilization by the president. This particular situation clearly exemplifies how the inadequate utilization of the foreign policy decision-making systems that were available during the Shagari Government caused that government to be low-profile in its foreign policy behavior.

On the whole, the inadequate use of the EOP to coordinate the various ministries, agencies, and units and to provide foreign policy guidelines and directions, made the Shagari Government fragmented, compartmentalized, and underdriven in its foreign policy decision-making processes. This situation significantly caused made the Shagari Government to manifest low-profile and non-proactive foreign policy behavior.

7
Love the Nation: The Buhari Era

THE BUHARI GOVERNMENT, WHICH FOLLOWED THE SECOND REPUBLIC, ushered in the second era of military governments. Decision-making structures and processes of the Buhari Government, naturally, reflected that reality. Muhammadu Buhari was the head of state during this period.

The Federal Ministry of External Affairs (MEA) performed its normal function of serving as the main structure charged with the management of Nigeria's foreign relations. At the apex of the ministry was the minister, who was the political head. The minister was a political appointee, who owed his position solely to the head of state and the Supreme Military Council. Ibrahim Gambari served as the minister of External Affairs. He brought to this position a wealth of academic knowledge of international affairs. As a professor of political science, he specialized in the area of international relations. His immediate former position, before becoming a minister, was that of the director-general of the Nigerian Institute of International Affairs (the premier foreign policy think tank that serves the government). As a minister, Gambari was a member of the Federal Executive Council (the council of ministers that served as an important decision-making body).

The permanent secretary was the second most important person in any ministry; and it was a position that, by tradition, was occupied by a career civil servant. In the MEA, below the permanent secretary, the structure of the ministry, as usual, was divided into various directorates or divisions, which were charged with responsibilities that dealt with geographical, functional or administrative issues. These divisions were headed by the director-generals. Within the divisions there were further subdivisions. Nigerian foreign missions, in various countries, also constituted an important segment of the structure of the MEA. In terms of routine home communication, the Nigerian foreign missions were coordinated through the relevant divisions within the ministry. However, in reality, depending on the status of individual envoys heading these foreign missions, and/or the importance of issues, envoys could have direct links with the minister of External Affairs, the Supreme Military Headquarters, and/or the head of state. The fact that, while some envoys were career diplomats, others were political appointees (with possible extensive political bases of their own), did affect the sort of access to power points that these envoys had back home, within the ministry, and the general governmental structure.

During the Buhari era, the Supreme Military Council (SMC), as in past military governments, was the highest decision-making body in the political system. As usual, it was mostly made up of military officers: it consisted of the head of state, the chief of staff of the Supreme Military Headquarters, the chiefs of staff of the army, the navy, and the air force, other key military officers, the inspector general of police, the secretary to the Federal Military Government, the attorney general, and the director-general of the Nigerian Security Organization (*West Africa* 9 January 1984, 86). The last three members were civilians. Being the highest national decision-making body, the SMC dealt only with very crucial foreign policy issues. The nature of this body also meant that it dealt with these issues in only a general manner.

The head of state's office also constituted a highly significant decision unit in the governmental structure. The appointment of envoys (especially the politically appointed envoys) had a lot to do with the head of state, although the SMC, possibly, had to formally approve the appointments of all envoys. In practice, consultations with (and recommendations from) the MEA also counted significantly. As chairman of the SMC, the head of state, Muhammadu Buhari, was clearly invested with considerable power. However, the fact that the SMC functioned as a body whose members fairly effectively participated in decision-making meant that Buhari did not have a monopoly on political power. The considerable power that Buhari allowed the chief of staff of the Supreme Military Headquarters to wield also meant that, in terms of the policy-making process (and in cases of foreign policy issues that moved up to the higher echelons of the government, in particular), Buhari shared much of his power with him (*Newswatch* 20 October 1986, 19). On the whole, Buhari's significant interest in foreign affairs resulted in some direct contacts with Nigerian envoys. For example, in an opening address to a 10-day seminar organized for all Nigerian heads of diplomatic missions at the Nigerian Institute of Strategic and Policy Studies, he spoke on detailed Nigerian foreign policy concerns and postures and on almost all global, regional, and bilateral issues that were relevant to Nigeria (*West Africa* 5 August 1985, 1612).

During the Buhari Government, the Supreme Military Headquarters, headed by the chief of staff (who was also the number two man in the government) served as the fulcrum for most policy-making activities (*Newswatch* 20 October 1986, 19). As indicated above, the chief of staff came to be vested with an enormous amount of power, due to the fact that the Buhari Government gave considerable responsibilities to that position (*Newswatch* 20 October 1986, 19). Additionally, whatever powers that

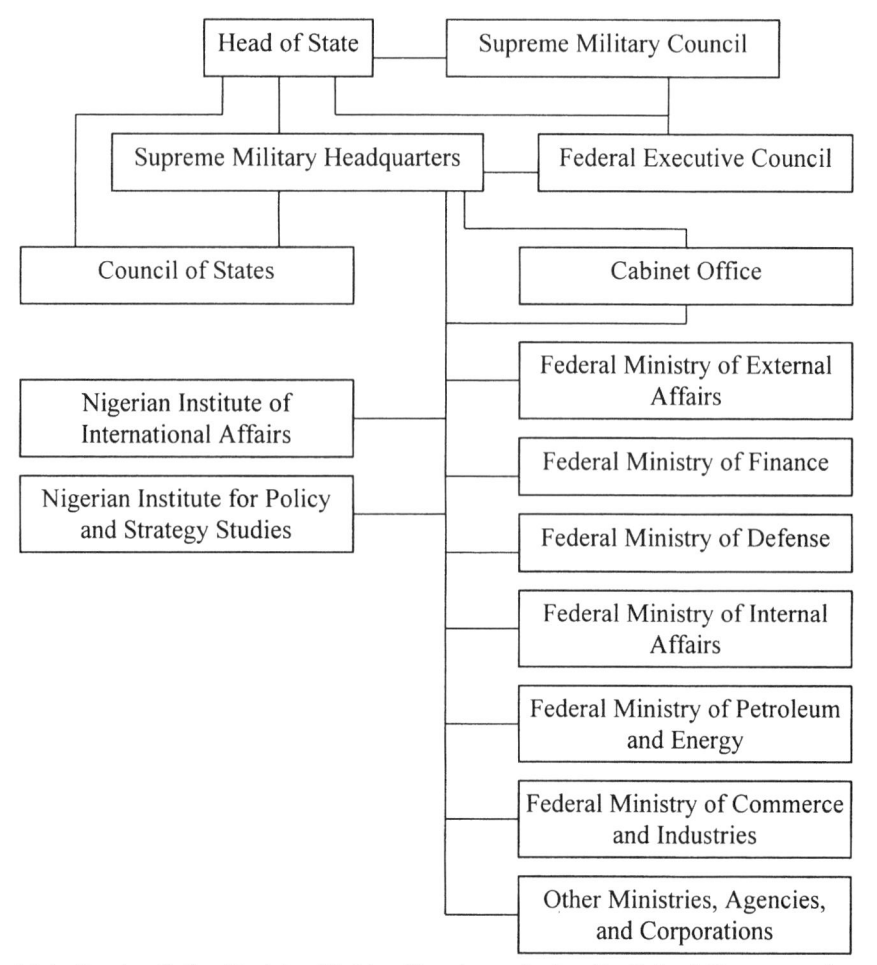

```
                    ┌──────────────────┐    ┌────────────────────────┐
                    │  Head of State   │────│ Supreme Military Council│
                    └──────────────────┘    └────────────────────────┘
                             │                         │
              ┌──────────────────────────────┐    ┌────────────────────────┐
              │ Supreme Military Headquarters│────│ Federal Executive Council│
              └──────────────────────────────┘    └────────────────────────┘
                     │                                  │
         ┌────────────────────┐              ┌────────────────────┐
         │  Council of States │              │   Cabinet Office   │
         └────────────────────┘              └────────────────────┘
```

Main Foreign Policy Decision-Making Structures during the Buhari Government

(Chart also shows: Nigerian Institute of International Affairs, Nigerian Institute for Policy and Strategy Studies, Federal Ministry of External Affairs, Federal Ministry of Finance, Federal Ministry of Defense, Federal Ministry of Internal Affairs, Federal Ministry of Petroleum and Energy, Federal Ministry of Commerce and Industries, Other Ministries, Agencies, and Corporations.)

were not vested in the position, Tunde Idiagbon, a very assertive individual who occupied this position, simply gave to himself (*Newswatch* 20 October 1986, 19). Thus, most of the foreign policy issues that seeped up to the higher echelons of government were invariably handled by him. He seemed to have been particularly interested in foreign policy issues that had significant national security ramifications (*West Africa* 16 July 1984, 1462; *West Africa* 22 April 1985, 805).

The Federal Executive Council (FEC) was another national decision-making structure. Thus, this was another decision forum at the higher echelon of government that was involved in major foreign policy decision-making. The minister of External Affairs, as a member of this body, invariably served as the key member of the FEC on foreign policy issues. The sort of foreign policy issues that reached this body were often those that required the coordination of policy design, development, implementation, and evaluation by various ministries: for examples, national security, immigration, international border disputes, and international trade issues. These issues prominently featured during the Buhari Government (thus the FEC dealt with significant numbers of foreign policy issues). Note must be taken of the fact that the FEC was clearly subordinated to the SMC. As the highest decision-making body, the SMC could change, or nullify, any FEC decision. Since the head of state chaired both bodies, and there were also significant membership overlappings between both bodies, the FEC decisions, invariably, were often those that could meet with the SMC's approval.

The National Council of States (a national body mostly composed of state governors), as usual, was also chaired by the head of state. Since state governors were directly under the chief of staff of the Supreme Military Headquarters (*Newswatch* 20 October 1986, 19), this National Council of States (NCS) was subordinated to the SMC, the head of state, and the chief of staff of the Supreme Military Headquarters. The NCS, as the forum of state governors, was, as usual, primarily concerned with domestic affairs. However, because there were perennial border disputes with neighboring countries and problems with undocumented immigrants during the Buhari Government, these prominent foreign policy issues meant the involvement of the NCS, though only tangentially. The state governments (of those states that shared borders with foreign countries) often served, as usual, as the immediate governmental level that bore the pressure of state residents who were threatened by international border disputes or conflicts. Since the national security and military forces, the Customs Department, and the Immigration Department have all always been controlled by the federal government, the affected state governors, as usual, had to work closely with the federal government, either individually or collectively. The NCS conveniently served as a forum for states to relate collectively to the federal government and to cooperate in handling border problems. During the Buhari era, both the citizens and the government, rightly or wrongly, often concluded that crime, moral decay, and certain societal upheavals (that had national security ramifications) were caused by undocumented foreign nationals from neighboring countries (Aluko 1985, 539–60).

The Cabinet Office, as usual, also served as a major structure in the decision-making process. It primarily served as the unit that bureaucratically, and routinely, coordinated all the ministries and agencies. Staffed by career civil servants, it exuded technocratic and bureaucratic bents, rather than political assertiveness. The fact that the head of state, or the Supreme Military Headquarters, could also deal directly with particular ministries or agencies further emphasized the routine and bureaucratic coordinating role of the Cabinet Office. However, the wealth of administrative proficiency and expertise in the areas of economics, financial management, social policy, policy analysis, and policy evaluation that is lodged in the Cabinet Office has, nevertheless, meant that this unit of government is often valued by Nigerian governments. While the government allowed the Cabinet Office to play its routine role, the assertive Tunde Idiagbon, as the number two man, clearly established the Supreme Military Headquarters as the fulcrum for national policy process and administration. Apart from a states' administration unit, his office also had a federal administration unit, which was headed by a senior air force officer (*Newswatch* 20 October 1986, 19; *West Africa* 16 July 1984, 1462). Thus, the Cabinet Office was mainly in the background, while the Supreme Military Headquarters was recognized as the pivotal unit in the policy-making process.

Apart from the MEA, other ministries were involved, as usual, in policies and activities, that related to Nigeria's relations with the outside world. One of the most important problems that the Buhari Government faced was the foreign debt burden (Olusanya 1984, 55–66). Thus, the management of the country's financial system and specifically, the negotiation of the best possible terms of payment of foreign debts in order to best minimize the negative impacts of the debt payments on the nation's economy, were critical functions. These functions were handled mainly by the Federal Ministry of Finance (FMF). As in all ministries, at the top of the FMF was the political head, the minister. Onaolapo Soleye, a university professor who had a prior government background, served as the minister. The permanent secretary, a career civil servant, was as usual at the number two position in the FMF hierarchy. Divisions, directorates, and some fairly autonomous units dominated the basic structure of the FMF. Throughout the Buhari era, the task of negotiating with foreign lenders and international financial institutions, like the International Monetary Fund (IMF) and the World Bank, for more agreeable debt payment arrangements was mainly borne by the minister, the permanent secretary, and the financial experts of the FMF (*West Africa* 15 October 1984, 2069–71). Because of the weak profile of the country's economy during this period, this task was the most critical aspect of Nigeria's international economic relations. Thus, the FMF was a major decision-making structure that handled the economic components of Nigerian foreign relations. For example, the FMF and the Federal Ministry of Petroleum and Energy (FMPE) entirely handled the counter trade transactions (which occurred during the Buhari Government)—the MEA was not involved in these transactions (Ofoegbu 1990, 89).

The Federal Ministry of Commerce and Industry (FMCI) was another major decision structure involved in international economic relations. This was mainly due to the fact that it handled the task of ensuring that Nigeria's international trade policy was one that would help the country handle its foreign debt burden, rather than aggravating it. Additionally, it was also in charge of efforts to encourage the development of raw materials sources within the country for Nigerian industries, rather than encouraging the importation of these items. The major planks of this policy were articulated by the minister in charge, and presented by Ganiyu Amusa-Eke, the assistant director of Industrial Policy and Planning in the FMCI (*West Africa* 10 December 1984, 2553). Incidentally, the forum for this presentation was a workshop, organized by the Department of Chemical Engineering of the University of Lagos, for those interested in the establishment of plants for the production of raw materials for Nigerian industries. On another occasion, Mahmud Tukur, the minister of Commerce and Industry, hinted about a plan to deny foreign exchange for the importation of raw materials for Nigerian industries if those raw materials could be produced within the country (*West Africa* 29 July 1985, 1556). Dr. Tukur's position, in terms of ensuring industrial self-sufficiency in Nigeria, showed much personal commitment. At times, it even appeared that he was leading the country in a crusade. In advocating that Nigerians be satisfied with only those things that Nigerian industries could produce, he developed a maxim that summed up his way of selling the Buhari Government's impact of the industrial policy; it ran thus: "If you can't get what you want, you must want what you can get" (Tukur, quoted in *West Africa* 29 July 1985, 1556). To the extent that the FMCI was the decision structure that created the industrial and international trade policies that were to help Nigeria develop a virile economy, it served as an important unit in the policy-making process dealing with international economic relations.

Another ministry that figured prominently in international economic relations was the Federal Ministry of Petroleum and Energy (FMPE). Its importance derived mainly from three of its numerous functions: its serving as the major unit that managed Nigeria's relations with OPEC; its role in the countertrade efforts; and its functioning as the main ministry in charge of the development of Nigerian petrochemical industries.

Nigeria is a country that, in its recent history, has been saddled with an economy much dominated by its petroleum industry sector. This results in its export trade being dominated by petroleum export trade. Since, during the Buhari era, Nigeria's economic problems figured importantly in its foreign relations, the FMPE became a major decision structure in Nigeria's relations with the outside world. Efforts that ensured a good price for crude oil, and Nigeria having a fair quota of crude oil export, meant that the FMPE served as the main structure that managed Nigeria's relation with

OPEC very effectively. The minister of Petroleum and Energy, a professor of virology, even transformed himself into an expert on petroleum affairs. He became a very effective voice in OPEC forums on behalf of Nigeria (*West Africa* 5 August 1985, 1594). He was strongly in favor of Nigeria remaining in OPEC (*West Africa* 15 April 1985, 758). The widespread and general conclusion of the policy elites seemed to have been that OPEC was the best existing framework that ensured fair prices for petroleum exports.

During the Buhari Government, as noted earlier, Nigeria also used countertrade practices as a means of handling the problems Nigeria faced in its international trade relations due to its foreign debt payment problems. Petroleum was the main product Nigeria used in the countertrade, through exchanging it for other products and services from other countries (*West Africa* 11 March 1985, 481; *West Africa* 27 May 1985, 1068; *West Africa* 5 August 1985, 1593–94). This factor enabled the FMPE to be a very significant decision structure in Nigeria's international trade relations.

The Buhari Government also intensified efforts to develop viable petrochemical plants in the country. The goal of the petrochemical industries was the production of the necessary raw materials that a viable industrialized economy needs (and thus help to stop the importation of these materials), and the exportation of some of these petrochemical products. These two goals were aimed at helping to improve Nigeria's international trade situation. Groundwork was also laid for the production of liquefied natural gas (LNG) for the export market (*West Africa* 17 December 1984, 2607). Through the construction of various petrochemical plants, petroleum and natural gas are converted into organic chemical products that are indispensable in most manufacturing industries (*West Africa* 9 April 1984, 794), for example, the pharmaceutical, paints, plastics, printing, textile, electronic, and automobile tire industries. As the FMPE also supervised the development of the petrochemical and LNG plants, the ministry's role in policies that affected Nigeria's international economic relations grew further. The FMPE efforts in the development of petrochemical plants during this period were so effective that by 1987 the plants in phase one of the petrochemical industries development were completed (*Newswatch* 13 October 1986, 23; *Newswatch* 12 January 1987, 37).

International relations, as noted earlier, can be divided into four main components—political, security, economic, and cultural. Likewise, the foreign policy profile of any country can be divided into these four components. The political and security components are often paid more attention, although in recent times many have justly given fair attention to the economic and cultural components. The fact that, during the Buhari era, Nigeria's relations with the outside world were significantly influenced by economic factors clearly demonstrated the need for students of international relations to adequately allocate attention to all four components. As shown above, the FMF, the FMCI and the FMPE were key decision structures in Nigeria's economic relations with the outside world during the Buhari era. As also shown above, the MEA was, specifically, in charge of Nigerian general international relations (with emphasis on the political component).

The security component of Nigerian foreign policy was also very significant. The Buhari Government foreign policy design, development, formulation, and implementation showed a thorough perception of the security needs and issues facing the country. A paper presented by Muhammadu Buhari at the Nigerian Institute of International Affairs (*West Africa* 17 December 1984, 2565–66) and one that Ibrahim Gambari (the minister of External Affairs) presented at a different forum (*West Africa* 22 October 1984, 2117), both demonstrated an acute perception of the security realities of Nigeria's foreign policy. The war in Chad, domestic social upheavals (that were linked to nationals from neighboring countries), and border conflicts were some of the important security issues that affected Nigeria's international relations during the Buhari era (Aluko 1985, 539–60). The dynamics of the regional security issues, which Nigeria has to manage continually, seem to be clear to various Nigerian governments (Nwokedi 1985, 195–209).

The former apartheid regime in South Africa was also often an important element in Nigeria's security perceptions. The regime was often seen as a potential source of aggression and conflict. South Africa's frequent aggression against and pressure on Angola and Mozambique seemed to have sharpened the security perceptions of the Buhari Government. Gambari noted that the "[S]trategic assessment of our borders demands that we re-equip to limit the activities of the apartheid government within its borders and deal with it there" (Gambari, quoted in *West Africa* 7 January 1985, 33).

The Federal Ministry of Defense (FMD), as usual, was the umbrella structure over Nigeria's military forces. The chief of army staff, Ibrahim Babangida (who later succeeded Buhari as head of state), presented a paper that showed that the military perceived that Nigeria's responsibilities, "whether we like it or not in the West African sub-region and Africa as a whole will continue to grow" (Babangida, quoted in *West Africa* 11 March 1985, 489). He also noted the national security necessity of Nigeria's plan to produce locally most of its military hardware (*West Africa* 11 March 1985, 489). This showed that the defense establishment provided security articulations and assessments that impacted on foreign policy. The fact that the Buhari Government was a military government made such impacts more significant.

Because massive expulsion of undocumented aliens and border closures were problems that greatly affected Nigeria's foreign relations during the

Buhari era, the Federal Ministry of Internal Affairs (FMIA) was another important decision structure that was involved in managing the security component of Nigeria's foreign relations (Aluko 1985, 539–60). Nigeria's borders, immigration affairs, and domestic law and order, as usual, were the responsibilities of the FMIA.

The Nigerian Institute of International Affairs (NIIA) continued its role during the Buhari era as an important structure in the Nigerian foreign policy process. However, it must be noted that the NIIA's role was that of a fairly independent body whose duty was to provide Nigerian leaders and the general society with adequate facts and analyses of international affairs (*Nigerian Journal of International Affairs* 1984, ii). Thus, the NIIA did not overtly engage in foreign policy-making. During the Buhari era, its relation with the government was, formally, through the chief of staff of the Supreme Military Headquarters. Thus, the NIIA had access to the Buhari Government at a very high level, and was also able to broaden the horizon of policy-makers in terms of the possible and available range of foreign policy options. The succeeding Babangida Government even formalized the NIIA's access to the national leadership, at this high level, through an official government gazette (*Thisweek* 20 October 1986, 18). The NIIA has often enjoyed a high status with most Nigerian governments. As noted earlier, the fact that the minister of External Affairs during the Buhari era and the first minister of External Affairs during the Babangida era were formerly director-generals of the NIIA attests to its national stature.

The National Institute for Policy and Strategic Studies (NIPSS) also continued to serve as a knowledge center that focused on major national policy issues (both domestic and foreign) as well as security issues. It has also developed the same sort of relationship with the government as did the NIIA (*Thisweek* 20 October 1986, 18). The fact that the NIPSS is located at Kuru, Jos, an area with very clement weather, made it a popular venue for the holding of seminars for high government officials, and also for the articulation of important policies (see *West Africa* 15 April 1985, 758; *West Africa* 5 August 1985, 1612). This further emphasized the importance of the NIPSS.

The Federal Ministry of Information, Youth, Sports, and Culture (FMIYSC), together with the MEA, managed the cultural component of Nigeria's foreign relations. This role emphasized international communications and arts and cultural exchange. For example, FMIYSC operated information centers in some foreign countries, engaged in international broadcasting, and promoted international arts and sports exchanges.

Apart from the above-mentioned decision structures, other ministries and agencies were also involved in activities that affected Nigeria's international relations. For example, the Federal Ministry of National Planning (FMNP) continued to serve as the major decision structure that was involved in the management of Nigeria's relations with the Economic Community of the West African States (ECOWAS). The efforts to handle the problems created by the allegations that the Buhari Government was involved in an almost successful effort to kidnap Umaru Dikko (a minister in the preceding Shagari Government who was accused of acts of corruption) from Britain, and then fly him to Nigeria for trial, might have involved some role being played by Nigerian intelligence bodies. Even organizations, like the Nigerian National Petroleum Corporation (NNPC), due to their huge and complex nature (with their own paraphernalia for the management of the international aspects of their activities), can also be seen as decision structures that figured significantly in Nigeria's relations with the outside world.

The Coordination Machinery and Processes

As the above evaluation of the major foreign policy decision-making structures shows, during the Buhari era, as is other periods, a significant number of ministries and agencies were involved in Nigeria's relations with the outside world. This, naturally, necessitated the usual need for coordination among these structures, so as to ensure concerted actions and the minimization of interorganizational conflicts.

The very prominent role played by Tunde Idiagbon, the chief of staff of the Supreme Military Headquarters, was the hallmark of the Buhari Government, Idiagbon, being a very assertive individual, and also having the trust of the head of state, almost controlled all the visible instruments of national political, governmental, and administrative powers (*Newswatch* 20 October 1986, 19). To most people, he was more visible than the head of state, and came to represent the very embodiment of that era. Apart from being the number two man, some even saw him as the real source of governmental power. Thus, he has been seen by some as exercising the power of a prime minister (the usual position of the head of government in a parliamentary system) (*African Concord* 30 October 1986, 31). This concentration of power in one office, and the hierarchical nature of a military government, meant that coordination was easily achieved. This coordination, which was mechanically induced rather than being voluntary organizational behavior, also derived from the fact that the stern military government saw excessive inter-organizational conflicts and strong interest groups pressures, as acts of societal indiscipline. The swift Nigerian actions immediately following the allegations that the Nigerian government was involved in the attempt to forcibly bring Dikko to Nigeria, the Nigerian border closure enforcement, and the massive expulsion of undocumented aliens all point to tight coordination of the ministries and organizations that were involved in these actions, with Idiagbon controlling the centerpoint. For example, while the undocumented aliens expulsion exercises during the preceding Shagari Government showed that the MEA did not cooperate in the actions, the opposite was the case during the Buhari era. During the Shagari Government, the MEA was not included in the inter-ministerial committee that was to formulate and implement a policy that would avoid the need to expel aliens (Aluko 1985, 539–60). This and other exclusions of the MEA resulted in the refusal of the minister of External Affairs to participate in the crisis management that followed the eventual expulsions (only junior MEA officials helped the minister of Internal Affairs) (Aluko 1985, 539–60). This sharply contrasted with the cooperation, and the active participation, of the MEA during the Buhari era in managing the expulsion exercises and their impact. For example, the minister of External Affairs said that plans had already been made to evacuate Nigerians from neighboring countries, if those countries retaliated by expelling Nigerians (*West Africa* 3 June 1985, 1136).

The Buhari Government also emphasized that the MEA, the main ministry concerned with foreign affairs, related well to other ministries and organizations and also learned to work with them. Thus, during a 10-day seminar at the NIPSS for all Nigerian heads of diplomatic missions, different ministers lectured on how their respective ministries related to the work of the envoys abroad (*West Africa* 5 August 1985, 1612). All newly recruited Nigerian external affairs officers, as part of their initial in-service training, usually have to tour all the states of the federation. This is to sensitize them to the political, economic, and cultural dynamics of all corners of the country, so they can adequately represent Nigerian interests abroad.

The praise Idiagbon lavished on Nigerian society as a whole and on the security agencies and the armed forces that had helped to handle the problems created by the alleged involvement of the Nigerian government in the Dikko affair (he called it "this test case"), showed how the person in charge appreciated the adequate coordination of efforts (*West Africa* 16 July 1984, 1462). However, it must be noted that all the effective coordination efforts achieved during the Buhari era may have been won at the cost of intolerance towards dissension, since that government detested any form of societal "indiscipline."

The Functioning of the Foreign Policy Machinery

The functions of designing, developing, implementing, and evaluating Nigerian foreign policy were handled by the above-mentioned decision structures. These structures emphasized each of the functions in varying degrees. The MEA, as the ministry specifically entrusted with Nigeria's relations with the outside world, carried out all the above functions. The policy planning unit of the MEA played a vital role in policy design and development. The detailed conceptualizations of the dynamics and principles that were to guide and inform Nigeria's foreign relations, as presented by Ibrahim Gambari (the minister for External Affairs) in a paper he wrote, showed that the policy planning unit of the MEA was very active (*West Africa* 22 October 1984, 2117–18). The national leadership seemed to have been sensitized to the various strands of new conceptualizations of foreign policy. The paper Buhari presented at the Nigerian Institute of International Affairs further elaborated on ideas that emerged from Gambari's paper (*West Africa* 17 December 1984, 2565–66). The NIIA, though not directly involved in designing the developing foreign policy, also contributed to this enterprise. Through the broadening of the horizon of the national leadership, the foreign policy elite, and the general public, with respect to possible various dynamics and policy options that might have been relevant to Nigeria's foreign policy behavior, the NIIA did influence and contribute to the foreign policy formulation process. The NIPSS, to some extent, fitted into the same mold in the policy process.

The head of state was much interested in foreign policy issues; at the apex of the foreign policy process, he was involved in the broad formulation and implementation of foreign policy. As a former commissioner for Petroleum and Energy, Buhari had managed Nigeria's relations with OPEC (*West Africa* 6 February 1984, 266). Though a rather narrow foreign affairs exposure, this experience had sensitized him to the dynamics of the international system. The SMC, the highest policy-making body, also had people with foreign affairs experience, for example, Major-general Sani Abacha, who commanded the Nigerian troops in Chad in 1978, and Mohammed Rafindadi, the director-general of the Nigerian Security Organization (the umbrella intelligence organization), who had served as an ambassador (*West Africa* 6 February 1984, 266). Buhari, who was perceived as a cautious gentleman (*The African Guardian* 17 July 1986, 19), also had an ascetic and stern personality. This, probably, partly accounted for the steadfast policies Nigeria manifested in some of its foreign policy behavior, for example, the expulsion of undocumented aliens, the border closure, and the Dikko affair.

As already shown above, the Buhari Government had Idiagbon, the chief of staff of the Supreme Military Headquarters, as the nerve center manager of the government (in simplified terms, Buhari was the effective full-time executive chairman of the government). Thus, Idiagbon, who ensured that everything that reached the head of state, and the SMC, passed through him, also ensured that the foreign policy arena merited his close supervision. As shown above, his interests were more acute in foreign policy matters that had security ramifications. Thus, the expulsion of undocumented aliens, border closure, and the crisis management after the Dikko incident in Britain were activities in which he closely coordinated the decision structures that were involved. Additionally, he also engaged in some routine diplomatic activities. For example, he signed, on behalf of Nigeria, cultural and educational cooperation and credit line agreements with a visiting Bulgarian delegation led by Prime Minister Grisha Filipov (*West Africa* 4 February 1985, 237). Idiagbon also paid an official visit to the former Soviet Union (*West Africa* 27 February 1984, 472). The fact that he was the person that a Chadian minister had to meet (instead of a Nigerian ministerial counterpart) in order to request transit for food aid to pass through to landlocked Chad (which was involved in a civil war), further demonstrated that Idiagbon was keenly interested in closely supervising foreign policy activities that were significantly intertwined with national security dynamics (*West Africa* 22 April 1985, 805).

The Cabinet Office, which often handled routine administrative supervision, did not generally play a pivotal role in the foreign policy process (though it was often involved). As shown above, the Supreme Military Headquarters, under the assertive Idiagbon, greatly decreased the standing of the Cabinet Office. Thus, the Cabinet Office's role in the foreign policy process during the Buhari era was routine and bureaucratic in nature.

The MEA, of all the decision structures in the foreign policy system, was the main routine structure. It managed Nigeria's foreign relations through its various directorates or divisions (which constituted its basic structures) as well as diplomatic missions abroad. The minister of External Affairs and certain ambassadors, depending on issues, had direct access to the chief of staff of the Supreme Military Headquarters and the head of state.

Under the leadership of Gambari, the MEA dealt with the thorny issue of the Saharawi Arab Democratic Republic (SADR); Nigeria recognized SADR and the Organization of African Unity (OAU) followed its lead in admitting SADR as a full member country (Ofoegbu 1990, 94).

Since, as shown above, the FMF, FMCI, FMPE, FMD, FMIA, FMYSC, NIIA, and NIPSS were the other major structures involved in Nigeria's relations with the outside world (some of these were virtually in charge of foreign economic relations or foreign security relations), the MEA had to liaise with most of these organizations. Functions did sometimes overlap. For example, the international economic unit of the MEA had to participate in a policy area that was primarily handled by some of the above-mentioned ministries. Conflicts were often endemic in these grey areas. The fact that Gambari sometimes provided detailed information on Nigeria's negotiation with international financial institutions (*West Africa* 26

March 1984, 657) showed that the MEA had adequate liaisons with some of these ministries.

Within the MEA, as usual, the career diplomats sometimes had intra-organization uneasiness with the political appointees (the minister of External Affairs and politically appointed envoys). This sort of problem was a house management issue that the political leadership had to come to terms with.

The Decision-Making System and Foreign Policy Behavior

As shown above, the tight coordination of the governance process by Idiagbon translated into a foreign policy process that tended to produce unity of purpose in the formulation and the execution of policy. Goals were relatively quickly formulated and prioritized, and the choice of means easily made on the basis of efficiency. This reality made foreign policy of the Buhari era fit more into the rational model of decision-making (Allison 1971). The hierarchical nature of the military government, which also discouraged strong interest groups' pressures and dissensions within the government (which it saw as a form of societal 'indiscipline'), also led to this form of decision-making. However, this reality also produced groups of decision-makers that might also have reflected the profile of the "group think" syndrome propounded by Janis (Janis 1972).

Most of the ministers in the Buhari government were technocrats who had little experience in partisan politics—for example, Gambari, Tukur, and Soleye. Being ministers who brought expertise, rather than political platforms, into government, they were more ready to fine-tune their ministries in order to achieve the goals set by the national leadership. This also contributed to the rational model being reflected more in foreign policy than behavior. The general dispensations of the Buhari Government also reflected this model.

8
Economic and Security Components Do Also Matter: The Babangida Years

THE BABANGIDA GOVERNMENT LASTED EXACTLY EIGHT YEARS. It started on 27 August 1985 and ended on 27 August 1993. It was a military government. The president was Ibrahim Badamasi Babangida, a general in the Nigerian army. Babangida was the first Nigerian military leader to be officially titled president; prior Nigerian military leaders were officially called head of state.

There were significant changes in the policy decision-making system throughout the Babangida era. This study examines these various changes in the general national policy decision-making system to appreciate how these changes, in turn, meant changes in the foreign policy decision-making system. Thus for the purpose of this study, the Babangida era is seen as having four phases. The first phase lasted from August 1985 to October 1988. During this period the General Headquarters, which was headed by the chief of general staff, was relatively separate from the Office of the President. Ebitu Ukiwe, a commodore in the Nigerian navy, was the chief of general staff from August 1985 to October 1986 (*West Africa* 10–16 September 1990, 2434). Augustus Aikhomu, an admiral in the Nigerian navy, was the chief of general staff for the remainder of the first phase (from November 1986 to October 1988) and beyond (until August 1990) (*West Africa* 10–16 September 1990, 2434). (The General Headquarters was the new name for the Supreme Military Headquarters of the Buhari Government and other, earlier military governments; and similarly, the chief of general staff was the new name for the chief of staff of the Supreme Military Headquarters.)

The second phase lasted from November 1988 to August 1990. During this period the General Headquarters, together with the chief of general staff, became an integral part of a new national decision-making structure called the Presidency (*West Africa* 17–23 October 1988, 1967). The Presidency was created in 1988 by the Babangida Government as an aspect of "important administrative reforms" and reorganizations (*West Africa* 17–23 October 1988, 1967). Through these administrative reforms and reorganizations, other important decision-making structures, such as the Cabinet Office, the Office of the Secretary to the Federal Government, the Code of Conduct Bureau, the National Population Commission, the offices of the minister for special duties and the minister of state for budget and planning, and some others, also were made part and parcel of the presidency (*West Africa* 17–23 October 1988, 1967). The Presidency, thus, was the central national policy decision-making structure, with many other important decision-making structures under its umbrella.

The third phase was not very different from the second phase. At the end of August 1990, the Office of the Vice President was created to replace that of the post of chief of general staff (*West Africa* 10–16 September 1990, 2434). The fact that Admiral Aikhomu (who was the chief of general staff) simply retired from the navy and became the vice president, and the fact that the Office of the Vice President, just like the post of chief of general staff, was an integral part of the Presidency, meant that the changes that ushered in the third phase of the Babangida Government were mainly cosmetic. Thus, in reality the second and third phases of the Babangida Government were very similar. However, the cosmetic changes of the third phase had significant symbolic value. The Office of the Vice President replacing the post of chief of general staff was an aspect of the political transition program (that was supposed to have eventually led to a civilian democratic polity replacing the military government of the Babangida era. Thus, the chief of general staff becoming the vice president symbolically signified an aspect of the progress toward the democratization and the civilianization (and, therefore, the demilitarization) of the government. The third phase of the Babangida Government lasted from the end of August 1990 to December 1992.

The fourth and final phase of the Babangida Government lasted from January 1993 to August 1993 (*West Africa* 7–13 December 1992, 2107; *West Africa* 6–12 September 1993, 1578). This phase was very different from the three earlier phases. This was the phase that was to directly serve as the transitional phase (that was to usher the country into a complete civilian democratic government and polity. During the Babangida Government, the Armed Forces Ruling Council (AFRC) was the highest and sovereign national policy decision-making structure. (AFRC was the new name for the Supreme Military Council of the Buhari Government and other prior military governments.) During the fourth and final phase of the Babangida Government, the AFRC was replaced by the National Defense and Security Council (NDSC) (*West Africa* 7–13 December 1992, 2107; *West Africa* 21–27 December 1992, 2203). Thus, during the fourth phase the NDSC was the highest and sovereign national policy decision-making structure. Other changes included the National Council of Ministers being replaced by the Transitional Council and the National Assembly becoming functional during the fourth phase (*West Africa* 7–13 December 1992, 2107; *West Africa* 21–27 December 1992, 2203). The Transitional Council served as the cabinet body that handled the daily governance of the country (*West Africa* 25–31 January 1993, 112), while the National Assembly (consisting of the Senate and House of Representatives) served as the national legislative structure. To underscore the fact that the fourth phase was to serve as the transitional phase for a return to full democratic rule, both the Transitional Council and the National Assembly had only civilian members. The Transitional Council consisted of appointed civilians (*West Africa* 21–27 December 1992, 2203) and the National Assembly consisted of elected civilians. Additionally, during the fourth phase, the vice president's role was restricted to the NDSC (of which he was one of the members) and thus he had no formal and direct links with the Transitional Council (*West Africa* 25–31 January 1993, 112) and the National Assembly. Nevertheless, the fourth and final phase of the Babangida Government was still a military government. To underscore this fact, the NDSC was the highest and sovereign national policy decision-making body. The NDSC and the Presidency generally supervised the work of the Transitional Council and National Assembly. Thus, the fourth phase was a hybrid government consisting of both civilian-controlled and military controlled decision-making structures. The civilian-controlled decision-making structures handled the day-to-day governing processes while the military-controlled decision-making structures mainly provided major policy guidelines and acted as the highest decision-making bodies. In reality, the fourth phase of the Babangida Government was well designed for a transition to democracy. However, the cancellation of the presidential election (which was to produce a democratically elected president for a new democratic polity) meant that the fourth and final phase of the Babangida Government did not lead the country to a full democratic government and polity as that phase of the government was supposed to do.

The Transitional Council was chaired by Ernest Shonekan (*West Africa* 25–31 January 1993, 112), a former business executive. Thus, during the fourth and final phase of the Babangida Government, Shonekan coordinated and/or directed the day-to-day governing processes, while Babangida (who chaired the NDSC) and other members of the NDSC set the major policy guidelines and oversaw and supervised the work of the Transitional Council.

Though the Babangida Government had four various phases, as analyzed above, most of the Babangida era consisted of the second and third phases. (While the Babangida Government lasted from 27 August 1985 to 27 August 1993, the second and third phases lasted from November 1988 to December 1993). As also noted earlier, the second and third phases were very similar. Thus, in analyzing the foreign policy decision-making structures, processes, and outputs during the Babangida era, the main focus will be on its second and third phases, although references will be made to the first and fourth phases when and where relevant.

It is also important to note that it was during the Babangida Government that the capital of the Federal Republic of Nigeria, legally and formally, changed from Lagos to Abuja. It was the Muhammed/Obasanjo Government that had initiated this decision, and the Muhammed/Obasanjo, Shagari, Buhari, and Babangida Governments all vigorously provided the financial, human, and material resources for the planning, design, development, and construction of the physical structures and facilities for Abuja, Federal Capital Territory. On 12 December 1991, President Babangida signed the official document that signified the formal transfer of the capital from Lagos to Abuja, and on had same day the president, his family, and the staff and officials of the Presidency left Lagos by air for Abuja (*West Africa* 23 December 1991–5 January 1992, 2162). The promulgation of 12 December 1992, which transferred the capital from Lagos to Abuja, was provided with the complete legal instruments on 18 December 1991 (*West Africa* 6–12 January 1992, 35).

During the Babangida era, there were many policy decision-making structures that were involved to a greater or lesser degree in the foreign policy decision-making processes. These various policy decision-making structures were the AFRC; the National Security Council; the National Defense Council; the National Council of Ministers; the National Council of States; the Presidency; the Ministry of External Affairs; the Ministry of Defense; and other ministries, agencies, and departments. Most of these policy decision-making structures will be evaluated individually, for the sake of analytic ease and clarity. Specifically, most will be analyzed in terms of their role in the foreign policy decision-making milieu, and in terms of how they impacted on foreign policy decision-making processes and outputs. (The General Headquarters and the Cabinet Office were freestanding organs only during the first phase of the Babangida Government—starting from the second phase, they became part and parcel of the Presidency—thus, for the purpose of this study, these two bodies are seen as being submerged within the Presidency.)

THE ARMED FORCES RULING COUNCIL

The Armed Forces Ruling Council (AFRC), as noted earlier, was the highest and sovereign national policy decision-making body during the first, second, and third phases of the Babangida Government. (As also noted earlier, NDSC replaced the AFRC during the fourth and final phase of the Babangida Government.)

The AFRC was both a legislative and an executive body—the highest in the government (Akindele 1990b, 247). It has also been portrayed as occupying the central position in the national security and defense organizational arrangements (*Nigeria: A Country Study* 1992, 276).

Though the AFRC had many changes in terms of its membership throughout the Babangida era, it was always a body composed mostly of military officers (for example, see *West Africa* 10–16 September 1990, 2434–35). Despite various changes, the president, vice president (during the first phase of the Babangida Government, this position did not exist; in its place was the chief of general staff, as noted earlier), the minister of Defense and chief of the Defense Staff, the chiefs of staff of the Nigerian army, navy, and air force, very senior military officers (especially those commanding important combat units of the army, air force, and navy), and the inspector general of the Nigerian police force were always members of the AFRC. The president was the chairman of the AFRC.

In terms of its functioning, the AFRC was always a body with many important senior military officers who were likely to make their voices heard in AFRC deliberations. Nevertheless, the president, due to his premier position in the political and military spheres, and due to his chairmanship of the AFRC, was the most important person in the AFRC. Thus, other members of the AFRC were likely to lean toward the president's position on policy issues . The fact that most members of the AFRC were military officers and the president was also the most senior military officer also meant that military values would have encouraged other AFRC members to defer often to the president on policy issues.

According to Akindele (1990b, 247), the AFRC was "the highest executive and legislative body" and also "the most important institutional mechanism for policy decision-making and coordination at the highest level." Thus, the AFRC handled both domestic and foreign policy issues. However, due to the fact that other subordinate policy decision-making, policy coordination, and/or policy advisory bodies handled most regular foreign policy issues, the AFRC mostly focused on providing broad foreign policy guidelines and goals. It directly handled foreign policy decision-making involving extremely important and urgent foreign policy issues, but merely gave final approval (or disapproval) for some important foreign policy decisions that were made by subordinate bodies. For example, other policy decision-making, policy coordination, and/or policy advisory bodies handled the issue of Nigeria's membership or non-membership in the Organization of Islamic Conference (OIC). The OIC issue persisted through a good portion of the Babangida era (see *West Africa* 3–9 June 1991, 913; *West Africa* 26 August–1 September 1991, 1420; *West Africa* 23 December 1991–5 January 1992, 2163). (Nigeria's membership in the OIC attracted vocal and sustained criticism by prominent public opinion leaders

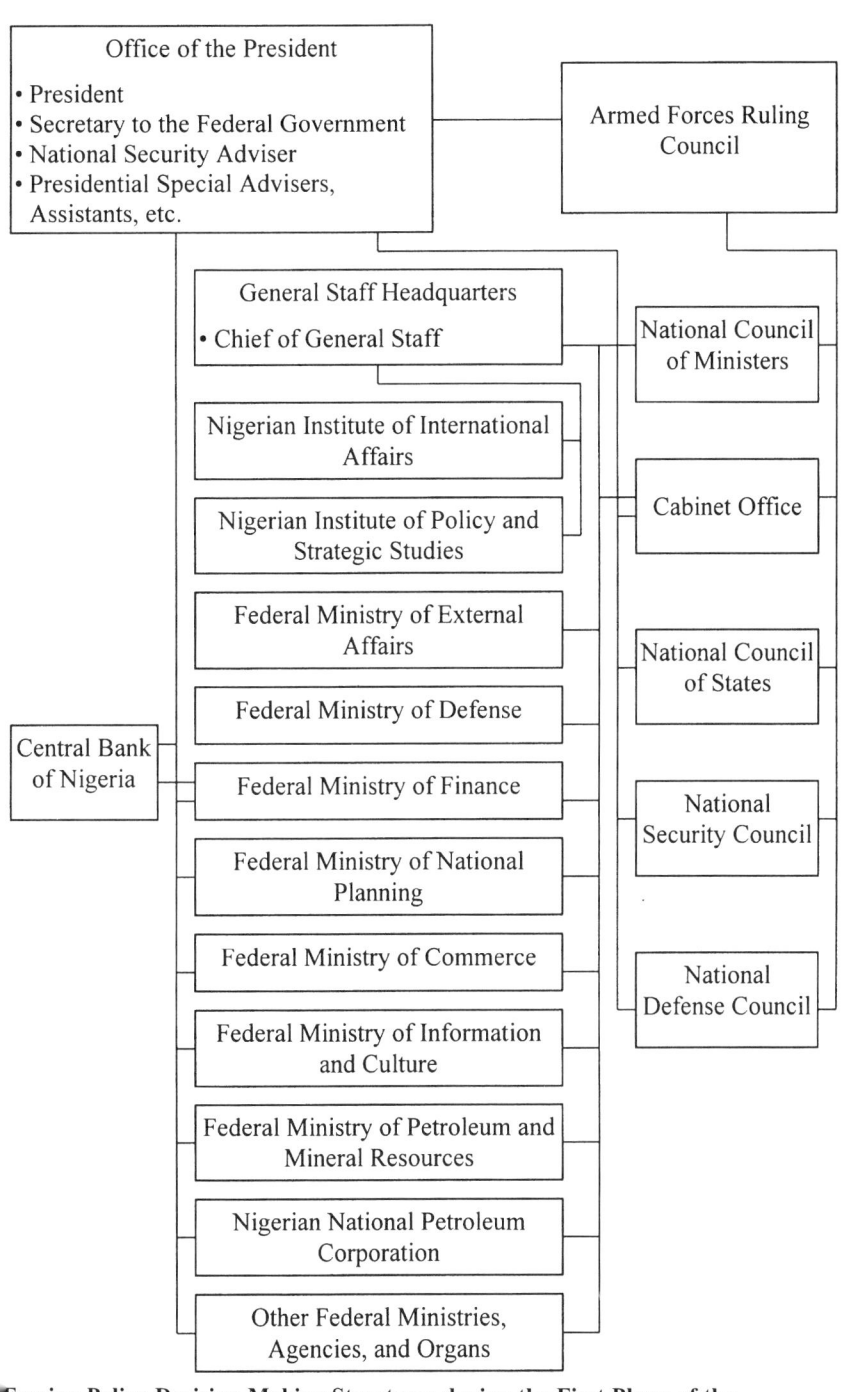

```
┌─────────────────────────────────┐     ┌──────────────────┐
│ Office of the President         │     │ Armed Forces     │
│ • President                     │─────│ Ruling Council   │
│ • Secretary to the Federal Gov. │     │                  │
│ • National Security Adviser     │     └──────────────────┘
│ • Presidential Special Advisers,│
│   Assistants, etc.              │
└─────────────────────────────────┘
```

- Office of the President
  - President
  - Secretary to the Federal Government
  - National Security Adviser
  - Presidential Special Advisers, Assistants, etc.

- Armed Forces Ruling Council

- General Staff Headquarters
  - Chief of General Staff

- Nigerian Institute of International Affairs
- Nigerian Institute of Policy and Strategic Studies
- Federal Ministry of External Affairs
- Federal Ministry of Defense
- Central Bank of Nigeria
- Federal Ministry of Finance
- Federal Ministry of National Planning
- Federal Ministry of Commerce
- Federal Ministry of Information and Culture
- Federal Ministry of Petroleum and Mineral Resources
- Nigerian National Petroleum Corporation
- Other Federal Ministries, Agencies, and Organs

- National Council of Ministers
- Cabinet Office
- National Council of States
- National Security Council
- National Defense Council

Foreign Policy Decision-Making Structures during the First Phase of the Babangida Government, August 1985 to October 1988

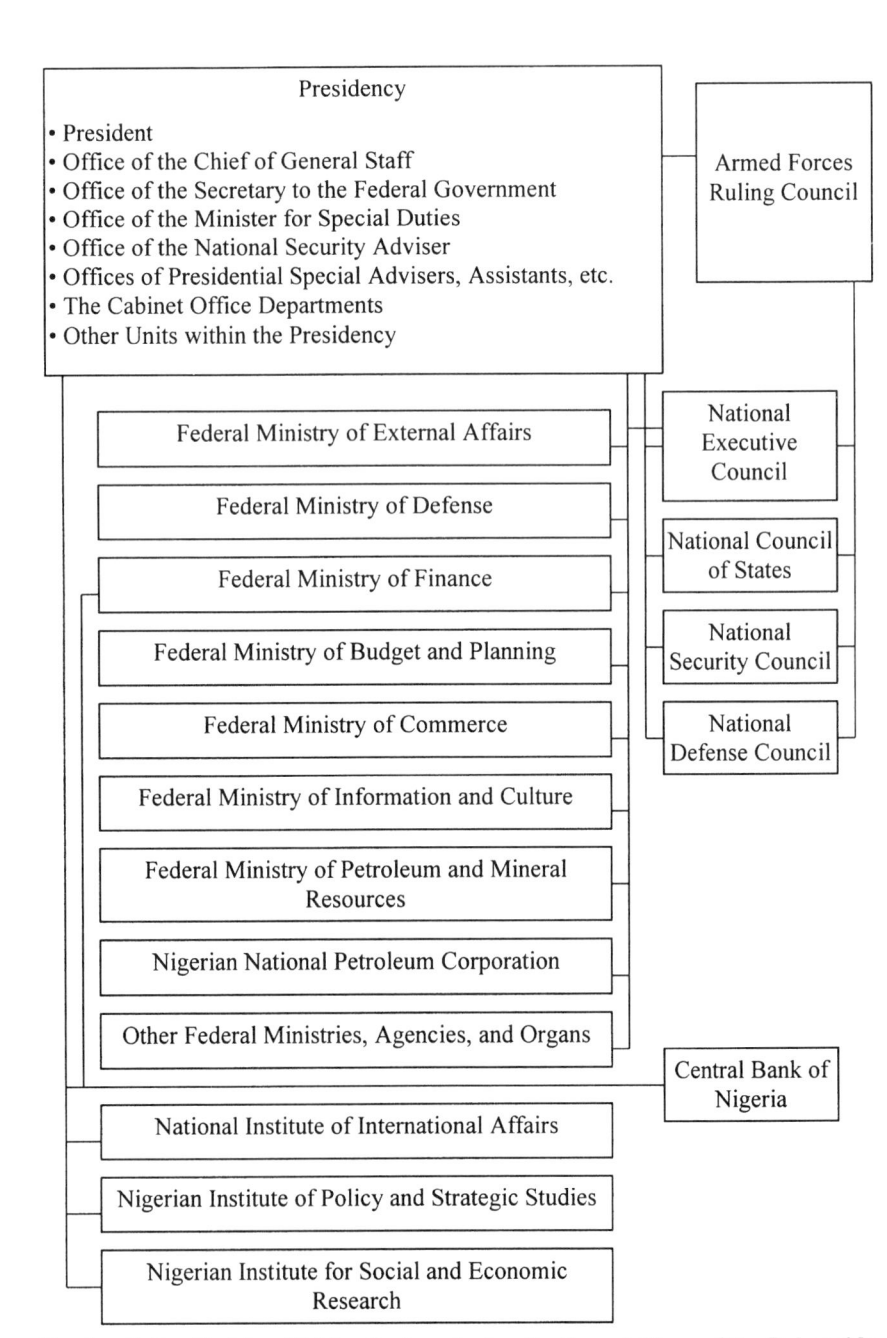

```
┌─────────────────────────────────────────────────────────────┐  ┌──────────────┐
│                         Presidency                          │  │              │
│ • President                                                 │  │ Armed Forces │
│ • Office of the Chief of General Staff                      │──│ Ruling Council│
│ • Office of the Secretary to the Federal Government         │  │              │
│ • Office of the Minister for Special Duties                 │  │              │
│ • Office of the National Security Adviser                   │  └──────────────┘
│ • Offices of Presidential Special Advisers, Assistants, etc.│
│ • The Cabinet Office Departments                            │
│ • Other Units within the Presidency                         │
└─────────────────────────────────────────────────────────────┘
```

- Federal Ministry of External Affairs
- Federal Ministry of Defense
- Federal Ministry of Finance
- Federal Ministry of Budget and Planning
- Federal Ministry of Commerce
- Federal Ministry of Information and Culture
- Federal Ministry of Petroleum and Mineral Resources
- Nigerian National Petroleum Corporation
- Other Federal Ministries, Agencies, and Organs
- National Institute of International Affairs
- Nigerian Institute of Policy and Strategic Studies
- Nigerian Institute for Social and Economic Research

Connected councils:
- National Executive Council
- National Council of States
- National Security Council
- National Defense Council
- Central Bank of Nigeria

Foreign Policy Decision-Making System during the Second Phase of the Babangida Government, November 1988 to Early August 1990

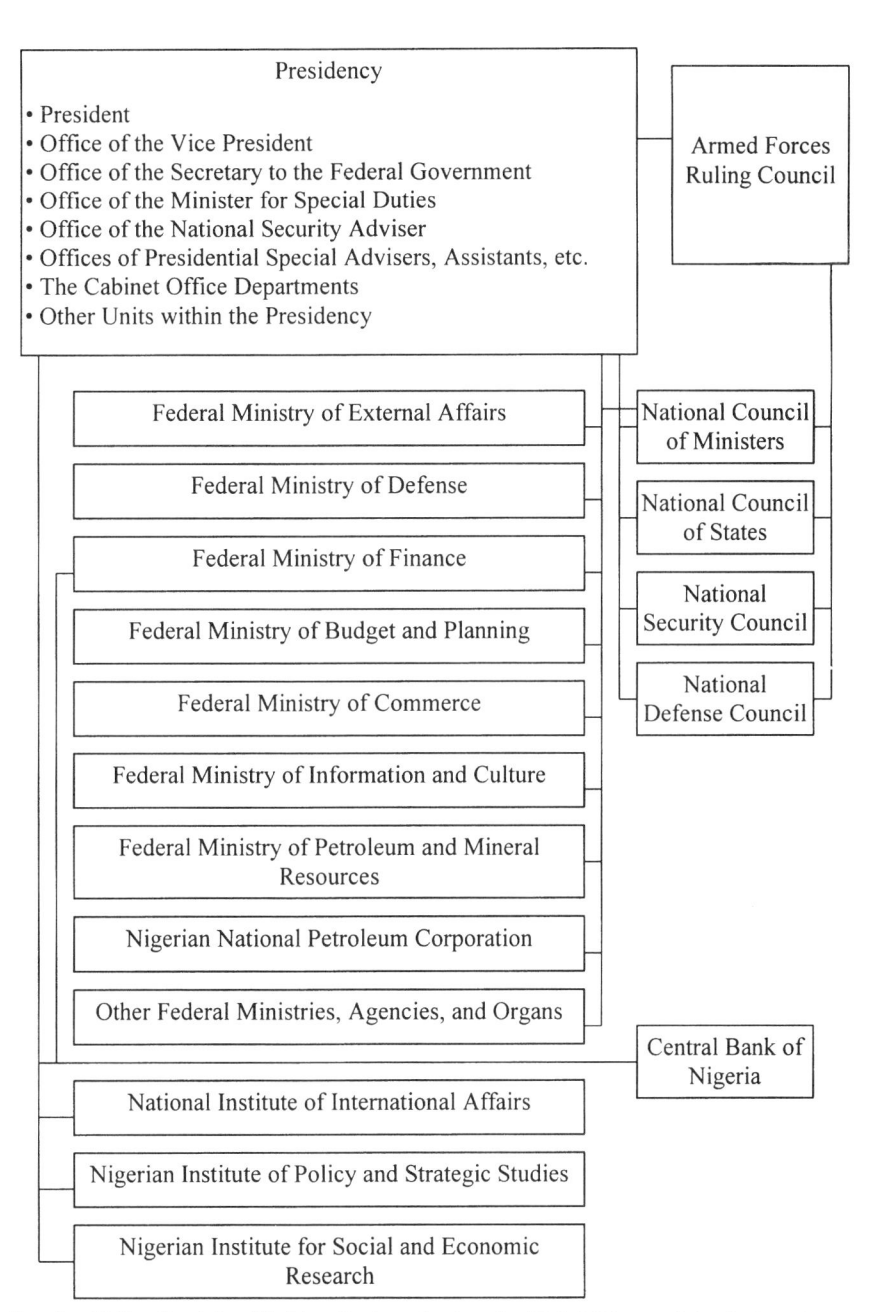

```
┌─────────────────────────────────────────────────────┐  ┌──────────────┐
│                    Presidency                       │  │              │
│ • President                                         │  │ Armed Forces │
│ • Office of the Vice President                      ├──┤ Ruling Council│
│ • Office of the Secretary to the Federal Government │  │              │
│ • Office of the Minister for Special Duties         │  │              │
│ • Office of the National Security Adviser           │  └──────────────┘
│ • Offices of Presidential Special Advisers, etc.    │
│ • The Cabinet Office Departments                    │
│ • Other Units within the Presidency                 │
└─────────────────────────────────────────────────────┘
```

- Federal Ministry of External Affairs
- Federal Ministry of Defense
- Federal Ministry of Finance
- Federal Ministry of Budget and Planning
- Federal Ministry of Commerce
- Federal Ministry of Information and Culture
- Federal Ministry of Petroleum and Mineral Resources
- Nigerian National Petroleum Corporation
- Other Federal Ministries, Agencies, and Organs
- National Institute of International Affairs
- Nigerian Institute of Policy and Strategic Studies
- Nigerian Institute for Social and Economic Research

- National Council of Ministers
- National Council of States
- National Security Council
- National Defense Council
- Central Bank of Nigeria

Foreign Policy Decision-Making System during the Third Phase of the Babangida Government, Late August 1990 to December 1992

```
┌─────────────────────────────────────────┐     ┌──────────────┐
│              Presidency                  │     │   National   │
│ • President                              │─────│  Defense and │
│ • Office of the Vice President           │     │Security Council│
│ • Offices of Presidential Advisers,      │     └──────────────┘
│   Assistants, etc.                       │
└─────────────────────────────────────────┘
         │
┌─────────────────────────────────────┐          ┌──────────────┐
│         Transitional Council         │          │   National   │
│ • Chairman of the Transitional Council│─────────│   Assembly   │
└─────────────────────────────────────┘          │ • Senate     │
         │                                        │ • House of   │
┌─────────────────────────────────────────┐      │ Representatives│
│   Federal Ministry of Foreign Affairs    │      └──────────────┘
├─────────────────────────────────────────┤
│       Federal Ministry of Defense        │
├─────────────────────────────────────────┤      ┌──────────────┐
│       Federal Ministry of Finance        │──────│ Central Bank │
├─────────────────────────────────────────┤      │  of Nigeria  │
│ Federal Ministry of Budget and Planning  │      └──────────────┘
├─────────────────────────────────────────┤
│       Federal Ministry of Commerce       │
├─────────────────────────────────────────┤
│ Federal Ministry of Information and Culture│
├─────────────────────────────────────────┤
│Federal Ministry of Petroleum and Mineral Resources│
├─────────────────────────────────────────┤
│  Nigerian National Petroleum Corporation │
├─────────────────────────────────────────┤
│Nigerian Institute for Social and Economic Research│
├─────────────────────────────────────────┤
│  National Institute of International Affairs│
├─────────────────────────────────────────┤
│Nigerian Institute of Policy and Strategic Studies│
├─────────────────────────────────────────┤
│  Other Federal Ministries, Agencies, and Organs│
└─────────────────────────────────────────┘
```

Foreign Policy Decision-Making System during the Fourth Phase (the Transitional Government Phase) of the Babangida Government, January 1993 to August 1993

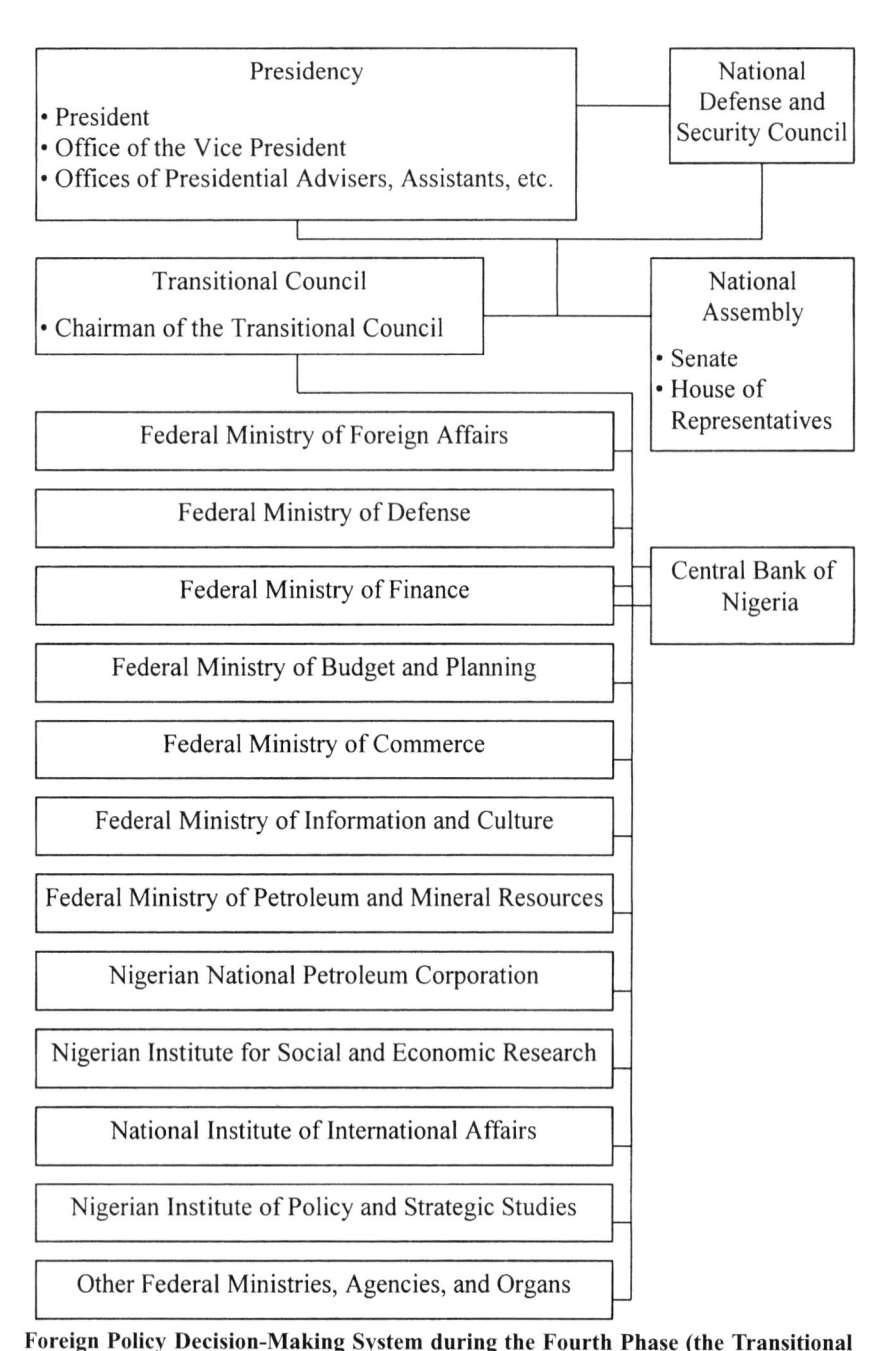

in Nigeria, who argued that Nigeria belonging to the OIC would compromise the secular nature of the country's political system and also fuel more religious conflicts in the country.) When in August 1991 the president announced that Nigeria had suspended its OIC membership, he noted that that decision was made based on "a recommendation by the Advisory Council on Religious Affairs" (*West Africa* 26 August -1 September 1991, 1420). (Interestingly, after this announcement most people were not sure whether Nigeria had permanently ended its OIC membership or just temporarily suspended it.) As noted above, the details of studying and providing policy options on the OIC issue was handled by an advisory body (the Advisory Council on Religious Affairs), not the AFRC. It has also been noted that the decision dynamics that led to Nigeria becoming a member of the OIC mainly involved the Office of the President (which became known as the Presidency during the second, third, and fourth phases of the Babangida Government), the Ministry of External Affairs (MEA), and internal and external pro-OIC lobby groups (Olukoshi 1990a, 488–504). According to Olukoshi, while the MEA expressed concern about Nigeria becoming an OIC member, the Office of the President shared the eagerness of the pro-OIC lobby groups; the last two organs prevailed and Nigeria became an OIC member. Thus, neither the decision to become an OIC member nor the later decision to suspend membership significantly involved the AFRC. In reality, most of the routine foreign relations issues and the framework and details of major foreign relations issues were handled by the Presidency, the MEA, and other ministries, agencies, and organs. The AFRC, as noted above, mostly focused on providing broad major foreign policy outputs and guidelines. Additionally, as the highest legislative and executive body, the AFRC had the role of ratifying all treaties that Nigeria entered into in order for such treaties to have full legal standing. For example, at the 1991 Organization of African Unity (OAU) Summit held at Abuja, Nigeria, the OAU adopted the African Economic Community Treaty "with the objective of creating an integrated common market" (*West Africa* 9–15 March 1992, 406). For that treaty, which Nigeria negotiated and adopted with other OAU member countries, to have full legal standing in Nigeria, the AFRC had to ratify it.

Since the president, vice president, and other important members of the government belonged to the AFRC, this organ was in position to provide adequate broad foreign policy outputs and guidelines.

The AFRC served as the supreme and sovereign legislative and executive body for the country during the first, second, and third phases of the Babangida Government. As noted earlier, it was abolished at the end of the third phase. During the fourth phase, the National Defense and Security Council (NDSC) replaced the AFRC (*West Africa* 7–13 December 1992,

2107; *West Africa* 21–27 December 1992, 2203; *West Africa* 25–31 January 1993, 112).

THE NATIONAL SECURITY COUNCIL AND THE NATIONAL DEFENSE COUNCIL

The National Security Council (NSC) and the National Defense Council (NDC) are two separate organs which are not to be confused with the NDSC. While the NDSC existed only during the fourth phase of the Babangida Government, the NSC and NDC were in existence right from the first phase. Most importantly, while the NSC and NDC functioned as national security coordination, management, and advisory structures during the Babangida era, the NDSC served as the supreme and sovereign legislative and executive decision-making body during its existence in the fourth phase of the Babangida Government.

The NSC and NDC maintained a very low profile in their role in the security components of the national policy milieu. This low profile also meant, quite predictably, that the NSC and NDC were not publicly perceived as active structures in the foreign policy decision-making milieu, even in the security dimensions of the foreign policy process. Some, like Peters (1986, 156–57), believe that even prior to the Babangida Government, the NSC and NDC lacked adequate leadership and sufficient staff and therefore were unable to play important roles in the coordination and management of the national security system. Though during the Babangida era there were some changes in the national security management system, the NSC and NDC were not perceived by the public as powerful structures in the foreign policy decision-making system and/or the national security management system, specifically.

The membership of both the NSC and NDC included the most senior and important military officers. In fact, the membership of the two bodies mostly overlapped. They were both also chaired by the president. Additionally, in terms of the organizational arrangements in the national security system, the two bodies were also well-positioned to be visible and important structures (see *Nigeria: A Country Study* 1992, 276). All the above factors show that in terms of composition and position, the NSC and NDC had the attributes to be significant decision structures in the national security system. However, these two bodies did not function adequately and were not significant and visible decision structures in the national security system (at least in terms of public perception). Had they had adequate staff, and had they been required by the national leadership to play a more robust role in the national security system, both the NSC and NDC could have been visible and important national security coordination, management, and advisory structures during the Babangida Government.

THE NATIONAL COUNCIL OF MINISTERS

The National Council of Ministers (NCM) was the formal name for the federal cabinet during the Babangida Government. Some prior governments called the federal cabinet the Federal Executive Council. It consisted of the ministers of all the federal ministries. The chairman of the NCM was the president, and the vice president (and during the first and second phases of the Babangida Government, the chief of general staff) was also a member of the NCM.

Its composition and profile made the NCM the main organ for the coordination and/or formulation of public policies. Though, formally, it was an advisory body for the president, the deliberations, activities, and decisions of the NCM greatly impacted on and shaped the coordination and/or formulation of public policies, since the president relied on the ministers' huge amount of information, data, and policy analyses and evaluations. However, in some cases the president could ignore the views of the members of the NCM, relying instead on the people and materials of the various units within the Presidency. President Babangida, who had great policy and organizational skills, was known to spend a lot of time listening to many people on various policy issues, and afterward making the decision he perceived as the most appropriate. The Babangida Government (especially its Presidency) was known for the utilization of many intellectuals on a temporary or permanent basis for advisory roles in numerous aspects of public policy. These intellectuals were advisory resources the president relied on when the input of the NCM was not adequate for him to reach a decision.

Nevertheless, in most policy cases, the president relied on the NCM to make major decisions; in fact, in most routine and regular public policy issues he allowed the various ministers and their ministries to handle the situation alone.

As noted earlier, the AFRC (and during the fourth phase of the Babangida Government the NDSC) was the highest legislative and executive body. Thus, though the NCM was the main executive branch council, it was subordinate to the AFRC (Akindele 1990b, 247). Thus, major national policies were ultimately made by the AFRC. Additionally, the AFRC could nullify, change, or affirm decisions that were made by the NCM. However, in reality, the NCM handled most policy coordination and/or formulation roles, while the AFRC mainly focused on major national policy issues.

In terms of foreign policy, the NCM had a significant role to play. As the federal cabinet, it played policy coordination and/or formulation roles in some foreign policy cases. Expectably, the ministers in the NCM who were normally more prominent in foreign policy issues were the ministers of External Affairs, Defense, Finance, Commerce, and Industries. The minister of External Affairs was prominent because he headed the main organ for the management of Nigeria's international relations. The minister of Defense was prominent due to the fact that his ministry was mainly in charge of the security/military components of foreign policy. The major role Nigeria played in the peacekeeping operations in Liberia and other roles in peacekeeping operations in Somalia and other countries meant that the MOD was a prominent organ in foreign affairs. The Babangida Government greatly emphasized the economic components of the country in order to boost the export of manufactured goods and other non-petroleum products to other countries (to reduce the country's dependence on the export of petroleum, and thus put the economy on a sounder footing). The emphasis on the economic components of international relations made the ministers and Ministries of Finance, Commerce, and Industries prominent in foreign affairs.

Thus, during the NCM meetings, the president had the opportunity to seekt he help of the ministers of External Affairs, Defense, Finance, Commerce, and Industries in coordinating and/or formulating foreign policies. Other ministers could also be prominent in helping the president, depending on the foreign policy issue. For example, the ministers of Petroleum Resources and Information were prominent in international petroleum issues and the cultural components of foreign policy/external publicity issues.

Scholars like Professor Akindele have thoroughly analyzed the role of the Federal Executive Council (which was often called the National Council of Ministers during the Babangida Government). According to him (Akindele 1990b, 247), this organ was "an institutional arrangement for policy management and coordination of policy-management issues on both domestic and external fronts." He also adds that the president and this organ, "separately or jointly, provide the institutional context for high level policy formulation and coordination within the machinery of government. Their effectiveness as institutional mechanisms for coordination of policies, including coordination of 'domestic' and 'foreign' policies, is not in doubt" (Akindele 1990b, 248).

The role the NCM played in Nigeria's decision to spearhead the creation of the African Petroleum Producer's Association (APPA) is a very good example of its place in the foreign policy decision-making system. As Nwoke notes (1990, 484), "[T]he final decision for Nigeria to initiate the formation of APPA was cleared by the Head of State, via the Council of

Ministers. . . ." This APPA case clearly shows the sort of significant role that the National Council of Ministers played in the foreign policy decision-making milieu.

However, there were also important foreign policy cases in which the NCM did not play a significant role. For example, in Olukoshi's analysis of the decision-making structures and processes that were involved in determining the nature of Nigeria's relationship with the Organization of Islamic Conference (OIC), the NCM was not mentioned as a significant part of that decision case (Olukoshi 1990a, 495–97). The very controversial and sensitive nature of the OIC issue might have accounted for the NCM not being able to play a significant role in that case. Nevertheless, generally, the NCM played an important role in helping the president to coordinate, manage, and/or formulate foreign policies.

The NCM was in existence during the first, second, and third phases of the Babangida Government. During the fourth, final, and transitional phase of the government the NCM was replaced by the Transitional Council (*West Africa* 7–13 December 1992, 2107; *West Africa* 21–27 December 1992, 2203; *West Africa* 25–31 January 1993, 112).

THE NATIONAL COUNCIL OF STATES

The National Council of States (NCS), as in most prior governments, was the national body primarily devoted to issues that affected state governments during the Babangida Government. The NCS was also the only formal national body that included the governors of all the states. Thus, it was the highest forum that enabled the Presidency to coordinate and manage intergovernmental relations (among the national, state, and local governments) and interstate relations in the federal system of government. Therefore, the NCS primarily focused on domestic issues. However, many states in Nigeria share some of their borders with one or more of the following countries: Republic of Benin, Chad, Cameroun, Equatorial Guinea (its Bioko Island portion), and Republic of Niger. This fact means that the NCS is often also a forum in which state governors discuss and seek solutions to international issues with the president and other prominent members of the federal government.

The members of the NCS during most of the Babangida era included the president (chairman of the NCS), the vice president (the deputy chairman of the NCS), former heads of states, former chief justices, former senate presidents, the state governors, the minister of Justice, and a traditional leader from each of the states (*West Africa* 20–26 April 1992, 685). This composition and profile of the NCS made it the most broadly based and representative national body of the Babangida Government, and might have also given it a lot of national legitimacy.

However, despite its appealing composition and profile, it was not one of the more prominent national bodies. It met less frequently than other organizations, and was merely an advisory body. The president had the choice of accepting, rejecting, or amending the views of the NCS. Most importantly, the NCS was a national body that was subordinate to the AFRC, which therefore also had the choice of accepting, rejecting, or amending tis views.

Additionally, though the NCS was the highest formal national body that focused primarily on intergovernmental and interstate relations within the context of the federal system, it was the chief of general staff (who later had the title the vice president) had the routine, continuous, and regular management of intergovernmental and interstate relations as one of his duties during the first three phases of the Babangida Government. The chief of general staff was formally assigned the management of national government and state governments relations, interstate government relations and national policy guidelines on local government system and administration (*Thisweek* 20 October 1986, 18; *Sunday Times* 23 April 1989, 1, 8). Thus, in reality, in terms of routine and regular relations with the national government, the state governors worked with the chief of general staff, who was also the deputy chairman of the NCS. During the fourth (final and transitional) phase of the Babangida Government, the Transitional Council created a Federal Ministry of State and Local Government Affairs (*West Africa* 25–31 January 1993, 113) to carry out the task of managing intergovernmental and interstate relations. Thus, throughout the Babangida era, while the NCS was the body for the deliberations on major issues that affected the states, the routine and regular management of intergovernmental relations was effected first by the chief of general staff and later by the Federal Ministry of State and Local Government Affairs.

As noted earlier, the NCS focused mostly on domestic issues, but sometimes dealt with also on international issues. For the purpose of this study, we are mainly looking at the NCS in terms of its role in international affairs.

Because many states in Nigeria share common borders with one or more foreign countries, as noted earlier, the NCS was a very appropriate forum for the state governors to work with the president, and other prominent members of the federal government, on related issues. The NCS is also a forum for states that do not share borders with foreign countries but face other international issues such as undocumented aliens in their states.

States that share some of their borders with foreign countries have economic, cultural, political, and security/military links with these countries. Routine and regular issues often involve international trade and financial transactions; the nature and regulation of cross-border movements of peoples (who may share a lot culturally with both sides of the international borders); the policies and actions of Nigerian customs and immigration officials; the activities of the customs and immigration officials of the bordering countries; and water and natural resources in the border areas. Sensitive and often problematic issues are those of disputed land and boundaries and the activities and behavior of the military forces—both Nigeria's and those of the bordering foreign countries. These issues sometimes result in border conflicts and clashes. Nevertheless, on the whole, Nigeria's relations with bordering foreign countries have been marked by cooperation usually, competition sometimes, and conflict occasionally.

The Babangida Government placed much emphasis on the economic components of Nigeria's foreign policy, so as to expand Nigeria's exports of manufactured goods. Neighboring countries and countries in the west African region were targeted as export markets. For example, the Babangida Government approved many manufactured products being exported to the west African region (*West Africa* 1–7 February 1993, 162). This acceleration of exports to the west African region necessitated fostering more cooperative relations with bordering countries. The states in Nigeria sharing common borders with some of these countries had to help this emphasis on economic ties by accelerating cooperative activities with the communities across the border, and for this the NCS was the natural forum.

One practical manifestation of this economic emphasis in Nigeria's foreign relations was the tradition of President Babangida always including many Nigerian businessmen in his official delegation when visiting foreign countries. (These businessmen were to transact business deals with nationals of the host countries in order to foster exports of Nigerian products and also promote foreign investment in Nigeria.) Another of President Babangida's traditions was the inclusion of some state governors in his official delegation when visiting foreign countries. This indicates that the states in Nigeria were playing important roles in helping to foster economic, cultural, political, and security links with foreign countries. The businessmen and state governors were thus another set of instruments in Nigeria foreign policy initiatives, policies, and actions. For example, during President Babangida's visit to Namibia, Clement Ebri (the governor of Cross River State), Ali Saa'du Birni Kudu (the governor of Jigawa State), and many Nigerian businessmen were part of the entourage; and the visit involved a lot of economic, cultural, political, and security issues being handled by Nigeria and Namibia (*African Concord* 18 May 1992, 37).

Though the Babangida era emphasized international cooperation (especially in the economic sphere), it could not avoid all conflicts, particularly border conflicts. The NCS was a significant instrument in the management of these conflicts, since the role of the state governors was to foster appropriate and cooperative behavior between their states and the border communities. Thus, the NCS was also seen as being part of the national security and defense organizational arrangements in the country (*Nigeria: A Country Study* 1992, 276).

Most of the prominent border conflicts during the Babangida era were with Cameroun, and these were all managed and minimized through dialogue between the Nigerian and Camerounian officials (*West Africa* 6–12 January 1992, 36–37; *West Africa* 17–23 August 1992, 1409).

Nigeria also had border issues with other neighboring countries, though these were minor conflicts. Nonetheless, persistent border conflicts create significant security problems in the states that experience them. Some of these conflicts even cause some states, rightly or wrongly, to believe that the federal government is not doing enough to provide adequate security and stability in the border areas. This sort of perception often leads to some state governors, either out of a genuine desire to help, or as an opportunistic move for the benefit of their political careers, to try to become more involved in the federal government's official political, security, cultural, and economic contacts with some of these bordering countries. Some analysts think that some of these state governors sometimes succeed in convincing the federal government to allow them to compete with the Ministry of External Affairs (MEA). According to Ofoegbu (1990, 88–89) "foreign policy towards our immediate neighbors" is one of the policy areas that "seem[s] to be persistently slipping off the hands of the Ministry of External Affairs." According to him

> Governors of neighboring states (Cross River, Gongola, Borno, Kano, Sokoto, Kwara, Ogun and Lagos States) had gradually but persistently waded into foreign affairs without training and without expert staff or Ministry of External Affairs support. . . .
> Nigeria's relations with its neighbors are serious matters. State Governors are serious and patriotic Nigerians. But they are untrained in diplomacy, and their staff lack the knowledge and experience to handle tough and difficult issues in (international) inter-State relations. They should, therefore, not be burdened with the responsibility. This does not mean they should not form part of a strong and knowledgeable federal delegation or team. Whether, therefore, the issues are territorial claims, oil prospecting, harassment of Nigerian border citizens, smuggling of persons and goods or raising and sustaining good and peaceful relations between Nigeria and its neighbors, Nigeria has Joint Commissions with these neighboring states. These joint and common institutions should be used.

The sort of issues raised abouve show how significant the NCS is in the foreign policy decision-making system, even though its primary focus is on domestic political and social issues. The NCS is one of the main forums through which the governors of states that share some of their borders with foreign countries can be made to play a more appropriate role. As Ofoegbu also notes above, such an appropriate role will mean state governors getting involved only in the policy issues with which the ministries and agencies of the federal government need their help. Undoubtedly, due to economic and cultural ties in the border areas, governors of such will have to continue to work positively with federal government ministries and agencies to promote cooperative relations with the neighboring countries. For example, it was noted that Sale Michika, the governor of Adamawa State in Nigeria (which shares some of its borders with the Republic of Cameroun) during the third and fourth phases of the Babangida Government,

> led a seven-strong delegation to Cameroon for bilateral talks on trans-border cooperation with three provincial governors in that neighboring country.
> During the five-day talks, the two sides also discussed the yearly flooding of Yola, Demsa and Furore local government areas by water from Cameroon's Lagado Dam. (*West Africa* 31 May–6 June 1993, 917)

Governor Michika's role in this incident is a good example of the positive, cooperative, and appropriate roles that governors can play. The NCS is a body that can enable state governors to know the sort of roles they should play in foreign affairs. During the Babangida Government, the Presidency was the most important and effective organ for the coordination and management of both domestic and foreign policies. Thus, the Presidency was even more well equipped and well positioned to guide the state governors in terms of the latter role in foreign affairs.

The Presidency

The Presidency formally came into existence in 1988 (*West Africa* 17–23 October 1988, 1967). It was preceded by the Office of the President. The Presidency included more units of the government than the Office of the President. The Office of the President was in existence during the first phase of the Babangida Government, while the Presidency was in existence during the second, third, and fourth phases. Since the Office of the president represented the power of the President to coordinate and manage domestic and foreign policies, just as the Presidency did (though this was a much larger organ), for the purpose of this study all the analyses under this section are applicable to both entities.

At the apex of the Presidency was the president. The major offices, units, and organs that came under the Presidency were the Office of the Vice President (from November 1988 to early August 1990, it was called the Office of the Chief of General Staff, and from late August 1990 to the end of the Babangida Government in August 1993 it was known as the Office of the Vice President), the Office of the Secretary to the Federal Government, the Office of the Minister for Special Duties, the Office of the National Security Adviser, the Offices of the Presidential Special Advisers and Assistants, the Cabinet Office, and others (*West Africa* 17–23 October 1988, 1967; *West Africa* 10–16 September 1990, 2434–35; *Sunday Times* 23 April 1989, 1, 8). Apart from the last two organs, which were mainly involved in domestic policy, all the others had significant roles in terms of foreign policy, in addition to their domestic policy roles. By placing all the above important organs under the Presidency, the Babangida Government provided the Presidency with the human and material assets that enabled it to play a very exalted role in the national policy milieu. The large number of organs, units, advisers, and assistants under the Presidency gave it a very enlarged, visible, and dominant role in the national policy and administrative milieus.

The President

The profile, functioning, and impact of the Presidency reflected the vision and goals of President Babangida. He designed, created, and operated the Presidency in such a way that it served as an effective instrument for the sort of transformation and changes in the political, economic, and social spheres that he envisioned.

Expectably, the profile and functioning of the Presidency reflected Babangida's background and worldview. Babangida was born into a very humble background in Minna, Niger State. Until he became the president, Babangida spent most of his adult life as a Nigerian army officer, serving mostly in purely military positions. He rose to the position of chief of staff of the Nigerian army, and from this position became the president of the country. Though none of the prior official positions was directly and primarily focused on foreign affairs, Babangida benefited from a rich educational experience. In 1979, he studied at the National Institute for Policy and Strategic Studies (NIPSS) in Kuru (*Newswatch* 27 November 1989, 16). The NIPSS is an institution devoted to the advancement of knowledge in both domestic and foreign policy studies. The two major units of the institute are the Department of Research and the Department of Studies (*Newswatch* 27 November 1989, 16). The Department of Research is engaged in wide-ranging policy research activities focused on providing policy solutions to various issues facing the country (*Newswatch* 27 November 1989, 16). Additionally, the results of these policy research activities are "published in the form of memoranda, monographs or books" (*Newswatch* 27 November 1989, 16). On the other hand, the Department of Studies provides high level policy studies education to those holding, or about to hold, important policy and/or administrative positions in the federal government, state governments, the military, intelligence organizations, the police, the private economic sector, labor union organizations, or the media (*Newswatch* 27 November 1989, 15–19). According to Ibrahim Alfa, a retired air marshal and a former chief of staff of the Nigerian air force, "the cream of the decision-makers in this country comes through NIPSS or, at least have lectured at NIPSS" (Alfa, quoted in *Newswatch* 27 November 1989, 15).

While studying at the NIPSS, Babangida was thoroughly exposed to both domestic and foreign policy studies. In fact, the Department of Studies has an excellent program that adeptly integrates domestic and foreign policy issues. The course program "covers six broad areas: policy and strategy, the domestic environment, regional studies, defense and security, international relations and international organization, and science and technology" (*Newswatch* 27 November 1989, 16). After taking the courses under the above six broad areas, Babangida emerged with a higher understanding of both domestic and foreign policy dynamics. Those who know the NIPSS well strongly believe that all who go through its programs are positively changed. According to Charles Ndiomu (quoted in *Newswatch* 27 November 1989, 16), a retired major-general and a former director-general of the NIPSS, "the training in the National Institute augurs very, very well for this nation and no man or woman who has passed through the walls of this institute is the same again." Also, according to Tunde Akogun (quoted in *Newswatch* 27 November 1989, 16), a colonel, "[A]nybody who gets in there will come out charged or fully re-charged to attack new assignments with renewed vigour, a new sense of patriotism and a broader outlook. This is because of the course content which extends one's horizon and frontiers of knowledge in a manner that one begins to look at national and international problems dispassionately and with patriotism."

Thus, Babangida, after completing his studies, was well prepared to deal with domestic and foreign policy issues and fashion solutions for them. Babandiga himself seemed to have been very aware and appreciative of the impact that the NIPSS had on his life and career. As president, he often visited the NIPSS in Kuru, the "serene village outside Jos, Plateau State," every October to attend the annual graduation ceremony (*Newswatch* 27 November 1989, 15). He was also a very active member of the alumni association. Additionally, during his tenure as the president of the country almost all the key positions in the government, military, intelligence organizations political organizations and police were held by graduates of the NIPSS (*Newswatch* 27 November 1989, 15–19).

The NIPSS, mainly through the policy research and publication activities of its Department of Research, is also a nationally influential think tank. During the Babangida Government numerous government policies were shaped by the institution's policy research outputs (*Newswatch* 27 November 1989, 17). Even the Department of Studies helped to shape public policies. A simulation program, organized by course participants, resulted in a solution that was immediately adopted by the Babangida Government as a way of organizing political parties in the country (*Newswatch* 27 November 1989, 17).

As a group, alumni of the NIPSS were also a major factor in the shaping of public policy during Babangida Government. "The NIPSS alumni association is a powerful union that has the ear of the president and rarely criticizes the administration openly. Twice a year, they meet in audience with the nation's number one citizen and exchange views with him on national questions. According to Ndiomu, 'the president and commander-in-chief pays the NIPSS alumni association a lot of attention. . . .'" (*Newswatch* 27 November 1989, 19). Thus, NIPSS graduates, whether in the public or private sectors, or whether in retirement or not, were able to help shape policies during the Babangida Government.

The knowledge President Babangida himself gained, while a student at the NIPSS, was seen as having direct impact on his policies and techniques of governing the country. According to T. B. Ogundeko (quoted in *Newswatch* 27 November 1989, 17), a retired major-general and the first director-general of the NIPSS, "[W]hen you look at some of the things happening in the Babangida administration . . . I often wonder whether this is not a rub-off on his participation at the NIPSS course because these are some of the issues they discussed thoroughly at syndicates and seminars." Also, according to Chris Okolie (quoted in *Newswatch* 27 November 1989, 17), a journalist, chief executive of his own media organization, and an alumnus of the NIPSS, "the techniques and strategies which Babangida is using to govern Nigeria today are the issues you cover at Kuru." Thus, apart from public policies of the Babangida era, the way the government was organized and how the country was generally governed also benefited from Babangida's educational experience. For example, the way he designed, structured, and operated the Presidency as the powerful fulcrum of national policy and administrative dynamics no doubt benefited from his policy studies education at the NIPSS.

Babangida was often perceived as a very intelligent, shrewd, and deliberate person who thoroughly knew how to manage, control, and use power. These personal traits, in addition to his educational and career backgrounds, helped to shape how Babangida designed, structured, and operated the various organs and units under the Presidency to formulate and implement policies, create and achieve his vision for the country, and govern the country.

While analyzing the structure of local government in the country, Ebo (1989, 127) notes that a governmental structure "is a functional tool designed to cater for the needs and interests set for it by those who designed it." Applying Ebo's logic to the Presidency, it can also be observed that the Presidency is a functional tool designed to serve the needs and interests set for it by the Babangida Government. A government like the Babangida Government, which aimed at making changes at the national, state, and local levels of government, and in the political, economic, and social spheres of the country, needed a structure like the Presidency to generate and implement the many new ideas these numerous changes required.

Changes in a complex society like Nigeria's necessitated some prudence. It has been observed that prudence is "a product of man's rational activity" and "the primary means of directing man to the good of human happiness" (Udoidem 1989, 114). Following this line of reasoning, the changes that the Babangida Government envisaged for the country needed some touch of prudence. The shrewd and tactful Babangida seems to have understood this reality more than most people. For example, when there was widespread public debate about the sort of ideological orientation the country should follow, the Babangida Government set up a Political Bureau to handle this issue (Ogundowole 1989, 87, 95 n. 1). In the end, the Babangida Government was perceived by the public as following policies that were a little bit to the right, and a little bit to the left of the ideological spectrum. Even the two political parties of the Babangida era were seen as representing that "little bit to the right, little bit to the left" profile of ideological orientations.

Babangida's shrewdness and prudence also entailed his respect for the national political consensus on some issues that was achieved during prior governments. He posited that there was "the need to preserve and respect the irreversibility of the wide measure of national consensus in the course of the political evolution of our nation" (Babangida, quoted in Akindele 1990a, 62).

However, Babangida's prudence in some policy areas did not mean that he was hesitant to use power. In fact, he was a master in terms of the management, control, and use of power to effect profound changes. The Presidency was designed, created, and operated in such a way that the seat of national government had adequate power to effect changes. Babangida himself noted that "the history of this country as far as economic development, political development is concerned, we have changed it, it will never remain the same again" (Babangida, quoted in *West Africa* 22–28 February 1993, 285). However, there was widespread public debate over these changes—whether they positively or negatively impacted on the society. There were many who strongly believed that the changes were negative economically, politically, and/or socially, at least in the short term.

Babangida's many initiatives in the domestic policy arena were matched by those in the foreign policy arena. For example, the Babangida Government was the first in the country that formally, and in practice, placed the economic dimensions of Nigerian foreign policy as the foremost aspect of that policy. During the Babangida Government, Nigeria was also involved in numerous peacekeeping operations in Liberia, Somalia, and many other countries. Nigeria was also involved in many other foreign policy initiatives in the west African region, the continent of Africa, and other countries worldwide. President Babangida himself was very much involved in designing, formulating, and/or implementing many of these initiatives. The various organs and units within the Presidency provided the president with the organizational resources he needed to perform these roles in the foreign policy arena.

Some of the important foreign policy initiatives that Nigeria engaged in during the Babangida Government included efforts to encourage faster transition to majority rule in South Africa (which was then under a white minority government) by replacing the policy of total isolation of South Africa with a policy of limited contacts aimed at making the last white minority government speedily and successfully make the transition to a black majority polity) (*West Africa* 25–31 May 1992, 874). Such a fundamental change in the foreign policy of Nigeria, no doubt, involved the change being initiated, or clearly approved, by the president. Another important foreign policy change was Nigeria's renewal of diplomatic ties with Israel (which had been broken off by Nigeria almost twenty years before) (*West Africa* 25–31 May 1992, 874). This was another fundamental foreign policy change that was initiated, or clearly approved, by the president. Alluding to these foreign policy changes, Babangida noted that "Nigeria must continue to remain relevant in the affairs of the world and as long as we want to remain relevant, as long as we want to be seen to play our role, I think we will go the whole hog to discuss and relate with virtually everybody in the world" (Babangida, quoted in *West Africa* 25–31 May 1992, 874)." Babangida added that "[N]ations must adapt to changes or be left behind." These statements clearly show that Babangida himself played a very important role in formulating and implementing these fundamental foreign policy changes.

As noted earlier, the Babangida Government also emphasized the economic components of Nigeria's foreign policy. In analyzing Nigeria's foreign policy during the Babangida Government, it had been observed that Nigeria's "diplomacy was compelled more by economic than political factors. Economic diplomacy, a new trend that emphasized trade not aid, has been pursued with an unwavering zeal since the inception of the Babangida administration" (*West Africa* 25–31 May 1992, 874). The Babangida Government saw the generation of economic growth in the country as one of its major goals. It was thus logical for Babangida to fashion economic diplomacy as the primary focus of Nigeria's diplomatic activities, so as to better harness Nigeria's international economic relations to enhance the country's economic growth. Economic growth was seen as an instrument that could help to lessen Nigeria's dependence on petroleum as its dominant export product. Economic diplomacy was thus seen as an instrument that could help the export of Nigerian manufactured products. This focus was also seen as having the added goal of helping to accelerate industrialization in Nigeria, which would lead to more employment, general economic growth, and a higher standard of living in the country. However, the poor profile and functioning of the country's economy during the Babangida Government meant that the economic diplomatic initiative did not seem to result in any significant improvement. Possibly, a persistent, continuous, and effective emphasis on economic diplomacy by present and future governments in the country will, in the future, bring the economic benefits of this foreign policy approach.

During the Babangida Government, Nigeria contributed most of the military forces that served as peacekeepers in Liberia under the auspices of the Economic Community of West African States (ECOWAS). (The peacekeeping operation in Liberia was organized as ECOWAS Monitoring Group [ECOMOG] force.) This enormous deployment of Nigerian military personnel and hardware in a foreign country with tense and complex internal military conflict meant that Babangida had to be a key player in shaping Nigeria's policy toward Liberia. Nigeria simply saw the situation in Liberia as one in which it had a duty to play a pivotal role (*West Africa* 25–31 May 1992, 874). During the Babangida Government, Nigerian military forces also served as peacekeepers in many other places in the world, including Somalia and Bosnia. Additionally, during this period the Nigerian government also tried to help the opposing political groups in Sudan, Somalia, and Ethiopia to engage in dialogues (*West Africa* 25–31 May 1992, 874).

President Babangida was also very involved in playing his role as the chief diplomat of the country, by visiting many foreign countries and attending many meetings of international organizations. For example, during Babangida's visits to Namibia in 1992, Nigeria established many bilateral agreements (*African Concord* 18 May 1992, 37). Reflecting the Babangida Government's emphasis on economic diplomacy, a significant number of these Nigeria-Namibian bilateral agreements were focused on economic issues, "and a array of Nigerian businessmen" followed Babangida to Namibia as part of the Nigerian official delegation, as noted earlier (*African Concord* 18 May 1992, 37). Babangida's visits to other foreign countries also almost always emphasized economic agreements and also included Nigerian businessmen. While the Nigerian government officials in the delegation were negotiating and concluding economic, political, and cultural agreements with the officials of the host countries, the private businessmen (which were part of Nigeria's official delegation) were negotiating and concluding business deals with the private businessmen of the host country. Thus, President Babangida himself also played a very direct role in helping to implement the Nigerian foreign policy of the primacy of economic diplomacy, which his government designed and formulated.

Babangida also played expansive leadership roles in the west African region and the continent of Africa. For example, he served an unprecedented extended term as chairman of ECOWAS (*African Events* October 1989, 25; *West Africa* 17–23 February 1992, 277). President Babangida also served as the chairman of the Organization of African Unity (OAU) in 1991. He assumed the OAU chairmanship at the OAU Summit he hosted in Abuja, Nigeria (*West Africa* 22–28 June 1992, 1044). The Abuja OAU Summit of 1991 clearly showed Babangida's diplomatic skills. "On the very first day of proceedings, the heads of state signed an historical document: a treaty to establish an African Economic Community (AEC)" (*West Africa* 22–28 June 1992, 1044). The AEC treaty has "the objective of creating an integrated common market" in Africa (*West Africa* 9–15 March 1992, 406). Babangida's diplomatic and organizational skills were also demonstrated by the fact that the summit had "a record attendance of 30 heads of State, 48 foreign ministers and three vice-ministers. Observers enthused that not since the OAU's inaugural summit in 1963 had Africa witnessed such a gathering" (*West Africa* 22–28 June 1992, 1044). In his capacity as the chairman of OAU in 1991, Babangida also used his diplomatic skills in mediation roles to help minimize conflicts in Sudan, Somalia, Rwanda, and Zaire (*West Africa* 26 August–1 September 1991, 1420; *West Africa* 2–8 December 1991, 2003).

As shown above, Babangida took one of his functions (that of the country's chief diplomat) very seriously. In terms of Nigeria's bilateral relations with foreign countries, and in terms of multilateral contexts such as the ECOWAS and the OAU, Babangida played very important leadership roles. He was able to perform his duties as the country's chief diplomat due to the organizational resources that the large and well-organized organs and units of the Presidency provided him (in addition, of course, to the organizational resources of the Ministry of External Affairs and other ministries and agencies).

The Vice President

One of the important units within the Presidency that assisted the president in performing his task in both domestic and foreign affairs was the Office of the Vice President. This office was formally in existence during the third and fourth phases of the Babangida Government (thus, from late August 1990 to August 1993). During the second phase of the Babangida Government (from November 1988 to early August 1990), this office existed as the Office of the Chief of General Staff, within the Presidency. Also, from August 1985 to October 1988 (the first phase of Babangida Government), this office existed as the General Headquarters (and was headed by the chief of general staff). (The General Staff Headquarters was closely linked to, but not formally part of, what was then called the Office of the President, during the first phase of Babangida Government.) However, in reality, the names General Staff Headquarters, the Office of the Chief of General Staff, and the Office of the Vice President refer to one and the same thing. The name changes were merely cosmetic changes. In fact one person (Admiral Augustus Aikhomu) headed this unit, under all its various names, for almost all the Babangida Government period. Ebitu Ukiwe, a commodore of the Nigerian navy (who retired from the navy when he lost his position in 1986) served briefly as the chief of general staff, from August 1985 to October 1986 (*West Africa* 10–16 September 1990, 2434). From October 1986 until the end of the Babangida Government in August 1993, Aikhomu served as the head of that unit. In 1990 he retired from the Nigerian navy but still continued to head this unit. Also in 1990 Aikhomu saw the title of his position change from the chief of general staff to that of the vice president of the Federal Republic of Nigeria. Throughout his tenure, the functions of his unit remained essentially the same; thus, as already noted above, in reality, the names General Headquarters, the Office of the Chief of General Staff, and the Office of the Vice President refer to one and the same thing. Thus, for the purpose of this study, all the various names will be used interchangeably, with the Office of the Vice President being more frequently used.

As noted above, Ebitu Ukiwe, served briefly as chief of general staff from August 1985 to October 1988. In this position, Ukiwe performed the usual role of representing the president in international meetings that the latter was unable to attend—visiting some foreign countries on behalf of the president and receiving some foreign officials and leaders visiting Nigeria. Such functions involved mostly ceremonial, rather than substantive, aspects of foreign relations. In some instances, Ukiwe seems to have been even significantly uninvolved in vital foreign policy issues. For an example, when the controversy over the membership or non-membership of Nigeria in the Organization of Islamic Conference (OIC) first emerged during the Babangida era, Ukiwe did not seem to be involved in the government decision-making dynamics.

On the whole, the briefness of Ukiwe's tenure as chief of general staff, and the fact that his relationship with the president was not cordial, might have accounted for Ukiwe not playing a significant role in the foreign policy decision-making milieu. On the other hand, Ukiwe was comparatively more significantly involved in domestic policy and administration issues.

Admiral Aikhomu, who replaced Ukiwe, and headed that unit from October 1986 until the end of Babangida Government in August 1993 (a very long tenure) seemed to have played a relatively more significant role in foreign affairs. However, just like Ukiwe, Aikhomu's roles had to do more with the ceremonial aspects of foreign relations than with vital foreign policy decision-making dynamics. Nevertheless, his very long tenure in office, and his more cordial relationship with the president, meant that Aikhomu had more to do with some of the substance of foreign policy than did Ukiwe. On the whole, however, Aikhomu too was more involved with domestic policy and administration issues than with foreign affairs.

As noted earlier, the chief of general staff was the new name given to the chief of staff of the Supreme Military Headquarters of the Bahari Government and other prior military governments. Just like the prior chief of staff of the Supreme Military Headquarters, the chief of general staff's main role was that of assisting the president in the governance and administration of the country. Note must be taken of the differences between the role of the chief of general staff and the chief of defense staff. While, as noted above, the chief of general staff was involved in helping the President govern and administer the country, the chief of defense staff coordinated the policies, programs, and operations of the various branches of the military by overseeing and coordinating the activities of the chiefs of staff of the army, navy, and air force. Thus, while the chief of general staff was a senior military officer involved in mostly governmental and political affairs of the country, the chief of defense staff was a senior military officer focusing on purely military affairs. The fact that both the chief of general staff and the chief of defense staff were often very senior and very visible military officers meant that conflicts sometimes developed between the two over the issue of which was the number two person in the country. This conflict was more visible when the chief of general staff had a military rank that was equal to, or lower than, that of the chief of defense staff. It was often perceived that this conflict could be resolved by taking the position that, in terms of political and governmental affairs, the chief of general staff was next in position to the president, while in terms of purely military affairs, the military ranks of the chief of general staff and the chief of defense staff was to determine which of them was next in position to the President—if the two officers had the same military rank, the one with the higher seniority in that military rank was, possibly, to be next in position to the president. However, it does not seem that this logic helped to significantly eliminate the conflict between the chief of general staff and the chief of defense staff when Ebitu Ukiwe was the chief of general staff. As a commodore of the navy, Ukiwe had a lower military rank than the chief of defense staff and some other military officers, and this contributed to conflicts between Ukiwe and higher-ranking senior military officers. When Ukiwe left the position of the chief of general staff in 1986 (*West Africa* 10–16 September 1990, 2434), he was replaced by Augustus Aikhomu, who at that time had the rank of rear admiral in the navy (*Newswatch Who's Who In Nigeria* 1990, 91–92). Aikhomu's military rank and personality helped him to have a more cordial relationship with other senior military officers. (Later, in 1990, Aikhomu retired from the navy with the rank of admiral.)

As noted earlier, the Office of the Chief of General Staff became a part of the Presidency in 1988 (*West Africa* 17–23 October 1988, 1967). According to the official document that announced the changes in relations to the Presidency, including the Office of the Chief of General Staff being made part of that office, "all staff working in the new Presidency will be treated as people working for a single organization regardless of the different units. . . . Efforts are being made to bring most of the units of The Presidency under one roof as a means of fostering a sense of belonging and promoting the organic unity of the new system" (a government circular, quoted in *West Africa* 17–23 October 1988, 1967). Thus, from 1988, Aikhomu and his Office of the Chief of General Staff were organically part of the Presidency. This meant that the Office of the Chief of General Staff became more directly linked with assisting the president in policy-making and administration, in terms of both domestic and foreign affairs.

On various occasions, the Babangida Government, formally stated the duties of the Office of the Chief of General Staff and other important official units and officials of the federal government. Such efforts were made, for example, in 1986 (*Thisweek* 20 October 1986, 18) and in 1989 (*Sunday Times* 23 April 1989, 1, 8). At both times the Office of the Chief of General Staff was in charge of such matters as administration of the various states of the federation, relations between and among the states in the federation, national policy guidelines on local government administration, appointments to the boards of the companies and corporations owned by the federal government, military liaison, and relations with the Public Complaints Commission, the National Population Commission, the Code of Conduct Bureau, the Nigerian Institute of Social and Economic Studies (NISER), the National Institute of Policy and Strategic Studies (NIPSS), and the Nigerian Institute of International Affairs (NIIA) (*Sunday Times* 23 April 1989, 1, 8; *Thisweek* 20 October 1986, 18). The powers of the Office of the Chief of General Staff (which were inherited by the Office of the Vice President), as shown by the above list of its duties, were enormous.

These duties show that the Office of the Vice President was the most important office within the Presidency, helping the President to govern and administer the country.

As also indicated by the list of functions noted above, some of the most important functions of the Office of the Vice President had to do with the management of intergovernmental relations in the federal system. The functions of the Office of the Vice President in these areas were the formulation, implementation, and evaluation of policies of the federal government toward the state and local governments. Thus, during the Babangida Government, the governors, officials, and governments of the various states, and the officials of the local government areas, related with the federal government through the Office of the Vice President. These responsibilities meant that in the three-tier federal system of the country (national, state, and local), the Office of the Vice President was mostly overseeing two tiers (state and local) for the Presidency. Thus, the Office of the Vice President was mostly directly in charge of managing the country's federal system of government for the Presidency: the heavy weight of these responsibilities made the office one of the most important units of the Presidency.

Obviously, the functions of the Office of the Vice President that were focused on overseeing the state and local governments for the Presidency were primarily related to domestic affairs. Most of the issues that the governors, officials, and governments of the states and officials of the local governments handled with the Office of the Vice President related to the federal government revenue allocations to state and local governments; guidelines for implementation of new policies (in terms of the roles of state and local governments in the implementation of the policies); inputs of state and/or local officials in relation to the formulation of new policies by the federal government; resolution of conflicts between or among states relating to boundaries, use of natural resources such as rivers that span more than one state, and other issues; resolution of conflicts relating to the proper roles of federal, state, and local governments; and roles and activities of federal ministries, agencies, institutions, and projects in the various states and local government areas. All these were issues of domestic policy and affairs.

However, as noted earlier, the overseeing of state and local government affairs for the Presidency by the Office of the Vice President also involved some foreign affairs issues. Many states and numerous local government areas of the country have common boundaries with foreign countries. A good number of these international boundaries have boundary dispute issues that often lead to tensions and conflicts. Whenever tensions or conflicts flare up, state governors and local officials (especially the state governors) liaise with the federal government to manage, minimize, and if possible resolve them. It is the Office of the Vice President that state governors first contact for the activation and/or coordination of the relevant federal ministries and agencies (for example, the Ministries of External Affairs and Defense). Thus, international boundary tensions often meant the Office of the Vice President being one of the major units of the Presidency helping to channel the input of the governor to the relevant ministries or agencies for the formulation of policies and actions for the management of the international boundary tensions and conflicts. Even during periods of calm and peace (which is more the norm) state and local officials often try to have input into the policies and actions of the Nigerian police force, the Immigration Department, the Customs Service, the air force, the navy, and the army (all federal government agencies and organs) in order to have adequate international border defense, effect safe movement of peoples and goods across the borders, and enhance international peace, tranquility, cooperation, and economic growth in the border areas. Sometimes, when state and local officials perceived that certain of these federal units were not cooperating with them to achieve the above goals, these state and local officials tried to influence the actions of these federal units by liaising with their head offices through the Office of the Vice President. In such cases, again the Office of the Vice President played a role in international affairs.

Some governors of states that share some of their boundaries with foreign countries like to visit the adjacent provinces of these neighboring countries and also host return visits in order to promote and enhance international peace and cooperation in the border areas. Since the Office of the Vice President oversaw the state governments, it was often the first point of contact for state governors who wished the cooperation of the Ministry of External Affairs and other federal ministries and agencies to facilitate their visits to neighboring countries and the hosting of visiting leaders. The role of the Office of the Vice President in this area also involved it in international affairs.

Many state governments sometimes developed contacts with foreign countries for purposes of international economic relations (for example, the promotion of foreign investments) or international cultural relations and with international organizations for the purpose of international cooperation development projects. Again, some of these international linkages involved the state governments liaising with and working through the Office of the Vice President.

All this involvement by the Office of the Vice President in matters related to international affairs meant, expectably, Vice President Aikhomu's involvement. During the Babangida Government, as noted earlier, Aikhomu headed the General Headquarters from 1986 to 1988, then became the head of the Office of the Chief of General Staff (within the

Presidency), and, then, later headed the Office of the Vice President (also within the Presidency).) The similar functions of the General Headquarters, the Office of the Chief of General Staff, and the Office of the Vice President can be shown by the fact that the foundation for a significant role in international affairs was even laid by the General Headquarters. For example, Nwoke (1990, 484) notes the significant (though mainly administrative) role of the General Headquarters in the decision-making processes that led to the formation of the African Petroleum Producers' Association (APPA), a grouping of important African petroleum producing countries. The Ministries of Petroleum Resources and External Affairs were said to have "informed General Headquarters at every stage in the decision process," and later, the president, the Council of Ministers, and the Ministry of Petroleum Resources made the decision that Nigeria should initiate the formation of APPA. In this context, the General Headquarters displayed the coordinating and administrative aspects of its functions (which spanned both domestic and foreign affairs) in helping the president and the national leadership in the decision-making system. The succeeding Offices of the Chief of General Staff and of the Vice President also had these coordinating and administrative aspects of their functions.

As noted earlier, Aikhomu, as the chief of general staff and later as vice president, visited foreign countries on behalf of the president. In this role he made some significant impact on international affairs. For example, his visit to Jamaica in 1989 helped to strengthen the relationship between that country and Nigeria (*The Jamaican Weekly Gleaner*) 7 August 1989, 14; *The Jamaican Weekly Gleaner* 14 August 1989, 25, 28). Many substantive Nigerian foreign policy goals were achieved during Aikhomu's visit to Jamaica. In a press conference there, Aikhomu noted that his visit had resulted in the government of Jamaica deciding to establish a foreign mission in Nigeria (an action that, Aikhomu noted, was very much needed since Nigeria had operated a foreign mission in Jamaica since 1974) (*The Jamaican Weekly Gleaner* 14 August 1989, 25). During Aikhoma's visit the government of Jamaica also announced that a former Jamaican minister of Foreign Affairs had been appointed to serve as the first Jamaican envoy to Nigeria, and the Jamaican-Nigerian Society was also launched in Jamaica (*The Jamaican Weekly Gleaner* 14 August 1989, 25). The fact that a former minister of Foreign Affairs was appointed to serve as the envoy showed that Jamaica regarded its relationship with Nigeria as very important. Aikhomu also used the occasion of his visit to seek Jamaica's support for the candidacy of Emeka Anyaoku (a Nigerian diplomat) for the position of the secretary-general of the Commonwealth of Nations (*The Jamaican Weekly Gleaner* 14 August 1989, 28). With the support of Jamaica and many other countries, Anyaoku won the position. Nigeria and Jamaica also signed a cultural and educational agreement, and Aikhomu also "said that a Nigerian trade and investment commission would be coming to Jamaica either this month or in September. Stating that he did not wish that visit to be an example of diplomatic rhetoric, he said, we want that visit to produce concrete results' (*The Jamaican Weekly Gleaner* 14 August 1989, 25). As shown by all the above diplomatic actions and initiatives taken during Aikhomu's visit to Jamaica, the visits of the vice president to foreign countries were sometimes important and significant occasions in terms of Nigerian foreign policy goals and objectives.

Even during the fourth (final and transitional) phase of the Babangida Government, the Office of the Vice President was still significant in foreign affairs. During the fourth phase, the Presidency (note that the Office of the Vice President was within the Presidency) as noted earlier, was to be replaced by the Transitional Council for the day-to-day governance of the country (*West Africa* 25–31 January 1993, 112). The Transitional Council oversaw the "political, economic, administrative and diplomatic matters," though, however, the members of the Transitional Council were "more or less answerable" to the National Defense and Security Council (NDSC) and the Presidency (Babangida, quoted in *West Africa* 25–31 January 1993, 112). Despite this changed situation, the Office of the Vice President was still somehow significant in the policy decision-making system, including the foreign policy decision-making system. For example, Aikhomu and secretary of external affairs, Matthew Mbu (a member of the Transitional Council) visited Cote d'Ivoire to reassure the government of that country of Nigeria's goodwill and friendship after a Nigerian air force plane serving with the ECOMOG (Economic Community of West African States' Monitoring Group) peacekeeping forces in Liberia mistakenly bombed a village in Cote d'Ivoire (*West Africa* 15–21 March 1993, 429).

Thus, it can be stated that the Office of the Vice President (like its predecessors the General Headquarters and the Office of the Chief of General Staff), which was within the Presidency, helped the Presidency to manage and/or coordinate foreign affairs throughout all the phases of the Babangida Government.

The Office of the Secretary to the Federal Government

The Office of the Secretary to the Federal Government was another important unit within the Presidency (*West Africa* 17–23 October 1988, 1967). The functions of this unit were varied and wide-ranging. Specifically, they included

> substantive issues of policy design, policy implementation and policy coordination as well as management of The Presidency.
> He [the Secretary] is also to manage such other Departments and Offices as, the Council Secretariat(s), Economic, Special Services and General Services

Department, as well as the Political Affairs, Planning, Research Statistics and Public Service Departments.

The Secretary is also to ensure effective monitoring and follow-up actions on the implementation of government decision and policies, by federal ministries and other Federal Government agencies, and is also in charge of Tribunal and other Commissions of Enquiry.

Other areas of the secretary's vast sphere of jurisdiction include the channelling of papers and directives of the President, awards of titles and honors and decorations, liaison with secretaries to state governments, control of common vote, and relations with the Judiciary, MAMSER, DFRRI, National Electoral Commission (NEC) and the Public Accounts Committee (PAC).

The Secretary's other duties include arranging meetings of Armed Forces Ruling Council (AFRC), National Council of State and National Council of ministers and ensuring that the conclusions of the meetings are produced and duly circulated to members of the respective councils.

He is also to ensure that council decisions are conveyed to the persons or authorities. (*Sunday Times* 23 April 1989, 1, 8)

The above duties of the secretary to the Federal Government were actually one of the lists of duties that the Babangida Government formally assigned to units within the Presidency and to other organs of the government. As shown by the above numerous and important duties, the Office of the Secretary to the Federal Government seemed to have been the main coordinating unit within the Presidency. Also, as specifically stated, the Office of the Secretary of the Federal Government was charged with the management of the Presidency. Though none of the listed duties directly and primarily focused on foreign affairs, obviously the numerous important roles it performed within the Presidency put the Office of the Secretary to the Federal Government in a position to exert some impact on foreign affairs (though, probably, mostly indirectly). The Presidency was the pivot of the national decision-making system, in terms of both domestic and foreign affairs. The mere fact that the Office of the Secretary to the Federal Government was the unit that coordinated and managed the Presidency itself made that office play some role in foreign affairs. For example, some of the duties of the Office of the Secretary to the Federal Government were the handling of substantive issues of policy design, policy implementation, and policy coordination in both domestic and foreign affairs.

The Office of the Secretary to the Federal Government monitored and supervised the implementation of government decisions and policies, of all federal government ministries, agencies and organs. Since these included the Ministries of External Affairs and Defense, as well as numerous other ministries and agencies that had something to do with the country's international relations, the Office of the Secretary to the Federal Government exerted significant influence in the foreign policy milieu, since it had the responsibility to decide how and when decisions and policies were to be implemented, and also whether or not they had been properly and effectively implemented.

Another set of the above listed duties of the Office of the Secretary to the Federal Government was the channeling of papers to the president, and the channeling of the directives from the president to various ministries, agencies, and organs of the government. By being in charge of the information that traveled to and from the president, the Office of the Secretary to the Federal Government was able to help shape policies in both domestic and foreign affairs. As commonly observed, information is power.

Another set of the above list of duties of the Office of the Secretary to the Federal Government had to do with the functioning of the major national policy decision-making bodies. The Office of the Secretary to the Federal Government was in charge of arranging the meetings of the Armed Forces Ruling Council (AFRC) (the highest policy-making body during the Babangida Government), the National Council of States (NCS), and the National Council of Ministers (NCM); producing and circulating the conclusions reached at the meetings of each of these three bodies to their respective members; and ensuring that the decisions of these three bodies were conveyed to the appropriate ministries, agencies, and individuals who were to implement the decisions. These duties gave the Office of the Secretary to the Federal Government control over another set of vital information (and thus more power and of influence) in terms of both domestic and foreign affairs.

As all the above sets of lists of duties show, the Office of the Secretary to the Federal Government had roles in coordinating and managing the Presidency that gave it much influence within the Presidency and in the government as a whole, and thus it had great opportunity to influence and shape both domestic and foreign policies.

The Office of the Minister for Special Duties

The reorganization of the Office of the President into the Presidency in 1988 also made the Office of the Minister for Special Duties become a part of the Presidency (*West Africa* 17–23 October 1988, 1967). The minister for Special Duties was a cabinet level official who was not in charge of any particular ministry but was assigned by the president to handle task forces, projects, policies, and programs as the need arose. These might have been in an area of domestic or foreign affairs that the Presidency believed required urgent and effective actions. By placing the Office of the Minister for Special Duties within the Presidency, the Babangida Government made it possible for the Presidency to closely monitor and supervise how urgent and effective actions were being taken in domestic and foreign policy issues that were very important to the government. Additionally, the fact that the minister for Special Duties was a cabinet-level official made it easier for him or her to elicit the cooperation of other cabinet-level ministers and heads of agencies.

The Office of the National Security Adviser

The Office of the National Security Adviser was another significant unit within the Presidency. Peters (1986, 156, 157) has noted that, during the Shagari Government, the Office of the National Security Adviser did not exert significant impact in the policy milieu. During the Babangida Government (just as during the Buhari Government), one can posit that the Office of the National Security Adviser continued to maintain a low profile (though this image did not mean that it did not exert significant impact in the policy milieu). The Office of the National Security Adviser seems to have been mostly a unit within the Presidency that coordinated the purely security organs of government that reported directly to the Presidency. The role of the Ministry of External Affairs in the area of foreign affairs, and the role of the Ministry of Defence in the area of military affairs, were never perceived by the public as being encroached upon by the Office of the National Security Adviser. This was due to the fact that the Office of the National Security Adviser, as noted above, focused mainly on its role within the Presidency in coordinating the security organs of Government which directly reported to the Presidency. The fact that those who served as National Security Advisers often seemed to be technocrats and career officials who had earlier served in security-related organs of the Government, rather than visible national political leaders with broad national political bases, might have also contributed to the Office of the National Security Adviser not being able to compete with the political leaders who were key officials in the foreign policy decision-making system. However, though the Office of the National Security Adviser was not operating as a major unit that helped to shape and fashion foreign policy, its role in coordinating the security organs that reported directly to the Presidency meant that it was in a position to provide information and data that were vital for both domestic and foreign policy formulation. It was as a provider of information, then, rather than as a decision-making unit, that the Office of the National Security Adviser contributed to foreign policy.

The Offices of the Presidential Special Advisers and Assistants

The Presidency during the Babangida Government also had many presidential special advisers and presidential special assistants. These special advisers and assistants were often intellectuals from academia. Within the

Presidency, they help to design, formulate, coordinate, implement, and evaluate policies in specific areas in both domestic and foreign affairs. The availability of these presidential special advisers and presidential special assistants, who were ready to be assigned to tackle any domestic or foreign policy issues, meant that the Presidency possessed additional powerful policy instruments. For example, G. Aforka Nweke, a noted political scientist, served as a special assistant to the Presidential Advisory Committee, a unit within the Presidency (Olusanya and Akindele 1990, xv). As academics who were often experts in various disciplines, these special advisers and special assistants provided the Presidency with acute intellectual minds used to help tackle important foreign policy issues (and, even more visibly, domestic policy issues).

The Cabinet Office

Before 1988, the Cabinet Office of the federal government existed as a separate organ and served as a unit for the coordination of the policy and administrative processes of the federal government. In 1988, "[T]he various departments of what used to be called the Cabinet Office" became part of the Presidency (*West Africa* 17–23 October 1988, 1967). The Cabinet Office departments coming under the umbrella of the Presidency provided the latter with resources that to strengthened its role as the fulcrum and nerve center of national policy and administrative processes for both domestic and foreign affairs.

The Presidency in Action

The units of the Presidency analyzed above, in addition to some others, constituted a huge organizational resource that made the Presidency a well-equipped machine for the coordination, management, and direction of policies in both the domestic and foreign policy spheres. The Office of the Vice President, the Office of the Secretary to the Federal Government, the Office of the Minister for Special Duties, the Office of the National Security Adviser, the Offices of the Presidential Special Advisers and Assistants, departments of the Cabinet Office, and other units within the Presidency constituted an awesome resource for the President.

The entire Presidency itself was designed, structured, and operated in such a way as to optimize its resources. For example, as noted earlier, all the personnel working for the Presidency were "treated as people working for a single organization regardless of the location of the different units," and efforts were exerted "to bring most of the units of The Presidency under one roof as a means of fostering a sense of belonging and promoting the organic unity of" the Presidency (a government document, quoted in *West Africa* 17–23 October 1988, 1967).

In terms of foreign policy decision-making dynamics, the policy coordination, management, and direction roles of the Presidency were very important, since many ministries, agencies and organs of the government often had overlapping roles in the area of foreign policy. The Office of the President (which was later reorganized and expanded into the larger, more effectively staffed body called the Presidency) established a good foundation for an effective foreign policy decision-making system. For example, in 1986 the minister of External Affairs, together with the Office of the President, decided that Nigeria would boycott the 1986 Commonwealth of Nations Games in Edinburgh to show Nigeria's displeasure that two South African athletes (now residents of the United Kingdom) were included in the United Kingdom's team, despite the fact that the international sporting community barred the participation of the then apartheid South Africa in international sporting events) (Olukoshi 1990b, 466–78). Professor Bolaji Akinyemi, the Minister of External Affairs, instructed the Policy Planning Unit of the Ministry of External Affairs to study the Edinburgh Games issue and prepare a case for the boycott (Olukoshi 1990b, 471). Thereafter, "Akinyemi, whose Policy Planning Unit had written a position paper arguing the case for a Nigerian boycott of Edinburgh," approached the president to discuss the Nigerian boycott.

According to Olukoshi (1990b, 472), "Akinyemi put across the case for a speedy decision in the knowledge that there were sections of the establishment that were opposed to the line of action recommended by" the Ministry of External Affairs. These sections of the establishment might have been those organs of the government that were focused on sports policies and programs, but the Ministry of External Affairs and the Office of the President were the only organs of government that were involved in the decision-making that led to the boycott of the Edinburgh Games. Interestingly, the Federal Ministry of Youth and Sports (FMYS), the Nigerian National Olympic Committee (NOC), and the National Sports Commission (NSC) (which, while the Ministry of External Affairs and the Office of the President were engaged in boycott discussions, were busy training Nigerian athletes for the Edinburgh Games) only heard about the boycott decision after it was leaked to a Lagos-based newspaper (Olukoshi 1990b, 472–73). The officials of the FMYS, NOC, and NSC, confused, protesting, and furious, phoned the chief press secretary to the president to ascertain the accuracy of the media report, and got the confirmation that the Games boycott decision had been taken (Olukoshi 1990b, 472–73). Considering the negative reactions of the FMYS, NOC, and NSC to the news, there is a possibility that the Office of the President and the Ministry of External Affairs purposely excluded them from the decision-making process in order to ensure that a boycott decision could be reached. The FMYS openly "protested vigorously at the failure of the MEA to consult with its officials prior to recommending a boycott" (Olukoshi 1990b, 473) to the Office of the President. There is a possibility that if the Office of the President and the MEA had included the FMYS, NOC, and NCS in the decision-making processes, the decision to boycott the Games might not have been taken, or at least might have been delayed through a deadlock.

It also seems that within the Office of the President, only the relevant policy units were involved with the Games issue. Despite the fact that officials of the MEA visited the Office of the President on several occasions to discuss the Games issues, interestingly the chief press secretary to the president was not aware of the boycott decision and only learned about it when the newspaper published it. "[T]he Chief Press Secretary to the President, Duro Onabule, upon reading the story in *The Guardian* on 9 July, 1986, went to the President, incredulous, to hear from him. General Babangida confirmed that a boycott decision had indeed been taken" (Olukoshi 1990b, 473). After this confirmation from the president, Onabule was able to brief officials of the FMYS, NOC, and NSC and others who telephoned to inquire about the news in *The Guardian* (Olukoshi 1990b, 473). The fact that the Office of the President kept the chief press secretary to the president uninformed about the boycott decision indicates the delicate nature of the Edinburgh Games issue decision-making process.

Nigeria was the first country to withdraw from the 1986 Commonwealth Games (Olukoshi 1990b, 473). This Nigerian action led to one of "the most successful sports boycotts in recent times" (Olukoshi 1990b, 473), since Nigeria's lead "was soon followed by many other Commonwealth countries in Africa, the Caribbean and the Pacific" (Olukoshi 1990b, 471). Essentially, Nigeria told the world that its boycott of the Edinburgh Games was its way of fighting against the apartheid system then current in South Africa (Olukoshi 1990b, 475).

When Akinyemi was the minister of External Affairs, his ministry proposed and designed the Technical Aid Corps (TAC) program, which sponsors and sends Nigerian doctors, nurses, teachers, engineers, architects, and other professionals as volunteers to work for two years in African, Caribbean, and Pacific countries, as a form of assistance to fellow developing countries. The Office of the President worked with the Ministry of External Affairs to bring the TAC program to fruition. In 1987, the president announced the establishment of the TAC program, which involved Nigeria paying for the salaries and traveling costs of the volunteer professionals (*West Africa* 17–23 February 1992, 277). The TAC program has been very successful and other developing countries are planning to follow Nigeria's example (*Newswatch* 9 April 1990, 16). For example, "Indonesia, warming up to start a voluntary service scheme like TAC, has invited Nigerian officials to share their experience with them," and "South

Korea, too, has started the programme following the Nigerian initiative" (*Newswatch* 9 April 1990, 16).

As noted earlier, another foreign policy issue that much involved the Office of the President was the issue of Nigeria's membership or nonmembership in the Organization of Islamic Conference (OIC). In 1986, the Office of the President decided to send a Nigerian delegation to an OIC meeting in Fez, Morocco (a delegation meant to operate as a full member of the OIC, (not as an observer), despite the fact that, when the Office of the President asked for the view of the Ministry of External Affairs on the OIC issue, the ministry advised against sending a participating delegation (Olukoshi 1990a, 495–97). In 1991 the president announced that Nigeria was not a member of the OIC (*West Africa* 3–9 June 1991, 913) and that Nigeria had suspended its OIC membership (*West Africa* 26 August–1 September 1991, 1420). However, the issue of Nigeria's membership or nonmembership appears to have remained a puzzle during the Babangida era (*West Africa* 23 December 1991–5 January 1992, 2163). Nonetheless, as shown above, in terms of the OIC issue the Office of the President was totally in charge.

After the Office of the President was reorganized, expanded, and transformed into a bigger outfit called the Presidency, the roles of the coordination, management, and direction of the foreign policy decision-making system were emanating even more vigorously from the nerve center of the federal government. One persistent foreign policy issue during the Babangida era was the border dispute issue with neighboring Cameroun (*West Africa* 6–12 January 1992, 36–37; *West Africa* 17–23 August 1992, 1409). Due to the fact that this sort of border dispute was bound to involve numerous Nigerian government organs, the Presidency had to play a very significant role in coordinating, managing, and directing the foreign policy decision-making system. Specifically, the Presidency had to coordinate, manage, and direct the roles of the Ministry of External Affairs, the Ministry of Defense (specifically the army, navy, and air force units in the border areas), the police force, the Customs Services, the Immigration Department, and other federal government organs involved in the handling of the border dispute. Additionally, the Presidency had to coordinate, manage, and direct the statements, policies, and actions of the state governments and local governments in the border dispute area in such a way that they would enhance (rather than hinder) the efforts of the federal Government to manage and/or resolve the border dispute.

As noted earlier, during the Babangida Government Nigeria played a pivotal role in the formation of the African Petroleum Producers' Association (APPA). The Ministry of Petroleum Resources and the Nigerian National Petroleum Corporation (NNPC) "were at the center of policy activities, with the active cooperation of the Ministry of National Planning and the Ministry of External Affairs' Multilateral Economic Department" (Nwoke 1990, 484). All the above organs administratively informed the General Headquarters of every stage in the decision processes, and in the end (with the minister of Petroleum Resources having convinced the government to approve the formation of APPA) the President, through the Council of Ministers, gave "[T]he final decision for Nigeria to initiate the formation of APPA" (Nwoke 1990, 484). In this particular case, the relevant ministries and units were more active, while the president's role was more passive. However, though the ministries and other units mostly designed and formulated the policy for the formation of APPA, it was the president who gave the final approval, and this action resulted in Nigeria leading other African petroleum producing countries in the formation of this common forum in 1987. One of APPA's major goals was the provision of a forum for African countries that belonged to OPEC, to attempt to harmonize their positions and thereby present a united front in OPEC meetings.

During the fourth (the final and transitional) phase of the Babangida Government, as noted earlier, the Presidency was still a significant factor in the coordination, management, and direction of the foreign policy decision-making system even though the Transitional Council was in charge of "day to day governance of the country," including the overseeing of "political, economic, administrative and diplomatic matters" (*West Africa* 25–31 January 1993, 112). For example, as noted earlier, the vice president (who was part of the Presidency) and the secretary of External Affairs (who was part of the Transitional Council) comprised the delegation Nigeria sent to Cote d'Ivoire to smooth things out with that country after a Nigerian air force aircraft mistakenly bombed a village in Cote d'Ivoire (*West Africa* 15–21 March 1993, 429). The fact that the vice president had to accompany the secretary of External Affairs on this mission shows that, during the fourth phase of the Babangida Government, the Presidency was still a major factor in the coordination, management, and direction of the foreign policy decision-making system, even though the Presidency was sharing these roles with the Transitional Council.

The Ministry of External Affairs

Although the Presidency coordinated, managed, and/or directed the foreign policy decision-making system and many ministries and other organs of government were involved in various aspects of Nigeria's international relations, the Ministry of External Affairs (MEA) was the main organ that was charged with the management of most aspects of Nigeria's international relations. Additionally, while the Presidency, the various ministries, and other organs of government dealt with domestic and foreign affairs, the MEA was unique in that its functions solely focused on Nigeria's foreign affairs. Thus, the MEA is often the major element in the foreign policy decision-making system. While the national policy decision-making nerve center (which during the Babangida Government was called the Presidency) is always the organ that oversees the foreign policy decision-making system and makes the final decisions on major foreign policy issues, the MEA manages most of the routine aspects of Nigeria's international relations and also implements most of the foreign policy decisions that have been made.

The Ministry of External Affairs was renamed the Ministry of Foreign Affairs towards the end of the Babangida Government (*West Africa* 6–12 January 1992, 37). However, due to the fact that during most governmental eras and, specifically, during most of the Babangida era, the name Ministry of External Affairs (MEA) has often been used for this ministry, that name is used for this study.

In various governmental eras, the nature and extent of the major role that the MEA plays in the foreign policy decision-making system depends on its effectiveness in the foreign policy decision-making milieu. Factors that determine the MEA's effectiveness are the nature of its leadership, organization, staff, functioning, relations with other governmental organs, and policy outputs.

The structure and organization of the MEA during the Babangida Government was both sophisticated and complex. As noted by Ofoegbu (1990, 94–99), the professionalization of all the federal ministries also meant the reorganization and professionalization of the MEA. Additionally, the 1988 reorganization of the MEA also reflected the "new economic orientation of the country's foreign policy" (Ofoegbu 1990, 94). This emphasis on the economic component of Nigerian foreign policy was "a deliberate effort to move away from the over preoccupation by earlier regimes on political issues to those who will support the rejuvenation of our national economy," and thus, aim "to achieve a happy balance between its political and economic content" (Major-General Ike Nwachukwu, the minister of External Affairs, quoted in Ofoegbu 1990, 94).

At the head of the organizational structure of the MEA was the Office of the Minister. In accordance with the 1988 Civil Service reform of the ministries, the Office of the Minister represented both the political and administrative leadership of MEA, since the minister was both the chief executive and the chief accounting officer of the ministry (Dlakwa 1992, 302). Some of the major units that were attached to the Office of the Minister were the Technical Aid Corps (TAC), the Public Relations unit, and the Foreign Service Academy. The TAC was the international assistance and cooperation program, noted earlier, which supplies Nigerian volunteer doctors, nurses, architects, teachers, and other professionals to work in many countries in Africa, the Caribbean, and the Pacific. The Public Relations unit handles public relations for the MEA. The Foreign Service Academy is the in-house academic institution of the MEA that provides professional diplomatic studies and training programs to the officials of the MEA.

The Office of the Minister consisted of seasoned officials who served as assistants and advisers to the minister. These advisers and assistants assisted the ministers in performing the task of policy design, policy planning, policy implementation, policy evaluation, management, and coordination of the MEA. During the Babangida Government, the first person to serve as the minister of External Affairs was Bolaji Akinyemi, a professor of political science and a noted international relations scholar who was also a former director-general of the Nigerian Institute of International Affairs (NIIA). Akinyemi was succeeded by Ike Nwachukwu, a major-general in the Nigerian army. Nwachukwu was, in turn, succeeded by Rilwanu Lukman, a mining engineer who had earlier served, at various periods, as the minister of Mines, Power, and Steel and minister of Petroleum Resources (*Newswatch Who's Who in Nigeria* 1990, 440). Interestingly, Lukman was succeeded by Nwachukwu, who thus served twice as the minister of External Affairs, probably because he was perceived as the major champion of the primacy of the economic components of Nigerian foreign policy, a position supported by the Babangida Government. Nwachukwu (after his second tenure) was succeeded by M. T. Mbu, a lawyer and a noted national politician who had served as a diplomat and as a minister in various ministries during the Balewa Government (*Newswatch Who's Who in Nigeria* 1990, 458–59). Mbu was the last person to head this ministry during the Babangida Government. As noted by the backgrounds of Akinyemi, Nwachukwu, Lukman, and Mbu, the MEA of the Babangida Government had ministers with strong policy-making, political, and leadership abilities.

During the Babangida Government, the MEA also contained the Office of the Minister of State (Ofoegbu 1990, 94). The minister of State was the junior minister in the MEA.

In accordance with the 1988 civil service reform, like all the federal ministries the MEA had a director-general who assisted the minister of External Affairs in managing the ministry. The civil service reform also required the ministries to be divided into only eight departments, but allowed the MEA to be subdivided into 10 departments, "in order to accommodate especially the Ministry's new thrusts in areas of international economic cooperation, as well as policy planning, research and statistics" (Ofoegbu 1990, 94). These departments were headed by directors who were the most senior career diplomats and officials in the MEA.

According to the 1988 civil service reform, the minister and the director-general of each ministry were to be political appointees, while the directors were to be career officials (Dlakwa 1992, 301–2). Thus, the highest position that any career official in the ministries could reach was that of the director (Dlakwa 1992, 302).

As the main organizational components of the MEA, the 10 departments carried out the functions of this ministry, and thus as the heads of the departments, the directors were the primary officials in charge of the main functions of the MEA, under the supervision and direction of the minister and the director-general. According to the 1988 civil service reform, the internal structure and organization of the departments in each ministry, including the MEA, were as follows: the departments were subdivided into divisions (headed by deputy directors), the divisions subdivided into branches (headed by assistant directors), the branches subdivided into sections (headed by chief officers), and the sections subdivided into other lower units (headed, in descending order, by assistant chief officers, principal officers, senior officers, officer I, and officer II) (Dlakwa 1992, 302, 304). However, while the MEA had internal units so designated, its professional diplomatic officials had universal diplomatic ranks or titles of ambassadors, ministers, minister-counselors, first secretaries, second secretaries, third secretaries, attachés, etc.

The ten departments of the MEA were the Planning, Research, and Statistics Department; the Finance and Supplies Department; the Personnel and Management Department; the Consular and Legal Department; the Regions Department; the African Affairs Department; the International Economic Cooperation Department; the International Organizations Department; the Protocol and Legal Department; and the Inspectorate Department (Ofoegbu 1990, 94–96). A closer examination of the departments reveals both the orientation and major dynamics of the MEA during the Babangida Government. The first three departments (Planning, Research, and Statistics; Finance and Supplies, and Personnel and Management) were mandated by the 1988 civil service reform for all ministries for the performance of basic staff functions, while the remaining seven were charged with basic line functions (Dlakwa 1992, 303). The Inspectorate Department had the task of ensuring that all the departments performed their functions effectively and efficiently. The Protocol and Legal Department, as the name connotes, handled protocol and related legal issues. The Consular and Legal Department likewise handled consular affairs and legal affairs. This departments was subdivided into the Consular Division, the Education Division, and the Legal Division (Ofoegbu 1990, 95). The International Organizations Department seems to have focused mainly on United Nations affairs, since it was subdivided into First United Nations Division and Second United Nations Division. As will be shown below, the Organization of African Unity (OAU) affairs and the Economic Community of West African States (ECOWAS) affairs were under the African Affairs Department. (ECOWAS affairs also came under the International Economic Cooperation Department [Ofoegbu 1990, 96].)

One of the most prominent departments of the MEA was the International Economic Cooperation Department, because the Babangida Government emphasized the economic components of Nigerian foreign policy (in the belief that such an emphasis would help build a strong, modern, and industrialized economy, which would help Nigeria become a major actor in the international community with a strong foreign policy posture. The department was subdivided into the Multilateral Economic Cooperation Division (MECD), the Bilateral Economic Cooperation Division (BECD), and the Trade and Investment Promotion Division (TIPD) (Ofoegbu 1990, 95–96). The MECD was in charge of the affairs of the United Nations Conference on Trade and Development (UNCTAD), the Group of 77, the International Monetary Fund (IMF), the World Bank, the General Agreement on Tariffs and Trade (GATT), and the ECOWAS (Ofoegbu 1990, 96). BECD seems to have been the workhorse of this department. Describing the functions of BECD during the Babangida Government, Ofoegbu (1990, 96) observed it

> handles technical and economic matters such as loans, aid, dormant bilateral agreements which the Department is also obligated to push to new heights. The new Directorate is to promote exports generally and, in particular, in the ECOWAS and the rest of Africa. It is expected to do this in various ways, especially by working jointly and in collaboration with the Ministries of Trade, Commerce, Industries, Immigration and Customs; by collaborating intimately with Bankers, Manufacturers Association of Nigeria (MAN), Chambers of Commerce, and Exporters Association; by judging the performance of Nigerian Diplomatic Missions in respect of their ability to attract new money, promote exports; and expand Nigeria's access to new technology; and by devising a strategy of realistic cooperation with the industrialized countries, South-South cooperation with other developing countries and an export oriented growth and development.

While the BECD focused on economic, trade, and investments relations on a bilateral basis, the TIPD focused on trade and investments activities and relations generally.

The African Affairs Department supervised and coordinated the activities of Nigerian diplomatic missions accredited to countries in Africa and handled inter-African affairs OAU affairs and ECOWAS affairs. The department was subdivided into the Inter-African (OAU) Division, the West African (ECOWAS) Division, the North Africa and Horn of Africa Division, and the East, Central, and Southern Africa Division (Ofoegbu 1990, 95). The Regions Department supervised and coordinated the activities of Nigerian diplomatic missions accredited to countries in the Americas, Asia, and Europe. This department was subdivided into the America Division, the Asia and Pacific Division, and the Europe Division (Ofoegbu 1990, 95). The very fact that Nigerian diplomatic missions in countries in Africa (one continent) had a department to themselves alone (the African Affairs Department), while the Nigerian diplomatic missions in other continents—Asia, Australia and the Pacific, Europe, North America, and South America—all shared just one department (the Regions Department) meant that the Babangida Government, like all other governments starting from the Muhammed/Obasanjo era, placed Africa as the centerpiece of Nigeria's foreign policy.

The continuous physical presence and impacts of the MEA in many foreign countries is through the Nigerian diplomatic missions (embassies) in those countries. These Nigerian embassies represent the continuous and regular instruments of Nigerian foreign policy in the countries in which they are located. During the Babangida Government, as noted above, the MEA mainly supervised and coordinated these embassies through the divisions within the African Affairs Department and the Regions Department. Within the above divisions there were country desks that handled matters relating to particular countries or particular groups of countries.

The prominence of the economic components of Nigerian foreign policy during the Babangida Government also affected the structure and functioning of the Nigerian diplomatic missions. The economic/commercial units of the diplomatic missions saw an increase in staff and resources. As noted earlier, Nigerian diplomatic missions during the Babangida Government were evaluated in terms of the amount and quality of economic and trade relations between Nigeria and the host country. Thus, the efficiency and effectiveness of each diplomatic mission were to a great extent judged on how well it helped to increase Nigeria's international economic relations (Ofoegbu 1990, 96). Thus, every Nigerian Ambassador and his/her entire embassy staff (both economic/commercial staff and noneconomic and noncommercial staff) worked harder to promote the economic components of Nigerian foreign policy.

The 1988 civil service reform was one of the most important things that happened to the MEA and other ministries, in terms of their structures and functioning, during the Babangida Government. Apart from the streamlining of the organizational structure of the MEA, reform also "granted the Ministry of External Affairs and other Ministries the autonomy to choose, recruit, train, promote and discipline their staff" (Ofoegbu 1990, 84). Before the reform, the Federal Public Service Commission directed and supervised these areas (Ofoegbu 1990, 84). This increased control over its staff meant that the MEA had more power to motivate its staff and to foster organizational values and orientations aimed at enhancing the efficiency, effectiveness, and attainment of the goals of the MEA.

As noted earlier, the minister of External Affairs headed the MEA, with the minister of state for External Affairs (a junior minister) also helping to provide the leadership for the ministry (Ofoegbu 1990, 95). Both these ministers were political appointees. However, some scholars, like Akindele (1990e, 535), seem not to have been very satisfied with the existence of the position of the minister of state for External Affairs during the Babangida Government, perhaps because the minister had "some specific responsibilities clearly assigned to him" (Akindele 1990e, 535). Additionally, Akindele notes that during the Balewa Government (which had two cabinet level ministers heading the MEA) and the Shagari Government (which had a minister of External Affairs and two ministers of state for External Affairs heading the MEA), there were significant conflicts between or among the minister of External Affairs and the minister(s) of state for External Affairs (Akindele 1990e, 535). This "dual or multiple leadership" of the MEA during the Babangida Government, Shagari Government, and Balewa Government contrasted with the streamlined "single-leadership" of the MEA during the Gowon Government, Muhammed/Obasanjo Government, and Buhari Government (Akindele 1990e, 535).

However, it must be noted that though the minister of state for External Affairs during the Babangida Government was assigned some specific responsibilities, this did not lead to very serious conflicts between him and the minister of External Affairs. The absence of such conflicts, most probably, was due to the high caliber of the persons who served as the ministers of External Affairs.

As noted earlier, those who served as the minister of External Affairs were Bolaji Akinyemi, Ike Nwachukwu (he served twice, before and after Lukman's tenure, Rilwanu Lukman, and Matthew Mbu.

As noted earlier, Akinyemi came to the MEA with a stellar academic background (both in theoretical and applied terms). He brought into office his background as a professor of political science with specialization and numerous publications in the area of international relations. He also had the experience of director-generalship of the NIIA. Naturally, as most academics, Akinyemi was a man who constantly generated new ideas for the MEA to develop, enact, and implement. However, the MEA was an institution mostly inhabited by cautious career diplomats who were, expectably, not very receptive to the idea of numerous bold and sweeping policy initiatives and changes. This factor, in addition to Akinyemi's somewhat direct, assertive, and intense personality made his tenure at the MEA sometimes frictional (Ate 1990, 447–65). Ate (1990, 452 has also noted that

Foreign Minister Akinyemi had a great deal of difficulty with the top echelon of the Foreign Ministry for a number of reasons. First, his initial contact with top officials of the Ministry, according to inside sources, was characterized by extreme hostility. He made his entry to the Ministry in the manner of an adversary entering a hostile territory. The ground for this initial adversarial encounter had been well prepared because of the totally inexplicable rivalry between the MEA and NIIA which reached its nadir at the time of Akinyemi's Director-generalship of the latter institution. But Akinyemi could have shorn his NIIA garb and mended fences on appointment to his new role, but did not. He had gone to the Ministry to 'do battle' with the old guard, in the words of his closest associates. Thus, he failed to portray himself as team member in an established institution. He consequently encouraged the perception among the senior staff of the institution which regarded him as an "outside", worse an upstart, in the practical world of foreign policy.

Apart from senior career foreign service officers, Akinyemi also managed to clash with some senior ambassadors who were political appointees. "Never afraid to spoil for war," Akinyemi clashed with some of these politically appointed senior ambassadors "who chose to side-step normal diplomatic channels by dealing directly with the" power center of the federal government at Dodan Barracks (*African Concord* 6 August 1990, 15). "One of those who found it difficult to deal with Akinyemi was Joe Garba," a retired Nigerian army major general and a former minister of External Affairs, who as the ambassador to the United Nations was "reprimanded for insubordination to Akinyemi by the director-general of the External Affairs ministry" (*African Concord* 6 August 1990, 15).

Given his intense and combative nature, Akinyemi was bent on realizing his goals as the minister, despite opposition to many of his bold foreign policy initiatives. Thanks to his persistence, some of them, like the Technical Aid Corps (TAC) program, have now become a very successful part of the country's foreign policy (*Newswatch* 9 April 1990, 16–17). His other bold foreign policy initiatives included the All-Nigeria Conference on Foreign Policy (a very visible national conference that allowed various individuals and groups in the general public of the country to make inputs into the foreign-policy decision-making milieu) and the Concert of Medium Power initiatives (which attempted to create an organization for medium-powers countries from all continents) (Ate 1990, 453). While the All-Nigeria Conference on Foreign Policy was successful, the Concert of Medium Power initiatives have so far not fully materialized.

Despite the resistance of the senior career officials of the MEA to him and his numerous new and bold foreign policy initiatives, Akinyemi was able to successfully create the TAC, convene the All-Nigerian Conference on Foreign Policy, and also carry out other initiatives and actions, due to new sources of support he created for himself within the MEA. Most of the new sources of support were erected by him around his immediate office and the Policy Planning Department of the MEA. According to Ate (1990, 452), Akinyemi used "the agency of his Special Assistants to mobilize a coterie of supportive staff made up of a number of young and intellectually agile officers mainly in the Policy Planning Department. This 'inner group' became the moving force in its ardent enthusiasm to advance the Minister's policy ideas." The "inner policy organ" mentioned above was a group that prominently featured "Mr. Olusegun Apata (then Acting Director, Policy Planning Department); Mr. Olufemi George (then Acting Deputy Director, Policy Planning Department), two Special Assistants to the Honorable Minister and the Minister himself as the team leader" (Ate 1990, 459–60). The members of this "inner group," who were young foreign service officers, were rewarded by Akinyemi "with choice postings" to the country's diplomatic missions abroad, "while the old guard protested," since "they were assigned to obscure" and undesirable diplomatic missions (Ate 1990, 452–53).

On the whole, Akinyemi, through persistence and his combativeness, was able to realize many of his goals, though his tenure at the MEA was somewhat frictional. In evaluating his own tenure long after he left the position, Professor Akinyemi, notes that "people cannot conceive that I have always been and I am still a nationalist with a capital N. I put Nigeria and Africa first, middle and last" (Akinyemi quoted in *African Concord* 6 August 1990, 15). He also adds that "It was a marvelous experience. I learnt a lot. It is the dream of every academic to be given an opportunity to practicalise his ideas. I am satisfied that I proved that my ideas could work. Some of them have brought fruits like the Technical Aid Scheme. I don't need to defend my period as External Affairs Minister, time would judge" (Akinyemi, quoted in *African Concord* 10 September 1990, 33).

Ike Nwachuckwu, who succeeded Akinyemi, was a Nigerian army major general. His calm and moderate leadership style contrasted with that of Akinyemi and also caused fewer problems with the senior career foreign service officers. His statement that "Foreign policy is based on principles and not expediency" (Nwachukwu, quoted in *West Africa* 5–11 September 1988, 1644) in a way crystallized his worldview, leadership style, and temperament.

His calm profile in no way meant he was not active as the minister for External Affairs. For example, he moved swiftly and effectively to smooth relations with the Republic of Equatorial Guinea and succeeded in making that country expel South African nationals (when the apartheid system still operated in South Africa)(*West Africa* 18–24 September, 1575). Additionally, he was the moving force behind the ascendancy of the economic components of the country's foreign policy. The prominence of the economic dimension of the country's foreign policy was the direct extension of the economic reforms of the Babangida Government aimed at revitalizing the country's economy (*West Africa* 9–15 October 1989, 1679). In recognition of Nwachukwu's role in the prominence of economic diplomacy during the Babangida Government, he has been referred to as "the main architect of the policy" (*West Africa* 9–15 October 1989, 1679). It has also been noted that when "he took over in 1987 . . . he chose a mercantile approach to foreign policy. According to him, his economic diplomacy was to help facilitate support measures with the international system for Nigeria's domestic economic policy and to harmonize the Babangida administration's domestic and foreign policy goals. The realization of this saw him on visits to 20 countries spanning three continents" (*African Concord* 17 September 1990, 12).

After two years as the minister of External Affairs, Major-General Ike Nwachukwu went back to the Nigerian army to handle a field military command position. Rilwanu Lukman succeeded him. As noted earlier, Lukman was a mining engineer who had earlier served, at various periods, as the minister of Mines, Power, and Steel and the minister of Petroleum Resources. Thus, Lukman brought to the job of Minister of External Affairs broad national policy-making experience. On the whole, Lukman seemed to have been a non-flamboyant technocrat, efficient and effective in the details of national policy-making. Lukman's tenure as minister of External Affairs was brief. Interestingly, as also noted earlier, he was replaced by the person whom he had succeeded in that position, Ike Nwachukwu. The key role Nwachukwu played in enthroning the prominence of the economic components of the country's foreign policy made the Babangida Government (which gave top priority to economic reforms and growth in the country) reappoint him (*African Concord* 17 September 1990, 12). The "charm, charisma and eloquence which he brought to" the position during his first tenure also made him welcome to return (an unnamed top government official quoted in *African Concord* 17 September 1990, 12). Professor Jide Oshuntokun, who was the special adviser to Nwachukwu during the latter's first tenure as minister of External Affairs, also noted that "[W]ithout being immodest, I can say Nwachukwu's tenure as Minister between December 1987 and December 1989 was about the best. He concentrated on making new friends for the country. His return is a tribute to his impressive credentials gained over that two-year period" (Oshuntokun, quoted in *African Concord* 17 September 1990, 12).

Nwachukwu was succeeded by M. T. Mbu, a lawyer and longstanding prominent national politician who had served as a diplomat and as a minister in various ministries during the Balewa Government. His long experience in the field of diplomacy made Mbu feel at home at the MEA. However, the fact that he served during the fourth (final and transitional) phase of the Babangida Government meant that his tenure was a period mostly focusing on the managing of ongoing foreign policies, rather than a period of initiating bold and new foreign policies.

On the whole, the MEA had varied and able leaders as ministers during the Babangida Government. Akinyemi brought numerous bold new foreign policy ideas and initiatives and fought gallantly to implement them. Nwachukwu, with his charisma, calm, eloquence, efficiency, and effectiveness, made economic components of the country's foreign policy prominent. Lukman gave the MEA his technocratic and efficient leadership. Finally, Mbu brought to the MEA a wealth of experience in the fields of diplomacy and national policy affairs. Thus, the MEA was provided with capable and effective leadership that allowed it to play its role as the main machinery for the management of the country's international relations.

This continuous effective leadership enabled the MEA to engage in numerous diplomatic offensives, for example, launching skilled and experienced Nigerians to prominent leadership positions in many international organizations (and thus share the skills and capabilities of these Nigerians with the international community). When Perez de Cueller left the position of the secretary-general of the United Nations, Nigeria promoted the candidacy of Olusegun Obasanjo (a former Nigerian head of state and a retired army general). However, the position went instead to Boutros Boutros-Ghali of Egypt. Nigeria also vigorously promoted the candidacy of Emeka Anyaoku for the secretary-generalship of the Commonwealth of Nations, and the candidacy of Joseph Garba (a retired army major general and then Nigerian ambassador to the United Nations) for a term as the president of the United Nations General Assembly (*African Events* October 1989, 25). Both candidates won (see *West Africa* 8–14 April 1991, 517; *West Africa* 7–13 November 1994, 1910). These diplomatic successes were due to the MEA deploying the diplomatic resources of its Office of the Minister, its senior officials, and Nigerian diplomatic missions abroad to effectively promote the candidacies of Anyaoku and Garba. That the MEA also worked closely with the Presidency to vigorously promote these two candidates worldwide also helped them to win the positions.

Also during the Babangida Government, Nigeria started to lay the foundations for the promotion of its candidacy as a permanent member of the Security Council of the United Nations. During the Babangida Government, Boutros Boutros-Ghali, the secretary-general of the United Nations, "proposed the inclusion of Nigeria, Germany, Japan, India and Brazil in an enlarged security council so as to reflect the global realities of the moment" (*West Africa* 23–29 March 1992, 513). However, it has been noted that, though not impossible, Nigeria being able to gain a permanent seat in the Security Council of the United Nations is "going to be a difficult objective to achieve," since the current five permanent members of the council "are far from enthusiastic about the idea at the present time" (*West Africa* 23–29 March 1992, 513).

Diplomatic offensives such as those noted above and other, more regular and routine diplomatic activities in the economic, political, cultural, and security areas, were effected through the proper and effective functioning of the decision-making processes of the MEA. Ofoegbu (1990, 101) superbly analyzes the decision-making processes of the MEA by noting that

> the Ministry of External Affairs has remained the principal state machinery for making and implementing foreign policy. Draft foreign policies are made in the Ministry of External Affairs after (a) extensive discussions and analysis of study reports, ideas and suggestions which might have originated from individuals, leaders or groups; (b) research and findings undertaken by the Nigerian Institute of International Affairs, the Nigerian Political Science Association or the National Institute of Policy and Strategic Studies; and (c) constant External Affairs review of embassy reports and recommendations which come in individually or from area conferences, or from joint conferences and seminars of Nigerian Ambassadors and High Commissioners with their counterparts in the Ministry of External Affairs.

Ofoegbu (1990, 98–102) additionally notes that the MEA also got foreign policy inputs from the Presidency, and even important elements in the general public, during the Babangida Government. In terms of inputs from the public, Ike Nwachukwu, as a minister of External Affairs (just as Joseph Garba as the commissioner of External Affairs during the Muhammed/Obasanjo Government did in Kaduna) invited the country's foreign policy elites to Lagos "to a review of the country's foreign policy. . . . [c]onfidence was shared, research findings and recommendations were also shared and criticized and, more especially, the content and conduct of foreign policy were subjected to informed criticisms" (Ofoegbu 1990, 99, 101). As can be imagined, this meeting provided Nwachukwu with new foreign policy ideas and insights that helped him, and senior officials of the MEA, to develop and manage the country's foreign relations. Also, as noted earlier, when Akinyemi was the minister of External Affairs, he organized the 1986 All-Nigerian Conference on Foreign Policy in Kuru (K. O. Mbadiwe, as adviser on African Affairs to the prime minister during the Balewa Government, organized the first such conference) to allow a broad section of the public (interest groups, civic leaders, academics, civic groups, etc.), to make foreign policy inputs that the MEA could use to improve the country's foreign relations (Ofoegbu 1990, 99, 101–2).

As shown above, the MEA had decision-making processes and foreign policy inputs dynamics that gave it the capacity to function adequately as the main machinery for the management of the country's foreign relations.

However, during the Babangida Government there were some few foreign policy issues in which the role of the MEA was constrained. The issue of Nigeria's membership or nonmembership in the Organization of Islamic Conference (OIC) was one such issues, as noted earlier. This was a foreign policy issue that had a very strong link with the country's domestic realities, as it concerned the nationally sensitive issue of religion. The OIC issue touched on the question of the nature and profile of the country as a secular entity. It also related to the relative impacts of Islam and Christianity (the two major religions in the country), and on the nature of relations between Muslims and Christians in the country. Perhaps because of the strong impact the OIC issue had on the country's domestic sociopolitical dynamics and stability, the power center of the federal government, as represented by Dodan Barracks, played the major role in this issue. An analysis of the country's decision-making processes in this issue (Olukoshi 1990a, 495–97) clearly shows these roles of Dodan Barracks and the MEA. For example, according to Olukoshi (1990a, 495):

> Dodan Barracks, in a memorandum to the MEA, the second of its type on the subject, sought the advice of the Ministry on the issue of whether Nigeria should or should not become a full member of the OIC.
> In a reply to the Dodan Barracks' memorandum, the MEA in a submission signed by the then External Affairs Minister, Professor Bolaji Akinyemi, argued against full membership and argued that the country's observer status in the OIC should be retained. Akinyemi quoted copiously from the earlier submission on the subject by his predecessor, Ibrahim Gambari, to General Buhari. Dodan Barracks was, however, not swayed by Akinyemi's submission.

As noted earlier, despite the opposition of the MEA, in 1986 a Nigerian delegation attended an OIC meeting in Fez, Morocco, as a full member (instead of as an observer, as previously, and as recommended by the MEA) (Olukoshi 1990a, 495–97). However, due to the serious controversy over the OIC issue, the status of Nigeria in relation to the OIC became very unclear. Twice in 1991, President Babangida noted that the country was not a member of the OIC (*West Africa* 3–9 June 1991, 913; *West Africa* 26 August–1 September 1991, 1420). The contentious nature of the OIC, however, meant that throughout the Babangida era the issue of the country's membership or nonmembership in the OIC seemed to have remained an unending puzzle (*West Africa* 23 December 1991–5 January 1992, 2163).

In the case just described, the role of the MEA was clearly subsidiary, probably because of the extremely sensitive nature of the issue on the domestic front. This might have accounted for Dodan Barracks playing the premier role. Such a situation, however, was more the exception than the rule: during the Babangida Government, the MEA played a central part in most foreign policy issues. For example, during the 1991–1992 period that President Babangida was the chairman of the Organization of African Unit (OAU) (*West Africa* 26 August–1 September 1991, 1420; *West Africa* 2–8 December 1991, 2003; *West Africa* 22–28 June 1992, 1044) the MEA human and material resources both in Lagos and in Nigerian diplomatic missions abroad were deployed in full gear in order to enable the president to carry out the function of the OAU chairmanship. As the chairman of the OAU, President Babangida had to articulate the interests of Africa in the international community, coordinate OAU activities, be a premier agent in intra-African affairs, help to mediate and manage conflicts in the continent, and engage in international visits in order to carry out these other functions. In order for Babangida to perform these roles, the MEA had to be very active in providing the necessary diplomatic resources, while also maintaining contacts with the OAU secretariat at Addis Ababa, Ethiopia. A centerpiece of Babangida's OAU chairmanship was the 1991 OAU Summit, in Abuja, Nigeria, which produced "the treaty establishing the African Economic Community, with the objective of creating an integrated common market" (*West Africa* 9–15 March 1992, 406). This sort of productive summit which involved the logistics of planning and managing a meeting of heads of state and/or governments and ministers of over 50 countries, meant that the MEA did a very good job.

During the Babangida Government, the country's external publicity and information activities substantially increased. This increase was linked, in a way, with the economic goals and reforms of the Babangida Government. The more deregulated economy of the country during that era saw some increase in Nigeria's non-petroleum sector exports (especially the export of manufactured goods), the increased modernization and industrialization of the economy, and the attraction of more foreign investments into the economy. Adequate international publicity and information about the country in general, and about the country's economic dynamics in particlar, helped to enhance the economic growth and reforms policies of the government.

As during previous governments, the function of handling the country's external publicity and information activities was mostly in the hands of the Federal Ministry of Information (FMOI) and not the MEA. However, many of the activities of the FMOI require that the two work together. As can be expected, such relations between two large established organizations are not always smooth. The MEA often perceives the role of the FMOI in the country's external publicity and information activities as the latter's encroachment into an area that the former often feels it is more competent to handle. The FMOI, in turn, often believes that as it is the ministry that is charged with information activities, all such information activities belong to it.

One of the areas in which the MEA and FMOI must cooperate is the information and cultural functions of the country's diplomatic missions abroad. The FMOI often seconds officials to Nigerian diplomatic missions to work as information attachés. During their tours of duty in the diplomatic missions, the FMOI officials, who are the information attachés, are working under MEA officials, who are the ambassadors and other grades of foreign service officers. As noted earlier for previous eras, the relations between the information attachés and the other members of the diplomatic missions is not always smooth. In some major countries of the world, the FMOI even operates a relatively autonomous outfit called Nigeria Information Service Centers (NISC) to handle Nigeria's external publicity and information activities. In these countries, the diplomatic missions often think that the FMOI officials (manning the NISCs are improperly autonomous, while the FMOI officials believe they need such relative autonomy in order to perform their jobs well. Nevertheless, the NISCs and the diplomatic missions have to maintain some significant links. One such link is in the area of financial matters. Since the diplomatic mission is seen as leading the country's foreign mission team in any country, it is often expected to come to the financial rescue of any Nigerian Government outfit in such particular countries. However, it seems that the MEA, (through its Nigerian Diplomatic Missions) used this financial role during the Babangida Government to show its displeasure with the FMOI over the latter's role in the external publicity and information area. In 1990, it was observed that

> ideally, if the centers should run into financial trouble, they can and should be bailed out by the Ministry of External Affairs (MEA). However, the matter is not as simple as that. MEA is often reluctant to come to the rescue of NISCs. It was, and probably remains apprehensive of the entire NISC idea, contending that the external publicity work is something it has facilities to absorb. It sought to show that it was better equipped (given its experience in external relations, privileged access to information on foreign policy goals and objectives, wide diplomatic contacts and experience, and access to intelligence) to handle external publicity; that conversely, without these strategic resources the ministry of information (MOI) was handicapped in this particular area and could even prove to be counter-productive.
>
> Thus, the MEA has always sought to co-opt the NISCs. It tried to direct their operations. In fact, initially, the external publicity personnel had worked out of the various embassies, and had had their subventions tied to embassies' funds. Worse still, their status was rendered far too inferior to that of external affairs officers. (*The African Guardian* 16 April 1990, 12)

As shown above, during the Babangida Government, as during previous governments, the MEA was not averse to making life sometimes uncomfortable for the FMOI. However, it seems that the Babangida Government did attempt to ameliorate the situation. For example, it was noted that "most of the friction" between the MEA and FMOI "had been removed. The external publicity personnel now carry diplomatic passport and are operationally independent" (*The African Guardian* 16 April 1990, 12). Interestingly, this government's way of resolving the problem between the MEA and FMOI seems to have involved FMOI officials having more autonomy, rather than emphasizing how MEA officials and FMOI officials, located in the same host country, should learn to work together. The government's solution was unsatisfactory, in that the autonomy given to the FMOI did not appear to be complete: the problem persisted between the MEA and FMOI. It was observed that "the remaining source of dispute is the question of what role, if any, MEA should play, in the first instance, should it become absolutely necessary for the NISCs to be bailed out financially, pending action from Lagos. MOI is under no illusion that the red tape permeating the funds remittance process will be minimized or eliminated soon, and has been trying to get MEA to agree to act as some kind of guarantor. The response has not been positive" (*The African Guardian* 16 April 1990, 12). The fact the government was not able to make these two ministries smooth over their perennial problem shows that, as in previous governments, the ministries still exerted their skills in protecting their turfs very well during the Babangida Government.

Despite this, the external publicity and information activities during the Babangida Government were vigorous. This government, particularly, prominently used advertisements and information inserts in major magazines and newspapers in some foreign countries (see, for example, *Newsweek* [Washington, D.C. edition] 2 September 1991 [a special 32-page advertising section placed after page 50 and before 51] and *Ebony* February 1990, 184–95). These special advertising inserts mostly focused on the changing economic profile and dynamics in Nigeria—thus buttressing the view that the country's external publicity and information activities served to advance the economic components of Nigeria's foreign policy and the general economic growth policies of the Babangida Government).

Though the FMOI mostly handled external publicity and information activities, including the advertisement activities noted above, MEA officials of the diplomatic missions, through the normal course of their diplomatic activities, contributed to the provision of information about the country in foreign countries. For example, Professor Adebowale Adefuye, as the Nigerian envoy in Jamaica, greatly enhanced the image of Nigeria in Jamaica through his excellent manner in relating to the public, media, and government officials in that country and thus, increased contacts between the two countries in political, economic, and cultural spheres (see, for example, *The Jamaican Weekly Gleaner Monday, 23 January 1989, 9; The Jamaican Weekly Gleaner Monday, 9 October 1989, 9; West Africa* 8–14

April 1991, 517). Later, as a deputy envoy to the United Kingdom, Adefuye sometimes even wrote articles in news magazines to highlight Nigeria's role in the international community (see, for example, Adefuye 1992).

Sometimes, even news items in foreign media sources seemed to relate to Nigeria foreign relations goals and external publicity goals. For example, in the early part of 1993, Jesse Jackson (a prominent United States political leader) noted in a U.S. news program (Cable News Network) that he had written the secretary of state of the United States advising a meeting between the president of the United States, Bill Clinton, and President Ibrahim Babangida of Nigeria (see *West Africa* 24–30 May 1993, 872). Though such a meeting did not occur, the news item was the kind of external publicity that might have been in line with the sort of international action Nigeria might have been wishing for.

Apart from the FMOI and MEA, other ministries and agencies helped to provide information about some aspects of Nigeria through their officials posted abroad. For example, the Nigerian Universities Commission (NUC), through officials posted to some Nigerian diplomatic missions, provides information about Nigerian universities as part of the function of its overseas representation. Thus, on the whole, though the FMOI was the main organ handling the country's external publicity and information activities, other government ministries and agencies also helped in this endeavor.

The Babangida Government seems to have also been formulating and/or implementing new strategies for the country's external image. It was noted the "Government is said to be putting together an international lobby for the express purpose of protecting Nigeria's image abroad. It will comprise of Nigerians as well as foreigners with interests in Nigeria' " (*West Africa* 24–30 May 1993, 873). Additionally "the nitty-gritty of the Nigerian lobby's brief will include monitoring foreign media reports on Nigeria and Nigerians as well as official thinking and attitude in the major world capitals" (*West Africa* 24–30 May 1993, 873). Interestingly, this *West Africa* magazine news item quoted officials of both the MEA and FMOI, meaning, very possibly, that the formulation and/or implementation of this new initiative on external publicity and lobbying were done by both the MEA and FMOI. This means that, during the Babangida Government, the two ministries could, in some instances, work well together.

The Technical Aid Corp (TAC) program was another important foreign policy initiative established by the Babangida Government. As noted earlier, this is a program through which Nigerian doctors, nurses, engineers, architects, teachers, lawyers, and other professionals are sent to work in countries in Africa, the Caribbean, and the Pacific for two years, and the federal government of Nigeria pays their salaries and traveling expenses

(Adefuye 1992, 276–77; *Newswatch* 9 April 1990, 16–17; *West Africa* 17–23 October 1988, 1967). The TAC is an international technical assistance program designed to provide help to other developing countries and enhance south-south global relations. Additionally, by providing Nigerian professionals, the TAC, also helps provide Nigeria with a positive image in the host countries where the program operates. Adefuye (1992, 277) has also noted that the TAC program "has been described by the *Gleaner* newspaper of Jamaica as a good example of South-South cooperation." Further explaining the rationale behind the TAC program, he adds that "Nigeria is admittedly a developing country but the rationale behind the scheme is best explained by a Yoruba adage which says that if you can afford only two meals a day and your brothers cannot afford any, it behoves you as your brother's keeper to share part of the two meals with them.'" In evaluating the TAC program, Adefuye continues: "the success of the scheme and the good will it has generated arising from the positive impact it makes on the manpower requirements of the receiving countries may well make the scheme one of the most enduring foreign policy legacies of the Babangida Government." Additionally, as noted earlier, the success of the TAC prompted Indonesia to request Nigeria's help in designing a similar program, and South Korea is also following the Nigerian example (*Newswatch* 9 April 1990, 17).

Since the TAC wholly managed and operated by the MEA, the success of the program also means the success of the ministry as an effective organization. The fact that the TAC program was placed as a unit within the Office of the Minister in the organizational structure of the MEA (Ofoegbu 1990, 95) meant that it received the attention and supervision of the highest office within the MEA. Additionally, the TAC unit was directly managed by an MEA official with an ambassadorial rank (*Newswatch* 9 April 1990, 16). The program was thus provided with the organizational structures, resources, and processes that enabled it to be managed and operated very successfully.

The decision-making processes that resulted in the Nigerian boycott of the 1986 Edinburgh Commonwealth Games, noted earlier, is another case that provides a very ample view of the profile, functioning, and impact of the MEA in the foreign policy decision-making milieu. The fact that the list of British athletes for the 1986 Edinburgh Commonwealth Games contained the name of British residents who were born in South Africa (a country then excluded from most international athletic competition due to the apartheid policy it subscribed to at that time) greatly displeased Nigeria and many other countries (Olukoshi 1990b, 471). The minister of External Affairs during that period, Akinyemi, requested the Policy Planning Unit of the MEA to study the course of action Nigeria should take. The Policy Planning Unit wrote "a position paper arguing the case for a Nigerian boycott of" the Commonwealth Games. After Akinyemi and President Babangida had discussed the Commonwealth Games issue a couple of times, on one occasion, "the President asked Akinyemi to submit a memorandum to his office on the matter. Akinyemi promptly sent a paper to the President's office in which he strongly recommended boycott as the most effective weapon available to Nigeria" (Olukoshi 1990b, 472).

> Although General Babangida gave what an MEA source described as an "implied endorsement" of Akinyemi's recommendation of a boycott action, there was concern in Dodan Barracks that the issue should not be rushed as the situation needed to be studied carefully to ensure that there was broad support in the Commonwealth for the Nigerian move. Yet in the view of MEA, there was a limit to which the country could delay action as time was not on Nigeria's side since the Games date was fast approaching. Akinyemi put across the case for a speedy decision in the knowledge that there were sections of the establishment that were opposed to the line of action recommended by MEA. The Ministry, however, took comfort in the fact that public opinion on the matter as expressed in various newspaper articles, was strongly on the side of a Nigerian boycott. . . .
>
> On the morning of Tuesday, 8 July, 1986, Akinyemi went to Dodan Barracks to hold further discussions on the Edinburgh Games with General Babangida. It was on that day that the President gave his firm endorsement of the MEA proposal for a boycott. The External Affairs Minister returned to his Ministry where he summoned a meeting of his top aides and announced the President's final approval of a Nigerian boycott of the Games. He discussed with them the appropriate time when the Nigerian decision should be announced to the public, the objective being to derive the maximum effect possible. (Olukoshi 1990b, 472)

However, the news of the Nigerian boycott of the Games was leaked to a Lagos newspaper, which published it on 9 July 1986, and this development led to the government confirming on that day that Nigeria had decided to boycott the Games (Olukoshi 1990b, 473). This leakage to the press, interestingly, actually was positive for Nigeria, as it led to Nigeria being the first to announce its boycott "and thus leading one of the most successful sports boycott in recent times," since "the days that followed saw many more countries following the Nigerian lead" (Olukoshi 1990b, 473).

As noted earlier in this study, the Federal Ministry of Youth and Sports (FMYS), the Nigerian National Olympic Committee (NOC), and the National Sports Commission (NSC) (which, as the government organs mainly responsible for sports activities, were directly in charge of Nigeria's participation in international sports events like the Commonwealth Games) were excluded from the decision-making processes that led to the Nigerian boycott; these organs only heard about the boycott when the Lagos newspaper published news about it (Olukoshi 1990b, 472–73). In fact, while the

Office of the President and the MEA were discussing the boycott, and even after they had arrived at their decision, these organs "went ahead with preparations for sending a Nigerian team on the assumption that the country will participate in the Games" (Olukoshi 1990b, 472). The fact that the MEA was able to exclude the FMYS, NOC, and NSC from the decision-making processes shows the dominant role it is often able to play in foreign policy decision-making milieus. Specifically, the MEA engineered the exclusion of the sports organizaitons out of fear that they would succeed in blocking efforts to boycott the Games. Furthermore, the MEA lobbied the Office of the President for a speedy boycott decision to avoid a delay allowing the FMYS, NOC, and/or NSC to later enter the decision-making processes and block the Games boycott decision being made. Not surprisingly, the FMYS, NOC, and NSC were openly displeased by this incident.

While the MEA took center stage in some foreign policy decision-making areas, like the 1986 Edinburgh Commonwealth Games decision-making analyzed above, its roles in other areas, like the decision-making processes associated with the formation of the African Petroleum Producers' Association (APPA), were in the periphery of the policy process, as also noted earlier. The Ministry of Petroleum Resources and the Nigerian National Petroleum Corporation (NNPC) "were at the center of policy activities," while the Ministry of National Planning and the Multilateral Economic Department of the MEA provided "active cooperation" (Nwoke 1990, 484). The very fact that the country's international petroleum affairs, such as those relating to OPEC, have been always mostly handled by the Ministry of Petroleum Resources, with the NNPC assisting with technical information and resources, meant that these two organizations were able to be at the center stage of the decision-making processes associated with the formation of the APPA, while organs like the MEA were at the periphery. The technical nature of petroleum international affairs meetings also meant that the Ministry of Petroleum Resources and the NNPC were better equipped than the MEA to play central roles in the decision-making processes associated with the formation of APPA.

In a few foreign policy decision-making areas during the Babangida Government, the role of the MEA was even insignificant. As noted earlier, the decision-making processes associated with the issue of Nigeria's membership or nonmembership in the Organization of Islamic Conference (OIC) was one such policy area (Olukoshi 1990a, 488–504). Despite the fact that the MEA advised Dodan Barracks against Nigeria attending the 1986 OIC meeting in Fez, Morocco, as a full member (but supported Nigeria continuing the tradition of attending OIC meetings in an observer status), Dodan Barracks sent a Nigerian delegation that had a full member status (Olukoshi 1990a, 495–97). Thus, the MEA's position on the OIC was totally ignored. As also noted earlier in this study, the sensitive nature of the OIC issue (in the sense that it related seriously to domestic sociopolitical stability—specifically, to the delicate issue of relations between Christians and Muslims in the country and the profile of Nigeria as a secular country) might have made Dodan Barracks take full charge of the OIC issue.

However, it is important to note that in most foreign policy issues during the Babangida Government, the MEA played a dominant or significant role; the OIC case was an exception rather than the rule for the MEA.

In numerous countries of the world, Nigerian diplomatic missions operate as the organs of the MEA. Since the MEA is the main machinery for the management of the country's international affairs, diplomatic missions are very important parts of the MEA. Thus, in order to have a more adequate understanding of the structure and functioning of the MEA, the structure and functioning of some diplomatic missions are also examined.

Expectably, an officer of the rank of ambassador heads a Nigerian diplomatic mission. Such a person may be a political appointee or a career external affairs officer. The structure of a particular diplomatic mission depends on the size of the mission, which, in turn, depends on the level of activities and importance of mission.

As noted earlier, the ranks of the external affairs officers below the ambassadors are, in descending order: minister, minister-counselor, counselor, first secretary, second secretary, and third secretary (and below the rank of the third secretary, other MEA officials in the missions include administrative attachés, financial attachés, and communications officers) (Akindele and Olusola 1990, 133). The political, economic, cultural, managerial, and consular functions of the embassies are mostly assigned to the ministers, minister-counselors, counselors, first secretaries, second secretaries, and third secretaries, while the administrative attachés obviously concentrate on technical administrative duties (Akindele and Olusola 1990, 132–38). The financial attachés handle financial, accounting, and auditing functions of an embassy, while the communications officers are in charge of an embassy's radio and communication links to other parts of the world (Akindele and Olusola 1990, 133–35).

Apart from the above officials of the MEA, other officials from other ministries and organs are also stationed in some embassies. For example, as noted earlier, officials from the Federal Ministry of Information (FMOI) are posted to some embassies as information attachés, to handle information, external publicity, cultural, and host country press relations functions of the embassies. Many embassies also have Nigerian army, navy, and/or air force officers as defense attachés, military attachés, naval attachés, and/or air attachés, to handle Nigeria's military relations with the host country. Apart from the above officials of the FMOI and Ministry of Defense

(MOD), some embassies, depending on their needs, do also have officials from other ministries and organs. While posted to the embassies, these non-MEA officials are supposed to see themselves as belonging to the Nigerian diplomatic mission and having the ambassador (an official of the MEA) as their leader. In reality, during the Babangida era (just as in other eras), some conflicts did develop between MEA and non-MEA officials in the Nigerian diplomatic missions, as shown earlier. Effective and efficient leadership, operation, and management of a Nigerian diplomatic mission also entailed the reduction and minimization of these conflicts.

The emphasis on the economic components of Nigerian foreign policy during the Babangida Government also meant the emphasis on the economic diplomacy functions of Nigerian embassies. As noted earlier, during that era ambassadors, other embassy officials, and each particular embassy as a whole were evaluated on how effective they were in increasing economic relations between Nigeria and each particular host country—for examples, through the increase of Nigerian exports (especially of Nigerian manufactured goods) to the host country and the encouragement of foreign investments in Nigeria. In fact, the Nigerian embassies were seen as one of the most important instruments for the implementation of the new MEA policy of emphasizing the economic dimension of the country's foreign policy, since they were the arms of the MEA physically positioned in many foreign countries. In order to effectively implement this new policy, the structure and functioning of the embassies, as noted earlier, had to change. This meant that the ambassadors, while still paying adequate attention to the supervision of their embassies' political, consular, security, managerial, and cultural functions, were now making the supervision and the leadership of the economic functions of their embassies their top priority duty. It also meant that a good number of the more competent external affairs officers (that is, the ministers, minister-counselors, counselors, first secretaries, second secretaries, and third secretaries) were assigned to handle the economic functions of the embassies.

On the whole, the Babangida Government seems to have perceived the ambassador as a key element in the efficiency and effectiveness of an embassy in all its functions: political, consular, cultural, security, managerial, and economic. For example, in explaining the delay in naming the ambassador for the reestablished Nigerian Embassy in Israel, G. Ihama, the head of the Foreign Department of the MEA, said that "Israel is a strategic country and the federal government wants to ensure that the person there as our ambassador has all it takes to run an embassy in such a place" (G. Ihama, quoted in *West Africa* 1–7 February 1993, 162). After Ignatius Chukwuemeka Olisemeka, a former Nigerian envoy to Canada and a career diplomat, was named the Nigerian ambassador to Israel, a statement issued by the MEA repeated that "Israel is a strategic country and [the] government wanted to ensure that the person [who goes] there has what it takes. . . ." (a statement by the MEA, quoted by *West Africa* 15–21 March 1993, 429).

Adequate attention being paid to the selection of ambassadors is very appropriate, since their role is very important and complex, both at high diplomatic levels and at levels more basic to human needs. For example, when Togo and Zaire were experiencing some sociopolitical instability, Nigeria's embassies in the respective capitals of these countries, Lome and Kinshasha, were instructed by the MEA "to convert themselves into sanctuaries in the event of the lives of Nigerians being threatened;" and then the MEA planned to later arrange for possible airlifts of Nigerians from those places (*West Africa* 15–21 February 1993, 253). In fact, in the early part of 1993, the families of the Nigerian Embassy staff in Kinshasha were already taking refuge in the residence of the Nigerian ambassador to Zaire (*West Africa* 15–21 February 1993, 253).

The Nigerian ambassadors stationed in countries with which Nigeria had a lot of ties were, expectably, involved in more interactions and important negotiations with the officials of the host countries. For example, it has been noted that Nigerian military instructors were needed by Sierra Leone to help train that country's military to fight rebels in their country (*West Africa* 8–14 March 1993, 384). The negotiations for Nigerian soldiers to go to Sierra Leone, and the adequate functioning of the soldiers after they arrived, expectably meant that the Nigerian envoy in Sierra Leone had more sustained and expanded interactions and negotiations with more officials of Sierra Leone. Other officials of the Nigerian diplomatic mission in Sierra Leone, expectably, were also involved in accomplishing such a task.

In line with the prominence given to the economic dimension of Nigerian foreign policy by the Babangida Government, Nigerian ambassadors, as noted earlier, were to effectively articulate, represent, and promote the international economic interests of Nigeria. Many ambassadors did their best to play these roles. For example, Zubair M. Kazaure, the Nigerian ambassador to the United States, noted to audiences in that country that "Nigeria needs no foreign aid but foreign investment" (Kazaure, quoted in *West Africa* 15–21 February 1993, 253). Also Dr. J. J. Lewu, the Nigerian ambassador to Brazil, negotiated with the government of Brazil to ensure that Nigerian entrepreneurs on business trips to Brazil were not impeded in their efforts to carry out their legitimate business activities (*West Africa* 15–21 February 1993, 254).

Close attention being paid to the selection of ambassadors (both career-diplomat ambassadors and politically appointed ambassadors) made a lot of positive difference during the Babangida Government. One very good example of this was the selection of Professor Adebowale Adefuye as the

Nigerian envoy to Jamaica. Even though he was not a career/professional diplomat (he is a professor of history at the University of Lagos and a politically appointed ambassador), he performed his job so well that he was one of the most effective envoys during the Babangida Government. He did a lot to improve Jamaican-Nigerian relations and Nigeria's links with the Caribbean generally. For example, during his tenure as the Nigerian envoy to Jamaica, the Nigerian diplomatic mission in Jamaica sponsored a workshop in Kingston, Jamaica, in order to provide adequate academic resources for the teaching of west African history in Jamaican schools, through the redesign of curriculums (*The Jamaican Weekly Gleaner* 23 January 1989, 9). Also, when Hurricane Hugo damaged some Caribbean countries in 1989, it was noted that Professor Adefuye went from Jamaica to visit "Antigua, St. Lucia and St. Kitts to assess the damage Hurricane Hugo wreaked on these islands with the view to recommending to his government how best they can be assisted" (*The Jamaican Weekly Gleaner* 9 October 1989, 9).

As the Nigerian envoy to Jamaica, Adefuye's accomplishments included the acceleration of Jamaican-Nigerian relations up to the point that Jamaica opened its diplomatic mission in Nigeria (*West Africa* 8–14 April 1991, 517). Also,

> Adefuye's influence in the Caribbean (he was also accredited to Belize, Haiti, St. Kitts, St. Lucia, Antigua and Grenada) was such that he was influential in persuading 12 of the 13 Commonwealth Caribbean countries to cast their vote for Emeka Anyaoku, Nigeria's candidate for Commonwealth Secretary-General at Kuala Lumpur in October 1989. The Caribbean vote clinched the election for Anyaoku.
>
> Other important accomplishments include the establishment in Jamaica of a Jamaican-Nigerian Society and the Technical Aid Corps programme in which Nigeria sends professionals to ACP countries. The programme operates in 18 countries and Jamaica has the largest contingent of these volunteers which include doctors, nurses, engineers and academics. (*West Africa* 8–14 April 1991, 517)

After completing the ususal three-year tenure of a Nigerian envoy, he was posted to the United Kingdom as a deputy envoy in 1991 (*West Africa* 8–14 April 1991, 517), where he also performed excellently.

Due to his accomplishments and personality, Professor Adefuye "was arguably the most popular diplomat" in Jamaica (*West Africa* 8–14 April 1991, 517). "Indeed, so closely had Adefuye identified with the people and country that it came as a considerable shock to many that he could be transferred elsewhere. His scholarship, seemingly inexhaustible energy, warmth, infectious enthusiasm for Jamaica-Nigeria relations so endeared him to Jamaicans of all walks of life that they took him into their hearts and homes. He had become family" (*West Africa* 8–14 April 1991, 517).

It was the performance of ambassadors like Professor Adefuye that made Nigerian embassies effective and able to achieve their goals during the Babangida Government. The ability of the ambassador to adequately structure, operate, and lead the embassy determined the level of the effectiveness of the embassy. An article by Akindele and Olusola (1990, 124–42), cited earlier, provides excellent information on how one particular embassy was structured, operated, and led. The backgrounds of the two authors might have helped to sharpen their insights. R. A. Akindele, as a research professor at the Nigerian Institute of International Affairs (NIIA) (Olusanya and Akindele 1990, xiii), and as a scholar who works in a foreign policy think tank, is very able in merging theory and practice in the field of foreign policy and diplomacy. Segun Olusola is a news media executive who attended the prestigious and influential National Institute for Policy and Strategic Studies (NIPSS) in Kuru, and later served as the Nigerian ambassador to Ethiopia, with additional accreditation to Djibouti (Olusanya and Akindele 1990, xvii). As a politically appointed ambassador (thus not a career diplomat of the MEA), he had the advantage of being an "outsider" able to see things a little more objectively and more ability and willingness to share his views. His background as someone who attended the NIPSS meant that he had a strong intellectual and policy-studies background to analyze and evaluate the structure and operation of the embassy that he led.

Akindele and Olusola have noted that among Nigerian embassies, the Nigerian Embassy in Addis Ababa, Ethiopia, is unique because Addis Ababa is the location of the headquarters of the Organization of African Unity (OAU). "Since Africa is the centerpiece of Nigeria's foreign policy, the OAU has quite understandably become an important instrument for the conduct of the country's foreign policy" (Akindele and Olusola 1990, 126). Thus, "Addis Ababa is both a bilateral and multilateral post for the conduct of" Nigeria's diplomacy (Akindele and Olusola 1990, 126). The bilateral relations aspects of the Nigerian Embassy in Addis Ababa focus on Nigeria-Ethiopa bilateral relations and (since the Nigerian Ambassador to Ethiopia is also accredited to the Republic of Djibouti) Nigeria-Djibouti bilateral relations. The multilateral relations aspects of the Nigerian Embassy in Addis Ababa focus on OAU affairs. The location of the United Nations Economic Commission for Africa in Addis Ababa, in addition to some other international organizations being located in that city, also adds to the multilateral relations aspects of the Nigerian Embassy there (Akindele and Olusola 1990, 126, 132–33). Due to OAU affairs and OAU regular meetings, the Nigerian Embassy "in Addis Ababa is the only post that plays host to the Nigerian Head of State or his Deputy annually, in addition to hosting the country's Minister of External Affairs twice a year" (Akindele and Olusola 1990, 126). This situation means that the Nigerian Embassy in Addis Ababa gears a lot of its activities toward OAU affairs. "In fact, it is estimated that close to seventy-five percent of the work of the Embassy is connected with the Organization of African Unity" (Akindele and Olusola 1990, 131). Additionally, the Nigerian Embassy in Addis Ababa "also functions as the key communications point between Nigeria and other African countries which have no Mission in Lagos" (Akindele and Olusola 1990, 131), since every African country has a diplomatic mission in Addis Ababa (because the headquarters of the OAU are located in that city).

The above bilateral and multilateral relations roles of the Nigerian Embassy in Addis Ababa greatly affect the structure and functioning of the embassy. In 1989, the embassy had the following personnel: the ambassador, one minister-counselor, one counselor, one first secretary, one second secretary, one third secretary, three administrative attachés, and one financial attaché (Akindele and Olusola 1990, 133–35).

The ambassador, expectably, headed the embassy in his capacity as the chief representative of the Nigerian government and Nigerian people in Ethiopia. Next in rank to the ambassador was the minister-counselor, who was also the principal adviser to the ambassador (Akindele and Olusola 1990, 134). Additionally, the minister-counselor had "special responsibility for bilateral relations with Ethiopia and Djibouti," and also coordinated and supervised Chancery reports and prepared "the annual confidential reports for the counter-signature of the" ambassador (Akindele and Olusola 1990, 134).

The counselor was primarily in charge of the multilateral relations functions of the embassy as it related to OAU affairs and the affairs of other international organizations located in Addis Ababa, in which he was assisted by the second secretary (Akindele and Olusola 1990, 134). The second secretary also handled "relations with local and international media and all non-governmental organizations" (Akindele and Olusola 1990, 134).

The first secretary was primarily in charge of consular affairs, and as the head of the Chancery in charge of management of financial resources, "all administrative and establishment matters, including the preparation of the annual estimates, budgets and reports;" and, additionally, he handled "all OAU administrative, personnel and recruitment matters" (Akindele and Olusola 1990, 134).

The third secretary assisted "the Minister-Counselor in bilateral matters with Ethiopia and Djibouti," provided "assistance to the First Secretary on

Consular matters," and also had "direct responsibility for staff welfare" (Akindele and Olusola 1990, 134).

The three Administrative Attaches divided among themselves administrative duties such as custody of classified documents; control, maintenance and disposition of official vehicles and drivers; discipline of local staff, maintenance, repair and security of government property; typing of reports from all political officers, protocol duties, including liaison with the Protocol Department of the Ethiopian Ministry of Foreign Affairs, and the Mission's communications links to the outside world. (Akindele and Olusola 1990, 134–35).

The Financial Attaché, who was a professional accountant, handled "general accounting, preparation of salaries, wages and allowances, banking and treasury transactions and audit queries, if any, from the Ministry of External Affairs in Lagos" (Akindele and Olusola 1990, 135).

During the tenure of Olusola as the ambassador, two types of meetings usually assisted the functioning of the embassy. One was the general meeting of the home-based staff, during which participants focused on "administrative, management and welfare issues bearing on the substantive work of the home-based staff," and the other meeting involved senior officers and the ambassador and focused on policy issues (Akindele and Olusola 1990, 136–37).

At the embassy, decision-making and policy recommendations involved "the process of *ad hoc* political discussion and consultation between the Ambassador and his appropriate top-level staff before 'despatches', based on the consensus and recommendations" which arose, were forwarded to the MEA in Lagos (Akindele and Olusola 1990, 137). The flow of messages, between the embassy in Addis Ababa and the MEA in Lagos often carried captions like "'directives', 'advice', 'recommendations' and 'request for approval', etc." (Akindele and Olusola 1990, 137). According to Akindele and Olusola (1990, 137), "In giving policy advice and making recommendation, the quality of reports and despatches sent to Lagos is equally as important as the quality of briefings and information about Nigeria received from Lagos. The latter enables the Mission to explain intelligently developments in Nigeria, and the background to Nigeria's position on various issues to both the government and people of the country of accreditation."

A seasoned career ambassador, Olu Adeniji (1990, 155), also contributes to the understanding of the nature of the communications linkages between embassies abroad and their ministries of external affairs in their home countries; according to him,

[T]he importance of the two-way contacts between the Ministry and Missions abroad can again be highlighted with regard to the flow of information. Missions are expected to convey constant flow of information from their host countries to their capital. By the same token the Ministry of External Affairs is expected to keep its overseas Missions informed of important developments at home. . . . An Ambassador's effectiveness with his host government depends extensively on how well-informed he is about developments in his own country. This necessitates a well-developed communications system both technically and methodically.

Adeniji (1990, 154), noting the importance of embassies having experienced diplomats, adds that

> the result of using well-trained officers in Missions is the attainment of many of the objectives set out. Often, reports from a Mission may prompt an examination of policy not just relating to the particular Mission but of general application. Ambassadors abroad sometimes see and elaborate in their report to the Foreign Ministry aspects of a problem which are not necessarily seen from the home setting. . . . When headquarters does not receive enough inputs from a particular Mission abroad, the leadership of the Mission may be the problem.

Adeniji (1990, 154–55) seems to be of the opinion that career ambassadors are more likely to lead an embassy more effectively than politically appointed ambassadors, which reflects his worldview and opinion as a career ambassador. In this vein, he further adds that "in the final analysis, it is the government symbolized in the Ministry of External Affairs by the Minister that makes foreign policy. However, the contributions of the professional diplomats whether at headquarters in the Ministry or in the diplomatic posts abroad have always cumulatively represented an indispensable ingredient in the process."

In reiterating the importance of adequate two-way communications between the embassies abroad and their Ministry of External Affairs at home, Adeniji (1990, 153–54) emphasizes that the quality of the leadership of each embassy abroad is also very important. According to him (Adeniji 1990, 154), "when a Mission is given proper guidance as to its focus in the pursuit of its country's foreign policy objectives, and proper leadership by the Head of Missions, it can obtain spectacular results."

As shown above, the structure, functioning, and leadership of Nigerian embassies abroad are very important elements in the structure, functioning, and leadership of the MEA and the Nigerian foreign policy decision-making system as a whole.

Another interesting aspect of the Nigerian foreign policy decision-making milieu during the Babangida Government was the significant role provided for private citizen diplomacy. A very good example of this was the role played by M. K. O. Abiola, a prominent Nigerian businessman. Abiola spearheaded a global campaign for "reparations for Africa's sufferings during the slave trade and colonialism" (*West Africa* 8–14 March 1993, 391). Abiola's reparation campaign resulted in his being asked "to look in depth at the matter and submit a report to the OAU for presentation at the UN," and also involved a series of conferences on the issue (*West Africa* 8–14 March 1993, 391). Additionally, the reparation campaign also involved Abiola flying in his private jet, in a well-publicized visit, to the Caribbean, with specific stops in Jamaica and Cuba (*West Africa* 8–14 March 1993, 391). In Jamaica, he held discussions with the governor-general, prime minister, foreign minister, and other representatives of that country, and in Cuba he met with "President Fidel Castro [and] several members of the Politburo," including the Minister of Foreign Affairs and the minister of Trade of that country (*West Africa* 8–14 March 1993, 391). Though the federal government of Nigeria was not aggressively pushing Abiola's campaign, there was a general impression that it was passively helping to facilitate Abiola's reparation campaign, though not openly identifying with it. The ease with which Abiola convened his conferences with prominent individuals from all over the world, the ability of the reparation campaign organization, as a nongovernmental body, to easily establish official working relationships with the OAU and the UN, the ease with which Abiola met with the highest government leaders of Jamaica and Cuba, and even more important the close relationships that Abiola had with the most important leaders of the Babangida Government, all point to the strong possibility that Abiola's reparation campaign got at least passive approval, if not active help, from the federal government of Nigeria. If the government did provide Abiola's reparation campaign with passive help, it meant that MEA human and material diplomatic resources might have, for example, facilitated Abiola's official contacts with the OAU, the UN, Jamaica, and Cuba. If such a situation did occur, it meant that during the Babangida Government, the MEA was, on some occasions, able to at least passively help to facilitate private citizen diplomatic activities that promoted the country's national interests or did not clash with those national interests.

During the Babangida Government there were the usual border problems with neighboring countries, as noted earlier. Specifically, the border problems between Nigeria and Cameroun continued to arise and efforts were often made by both countries to manage and minimize the conflicts adequately (see *West Africa* 2–8 July 1990, 2029–30; *West Africa* 6–12 January 1992, 36–37; and *West Africa* 17–23 August 1992, 1409). As noted earlier, the management of these sort of conflicts often involved the MEA working closely with the Presidency, the Ministry of Defense, the Nigerian police force, the Nigerian Immigration Department, the Nigerian Custom Service, other federal ministries and organs, and state and local governments that share some of their borders with foreign countries. As also noted earlier, the significant involvement of so many federal ministries and organs as well as state and local governments often meant more cumbersome foreign policy decision-making. All these government ministries and organs had to work together to decide on Nigeria's policy positions, negotiating strategies, and tactics, even before negotiations began with the government of the neighboring country.

Nigerian diplomatic missions in neighboring countries were often very helpful instruments of the MEA in the management of the border disputes not only because of the information they sent to the MEA, but through their actions and general behavior—the statements they made to the governments and peoples of the neighboring countries and the nature of their general diplomatic activities before, during, and after border or other forms of conflicts. For example, the Nigerian Embassy in Cameroun staged a pre-planned five-day commercial and industrial exhibition "in Party House, Douala, Cameroun's centerpiece of commerce and industry," despite the fact there were tensions in Nigeria-Cameroun relations (*West Africa* 2–8 July 1990, 2029–30). Alhaji Mohammed Saidu, the Nigerian ambassador to Cameroun, noted that the exhibition "had long been planned before the recent misunderstanding" (Ambassador Saidu, quoted in *West Africa* 2–8 July 1990, 2030). In diplomatic circles it was hoped that the exhibition would help to "ease the tension between both countries, which arose as a result of allegations of harassment and inhumane treatment of Nigerian residents in Cameroun, leading to their detention and the recent death of a Nigerian businessman" (*West Africa* 2–8 July 1990, 2030). Notably, "the opening ceremony for the exhibition . . . was attended by the Cameroun government officials" (*West Africa* 2–8 July 1990, 2030). The very fact that the officials of the government of Cameroun attended the opening ceremony meant that the exhibition helped to ease the crisis by giving the officials of the two countries a relaxed forum to renew contacts. Thus, the Nigerian Embassy in Cameroun was right in staging the exhibition as was planned, despite the tension. This shows the kind of roles that the Nigerian embassies (which are arms of the MEA) often play in this sort of situation.

During the Babangida Government, tension also rose between Nigeria and Equatorial Guinea (a country Nigeria shares an Atlantic Ocean border with) over the presence of South Africans in the latter country at a time when sanctions and international isolation were waged against South Africa, then under the apartheid system (*West Africa* 24 December 1990–6 January 1991, 3117). Nigeria managed the resultant strains in relations, and indeed removed these tensions, by increasing diplomatic and economic relations with Equatorial Guinea. The presidents of the two countries visited each other's country and Nigeria extended economic assistance to Equatorial Guinea (*West Africa* 24 December 1990–6 January

1991, 3117), providing a 10 million Naira credit line (for the export of petroleum products and cement from Nigeria to Equatorial Guinea), building a 30-bed hospital-polyclinic, and subsidizing a 1.25 million Naira agricultural venture in Equatorial Guinea. Nigeria "also donated about $5m towards Equatorial Guinea's bid to host the international conference of economic and customs unions of African states" (*West Africa* 24 December 1990–6 January 1991, 3117). These Nigerian accelerated and expansive diplomatic and economic activities obviously involved the MEA working very closely with various other Nigerian government ministries and organs to formulate and implement the actions. The new diplomatic and economic ties between Nigeria and Equatorial Guinea resulted in the latter expelling the South Africans (who were commercial farmers) from that country (*West Africa* 18–24 September 1989, 1575).

The Liberian crisis was an important foreign policy issue for the Babangida Government. With Nigeria providing most of the troops for the ECOMOG forces and also being seen as a key element in the Liberian situation, MEA resources were heavily involved in helping to search for political solutions to the problems and in organizing liaison with, and on behalf of, the Nigerian military forces that were part of the ECOMOG forces. The nature of the Liberian situation had to involve the MEA and the Nigerian Ministry of Defense doing their best to work closely together. Ambassador Joshua Iroha, a retired Nigerian diplomat (and thus a former employee of the MEA), who was brought out of retirement to serve as the representative of the executive secretary of the Economic Commission of West African States (ECOWAS) in Liberia, was seen as having a very good working relationship with Major-General Ishaya Bakut, a Nigerian army officer who was the field commander of the ECOMOG forces in Liberia (*West Africa* 25–31 May 1992, 873).

It also seems that during the Babangida Government, the MEA and the National Intelligence Agency (NIA) (the Nigerian external intelligence organization) had good relations. The fact that Ambassador A. I. Atta (who was either a former official of the MEA or a current official of the MEA on secondment to the NIA) was the director-general of the NIA (possibly the second most important official of the NIA) (*African Concord* 9 November 1992, 49). The fact that a current or former official of the MEA was the second most important official of the NIA is a possible indication of a good relationship between the two organizations during the Babangida Government. Also, the fact that both the MEA and the NIA focus on the external arena made such a good relationship logical. The fact that Ambassador Atta played a nationally visible role for the NIA also buttresses the possibility that he was a very important official of the NIA. For example, he delivered a paper on behalf of Brigadier General Alilu Akilu, the head of the NIA, at a public seminar in Lagos that focused on the dynamics that intertwine national security, mass media, and the law (*African Concord* 9 November 1992, 49).

Because the Babangida Government emphasized economic dimensions as the most important components of Nigerian foreign policy (*African Events* October 1989, 25; *West Africa* 9–15 October 1989, 1679–80; *West Africa* 25–31 May 1992, 874), the relationship between the MEA and the ministries and organs that focused on economic matters were even more expansive (though often somewhat uneasy, due to various ministries and organs attempting to protect their turf). For example, the 10 million Naira line of credit extended by Nigeria to "Equatorial Guinea for the purchase of essential commodities, including oil by-products, kerosene, canned fish and meat products" (*West Africa* 4–10 December 1989, 2029), very likely involved the MEA working closely with the Federal Ministry of Finance (FMOF), the Federal Ministry of Commerce (FMOC), the Federal Ministry of Petroleum Resources (FMPR), the Nigerian National Petroleum Corporation (NNPC), the Central Bank of Nigeria (CBN), and the Presidency to formulate and implement this policy.

The MEA must work together with other ministries and organs in the area of international economic matters, for these others have the primary responsibility for such matters. As excellently analyzed by Professor Akindele (1990c, 106–23), the Federal Ministry of Finance (FMOF) often has the primary responsibility for most international financial matters and relations, the Federal Ministry of Commerce (FMOC) often has the primary responsibility for most international trade matters and relations (excluding petroleum issues); the Federal Ministry of Petroleum Resources (FMPR) often has the primary responsibility for international petroleum matters and relations, and the Federal Ministry of National Planning (FMNP) has the primary responsibility for relations with international organizations and agencies that dwell wholly or partially with international economic and development issues. In fact, according to Akindele (1990c, 109–10), the four ministries named above have the primary responsibilities for most of the country international economic matters and relations. It is "patently and indisputably clear . . . that the Ministry of External Affairs has no primary responsibility for the country's external economic relations" (Akindele 1990c, 110). This situation thus means that

> in the areas of foreign economic policies, what the Ministry of External Affairs does is . . . "to complement and reinforce the activities of . . . other organs of government." According to Professor Akinyemi, MEA's Directorate of International Economic Cooperation "provides a useful link between it and the various economic home ministires." It provides them with ideas and policy prescriptions based on its activities in the economic field with foreign countries and international organizations. This facilitated by the existence of economic desks in all Nigerian missions abroad, charged with the responsibility of moni-

toring and reporting economic issues and identifying the prospects for enhanced bilateral economic cooperation between Nigeria and the host countries (Akindele 1990c, 110–111).

However, during the period Akinyemi headed the ministry (a period during which it was always brimming with new ideas and was also always ready to expand its activities and actions), the MEA tried to play a prominent role in the country's relations with ECOWAS (despite the fact that the FMNP had, and had always had, the primary responsibility for this. It was the assertiveness of Professor Akinyemi, as minister of External Affairs, that enabled the Ministry of External Affairs to wade forcefully into a policy area not hitherto its own. The bold incursion of the MEA into ECOWAS affairs was exemplified by the fact that it was through "Akinyemi's bold efforts" that "communications and contact" were restored "between Nigeria and ECOWAS States by lifting the boundary closures of 1984 and 1985" (Ofoegbu 1990, 89). It was also Akinyemi's "shuttle diplomacy which mediated the Mali-Burkino Faso frontier wars of 1986" (Ofoegbu 1990, 89). Additionally, "until the . . . visits of President Ibrahim Babangida to Sierra Leone, Cape Verde, Liberia, Ghana, Togo, Benin and Cote d'Ivoire which were arranged and conducted by the Ministry of External Affairs, Nigeria's relations with the ECOWAS was outside the sphere of responsibility [of] the Ministry of External Affairs, or seemed to be so" (Ofoegbu 1990, 89).

The MEA's actions did not go unchallenged by the FMNP. In fact, the Federal Ministry of National Planning (which at some periods is also called the Federal Ministry of Economic Development) seems to have seriously battled the prominent incursion of the MEA into ECOWAS affairs. According to Ofoegbu (1990, 89), "Nigeria's Minister of Economic Development rather than the Minister of External Affairs chaired meetings of the ECOWAS Council of Ministers during Nigeria's Presidency of ECOWAS," despite the fact that "Bolaji Akinyemi tried to break this tradition." This reality was very significant. The fact that the minister of External Affairs was not able to chair the meetings of ECOWAS Council of Ministers meant that the Federal Ministry of National Planning (FMNP) still had the primary responsibility for ECOWAS affairs, despite the forceful moves the MEA made, under Akinyemi's leadership, into ECOWAS affairs. Thus, the incursions the MEA made into ECOWAS affairs were peripheral. They were also likely temporary, since ministers of External Affairs who came after Akinyemi mostly likely preferred to avoid tensions, bruised feelings, and constant serious turf battles with the FMNP over ECOWAS affairs. The Ministry of External Affairs, in most periods, often works with the FMNP in relation to ECOWAS affairs, instead of trying to wrest primary responsibility from the FMNP.

During the Babangida Government, the Federal Ministry of Finance (FMF) and the Central Bank of Nigeria (CBN) continued their tradition of being the major organs in charge of Nigeria's international financial relations (Ofoegbu 1990, 88). The MEA mainly works with the FMF and CBN in helping to guide and manage the country's international financial relations. Some, like Ofoegbu (1990, 90), are of the view that the MEA should be leading in this sphere, but the reality is that, as in other areas of international economic relations, the MEA's role in the area of international financial relations continues to be a secondary and supporting one. Nevertheless, due to the emphasis on the economic components of Nigeria's foreign policy during the Babangida Government, the MEA, though not playing the dominant role in the country's international economic relations, increased its role in this policy area. For example, the MEA and its foreign missions overseas were more endowed and empowered to play an important role in Nigeria's bilateral economic relations (Adeniji 1990, 156–57), whereas prior to the Babangida Government the MEA mostly focused on multilateral economic relations.

This expanded role for the MEA in international economic relations necessarily meant more conflicts between it and other ministries and agencies. Apart from the conflicts between the MEA and FMNP over the control of Nigeria's relations with ECOWAS, there were numerous other conflicts. For example, in 1990 there was "serious in-fighting between the staff of the Nigerian Embassy in Brussels" and the staff of the Nigerian Export Promotion Council (NEPC) posted to Brussels (*Newswatch* 24 May 1993, 31). It was alleged that the "embassy officials did not give NEPC staff a free hand to operate a trade center within the embassy" (*Newswatch* 24 May 1993, 31). It was also alleged that when the NEPC staff attempted to secure office space outside the embassy (without involving the ambassador in the efforts), the embassy frustrated and possibly thwarted this goal (*Newswatch* 24 May 1993, 31–32). This sort of conflict between the embassy and the NEPC incidates a need to streamline and clearly delineate the roles of the MEA and other ministries and agencies in the area of international economic relations. Even more importantly, mechanisms to foster more cooperation need to be designed, formulated, and activated. Such cooperative mechanisms are very important, since there will always be an overlapping of functions between the MEA and other ministries and agencies in the area of international economic relations. For example, the Trade and Investment Division of the MEA is in a position to make such positive contributions. Specifically, "the job of the Trade and Investment Division in the Ministry of External Affairs remains first and foremost to improve the information flow between government ministries, the external affairs ministry, the planning and economic ministry and with the organized private sector" (*West Africa* 9–15 October 1989, 1679).

The Nigerian effort to emphasize the economic component of its foreign policy also resulted in Nigeria staging various trade fairs in foreign countries and sending trade missions abroad (*West Africa* 9–15 October 1989, 1679–80). These activities gave the MEA (with its embassies abroad) ample opportunities to work together with various other ministries and agencies—for example, the Federal Ministries of Commerce, Industries, National Planning, and Finance; the Central Bank of Nigeria; and the Nigerian Export Promotion Council—to promote and bolster the Nigerian manufactured products in foreign countries.

On the whole, throughout the Babangida Government the MEA was a very important instrument in the management of Nigeria's international relations. Able leadership of the MEA during this period enabled the ministry to grow stronger. Two ministers of External Affairs provide very interesting contrasting styles and profiles of leadership. Akinyemi led the MEA to design and implement big and expansive goals: for example, the Technical Aid Corps (TAC) program, that Forum of Medium Powers, and bold moves to give the MEA more roles in ECOWAS affairs (Ofoegbu 1990, 93–94). On the other hand, under Nwachukwu, the MEA human and material resources were fine-tuned and activated to focus heavily on the economic components of Nigeria's foreign policy (Ofoegbu 1990, 94–98).

Throughout the Babangida era (as in most other eras), the MEA, on the whole, mostly dominated the political aspects of Nigeria's international relations, while it shared the security, cultural, and economic aspects with other ministries and agencies of the government.

Ministry of Defense

During the Babangida Government, as in other periods, the Ministry of Defense (MOD) was the most prominent organ in terms of the security aspects of the country's international relations.

Like other ministries, the MOD was streamlined in accordance with the 1988 Civil Service Reform (Dlakwa 1992, 297–311). General Domkat Bali was the minister of defense and the chief of defense staff in the early part of the Babangida Government. From December 1989 to August 1990, President Babangida held the defense ministership, while General Sanni Abacha, who had been the chief of army staff since 1985, also simultaneously served as the chief of defense staff (*Newswatch Who's Who in Nigeria* 1990, 9; *Nigeria: A Country Study* 1992, 272; *West Africa* 10–16 September 1990, 2434–35). In September 1990, General Sanni Abacha became the minister of defense as well as the chief of defense staff, while Major-General Saliu Ibrahim became the chief of army staff (*Nigeria: A Country Study* 1992, 272; *West Africa* 10–16 September 1990, 2434). Bali and Abacha were both very senior, experienced, and influential generals of the Nigerian army. Thus, during the Babangida Government the MOD had leaders with enormous stature and influence (thereby enabling the ministry also to have stature and influence in the national policy milieu—especially in terms of the ministry's interactions and liaisons with other ministries). By simultaneously holding the positions of minister of Defense and chief of defense staff Bali, and later Abacha, provided policy and administrative leadership to the ministry while, at the same time, also being directly in charge of the coordination of the army, navy, and air force.

As aforementioned, the position of chief of defense staff and the position of chief of general staff were two different and separate positions. As noted above, the chief of defense staff is a position within the MOD for the coordination and supervision of the activities of the Nigerian army, navy, and air force. On the other hand, as noted earlier, the chief of general staff headed the General Staff Headquarters, which was part of the Office of the President (later called the Presidency). As also noted earlier, the chief of defense staff was a very senior military officer who supervised the chiefs of staff of the various military service branches, while the chief of general staff was a very senior military officer who (heading a group of military officers who were seconded to the Presidency) assisted President Babangida (who headed a military government) in the governance of the country. Thus, the chief of defense staff dealt with purely military matters, while the chief of general staff dealt with mostly national policy, political, and administrative matters.

The chief of general staff was the number two leader and next to the president. However, as also noted earlier, there was always some competition for power between the chief of general staff and the chief of defense staff (who was often also the minister of defense during the Babangida Government). This tension was very intense during the very early phase of the Babangida Government, partly due to the fact that Ebitu Ukiwe, a commodore in the navy, had a lower military rank than the chief of defense staff (who was also the minister of defense). Ukiwe lost this position in 1986 (*West Africa* 10–16 September 1990, 2434), and was replaced by August Aikhomu, a flag officer of the Nigerian navy who was higher in rank than Ukiwe. After Ukiwe's replacement, the tension between the chief of general staff and the chief of defense staff was no more very prominent.

The tensions between the chief of general staff and the chief of defense staff revolved around the fact that some perceived the chief of general staff as being the next in power to the president in all areas and circumstances, while others perceived him as being next in power to the president only in terms of national policy, political, and administrative issues, while the chief of defense staff (who was also the minister of Defense) was next in power to the president in terms of purely military matters.

The position of the chief of general staff, as aforementioned, was called the chief of staff of the supreme military headquarters during previous military governments. As also aforementioned, the position of chief of general staff existed only during the first and second phases of the Babangida Government. The position of vice president was created to replace it. During the third phase and the fourth (final and transitional) phase of the Babangida Government, the vice president (who, interestingly, as aforementioned, was the same Aikhomu who was formerly the chief of general staff, though he retired from the navy just before he assumed the new title of vice president) essentially performed the same functions that were formerly performed by the chief of general staff. With the position of vice president replacing the position of chief of general staff, the chief of defense staff (who was also the minister of defense) no more (at least openly) contested for second position to the president, since the title of vice president clearly and obviously denoted resolved the rivalry.

The minister of defense was clearly the head of one of the most important ministries due to the size of the ministry and the prominent role of the military in the country's political system. The very fact that the MOD was the umbrella organization for the Nigerian army, Navy, and air force makes it the major organization in the national security milieu of the country. Thus, the MOD is the major organ for the articulation, planning, formulation, and implementation of the security components of the country's foreign policy. During the Babangida Government, the MOD continued to play this major role.

During the Babngida era, the various military branches sought to meet the goals and demands of the country's security needs in terms of the quality and quantity of military personnel and hardware (*Nigeria: A Country Study* 1992, 257–301). The training, combat readiness, and weapon systems of the military were, thus, geared toward these goals.

The major combat components of the Nigerian army during the Babangida era were the 1st Mechanized Infantry Division, headquartered in Kaduna; the 2nd Mechanized Infantry Division, headquartered in Ibadan; the 3rd Armoured Division, headquartered in Jos; the 82nd Airborne Division, headquartered in Enugu; the Artillery Command; and the Guard Brigade (*Nigeria: A Country Study* 1992, 274). For the Nigerian navy, the major combat components were the Western Command, headquartered in Lagos; the Eastern Command, headquartered in Calabar; and the Naval Training Command (*Nigeria: A Country Study* 1992, 274). For the Nigerian air force the major combat components were the Tactical Air Command, headquartered in Makurdi; the Training Command, headquartered in Kaduna; the Logistics Command, headquartered in Ikeja; and the Airlift Command headquartered in Ibadan (*Nigeria: A Country Study* 1992, 274).

The Nigerian Defense Academy at Kaduna, the Command and Staff College at Jaji, and the National Institute for Policy and Strategic Studies provide officers training facilities for all the military branches, while the army, navy, and air force also have various specialized training schools and programs for officers and enlisted members (*Nigeria: A Country Study* 1992, 287–94). During the Babangida Government, the Nigerian War College was established to provide another training facility for senior military officers (*West Africa* 2–8 July 1990, 2029; *West Africa* 29 March–4 April 1993, 518).

There were also increased efforts to produce some military hardwares in the country (while other military hardwares were still imported from other countries). For example, by 1988, the Defense Industries Corporation in Kaduna "was reported to be relying entirely on local materials and to be producing all the basic rifles and ammunition the army and police used" (*Nigeria: A Country Study* 1992, 285–86). Additionally,

> newer facilities for the assembly of armored fighting vehicles and light tanks were under development at Bauchi in 1990. . . . Indications of a nascent commercial defense industry included a manufacturer in Anambra State whose inexpensive jeeps included military models being tested by the army; a local service industry to supply uniforms, accoutrements, and selected ordnance matériel; and increased domestic sourcing for aircraft and naval ship components and maintenance services. . . .
>
> On its silver anniversary April 22, 1989, the air force unveiled and conducted a test flight of a prototype of Nigeria's first domestically built aircraft, the Air Beetle. . . . This two-seat, single engine airplane was intended to be the primary trainer for the NAF. . . . The production program called for sixty units by 1992 and eventual development of an improved version, the Super Air Beetle. In early 1990, the first export orders were reported, and forty aircraft of the first production run were scheduled for delivery to foreign customers. . . .

The navy also turned increasingly to local suppliers for spare parts and maintenance services. In mid-1989 about 40 percent of the spare parts for naval vessels reportedly had been produced in Nigeria . . . including propeller shafts and generator parts. The new navy dockyard, opened at the end of 1990 at Victoria Island near Lagos, will eventually have the capacity to boost domestic production of spare parts for ships to 70 percent of requirements and to permit future modification and even construction of ships. (*Nigeria: A Country Study* 1992, 286–87).

On the whole, as indicated by the above structures and organizations, training facilities, and the military hardware systems development programs, the army, navy, and air force, seem to have sought to provide the country with the military profile and capabilities that would enable it to meet its national and international security needs. For example, the training programs and military field, combat, and staff assignments produced seasoned officers who were able to lead some of the United Nations' peacekeeping efforts. Some of these officers were Major-General Edward Unimna, who was the United Nations' chief military observer in Angola; Major-General Chris Garba, who succeeded Unimna; and Major-General Ekundayo Opaleye, who was appointed the commander of the United Nations' observer team in Rwanda and Uganda (*West Africa* 23–29 September 1991, 1604; *West Africa* 15–21 March 1993, 428).

The ability of the MOD to adequately articulate, plan, formulate, implement, and evaluate the security components of the country's foreign policy, depends largely on the profile and capabilities of the military and the quality of the leadership of the MOD. During the Babangida Government, Nigeria's involvement in numerous international peacekeeping operations, many international multilateral and bilateral military cooperations, and border conflicts greatly heightened the need for the MOD to play an adequate role in the area of the security dimension of the country's foreign policy. This might have prompted some, like Jimi Peters and A. L. Aminu, to proffer ways the leadership structure of the MOD could be equipped to have, process, analyze, and utilize information on international issues to better play its important role. According to Peters and Aminu (1986, 97),

> there may be a need for the Ministry of Defense to create a small department in the office of the Minister of Defense to service the needs of the armed forces in the area of foreign policy and international security analysis. That will not be different from the idea behind the Defence Intelligence Agency (DIA) created for military-related internal and external intelligence and reporting directly to the Minister of Defense, the National Intelligence Agency (NIA) responsible for external intelligence and the State Security Service (SSS) for internal intelligence and reporting to President.

> Of course, such a unit will necessarily have to cooperate with institutions such as the Nigerian Institute of International Affairs (NIIA) and the National Institute of Policy and Strategic Studies (NIPSS) as well as with the various political science and international relations departments in the various universities to tap the available resources for the maximum benefit of the military. But the essential thing is that the military should be able to conduct research on foreign policy and international security issues from its own perspectives, with a view to giving it a greater say in the foreign policy process. After all, it provides or should provide the backbone for the achievement of foreign policy objectives.

The above recommendations by Peters and Aminu aim at helping the MOD leadership structure to acquire the capacity to articulate, plan, formulate, implement, and evaluate the security components of the country's foreign policy. In fact Peters and Aminu (1986, 95) see the adequate "review of the National Security management structure" of the country, in such a way as to fully "integrate the foreign, military and intelligence arms of the government," as the general approach that should be taken in order to strengthen the security components of the country's foreign policy.

The above views of Peters and Aminu was published in an academic journal in 1986. A series of papers were "commissioned in 1988 by the Nigerian Joint Chiefs of Staff, Ministry of Defense, for a national seminar on 'Nigeria's National Interests and Values.' Of the 15 papers presented in that seminar, 11 identified national security as the foremost national interest of Nigeria" (Asobie 1990, 10). Whether or not this effort by the joint chiefs of staff to provide a forum for the probing of an aspect of the country's national security dynamics was influenced by Peters and Aminu's article, the MOD was starting to harness and utilize intellectual inputs for the adequate handling of the security components of the country's foreign policy—in the manner recommended by Peters and Aminu.

During the Babangida Government there were also efforts to create infrastructures for the development of capability to harness and utilize nuclear energy for peaceful purpose. This "fresh effort to acquire nuclear capability" by the Babangida Government was in fact a continuation of "a policy which has occupied the attention of successive governments over the years" (*West Africa* 20–26 May 1991, 812). Although Nigeria's desire to develop nuclear capability has often been formally stated as being motivated by the need for peaceful uses "in the energy, agricultural and medical sectors" (*West Africa* 5–11 June 1989, 937), there has often been a perception that the military encourages the development of nuclear energy capacity. Though the military officers know that nuclear energy capability, when and if developed by Nigeria, will most probably be utilized for peaceful purposes in the country, they are aware of the potential national security value it would provide for the country in the international system. Thus, in a way, the nuclear energy issue may reflect that an increasing number of the military officers are very sensitized to international security issues and affairs as they relate to the country.

During the Babangida Government, a "team of researchers at Ahmadu Bello University, Zaria, is said to have developed a formula for manufacturing the so-called 'yellow cake' or uranium oxide which can be processed chemically with rain water to produce nuclear power" (*West Africa* 22–28 May 1989, 845). The government's strong interest in this development was indicated by the fact that Professor Emovon, the federal minister for Science and Technology, commended this achievement by the Center for Energy Research and Training (CERT) of the Ahmadu Bello University (ABU) (*West Africa* 22–28 May 1989, 845). Dr. Shamsideen Elegba, the Director of CERT, commented that "whether or not uranium exists in the country in commercial quantities, whatever is available should be exploited as a matter of national policy and developed into yellow cakes, using CERT's technique" (*West Africa* 22–28 May 1989, 845). It was also noted that CERT's ultimate goal was "to perfect a formula for enriched uranium, otherwise known as uranium exflouride" (*West Africa* 22–28 May 1989, 845).

A further indication of a strong interest in the nuclear energy policy by the Babangida Government was the fact that, during President Babangida's visit to France in 1989, the president had "apparently been advised" by Nigerian government officials "to seek an updated and expanded" economic and technical cooperation accord, "with a bias towards nuclear and solar energy research" (*West Africa* 5–June 1989, 937). Furthermore, it was noted that "Nigeria's science and technology ministry is said to be seeking a joint venture with the French nuclear center at Strasbourg. If an agreement is reached, the center would work closely with ABU, Obafemi Awolowo University, Ile-lfe, and the University of Nigeria, Nsukka—the three institutions handling Nigeria's nuclear research programme" (*West Africa* 5–11 June 1989, 937).

The interest that the military officers might have had in the nuclear energy policy probably is a general reflection of the growing realization among them that the general quality of science and technology, and the general level of research and education in the country, also help to determine the quality and capabilities of the country's military. During the twenty-fifth year anniversary celebrations of the founding of the Nigerian air force (NAF), in 1989, the development of the trainer aircraft industry in Nigeria was a major focus (*African Concord* 15 May 1989, 50). It was also noted "that the NAF has been able to attract some of the brightest brains in the country" (*African Concord* 15 May 1989, 50). These sorts of facts and factors that were part of the highlights of the NAF anniversary celebrations were probably a good indication of the importance and value the NAF places on science, technology, research, and education.

The training of military officers in the educational institutions for military officers in the country helps to foster the interest of the military officers in intellectual areas. Thus, it has been noted that these Nigerian military educational institutions emphasize "the learning of not only military subjects but also an understanding of international and domestic issues" (Peters and Aminu 1986, 95). Such an educational which includes knowledge of international affairs, is important for military officers in the contemporary international system. The military officers having formal knowledge of the dynamics of international relations particularly aided the country in the various international peacekeeping and peacemaking efforts the military was involved in during the Babangida Government. The prominence of peacekeeping and peacemaking efforts in the security components of Nigerian foreign policy during the Babangida Government was underlined by the strong interest of the president in these efforts. In 1993, it was reported that

> the Nigerian War College has been directed by President Ibrahim Babangida to establish a training program for military officers from member-countries of OAU. Such officers will, in future, be deployed for peace-keeping duty.
> The initiative has been communicated in writing to Salim Ahmed Salim, OAU Secretary-General and Dr. Boutros Bourtros-Ghali, UN Secretary-General. (*West Africa* 29 March–4 April 1993, 518).

To further emphasize the importance of this action, "the note was delivered to Mr. Salim in Addis Ababa by a delegation led by Colonel Lawan Gwadabe," while "Mr. Matthew Mbu, external affairs secretary, led the delegation that visited Dr. Boutros-Ghali in New York" (*West Africa* 29 March–4 April 1993, 518).

In order to be able to perform international peacekeeping and peacemaking roles while at the same time being able to adequately defend Nigeria, all branches of the military needed also to maintain adequate combat readiness. Thus, "in line with the drive towards greater combat readiness of the Nigerian military, the navy" had noted that it "created its own 'rapid deployment force' of vessels" (*West Africa* 18–24 September 1989, 1574). Additionally, "The acting Chief of Naval Staff, Rear Admiral Promise Fingesi," had noted "that the vessels, stationed at the Lagos base of the western naval command, were combat ready and could be deployed within 24 hours" (*West Africa* 18–24 September 1989, 1574). Fingesi had also "made a case for the creation of a submarine arm," noting "that the navy's strategy already envisaged a submarine role" (*West Africa* 18–24 September 1989, 1574).

From another angle, the chief of army staff, Lieutenant General Salihu Ibrahim, focused on pushing "the attitude of the officers and soldiers towards greater emphasis on military professionalism than any other interests" (*West Africa* 6–12 January 1992, 36). Given the long history of military intervention and prominence in the country's political system, Lieutenant Ibrahim's emphasis on military professionalism (thus emphasizing that politics is not a proper sphere for the military) was admirable. Professionalism in the military leads to higher quality of military personnel, and thus enhances the combat readiness of the military. Logically, an enhanced combat readiness status of the military means that the capabilities for international peacekeeping activities and the defense needs of the country can be simultaneously achieved at adequate levels.

Due to the numerous peacekeeping activities Nigerian military forces were engaged in and the many border conflicts Nigeria was often also involved with, during the Babangida Government the Nigerian military forces' quality of personnel and weapon systems and its general combat readiness) were very important.

Nigeria had a significant commitment of military resources in Sierra Leone during the Babangida Government. Sierra Leone "had requested a Nigerian 'peacekeeping force' to help it fight rebel forces in the eastern part of Sierra Leone" (*West Africa* 8–14 March 1993, 384). The Nigerian government was said to have "rejected the idea, opting instead to train Sierra Leonians to do the fighting themselves" (*West Africa* 8–14 March 1993, 384). Thus, Nigerian military personnel were "to be sent to Sierra Leone to help that country establish an efficient fighting force," and "instructors, numbering 52 in all," had "already been selected by the Nigerian Army" (*West Africa* 8–14 March 1993, 384). This Nigerian military role in Sierra Leone seems to have become more elaborate and long-lasting than had been envisaged (in fact, the mission continued after the end of the Babangida Government).

Even more elaborate, complex, costly, and intense was the role of Nigerian military forces in Liberia during the Babangida Government. The peacekeeping force, which was organized by the Economic Community of West African States (ECOWAS),, and named the ECOWAS Monitoring Group (ECOMOG), was created to stabilize Liberia (which had experienced total breakdown of its governmental and political system and consequent socioeconomic chaos) and was for most of the time made up mostly of Nigerian military forces. Nigeria's premier role in ECOMOG also resulted in it providing most of the military commanders for ECOMOG. For example, in 1991, when Major-General Rufus Kupolati, the field commander of ECOMOG and a Nigerian, completed his tour of duty, he was replaced by Major-General Ishaya Bakut, another Nigerian (*West Africa* 23–29 September 1991, 1604).

Sometimes the activities of Nigerian military forces serving with ECOMOG threatened to negatively affect Nigeria's relations with countries bordering Liberia. For example, in 1993, the government of Cote d'Ivoire complained that aircrafts belonging to ECOMOG "had bombed Ivorian territory, killing and wounding customs officers, military personnel and civilians (*West Africa* 8–14 March 1993, 389). The foreign minister of Cote d'Ivoire, "in a strongly-worded protest letter," noted that "the raids had occurred in an area where there was a large number of Liberian refugees with ethnic affiliation to Cote d'Ivoire," and that "there were no armed . . . fighters" of a Liberian factional group in that area, and further 'commented that ECOMOG had exceeded its right to defend itself when attacked" (*West Africa* 8–14 March 1993, 389). It was reported that the air "raids were carried out . . . by four Nigerian Alpha aircrafts serving under ECOMOG," and that the "bombs were dropped near Danene, an Ivorian village near the border with Liberia" (*West Africa* 8–14 March 1993, 389).

Major-General Olatunji Olurin, the Nigerian commander of ECOMOG, said in his assessment of this incident that "the border is 580 km long and the same people live on each side of it. It is sometimes difficult to know who is Ivorian and who is Liberian. I would be surprised if this region [Danene], where there are only refugees, has really been bombed" (Olurin, quoted in *West Africa* 8–14 March 1993, 389). However, Olurin also commented that a Liberian factional group "had deployed a certain number of troops in the areas bordering Cote d'Ivoire and warned that ECOMOG would not hesitate to bomb military targets there" (*West Africa* 8–14 March 1993, 389).

Apart from foreign military missions, the Nigerian military forces also had to deal with many border conflicts during the Babangida Government. The border conflicts with Cameroun were the most prominent; luckily, however, they were often contained through diplomatic contacts between Nigerian and Camerounian officials (*West Africa* 6–12 January 1992, 35; *West Africa* 17–23 August 1992, 1409; and *West Africa* 8–14 March 1993, 384).

United Nations' peacekeeping operations represented another area that the Nigerian military was significantly involved in during the Babangida Government. Apart from the aforementioned roles of the Nigerian military in the United Nations peace-keeping missions in Angola and Rwanda/Uganda, the Somali United Nations' peacekeeping operations was also one of the United Nations missions in which the Nigerian military was involved in (*West Africa* 15–21 February 1993, 253; *West Africa* 8–14 March 1993, 384). The Nigerian military contingent to the Somali United Nations' peacekeeping mission was "led by Lieutenant-Colonel Ola Oyinlola" and consisted of "39 officers and 621 other ranks," and all of them "belonged to the military cantonment in Ikeja, Lagos" (*West Africa* 15–21 February 1993, 253).

As has been shown, during the Babangida Government the security components of Nigerian foreign policy were elaborate and significant, and Nigerian military forces played a very large role in their implementation. As shown by the above examples, the foreign activities of the Nigerian military mostly focused on Africa. Logically, this flowed from the long-standing conceptualization of Africa as the centerpiece of Nigeria's foreign policy.

This conceptualization is often associated with Nigeria's desire to play a leadership role in Africa. The role of France in Africa (especially through that country's visible roles in former French colonies) is often seen as a factor that militates against Nigeria's interests in Africa (Akinterinwa

1989, 91–122). Akinterinwa (1989, 118) sees the Nigerian military as one of the major instruments Nigeria can use in dealing with the role of France in Africa. According to him,

> if Nigeria is to be able to cope with French influence, the Nigerian Armed Forces must be made very strong. The determination of strongness should not be by comparison with African armies but with African-based French troops. This will be very costly, nonetheless, the problem is that of choice between whether to be, or not to be a great sub-regional power, economically and military wise. If Nigeria is to be, whatever is required has to be given, self and national sacrifice should be foremost in this case. The essential thing is to get the majority of Nigerians to agree with the national objective; which should be a "greater and well-respected Nigeria."

Akinterinwa even sees the role of France in Africa as being beneficial to the Nigerian military forces, because

> using France as a yardstick, it would be discovered that French military posture in Africa is regarded as a challenge. This will bring about the desire to improve. It is in this light that French military posture constitutes a catalyst in the process of Nigeria's military growth and development. It constitutes a blessing in different respects: French military presence cannot be perpetuated as it will be obliged to reckon with Nigeria. So will the Francophones be forced to reckon more with Nigeria. The Nigerian military would have been forced to develop and modernize and above all, a strong Nigeria will naturally start to attract international respect. (Akinterinwa 1989, 118–19)

Like Akinterinwa, other intellectuals have given their attention to the security components of Nigeria's foreign policy. Ate (1985, 66) sees Nigeria and South Africa (now ruled by the majority of its population) as possible future power centers in Africa that may be able to reduce or eliminate the influence of non-African countries in Africa. According to Ate, "what is envisaged is that the inevitable development of indigenous centers of power in Africa will serve as a rallying point in the ultimate task of constructing a truly post-colonial security order which, over time, will render redundant, and thus delegitimize the historical role of foreign powers in the management of African security" (Ate 1985, 66).

Despite its political and economic problems during the Babangida Government, Nigeria was beginning to lay the foundations for some of the actions suggested by Akinterinwa and Ate. Whether Nigeria, or Nigeria together with South Africa, will fully accomplish such goals will depend on political and economic developments in Nigeria and South Africa, the situations in and behavior of other African countries, and the behavior of non-African countries. The role that the Babangida Government played in organizing other west African countries, through ECOMOG, to intervene militarily in Liberia to stabilize the chaotic political situation there fits in well with the sort of role scholars like Akinterinwa and Ate suggested for Nigeria. Such an incident shows that African military forces (if they quickly and adequately assert themselves) can manage security crises in other African countries: thus reducing the possibility of non-African countries leading the management of security crises in African countries.

The prominent role that the Nigerian military played in the west Africa region in particular during the Babangida Government resulted in more countries in the region requesting the help of the Nigerian military in the management of their national security needs. For example, as a result of an agreement between Nigerian and Gambia "a Nigerian military officer, Col. Abubakar Dada," was appointed to "the post of Chief of Staff of the Gambian Army" and Nigerian army personnel "arrived in Banjul to train men of the Gambian army" (*West Africa* 6–12 April 1992, 600).

As shown above, in places like Gambia, Sierra Leone, Liberia, Somalia, Rwanda, and Angola, the Ministry of Defense (through the Nigerian military forces) played a very major role in articulating, planning, formulating, and implementing the security components of Nigerian foreign policy during the Babangida Government.

OTHER MINISTRIES AND AGENCIES

Many other ministries and agencies were also involved in foreign policy decision-making during the Babangida Government. However, it is important to note that for many of these other ministries and agencies the primary focus was on domestic policy issues, and their involvement in foreign policy was often incidental and/or intermittent. As aforementioned, it is possible to assume that during any governmental era almost all organs, ministries, and agencies of the federal government of Nigeria are, more or less, fully or partially, continuously or intermittently, involved in foreign policy decision-making. It is also important to note that in any foreign policy area (be it the political, security, economic, or cultural aspects of foreign policy), more than one ministry or agency is often involved in the formulation and implementation of policy; although usually only one plays the dominant role in shaping each particular foreign policy area or issue.

Thus, though the Ministry of Defense played the dominant role in the security components of the country's foreign policy during the Babangida Government, other government ministries and agencies were also involved in these components of foreign policy: for example, organizations within the intelligence community. As aforementioned, prior to the Babangida Government the Nigerian Security Organization (NSO) was a behemoth that dominated the intelligence community. The NSO's role as "first among equals in the Nigerian intelligence community . . . was in fact resented by the other agencies, especially the military and police" (Peters 1986, 152–53). In reality the NSO's "authority was never quite accepted" by other agencies (Peter 1986, 153). These frictions helped persuade the Babangida Government to abolish the NSO. In its place in 1986, emerged the National Intelligence Agency (NIA) for external intelligence activities, the State Security Service (SSS) for internal intelligence activities, and the Defense Intelligence Agency (DIA) (which was actually created in 1984, its existence merely formalized in 1986) for internal and external defense intelligence activities (Peters 1986, 158; Peters and Aminu 1986, 97, and 98 n. 9). The year 1986 also witnessed the "creation of the office of the Coordinator of National Security . . . as the head of the intelligence community" (Peters 1986, 158). It is important to note that with this creation of the coordinator of national security, the intelligence community now had a leader who had "no primary intelligence collection role" (Peters 1986, 158). With such a profile, the head of the intelligence community was in a position to concentrate on advising the president on intelligence matters and on coordinating all the organizations in the intelligence community without being biased toward any of them and, thus, receiving more cooperation from them all—and therefore increasing the efficiency and productivity of the entire intelligence community.

As the above roles and functions of the Office of the Coordinator of National Security, the National Intelligence Agency, the State Security Service, and the Defense Intelligence Agency show, during the Babangida Government these organizations most probably played significant roles in the security components of the country's foreign policy, especially as they related to the management of numerous border conflicts, the country's significant involvement in international security management operations in some west African countries, and the fastly evolving situations in the countries in southern Africa.

The Defense Intelligence Agency activities are often enhanced by the roles of the intelligence units of the various branches of the armed forces. The Directorate of Military Intelligence (DMI) of army supplies the army with information about the command structures, personnel profile, weapon systems, and general capability of armies of countries that may pose a threat to Nigeria; the Directorate of Naval Intelligence (DNI) does the same for the navy, and the Directorate of Air Intelligence (DAI) fulfills this role for the air force (Peters 1986, 153–54). The Defense Intelligence Agency provides a place where the outputs of the DMI, DNI, and DAI can be coordinated and made centrally available for use by government officials. The fact that the Defense Intelligence Agency is part of the Office of the Minister of Defense (Peters 1986, 154) greatly enhances its ability to play significant roles in the security components of the country's foreign policy. Interestingly, the roles of the Defense Intelligence Agency, DMI, DNI and DAI, as intelligence organizations within the Ministry of Defense, further strengthen the role of the Ministry of Defense.

Two other relevant Nigerian intelligence organizations are the Petroleum Intelligence Agency and Price Intelligence Agency (Peters 1986, 155), which are focused on the internal and external monitoring of the petroleum industry and the internal and external monitoring of prices of commodities, respectively. Peters (1986, 155) sees these two bodies as being able to supply relevant information for use in the conduct of Nigeria's foreign relations.

The Nigerian police force has the Federal Intelligence and Investigative Bureau (FIIB) at the national level of its organization and the State Intelligence and Investigation Bureaus (SIIBs) at the state level (*Newswatch* 3 April 1995, 20–21). The FIIB and the SIIBs, though focused on domestic intelligence and investigative work for normal policing and law enforcement needs, may stumble on intelligence that has international significance. It was during the Babangida Government that an organization called National Drug Law Enforcement Agency (NDLEA) was created for combating the drug problem. Due to the international nature of the trafficking of some drugs, the NDLEA has to continually develop and maintain relations with similar bodies in other countries, thus it is involved in the security components of the country's foreign policy.

As aforementioned, the economic components of foreign policy were of paramount importance during the Babangida Government (*West Africa* 9–15 October 1989, 1679; *West Africa* 25–31 May 1992, 874; *African Events* October 1989, 25; *African Concord* 24 May 1993, 34). The writings of many scholars also emphasized this importance during the Babangida era (for example, see Akindele 1990c, 106–23; Ayodele 1989, 140–57). Even before the Babangida Government, some scholars, like Olusanya (1984, 55–66), had called attention to the importance of the economic dimensions of the country's foreign policy. Thus, the foreign policy elite, both in academia and the world of practice, agreed that the economic aspects of the country's foreign policy should be emphasized. Also, the severe economic strains and stresses the country experienced during the Babangida Government elevated the economic components of foreign policy to a higher level, in order to help boost the economic performance of the country through international economic relations.

It is in this context of the push for economic diplomacy that explains Nigeria successfully leading and helping African countries to adopt the treaty establishing the African Economic Community, with the future "objective of creating an integrated common market" in Africa, during the 1991 Organization of African Unity Summit in Abuja (*West Africa* 9–15 March 1992, 406). Apart from multilateral economic diplomatic initiatives, such as the African Economic Community Treaty, Nigeria focused even more on bilateral international economic relations, for such bilateral trade and financial transactions with other countries were more concrete actions aimed at boosting Nigeria's economy through vigorous economic diplomacy.

During the Babangida era, as in other eras, numerous ministries and agencies were involved in helping to advance Nigeria's bilateral and multilateral international economic relations. The Federal Ministry of Trade (sometimes called the Federal Ministry of Commerce) was mainly in charge of international trade relations; the Federal Ministry of Petroleum Resources was mainly in charge of international relations in the area of petroleum resources affairs (for example, relations with OPEC); the Federal Ministry of National Planning (sometimes called the Federal Ministry of Economic Development) was mainly in charge of the management of relations with key international economic organizations (for example, ECOWAS); and the Federal Ministry of Finance and the Central Bank of Nigeria managed international financial relations (Akindele 1990c, 106–23; Ofoegbu 1990, 88–90). All the above ministries mostly deal with domestic economic policy issues and devote only some segments of their resources to their assigned roles in the area of international economic relations. In order to carry out their international roles, these ministries often relate with the Ministry of External Affairs, though such liaisons sometimes cause conflict due to the overlapping of roles (Akindele 1990c, 106–23; Ofoegbu 1990, 88–90). Also, for a period of time during the Babangida Government, there was a minister of state for Budgeting and Planning under the umbrella of the Presidency (*West Africa* 17–23 October 1988, 1967) and, later, a minister of Budgeting and Planning as full-fledged cabinet minister (*West Africa* 10–16 September 1990, 2434–35). This means that budgetary matters (which often belong to the Federal Ministry of Finance) were paired with the Planning Ministry for a period of time.

Apart from the above ministries, many other ministries and agencies were to some extent involved in some aspects of Nigeria's international economic relations, on a continuous or intermittent basis. For example, the Federal Ministry of Agriculture was involved in international issues that related to agriculture and food resources.

The major factor for strains and stresses in the country's economy during the Babangida Government was the enormous debt problem (especially external debts), which that government had inherited from prior governments. In fact, in order to handle the debt problem, the Babangida Government engaged in a series of negotiations with the International Monetary Fund (IMF) and other international financial bodies, and also instituted structural adjustment programs in the country's economy

(Biersteker 1989; *West Africa* 2–8 July 1990, 2031). Throughout the period of the Babangida Government, the management of the economy was a major preoccupation; the government emphasized the economic components of the country's foreign policy in order to enlist external economic dynamics to help boost the economy through more exports of Nigerian especially manufactured products and other non-petroleum products, and through the attraction of foreign investments into the country's economy.

The Babangida Government, however, also realized that the best way of improving a country's economy is through an internal effort to make the economy more efficient and productive. Enhancing the managerial skills in the economy is one way of achieving this goal. The Center for Management and Development (CMD), the Administrative Staff College of Nigeria (ASCON), the Industrial Training Fund (ITF), and the Institute of Management (NIM) (Chilaka and Imanyi 1989, 213) existed to meet this need. Management studies programs in polytechnic colleges and the undergraduate and graduate programs in business administration and public administration in the country's universities provided management education for both the private and public sectors of the economy. This effort to increase the managerial capacity in the entire economy was one good way to boost economic productivity.

During the Babangida Government, increases in the scientific and technological levels of the society were seen as other important ways of increasing the efficiency and productivity in the economy. In this vein, the Babangida Government established the National Commission on Science and Engineering Infrastructure (NASENI) to supervise all science and engineering research and development bodies and also to ensure that the outputs of these bodies were utilized and made commercially viable by industrial plants and companies. In explaining how NASENI would achieve its goals, its chairman; Professor Gordian Ezekwe, commented that

> the Science and Technology Infrastructure will enable the country to begin to master science and technology and convert this into hardware for development. For example, hardware for the establishment of industry, hardware for the implementation of agricultural projects, hardware for defense, education, etc. The possession of such hardware hinges on our capability to translate science principles through engineering into equipment, and we have to have an infrastructure to be able to engineer those capital products to build, design machinery and test them, and finally hand them over to industries to produce. (Ezekwe, quoted in *African Concord* 26 October 1992, 34)

On another occasion, Professor Ezekwe announced that NASENI was planning to post "attaches to selected Nigerian diplomatic missions abroad" and "certain international organizations" (*West Africa* 28 December 1992–10 January 1993, 2247–48). He added that the attachés were "to gather the latest information on new and advanced technologies" and that such "information supplied by the attaches would be stored for use by those implementing Nigeria's infrastructural development programmes" (*West Africa* 28 December 1991–10 January 1993, 2248). This move underscores the fact that NASENI was being prepared to help enhance the economic components of the country's foreign policy.

Another government agency that was very significant in helping to strengthen the economic components of the country's foreign policy was the Nigerian Export Promotion Council (NEPC). In fact, the NEPC was a frontline organ in the efforts of the Babangida Government to boost the country's international economic relations. For the government, the NEPC was one of the key elements capable of helping the private economic sector to dramatically increase Nigeria's export of manufactured goods and other non-petroleum exports. The plan was that, in the long term, such a strategy would help the country to build a modern industrialized economy not overly dependent on the export of petroleum resources.

The NEPC was important in the economic components of the country's foreign policy because the functions of the organization involved helping Nigerian businessmen contact, conclude, and transact trade deals with businessmen in other countries who wished to import Nigerian products. In order to carry out such functions, some NEPC officials were stationed in Nigerian foreign diplomatic missions (*Newswatch* 24 May 1993, 31–32) in countries that were considered vital to Nigeria's export drive. These NEPC officials posted to foreign countries were in good positions to aid Nigerian businessmen who wished to export to those countries.

The organization of trade exhibitions was another NEPC activity aimed at resulting in the promoting Nigerian exports and the actual contacts, conclusions, and transactions of deals between foreign and Nigerian businessmen. During the Babangida Government, the NEPC was especially active in this role. For example, in 1991 it was reported that "Nigeria secured trade deals worth $92.45m during the solo exhibitions . . . organized by the Nigerian Export Promotion Council (NEPC) in various African countries and abroad" (*West Africa* 2–8 March 1992, 377). On the occasion of this announcement Mahmud Yahaya, the minister of commerce and tourism, was reported to have enjoined the private sector in the country to "reciprocate the kind gesture of the government by expanding and diversifying production" (Yahaya, quoted in *West Africa* 2–8 March 1992, 377). Elaborating further, Yahaya added that "our performance in the export market will be determined by diversifying the volume of production, cost efficiency, quality of production packaging and labelling." Since Nigeria's push to increase exports was also accompanied by efforts to reduce imports into Nigeria, Yahaya also urged "private sector's participation in the present research and development programme on local sourcing of raw materials especially in the industrial, petrochemical and agro-allied sectors."

On the whole, the government was very happy about the exports of Nigerian products generated by trade exhibitions organized in foreign countries by the NEPC in 1991. It was reported that "the success of the export has been hailed by the government as another proof of its determination to encourage the private sector" (*West Africa* 2–8 March 1992, 377).

The Nigerian Export-Import Bank (NEXIM) was another frontline agency employed by the Babangida Government to translate the policy of encouraging exports of Nigerian products into a reality. NEXIM's main role is the provision of financial incentives to Nigerian companies that are involved in the export of Nigerian products to other countries. NEXIM also collaborates with commercial banks in the country to achieve its goals. For example, NEXIM gave an award to Commerce Bank Plc as "the top export financing bank in 1992." It was reported that "Commerce Bank used NEXIM's facilities to generate $8.2 million in 1992" (*Newswatch* 24 May 1993, 32). According to NEXIM, "Commerce Bank excelled its peers in the 1992 export year by contributing optimally to the realization of an export-led economic recovery."

There are many examples of these efforts to increase Nigeria's exports and general external economic activities resulting in some concrete results during the Babangida Government. In 1993 "the formation of Liberia's first airline" was made possible by the help of a Nigerian airline (*Newswatch* 6 December 1993, 28). "The airline, ADC Airlines Liberia Incorporated," was "the initiative of a Nigerian private airline, ADC Airlines, which owns 49 percent of the equity holding," and "Liberians own the remaining 51 percent" (*Newswatch* 6 December 1993, 28). With this business foothold in Liberia, ADC Airlines was able to take "over at least ten bilateral services agreements signed by Liberia with other countries in Africa, Europe and America," and thus secure the rights "to operate scheduled services" to several countries in many continents (*Newswatch* 6 December 1993, 28; *Newswatch* 28 March 1994, 31). Augustine Okon, the chief executive officer of ADC Airlines, asserted that "his airline would use whatever competitive advantages are available in the joint venture" (*Newswatch* 6 December 1993, 29).

In 1991 Concord Airlines, another Nigerian private airline, "signed an air agreement with the government of Equatorial Guinea"; "under the pact, Concord Airlines will assist in providing a reliable air transport arrangement to link Nigeria with Equatorial Guinea" (*African Concord* 1 July 1991, 43). At the time this agreement was publicized it was also reported that Concord Airlines had already "increased its flight schedule to Equatorial Guinea" (*Africa Concord* 1 July 1991, 43). Commenting about this agreement, Bashorun M. K. O. Abiola (the owner of Concord Airlines) described the agreement as a "practical demonstration of the federal government's policy of economic diplomacy" (Abiola, quoted in *African Concord* 1 July 1991, 43). In fact, the later ADC Airlines pact with Liberia in 1993 was a continuation of this Nigerian government's efforts help Nigerian businessmen to succeed in foreign markets.

There are other examples of the government's effort to enhance the economic components of the country's foreign policy. The minister of Budget and Planning led a Nigerian delegation to Indonesia to sig a cooperation agreement between the two countries "in the fields of agriculture, family planning, industry, civil engineering, construction, trade, mining, petroleum and gas, banking and finance and communications" (*West Africa* 8–14 October 1990, 2623), and the government cabinet member in charge of commerce and tourism led "a high-powered trade mission" to Taiwan (*West Africa* 15–21 February 1993, 254). The Nigerian team that went to Taiwan was "comprised of government officials and representatives of three bodies: the Nigerian Association of Chambers of Commerce, Industry, Mines and Agriculture (NACCIMA); the Association of Nigerian Exporters (ANE); and the Manufacturers Association of Nigeria (MAN)" (*West Africa* 15–21 February 1993, 254). The fact that this trade delegation to Taiwan included the representatives of these important bodies of the private sector of the Nigerian economy meant that it aimed primarily at helping the Nigerian companies transact and conclude business deals with their counterparts in Taiwan.

The visit of the prime minister of Trinidad and Tobago to Nigeria in 1991, apart from being wrapped in warm hospitality, also had strong undertones of economic ties. Prime Minister Arthur Robinson arrived in Nigeria "aboard a Nigerian Airways DC 10"; departed aboard "Nigeria's Presidential plane"; was "treated to a durbar at the Emir of Kano's palace"; was given a traditional title by the Oba Okunade Sijuwade (the Oni of Ife); and was awarded an honorary doctoral degree by Obafemi Awolowo University (*African Concord* 28 October 1991, 25). Accompanying this hospitality was a strong Nigerian desire to cement economic ties with Trinidad and Tobago. During this visit, the vice president of Nigeria, Augustus Aikhomu, enthused that "we have been authorized by our President to come into some very concrete agreements" (Aikhomu quoted in *African Concord* 28 October 1991, 25). These economic negotiations resulted in Nigeria and Trinidad and Tobago signing an agreement to cooperate in the area of petroleum resources (*African Concord* 28 October 1991, 25).

During the Babangida Government, Nigeria also reestablished diplomatic relations with Israel, as aforementioned. This resumption of links with

Israel was perceived by Nigeria as portending significant expansion of economic ties between the two countries (*African Concord* 18 May 1992, 21).

The petroleum industry, the backbone of the Nigerian economy, was not left behind in the efforts to increase the country's international economic links through export of products and services to other countries. Already the country's predominant exporter, the petroleum industry also sought to establish international economic ties in other ways. For example, it was reported that the Nigerian National Petroleum Corporation (NNPC), the umbrella organization of the petroleum industry, was trying to buy refineries in other countries in order to improve market conditions for Nigerian crude oil (*West Africa* 18–24 June 1990, 1039). Additionally, Integrated Data Services Limited (IDSL), a subsidiary of the NNPC, was able to compete with international petroleum services companies and win an important contract in Ghana (*Newswatch* 16 July 1990, 27–28; *West Africa* 3–9 July 1989, 1108–9; *West Africa* 22–28 January 1990, 104–5; *West Africa* 10–16 June 1991, 956). The IDSL contract in Ghana involved the company enabling Ghana to acquire seismic data and training Ghanaians "in seismic administration, equipment operations and seismic drilling" (*Newswatch* 16 July 1990, 27).

The success of the IDSL was a result of efforts to strengthen the Nigerian petroleum industry both scientifically and technologically. Another major development in the country's petroleum industry was the conscious effort of the government to ensure that Nigerians were directly involved in all aspects of the petroleum industry, as owner and operators. While Nigerians had long been much in control in terms of direct ownership and operation of transportation, refining, and marketing of petroleum products in the country, foreign oil companies were the major contractors employed by the NNPC for petroleum explorations and drilling activities. The Babangida Government adopted a policy aimed at making Nigerian-owned and -operated companies also active in petroleum exploration and drilling activities. It was noted that

> an important strategy in the "upstream" sector is the conscious decision that Nigerian entrepreneurship should be encouraged to participate in exploration and production activities. It is the most important strategic policy ever made by any Nigerian administration and involves a fundamental review of policy and the offer of special assistance and incentives for qualified and interested Nigerians. Nigerian entrepreneurs have responded with enthusiasm, and so far, they have performed with commendable skill and have achieved early and encouraging sources in exploration. (*West Africa* 4–10 May 1992, 752)

As a result of this support given to Nigerian entrepreneurs, two Nigerian-owned and -operated petroleum exploration and drilling companies, Summit Oil (owned by Bashorun M. K. O. Abiola) and Consolidated Oil (owned by Michael Adenuga), were able to drill productive oil wells by 1992 (*African Concord* 23 March 1992, 43; *West Africa* 4–10 May 1992, 753).

These efforts in the petroleum industry show that the Babangida Government policy to boost export of wide array of Nigerian products and services was complemented by efforts to create a modern and viable industrialized economy in the country that would sustain and accelerate such export drives.

As aforementioned, apart from its economic, political, and security dimensions, another major dimension of foreign policy is cultural. The cultural dimension of a country's policy covers the areas of external information, publicity, and general cultural activities aimed at other countries. The Federal Ministry of Information (FMOI), as usual, was the main organ in charge of these activities (*Africa Guardian* 16 April 1990, 12). As also aforementioned, the FMOI relates with the Ministry of External Affairs (MEA) in order to carry out many of its activities, and sometimes conflicts do develop over the role each should play (*African Guardian* 16 April 1990, 12) and, at other times, both FMOI and MEA seem to cooperate in carrying out these activities (*West Africa* 24–30 May 1993, 873). During the Babangida Government, the FMOI operated Nigeria Information Service Centers (NISCs) in some countries (*African Guardian* 16 April 1990, 12; *West Africa* 17–23 February 1992, 292). It is also important to note that Voice of Nigeria, an external radio broadcasting service, is an arm of the Federal Radio Corporation of Nigeria (FRCN), which is a corporation within the FMOI. Voice of Nigeria serves as another important instrument for external information, publicity, and general cultural activities aimed at other countries.

During the Babangida Government, organizations such as the Nigerian Institute of International Affairs (NIIA), the National Institute for Policy and Strategy (NIPSS), and the National Institute for Social and Economic Research (NISER) continued their tradition of serving as think tanks that provided the government with advisory inputs in foreign policy analysis and alternative foreign policy options. Some, like Banjo (1986), as shown earlier, have chronicled and analyzed the rich history and tradition of the NIIA in the country's foreign policy decision-making milieu. Olusanya (1990, 237–40) has also analyzed the various ways in which the NIIA has continued to have impact on the country's foreign policy decision-making, noting particularly its indirect roles ("lectures, seminars, symposia, radio and television discussions and debates" organized by NIIA), its numerous publications, its members' participation "in crucial discussions and decision-making at various levels", and its "direct input of research findings into the policy-making process." Speaking of the last-named contribution, Olusanya (1990, 237), a former director-general of the NIIA, adds that these direct inputs

> can be achieved by the preparations, on request of government or its agencies, of policy papers for use by government either in direct negotiations with foreign governments or bodies or as background information for such negotiations and there is evidence to show that such papers have been found useful by policy-makers. This can be discerned in two ways. One is by studying the outcome of such negotiations vis-a-vis the policy papers submitted. And, in any case, the very fact that such requests keep coming is an evidence that those so far produced have been found useful.

In terms of the participation of NIIA officials in the actual foreign policy decision-making processes, Olusanya (1990, 237) mentions, for example, "the participation of members of the research staff of" the NIIA "on various inter-ministerial meetings organized by the Ministry of External Affairs to deal with specific issues" and problems, "the membership of the Director-General" of the NIIA "on the Crisis Management Committee of the Ministry" of External Affairs, and the fact that, as a result of the Babangida Government's policy of appointing special advisers for ministers, two officials of the NIIA were seconded to the Ministry of External Affairs to serve, at various times, as the special advisers to the minister of External Affairs.

Professor Olusanya (1990, 238–39) also asserts that, during the Babangida Government, "the most significant evidence of the role of" the NIIA "in the foreign policy formulation was its pioneering of the current policy thrust of the Federal Military Government with its heavy emphasis on economic diplomacy. It is true that formal government pronouncement was made in June 1988 at a lecture delivered by the Minister of External Affairs, but" the NIIA had "been pushing the idea for months before."

On the whole, the positive impact of the NIIA in the foreign policy decision-making milieu was appreciated by many officials during the Babangida Government, including the president himself. President Babangida (quoted in Olusanya 1990, 240) said in 1986, "permit me to state, without equivocation that the Nigerian Institute of International Affairs has, in the past twenty-four years of its life, discharged, with distinction, those national objectives entrusted to it, and has thereby amply fulfilled the noble expectations of its founding fathers." He added that the NIIA has been seen as "one of the foremost International Affairs Research Institutions in the world."

Another major think tank that has a significant role in the foreign policy decision-making milieu is the National Institute for Policy and Strategy (NIPSS). While the NIIA devotes itself to policy oriented research in international affairs, the NIPSS covers national security policy issues, domestic policy issues, economic policy issues, and foreign policy issues. Unlike the NIIA, the NIPSS combines policy oriented research activities with a very prominent advanced policy studies program. This program lasts for about one year and those who undergo it are high-ranking members of the Nigerian military forces; senior members of other national security organizations; senior officials of federal and state ministries, agencies, and organs; senior members of the media; high-level managers from the private sector; leaders of labor organizations; and seasoned members of academia (*Newswatch* 27 November 1989, 15–19). Graduates of the NIPSS studies program in the Babangida era were the president; vice president; many senior members of the army, air force, and navy in charge of important command and staff positions; and many senior officials of the government, causing many to perceive the NIPSS as a dominate factor in the general policy decision-making milieu (*Newswatch* 27 November 1989, 15–19). The additional fact that the graduates of the NIPSS studies program maintain a contact through the NIPSS alumni organization and other avenues further strengthens the impact of the NIPSS. The NIPSS also impacts on the general policy decision-making milieu (including the foreign policy decision-making sector) through the outputs of its research and publications units.

Another significant think tank is the aforementioned Nigerian Institute of Social and Economic Research (NISER) (*Sunday Times* 23 April 1989, 1, 8). The NISER concentrates on research and publications mainly in the area of economics and social issues. Its research and publications in the spheres of international economics, trade issues, finance matters, and other related areas impact on the foreign policy decision-making milieu.

During the Babangida Government, the National Commission for Refugees (NCFR) was created to handle the influx of political and economic refugees from other African countries (*Newswatch* 23 August 1993, 3–4). The functions of the NCFR include the processing, settlement, and transit movement of refugees and other related matters (*Newswatch* 23 August 1993, 3–4). The very nature of its functions makes the NCFR a part of the foreign policy decision-making system, and also necessitates routine and significant relations with such organizations as the Ministry of External Affairs. The governing board of the NCFR, during the Babangida Government, included officials from the Ministry of External Affairs and the Presidency (*Newswatch* 23 August 1993, 3), a composition most probably designed to facilitate these liaisons.

On the whole, as shown above, numerous ministries, agencies, and organs were involved in the formulation and implementation of foreign policy during the Babangida Government, with varying roles and impacts.

Structures and Processes of Foreign Policy Decision-Making Coordination

The very fact that so many organizations were involved in the foreign policy decision-making milieu during the Babangida Government necessitated elaborate structures and processes for foreign policy decision-making coordination.

As shown above, the functions of the various ministries, organs, and agencies often overlapped, since many of them played roles in a particular broad policy area. For example, the Federal Ministry of Finance, the Federal Ministry of Trade, the Federal Ministry of National Planning, the Ministry of External Affairs, the Ministry of Petroleum Resources, the Nigerian National Petroleum Corporation, the Nigerian Export Promotion Council, the Nigerian Export Import Bank, and other organizations were all involved in managing various aspects of the country's international economic relations; and the Federal Ministry of Information and the Ministry of External Affairs worked together to manage the country's external information, publicity and cultural activities (Akindele 1990c, 106–23; Ofoegbu 1990, 85–105). Due to the inevitable overlapping of functions and bureaucratic turf protections, some conflicts did occur between and/or among some ministries and agencies, as shown earlier.

In order to minimize and manage such conflicts, foreign policy decision-making coordination machinery was needed. The structures and processes for foreign policy decision-making coordination can be viewed as having existed in three forms during the Babangida Government. One form involved officials from a ministry or agency that had the primary responsibility for a particular foreign policy issue chairing an inter-ministerial committee of officials from ministries and/or agencies that also had some responsibilities for that particular issue. Olusanya (1990, 237) has mentioned "a number of committees and Task Forces set up by government to look into one aspect or another of our external relations"; "various inter-ministerial meetings organized by the Ministry of External Affairs to deal with specific issues"; and "the Crisis Management Committee of the Ministry" of External Affairs, which all existed during the Babangida Government. Akindele (1990c, 117) has also noted how "the existence of often complex issue-linkages and policy interrelatedness in public life and the necessity for involving all relevant interests in decision-making have visually led to the creation of inter-ministerial committees for consideration and recommendation of policy proposals for final approval, sometimes at the highest political and governmental level."

Another form of foreign policy decision-making coordination consisted of broad national policy-making bodies at high political and governmental levels, as noted above by Akindele. As he has also noted, issues that were handled at departmental levels by inter-ministerial committees led to recommendations that were approved, modified, or disapproved by these national bodies. These national policy-making bodies were the National Council of Ministers (NCM) (the federal cabinet body) and the Armed Forces Ruling Council (the highest policy decision-making body in the country for all issues—both domestic and foreign) (Akindele 1990c, 118; Akindele 1990b, 247).

Another form of foreign policy coordination came into play when the Presidency decided to take charge of the foreign policy decision-making, with the Ministry of External Affairs and others playing only subordinate roles. In such circumstances the Presidency acted as a vigorous coordinating body that sometimes did ignore other views. In practice, this occurred infrequently (only when the Presidency had a very strong interest in a particular issue). One example of this was the foreign policy decision-making dynamics in deciding the sort of relationship Nigeria was to have with the Organization of Islamic Conference (Olukoshi 1990a, 495–97).

In practice, foreign policy decision-making coordination during the Babangida Government seems to have usually involved all the above forms of coordination. For example, in the decision-making that led to Nigeria's boycott of the 1986 Edinburgh Commonwealth Games, the Ministry of External Affairs and the Presidency cooperated as equal partners (while, however, excluding some ministries that they thought might have opposing views) to reach a decision (Olukoshi 1990b, 471–73). In another example, in the decision to create the African Petroleum Producers' Association (APPA), ministerial committees or groups worked on the detail, and technical issues and laid the policy foundations (keeping the Presidency informed throughout their deliberations), and the president, through the National Council of Ministers, made the final decision to create APPA (Nwoke 1990, 484).

In the fourth (final and transitional) phase of the Babangida Government, as noted earlier, the Armed Forces Ruling Council (AFRC) was replaced by the National Defense and Security Council (NDSC), and the National Council of Ministers (NCM) was replaced by the Transitional Council (*West Africa* 7–13 December 1992, 2107). Thus, during that phase the NDSC and the Transitional Council played the foreign policy coordinating roles that the AFRC and the NCM had formerly played. Additionally, the transitional phase also had a National Assembly (consisting of the Senate and House). Though the National Assembly had a somewhat restricted legislative role and the NDSC was the highest policy-making body (*West Africa* 25–31 January 1993, 112; *West Africa* 24–30 May 1993, 871), the National Assembly was in a position to help coordinate foreign policy (though in a very limited way) during the final and transitional phase of the Babangida Government.

Conclusion

A general overview shows that the foreign policy decision-making structures, processes, and outputs were varied during the Babangida Government. As in other governmental eras, most of the country's political, security, economic, and cultural relations with other countries dealt with routine issues. In most cases, these routine issues were handled by one particular ministry or agency, or by a cooperative effort of some ministries and/or agencies. Here the foreign policy decision-making dynamics mostly conformed to the organizational process decision-making model, since decisions were based on standard operating procedures of the organization(s).

However, in cases of major foreign policy issues the foreign policy decision-making dynamics were more elaborate and complex. For example, in another study (Inamete 1990, 39–50), the author has noted how the foreign policy decision-making dynamics in relation to the country's handling of the issue of acceptance or non-acceptance of International Monetary Fund (IMF) loan arrangements during the Babangida Government were so highly unusual that they could not be classified into any of the prevailing decision-making models (and thus necessitated a suggestion of a new decision-making model). This IMF loan issue was essentially handled by national public debating forums across all parts of the country, with the national leadership merely validating the consensus of that national debate; in this case the various important ministries that handle the economic components of Nigeria foreign policy did not have their usual prominent impact on the decision.

In the 1986 Edinburgh Commonwealth Games issue, the initial decision-making dynamics might have involved the federal ministry in charge of sports being lukewarm about the boycott of the games (since such a boycott would diminish its own activities, while the Ministry of External Affairs supported a boycott in order to support a foreign policy principle and interests (and thus, also enhance the diplomatic activities and general importance of the MEA). Thus, in the initial stage, the decision-making dynamics seem to have been poised to follow the bureaucratic politics decision-making model, with the ministries and agencies advancing divergent policy positions (which mostly served the interests of the respective ministries and agencies), which would probably lead to bargaining and then compromises among the ministries and agencies in order to reach a decision. However, the MEA co-opted the Presidency, and these two units worked together in secrecy to reach a decision to boycott the games with other interested ministries and agencies protesting the decision when they were finally informed about it through the media (Olukoshi 1990b, 471–75). Thus, the final stages of the decision-making dynamics mostly conformed to the rational actor decision-making model, since the MEA and the Presidency considered the issue of the Games in terms of national interest and costs and benefits to foreign policy goals and principles. In addition, with ministries or agencies that would have brought divergent views being frozen out of the decision-making system, the decision processes focused more on how to use the country's position on the Games to advance foreign policy goals, rather than also taking into account the interests of athletes (who had been training for years to win sports honors for themselves and their country), sports officials and officials of the ministry in charge of sports (who had been working hard for months to show the world and the country the seasoned athletes the sports management had been able to produce), and private sector sports sponsors (who had hoped to gain public relations and advertising benefits for the resources they had spent in promoting sports).

The decision-making processes associated with the issue of Nigeria's membership or nonmembership in the Organization of Islamice Conference (OIC) presented yet another category of decision-making dynamics. The OIC decision-making dynamics were much affected by religious and cultural groups who strongly sought Nigeria's full membership in the OIC, and equally by other religious and cultural groups who strongly opposed Nigeria attaining full membership in the OIC. The fact that the OIC issue was a very sensitive and potentially explosive one made the Presidency directly take charge of the decision-making (with the Ministry of External Affairs playing a subordinate role). Possibly the Presidency acted as it did to avoid decision-making chaos or paralysis. However, this seems to have resulted in a kind of decision-making milieu that fostered group-think syndrome, which Janis (1972) had discovered in similar decision-making settings. The OIC issue decision-making system seems to have involved mainly the president and a few officials who shared similar worldviews, or were not capable of providing divergent and/or correcting inputs if a member of the decision-making group was making erroneous assumptions or conclusions. On the whole, the OIC issue decision-making system seems to have had a very narrow base of inputs. Thus, as a true product of a group-think syndrome decision-making milieu, the OIC issue produced an inadequate decision (which also caused significant disaffection in some segments of the population and resulted in drawn-out public controversy). Inevitably, the negative public reaction made the president waffle on this issue up to the end of that government.

In contrast, the Babangida Government employed a decision-making system for the African Petroleum Producers' Association (APPA) issue that was a classic reflection of the rational actor model of decision-making. As shown above, various ministries and agencies worked together to provide policy details and technical information and build policy foundations, while continually briefing the Presidency on progress; and after being provided with the outcome of their deliberations, the president, through the National Council of Ministers, made the decision to create APPA (Nwoke 1990, 484). In this decision-making system, all the relevant ministries and agencies were eager to work together to lay the foundations for an organization that would help Nigeria and other African petroleum producers to enhance their positions within OPEC and the general global petroleum industry.

On the whole, as shown above, on routine foreign policy issues, the organizational process decision-making model was used, while on major foreign policy issues, the decision-making dynamics varied with each particular issue (thus, variously reflecting the group-think syndrome model of decision-making, the bureaucratic politics decision-making model, and the rational-actor decision-making model).

A general overview of the Babangida Government also shows that it paid a great deal of attention to the economic components of the country's foreign policy. It was the first government in the country to formally declare (and actively implement) a foreign policy that positioned the economic components of foreign policy as the most important; prior governments paid more attention to the political components of foreign policy.

As also shown by Nigeria's role in international security management in Liberia, Sierra Leone, and Gambia, and in United Nations peacekeeping missions in Somalia, Rwanda, and Angola, the Babangida Government also devoted attention to the security components of the country's foreign policy. That most of these international security management operations focused on Africa also shows that the Babangida Government continued the tradition of placing Africa as the centerpiece of Nigeria's foreign policy.

9
The Shonekan Government Interlude

THE FOURTH (FINAL AND TRANSITIONAL) PHASE OF THE BABANGIDA Government did not lead to a fully democratic government in the country due to the abortion of the presidential election that was to produce an elected president to complement the already elected members of the National Assembly (consisting of the Senate and House of Representatives), elected state governors, elected members of state legislatures, elected local government chairmen, and elected members of the local government councils. President Babangida handed over power to an appointed president to head an interim government that was to prepare the country for full democracy. The president of the interim government was Ernest Shonekan. The Shonekan Government was very brief, lasting from late August 1993 to the middle of November 1993 (*West Africa* 29 November–5 December 1993, 2153–56).

Shonekan was a business executive until he was appointed the head of the Transitional Council during the fourth (final and transitional) of the Babangida Government. After the abortion of the presidential elections, Babangida stepped down as president, leaving Shonekan to lead the country. It was widely perceived that Shonekan did not have a full grip on the interim government he headed; Sanni Abacha (a general in the army and the head of the Ministry of Defense) was believed to be the real source of power in that government (*West Africa* 29 November–5 December 1993, 2153–56). When Shonekan resigned (some suggested he was forced to resign), Abacha replaced him as president.

The very brief duration of the Shonekan Government and the perception that Shonekan did not have an adequate grip on power meant that the government had little impact on the foreign policy arena. Additionally, the widespread public disaffection with the abortion of the presidential election (and thus the disaffection with the interim government itself, which some segments of the population even tried not to recognize) caused significant sociopolitical instability. The Shonekan Government, thus, had to concentrate much of its attention on the domestic front.

Whatever attention the Shonekan Government paid to foreign policy was mainly reactive, trying to contain and minimize the negative reactions in many important countries of the world, which were displeased with political developments in Nigeria not leading to a democratic government.

The decision-making structures (including foreign policy decision-making structures) during the Shonekan Government were not much different from those of the Babangida Government, especially those of the fourth phase of the Babangida Government. The highest executive body was the Interim National Government (ING), headed by Shonekan and which included the political heads of the ministries, the secretary to the ING, the chairman of the National Planning Commission, and three National Assembly liaison officers (*West Africa* 6–12 September 1993, 1575). There was also the National Assembly (consisting of the Senate and the House of Representatives), which served as the legislative arm of the government. The federal ministries and agencies were more or less as they were during the period of the Babangida Government, with some of them having new political heads. Thus, on the whole the decision-making system, and more specifically the foreign policy decision-making system, was not much different from that of the prior Babangida Government. However, the government's very short duration and tenuous position meant that it was not able to focus adequately on foreign policy issues. This reality might have contributed to the Shonekan Government's attempt to withdraw "Nigerian troops out of the ECOWAS peace-monitoring group (ECOMOG) in war-torn Liberia," though Shonekan later decided not to withdraw the troops after a meeting in Abuja with the head of the Liberian government, since that meeting concluded that "Nigeria's sacrifices so far should not be negated by an untimely withdrawal" (*West Africa* 22–28 November 1993, 2117).

The lull in foreign policy activities was due to the above political situation rather than the nature and strength of the foreign policy and national security policy decision-making structures and processes. As was demonstrated by the handling of an attempted hijacking of a Nigerian airline, these decision-making structures were as efficient and effective as ever (*Newswatch* 15 November 1993, 18–20). Shonekan was attending a Commonwealth of Nations summit in Cyprus when the attempted hijacking happened, but the national security, foreign policy, and aviation organizations were able to successfully end the crisis before he was back in the country. As soon as Captain Makpo of Airbus A310 of Nigerian Airways (which was making a scheduled passenger flight from Lagos to Abuja) reported the hijacking to the control towers at Abuja and Kano and also filed distress signals, three aircrafts within Nigerian airspace picked up the signals (a Nigerian Airways aircraft returning from Saudi Arabia, another Nigerian Airways aircraft flying from Yola, and a G4 jet aircraft belonging to the presidential aircraft fleet of the Nigerian leadership that was conveying Ismaila Gwarzo, the national security adviser to The nigerian President, to Maiduguri). Changing the course of his aircraft to pursue the hijacked aircraft, Gwarzo, still airborne, was able to persuade the government of Chad to forbid the hijacked aircraft to land in N'djamena, Chad, to refuel enroute to Germany. The hijackers (four Nigerians) then ordered the plane to fly to Niamey, Niger Republic. Eight minutes later, Gwarzo also arrived at Niamey International Airport and immediately met with officials of the Republic of Niger and with Ja'affa Koguna, Nigeria's ambassador to the Republic of Niger, to make plans and to communicate with the hijackers. Meanwhile, in Nigeria, a task force was set up "to monitor the crisis and work out strategies for getting out of the mess. With the approval of Mustapha Umara, secretary to the Interim Government of Nigeria, and Bashir Dalhatu, the head of the Ministry of Transport and Aviation, the task force arranged for a rescue plane to bring back the freed passenger to Nigeria. Dalhatu, accompanied by Tijani Ahmed, the chairman of the Senate Committee on Transport and Aviation, and other officials, went to the Republic of Niger to supervise the return of the passengers to Nigeria. Another team of officials from Nigeria, consisting of officials "from the ministry of foreign affairs, the Nigerian Intelligence Agency, NIA, and the Defense Intelligence Service" and headed by Kabir Ahmed, an official of the Ministry of Foreign Affairs, flew to Niamey to help manage the crisis; and the team also brought with them "communication equipment with which contact was made with Shonekan, who was in Cyprus for the Commonwealth Summit", and thus, "fax, telex, radio and telephone communication with the world were established at the airport and the Nigerian embassy" (*Newswatch* 15 November 1993, 20). After a series of negotiations and ploys to wear down the hijackers, and one day after the team from Nigeria (led by Kabir Ahmed of the Ministry of Foreign Affairs) arrived in the Republic of Niger, the commando forces of Republic of Niger stormed the hijacked aircraft and the hijackers were overpowered and taken into custody for their trial.

This stellar performance by the Ministry of Foreign Affairs, the other national security organizations, and the aviation officials shows that the foreign policy decision-making structures and processes were still very efficient and effective during the Shonekan Government. However, as noted earlier, the vrevity of the government, the inability of Shonekan to control the government, and the sociopolitical instability caused by the delays to full democracy meant that the Shonekan Government which could not afford to adequately focus on foreign policy issues.

10
The Abacha Government

THE ABACHA GOVERNMENT CAME INTO EXISTENCE IN NOVEMBER 1993 (*West Africa* 29 November–5 December 1993, 2155–56) and lasted until President Sani Abacha's death in June 1998.

The political problems in the country caused by the cancellation of the 1993 presidential election and the failure to restore deomcracy, which had plagued the Shonekan Government, continued during the Abacha Government. The fact that the solutions to these political problems seem to have been even more elusive during the Abacha Government heightened the turmoil. Like the Shonekan Government, the Abacha Government also faced pressures from many important countries of the world that were displeased with Nigeria's continuance of non-democratic polity. For example, pro-democracy Nigerian activists who traveled to Western countries were well received and some countries, such as the United States, imposed sanctions against Nigeria (*West Africa* 22–28 August 1994; 1474; *West Africa* 23–29 January 1995, 119). Additionally, the Abacha Government still had to deal with many other foreign policy issues, such as the role of Nigeria in peacekeeping activities in Liberia, Sierra Leone, and other countries and the perennial border conflicts.

The Abacha Government was a military government headed by President Sani Abacha. The highest decision-making body during this government was the Provisional Ruling Council (PRC) (*West Africa* 29 November–5 December 1993, 2153–55). Another important national body was the Federal Executive Council (FEC) (*West Africa* 6–12 December 1993, 2204–05; *West Africa* 27 March–2 April 1995, 466), which was the executive cabinet body. Additionally, the Presidency continued to be the important nerve center for important national policy-making. The relevant various federal ministries and agencies also continued their traditional roles in the area of foreign policy. The functioning and roles of the PRC, the FEC, the Presidency, and other national bodies, together with those of the federal ministries and agencies in the area of foreign policy decision-making will be examined in this section, starting with the PRC.

The PRC consisted of the president (as the chairman), the minister of Defense, the chief of Defense Staff, the chiefs of staff of the Nigerian army, navy, and air force, the inspector general of police, senior military officers, national security advisers, and a few ministers heading ministries with some national security related functions (*West Africa* 29 November–5 December 1993, 2153–2155). The PRC, as the highest decision-making body in the country, dealt with important, vital national policy issues (both domestic and foreign). The domestic and foreign policy issues that reached the PRC were often those that had been weighed and analyzed by other national bodies and/or ministries and agencies; the PRC was mainly to provide the decisions. In the case of regular and routine foreign policy issues, the FEC, the Presidency, the Ministry of Foreign Affairs, the Ministry of Defense, and many other ministries, organs, were able to decide.

The FEC consisted of the president, as chairman, and the ministers of the various ministries (*West Africa* 6–12 December 1993, 2204–5; *West Africa* 27 March–2 April 1995, 466). As the executive cabinet body consisting of the heads of the ministries, the FEC was a very important decision-making body for both domestic and foreign policy issues, since it enabled those in charge of the various functions of the government to collectively deliberate, share information, and, through their collective insights, help make decisions. Very important decisions of the FEC most likely had to receive the final approval of the PRC.

In the area of external relations matters, the FEC was a very suitable body. Since the political, security, economic, and cultural components of foreign policy are often policy areas in which many ministries had to work together, the FEC provided a good forum for the heads of these ministries to deliberate together in order to reach more harmonious decisions.

The Presidency was another important national decision-making body. It continued as the organ that provided the president with elaborate and complex machinery for national governance and administration. Expectedly, the governance, management, and leadership style of President Abacha affected how the Presidency was structured, and how it functioned, during the Abacha Government. It can be said that Abacha had a complex leadership style. He wielded enormous power, while at the same time allowing his cabinet officials and other senior officials adequate freedom to lead and administer their respective ministries or departments. Abacha was tough and tenacious, but at the same time known for his shyness and his love of listening to others talk. he himself rarely spoke, and on those very rare occasions whe he did, his tone was very low and almost inaudible. Abacha spoke

> softly, almost inaudibly, like in a whisper and you have to strain your ears to hear him. Perhaps that is a strategy, the strategy of a consummate wielder of power to get his listeners to truly listen. . . . Some who know Abacha think he is a shy man but that may not be the reason for his near-whisper level of

discussion. They think he is not a man of emotion, that he never really raises his voice even when he is angry but that he lets actions, not thunderous words, speak for him. Which is why some who don't know him well, but who have listened to him talk softly are surprised by his tough guy actions. (*Newswatch* 24 November 1997, 10–11)

Mohammed Abukakar Rimi (a former minister of Communications in the Abacha Government who, after leaving his cabinet post, became a very strong critic of the government and was indeed jailed by that government) analyzed how Abacha's tendency not to talk affected the style he (Abacha) used in running the cabinet and the government. According to Rimi, Abacha "was the most patient man on earth. We would hold a cabinet meeting for three hours and he would not say a word. . . . I am sure he understood what was happening. And also he cracked a joke one day and said that people shouldn't bother if he was not speaking at cabinet meetings, that he was learning. Because this cabinet was made up of distinguished Nigerians, distinguished ministers and the amount of grammar they spoke impressed him a lot" (Rimi, quoted in *Newswatch*, 1 February 1999, 20). Abacha was probably also using the cabinet meetings to gauge the strengths and weaknesses of the cabinet members, in terms of their ability to head their respective government ministries. This evaluation of the cabinet members might have accounted for the change in Abacha's style of working with them. According to Rimi, "Later I think he changed the style of meeting. He was dealing with the ministers on [a] one to one basis" (Rimi, quoted in *Newswatch* 1 February 1999, 20). Other observers have noted that "Abacha's strength lies not simply in the fact that he keeps his cards close to his chest since he says very little about anything, but also in the fact that his opponents grossly underrate him. They say that he doesn't read much, can't sustain a prolonged discussion so what has he got to offer? Not much, they say until he pulls the rug from under their feet. As a patient listener Abacha must have picked up along the way by virtue of the offices he's held, a lot of political savvy" (*Newswatch* 24 November 1997, 13). It has also been noted that, even though Nigerians have had many strong military leaders before,

it does appear, by hindsight, that all of them were manufactured from concentrates. Now we have the real thing: Abacha. . . . Abacha is a hammer without velvet. . . . Abacha is a patient man, one who is willing to give you a long rope to tie yourself with. That stands him out as a long term planner and strategist. Which is why those who expect quick action from him often feel disappointed.

Abacha's tenacity, some call it obduracy, is evident in the government's hand combat with the Commonwealth, Britain and the United States in the last three years. That no biting sanctions or no severer action has been taken against Nigeria is a tribute to Abacha's ability to face his opponents eyeball to eyeball while dangling some carrots to African communities, and the former socialist states as a means of melting the solidarity block that was needed to drown Nigeria (*Newswatch* 24 November 1997, 14).

Another important aspect of the leadership style of Abacha was his tendency to be inaccessible to many top officials of his government. This situation resulted in some occasions when key officials gave contradictory views on the government's position on some issues (*Theweek* 2 June 1997, 15). Another paradox of Abacha is that though he was the only dominant force in his government, he allowed his ministers a lot of freedom to run their ministries, and even allowed ministers to openly debate and/or disagree with fellow ministers on policy issues (*Theweek* 7 July 1997, 10–15; *Theweek* 28 July 1997, 5; *Theweek* 4 August 1997, 11–14). For an example, Anthony Ani, the minister of Finance, strongly criticized Dan Etete, the minister of Petroleum Resources, over the fuel scarcity situation in the country, by saying that "with sound planning and a good oil and gas policy, Nigeria should no longer be scandalized by the persistent fuel shortage as we have seen recently" (*Theweek* 4 August 1997, 12).

> Ani's attack on Etete . . . signalled the commencement of another verbal warfare among top government officials. The first reaction from the ministry of petroleum resources as good as called the finance minister a madman. Giving the impression that Etete was not interested in a confrontation, the statement said that "the honourable minister of petroleum resources believes that sensible neighbours do not adopt the antics of a madman who chooses to dance naked at the village square." The statement described Ani's claim as "a deliberate falsehood with intent to incite Nigerian masses and pitch the international community against not only the ministry of petroleum resources . . . but to embarrass and discredit the present administration. (*Theweek* 4 August 1997, 12–13)

Also, when Mohammed Marwa, the administrator of Lagos State, criticized how the petroleum industry was managed, Etete described Marwa as being "very very childish" (Etete, quoted in *Theweek* 4 August 1997, 13). The fact that despite these utterances all three officials (Ani, Etete, and Marwa) were able to hold their official posts until the end of the Abacha Government shows that the all powerful Abacha tended to give free rein to his top officials. Giving a clue to how the Presidency functioned in controlling the ministries and agencies, it has been noted that during the tense exchanges between Ani and Etete

> the presidency, though unamused, followed it keenly. Abacha's interest in the whole drama of the absurd was to empanel investigators to look into the claims and counter-claims being made by the combatants in government to determine

whether funds have been wasted or misappropriated. The head of state, according to the high level source, already aware of the personality clash between two ministers who are very close to him, was said to have refused to interfere in the verbal war. The aim, it was learnt further, was for the head of state to be able to gather enough intelligence on the two men. (*Theweek* 7 July 1997, 12)

On the whole, a general evaluation of the Abacha Government is that Abacha was a president who, while being in full control of the governing machinery, allowed his ministers, advisers, and assistants to have some measure of autonomous power (*Newswatch* 25 September 1995, 10–15). Abacha was also perceived as a leader who, while insisting on stamping his approval on all vital domestic and foreign policies, did not like being burdened with elaborate policy briefing papers (he preferred about two pages of recommendations papers); was very reluctant to provide time to meet with many ministers, state governors, and other high government officials and public leaders who sought appointments with him (though his few trusted friends, inside and outside the government, could easily meet with him); and convened the meetings of the PRC and FEC very infrequently (*Newswatch* 25 September 1995, 10–15). All these dynamics combined to make the Presidency a very powerful nerve center for public policy decision-making (both in domestic and foreign policy areas) during the Abacha era.

Within the Presidency was the Office of the Chief of General Staff headed by the chief of General Staff, who was Lieutenant General Oladipo Diya for most of the Abacha era. He served in this position from the beginning of the Abacha Government until the last few months of that government. Diya was removed from that position after he was said to have been involved in planning a coup (*Newswatch* 2 March 1998, 8–14; *The New York Times* 16 February 1998, A4). The position of the chief of General Staff was left vacant by the Abacha Government for the last few months of that government and the sudden death of President Abacha, a few months after Diya's removal, meant that the position was not filled. There is a possibility that the Abacha Government never intended to fill the position, since there was a plan to replace the military government with a civilian government in October 1998. As the number two person in the country, the chief of General Staff, just as during the Babangida era, assisted the president in overseeing federal government relations with state and local governments, the supervision of some organizations deputizing for the president in events and meetings the president was not able to attend, and many other duties the president shifted to him.

The Office of the secretary to the Federal Government, headed by the Secretary to the Federal Government, was another important unit within the Presidency. The Office of the Secretary to the Federal Government is the unit through which most of the paper flow from the various ministries and agencies reaches the Presidency; additionally, this unit ensures the proper scheduling and documentation of the deliberations of the meetings of various national bodies like the PRC and FEC, and the proper transmission of action orders from these bodies to the specific ministries and agencies charged with the implementation of those decisions. Normally, the Office of the Secretary to the Federal Government is a low-key (though a very vital) policy and administrative coordinating unit within the Presidency. However, during the Abacha Government this unit seems to have become a very high-profile and visible policy and administrative unit of the Presidency. Additionally, the Office of the Secretary to the Federal Government seems to have acquired a lot more power. The dramatic increase in the profile, visibility, and power of this office, for an example, was demonstrated by the fact that it was the Office of the Secretary of the Federal Government that organized a seminar in 1995 in Abuja to formally mark the beginning of public discourse, and canvassing of public inputs, in relation to the country's draft constitution (*Newswatch* 14 August 1995, 7, 19–20). In 1995, the head of this office, Aminu Saleh (the secretary to the Federal Government), was also seen as one of the most influential officials of the Abacha Government (*Newswatch* 14 August 1995, 7, 19–20; *Newswatch* 25 September 1995, 14–15; *Newswatch* 2 October 1995, 11). The power the secretary to the Federal Government (and his office) acquired was directly at the expense of the power of the chief of general staff (and his office) (*Newswatch* 2 October 1995, 11). The erosion of the power of Lieutenant-General Oladipo Diya, the chief of general staff (CGS) was so severe that in 1995 it was even speculated that "the office of the CGS was made redundant because apart from Abacha himself, most other decisions are taken by Aminu Saleh" (*Newswatch* 2 October 1995, 11). Thus, in 1995, though Diya was formally the person next in position to the president, Saleh was in reality the second most powerful person in the country. Interestingly, therefore, in the military Abacha Government a civilian (at least in 1995) was the second most powerful person in that government, even though a lieutenant-general in the Nigerian army formally held the second most important position. The power of the Office of the Chief of General Staff was so severely eroded by Aminu Saleh and his Office of the Secretary to the Federal Government that, in 1995, there were even speculations that Diya "may be retired and removed from his position" (*Newswatch* 2 October 1995, 11). However, in accordance with the reality of the vicissitudes of power configurations and the arena of politics, it was Saleh, not Diya, who lost his position. Soon after predictions by the national media that the tremendous growth of the powers of the Office of the Secretary to the Federal Government would force Diya, suddenly lost his position in October 1995 (*Newswatch* 30 October 1995, 14–19). Apparently, even Abacha had finally come to the conclusion that Saleh was exercising powers that far exceeded those that properly belonged to the Office of the Secretary to the Federal Government, and thus decided to remove Saleh from his position (*Newswatch* 30 October 1995, 14–19). Saleh was replaced by Gidado Idris, whose last position was that of director-general in the Federal Ministry of Finance (*Newswatch* 30 October 1995, 14–19).

The increased profile, visibility, and power of the Office of the Secretary to the Federal Government meant that this unit of the Presidency was able to have more impact on policy-making (in both domestic and foreign policy arenas).

Within the Presidency there were also various presidential special advisers and presidential assistants who aided the president in handling domestic and/or foreign policies. During the Abacha Government one such official was Sule Hamma, presidential special adviser on Political Affairs. One prominent foreign affairs role Hamma played was that of coordinator of an observer mission to monitor the elections in Liberia in 1997 (*Theweek* 28 July 1997, 28). Also, as the presidential adviser on Legal Matters, Professor Auwalu Yadudu, was involved in helping to handle "the Nigerian-Cameroun case over the disputed Bakasi peninsula at the World Court in The Hague, Netherlands" (*Newswatch* 12 October 1998, 10). Yadudu was also the Nigerian official who told officials of the United Nations Commission on Human Rights, who were visiting Nigeria to assess the human rights situation, what their mandate in Nigeria consisted of (*Theweek* 10 March 1997, 19). Major General Lawrence Onoja, a general staff officer in the Presidency, was also one of the officials who made pronouncements on foreign policy issues (*Newswatch* 10 November 1997, 25). Onoja made a statement that Nigeria should be made a permanent member of the United Nations' Security Council, and added that "there was no point paying lip service to democracy if the UN is not democratised by expanding the security council to give new members veto power" (*Newswatch* 10 November 1997, 25). Admission of Nigeria as a permanent member of the United Nations' Security Council was an ambition the Abacha Government took very seriously (*Theweek* 7 April 1997, 26).

Wada Nas was a presidential special adviser who particularly specialized in making strong statements on foreign policy issues in order to make some countries uncomfortable (*Theweek* 15 June 1998, 14). There were also officials within the Presidency who were seconded from the Ministry of Foreign Affairs: Ambassador Emenyi Asuquo (the state chief of protocol), Aliyu Dagari (the protocol officer), and Umar Ahmed (the presidential liaison officer) (*Newswatch* 12 October 1998, 9). As the title of the positions of these three officials of the Presidency clearly indicate, they focused on foreign policy matters. Another official of the Presidency who was very vital in foreign policy matters was the national security adviser, Ismaila Gwarzo, who had also served in the same position during the Shonekan Government. Gwarzo's role in thwarting the hijacking of a Nigerian Airways plane, described earlier, shows that he had an excellent ability to serve the Abacha Government very well as the national security adviser. On the whole during the Abacha Government, as in other previous governments, the national security adviser concentrated mostly on security matters, without very visible and public efforts to compete with the Ministry of Foreign Affairs over the control of general foreign policy decision-making. Nonetheless, Gwarzo was one of the presidential advisers strongly associated with power excesses during the Abacha era (*Newswatch* 13 July 1998, 13–14; *Theweek* 13 July 1998, 15–16). The Presidency also had advisers and special assistants in many other areas—for example, in economic matters and media relations.

Thus, on the whole, the Presidency was a structure with numerous units, special advisers, and assistants. Therefore, the president had an adequate immediate staff who assisted him in domestic policy decision-making, foreign policy decision-making, and administrative duties. In terms of foreign affairs, in particular, the president thus had adequate decision units, advisers, and assistants to help him perform his duties. During his meetings with leaders, officials, and other important visitors from other countries (for example, see *West Africa* 20–26 March 1995, 431; *West Africa* 27 March–2 April 1995, 472); during his visits to other countries; and during the periods he was engaging in foreign policy decision-making, it was these various units, special advisers, and assistants who were in the position to supply the President with the information, analyses, and advice that enabled him to perform his duties.

As noted earlier, the displeasures and pressures of many countries (especially those in the West) in relation to the non-democratization of the Nigerian political system was one of the major foreign policy issues that occupied the attention of the Abacha Government. Efforts to minimize these external pressures became one of the important foreign policy goals of the Abacha Government. The president himself was directly involved in this effort. For an example, he gave an extensive interview about the political situation in Nigeria to Cable Network News (CNN) based in Atlanta, Georgia (*Newswatch* 1 May 1995, 10–11). Most probably, advisers, assistants, and other officials, of the Presidency as well as officials from other ministries and agencies did their normal job of thoroughly briefing the president and presenting him with all the information, analysis, and advice he needed for the interview with CNN. The president, as expected, presented his view of the political situation and developments in Nigeria to the worldwide audience of CNN; and as also expected, after the

CNN interview, Nigerian critics of the government told the Nigerian media that many assertions of the president during the CNN interview were not correct (*Newswatch* 1 May 1995, 10–11).

Other major foreign policy issues that faced the Abacha Government were border conflicts with Cameroun, Nigerian roles in international security management operations in Liberia and Sierra Leone, and Nigerian roles in many United Nations peace-keeping operations.

Important and sensitive foreign policy issues were often referred to the Presidency for final decisions, while the Ministry of Foreign Affairs and other ministries and agencies handled regular and routine foreign relations matters. This meant that, as was also often the case in most other previous governments, while the Presidency was an important and crucial foreign policy decision-making system, most of the foreign relations matters were handled at the Ministry of Foreign Affairs. Thus, the Ministry of Foreign Affairs, as in most previous governments, was the hub of foreign policy decision-making during the Abacha Government.

The nature and functioning of the Ministry of Foreign Affairs and other ministries and agencies were mostly the same as they had been during the Babangida Government and the very brief Shonekan Government. During the Abacha Government the Ministry of Foreign Affairs thus continued its traditional role as the main decision-making structure for the management of the country's foreign relations. Particularly, the ministry played a very major role in the Abacha Government's effort to minimize the significant displeasure of and pressures from foreign countries due to the nonrestoration of democratic polity in the country. For an example, in one news item, three important officials of the Ministry of Foreign Affairs, in three separate forums, were focusing on the minimization of the external pressures the country was facing. The minister of Foreign Affairs, Tom Ikimi, while addressing the senior officials of his ministry, asked them "to cooperate with him in realizing his objective of a better image for the country"; the country's permanent representative to the United Nations, Ibrahim Gambari, while addressing a symposium in a city in the United States, told his audience that "Nigerians are democratic by nature and free enterprise is in their blood"; and the country's ambassador to the United States, Zubairu Mahmud Kazaure, while receiving the traditional title of Baraden Kazaure, told his audience, rightly or wrongly, that the United States was going to reduce its pressures on Nigeria (*West Africa* 3–9 April 1995, 511).

The Ministry of Foreign Affairs was also very active in placing its officials in important positions in international organizations in order to help advance Nigerian foreign policy goals and activities. For an example, in 1995 the country's permanent representative to the United Nations, Professor Ibrahim Gambari, was elected as the chairman of the United Nations Special Committee on Peacekeeping Operations (*Nigerian Record*

May 1995, 2). With Nigerian military forces serving in numerous United Nations peacekeeping operations, as the chairman of the committee, Professor Gambari was in a position to help the United Nations fashion and implement good and effective peacekeeping policies and operations. Also in 1995, Chiedu Osakwe, the counselor in charge of economic affairs at the Nigerian Mission to the United Nations in Geneva, was elected as chairman of the World Trade Organization's Committee on Rules of Origin, which "is charged with harmonising and clarifying rules of origin governing tariff and other treatment of foreign products in a domestic market" (*Nigerian Record* May 1995, 6). As the chairman of a committee with such significant functions in the very important World Trade Organization (WTO), which "sets out the rule of law in international trade" (*Nigerian Record* May 1995, 6), Osakwe was in a position to help the WTO make important rulings that had vital impacts on the international trade relations and general economy of 120 countries, including Nigeria.

Apart from efforts in international multilateral bodies, the Ministry of Foreign Affairs also continued its traditional role of helping to strengthen bilateral links with other countries. For an example, in 1994 Nigeria and Venezuela signed an economic, technical, and scientific pact; during the signing ceremony, Anthony Ani, who was then the junior minister in the Nigerian Ministry of Foreign Affairs, commented that the bilateral pact between Nigeria and Venezuela offered "credible proof of our decisive will to take letters of south-south cooperation from theory of classroom and flowery talks of conference rooms to concrete actions" (*West Africa* 18–24 July 1994, 1273).

Nigerian embassies were also very active in various countries of the world. The influential Alhaji Abubakar Alhaji, as the Nigerian envoy to the United Kingdom, was very active in promoting Nigerian interests in the United Kingdom. For example, he used the occasion of the 34th anniversary of Nigeria's independence celebration in London to court the goodwill of the people and officials of the United Kingdom and the members of the diplomatic missions in London (*Diplomat* January/February 1995, 32). Alhaji was also able to secure important forums to communicate with important and significant segments of the population in the United Kingdom; for an example, he used an address he gave at the Army and Navy Club in London to analyze economic policies, conditions, and dynamics in Nigeria for his audience (*West Africa* 17–23 April 1995, 593).

Dr. J. J. Lewu, the Nigerian ambassador to Brazil, was active in promoting the interests of Nigeria in that country. For example, while visiting the research and development center of Petrobras (the major petroleum company in Brazil) in Rio de Janeiro, Lewu said that he was going to work for close cooperation between the Nigerian National Petroleum Corporation (NNPC) and Petrobras (*Nigeria News Update* 20 May–3 June 1994, 3). On another occasion, in a paper written by Dr. Lewu and read by Oku Ayodeji (an official of the embassy of Nigeria in Brasilia) at a conference in Recife, Brazil, the media in Brazil were accused of "marginalising and defaming" black Brazilians (Lewu, quoted by *Nigeria News Update* 20 May–3 June 1994, 3).

The leaders and senior officials of the Ministry of Foreign Affairs were also active in articulating and expressing their views on foreign policy issues, thus having enormous impact on the country's foreign policy decision-making system. For an example, Tom Ikimi, who became the minister of Foreign Affairs in 1995, was of the view that Nigeria, as the country with the biggest population of black people in the world, should try to look after the interests of "all the black people everywhere in the world" (*Newswatch* 24 April 1995, 19). (This sort of position, in a way, supported the view Dr. Lewu had earlier expressed in Brazil in 1994, as noted above.) Ikimi also noted that, in order to advance the prominence of the economic components of Nigeria's foreign policy and diplomacy, "Nigeria's economic relations with Asia, the Pacific and Latin America will be strengthened" (*Newswatch* 24 April 1995, 19). Ikimi (whose combative and aggressive personality has prompted some to describe him as "ebullient," "no-nonsense," "almost spitting fire," "swashbuckling," and as a person who often "stirred the hornet's nest") also often took delight in going on the offense against the forces he perceived as working against the interests of Nigeria and the whole of Africa (*West Africa* 26 January–1 February 1998, 112–13). He strongly believed that there were efforts by non-African countries to weaken Africa through the encouragement of divisions between francophone and anglophone African peacekeeping forces, and he voiced his concerns during the Fourth ECOWAS Extraordinary Summit, which was held in Lome, Togo in 1997 (*West Africa* 26 January–1 February 1998, 112–13). Ikimi was even more blunt and elaborate while addressing an Organization of African Unity (OAU) Council of Ministers meeting in Addis Ababa, Ethiopia, in 1998.

> During the crucial period in which Nigerian forces were restoring President Tejan Kabbah to power in Freetown, British, French and American troops were conducting peacekeeping exercises for African soldiers in West Africa.
> To . . . Ikimi, these Western powers appeared to be trying to steal Africa's thunder. After yet another African success in the West African sub-region, the Nigerian foreign minister felt that the continent was finally getting it right on the issue of peacekeeping. But the West was again intervening at the wrong time.
> Noted . . . Ikimi: "It is a matter for concern that every time Africa succeeds in formulating a common position on any critical issue, our external friends always manage to come up with an alternative solution. This has become a pattern on political, economic and social issues.

"When the priority of the OAU was focused on the liberation of the continent from colonialism, racism and apartheid, they come up with a formula for human rights and democratisation. When we moved on to economic liberation, they came up with structural adjustment, liberalisation and globalisation.

"Now that we have succeeded in establishing a continental mechanism for conflict prevention, management and resolution, we are being confronted with uncoordinated initiatives ostensibly designed to enhance our capacities in peace support operations."

He said that the Central Organ of the OAU's Mechanism for the Prevention, Management and Resolution of Conflict, which was established in Cairo in 1993, was meant to "evolve into a mechanism equivalent" to the UN Security Council. "The evolutionary process is being interrupted by the interventionist and divisive policies of countries outside the continent," . . . Ikimi said. "The naked pursuit of their own political and economic interests often ignores Africa's own interests. A new scramble for Africa appears to be now underway."

. . . Ikimi wondered whether such foreign-oriented peacekeeping exercises would be of much use to Africa, given the continent's peculiar circumstances. He noted that external forces failed in Somalia, which was "abandoned . . . after the tragic loss of a few soldiers. This loss would have been avoided if they had paid appropriate attention to the complexities of the local situation in their training and preparations."

. . . Ikimi added: ". . . There is a clear difference between releasing cruise missiles from secure aircraft carriers, designed to engage targets thousands of kilometers away, and the art of guerilla warfare in impenetrable jungles in African locations such as in Liberia, Sierra Leone, the Congo or Central African Republic." (*West Africa* 4–17 May 1998, 430)

The combative style of Ikimi, as shown above in his handling of foreign policy issues, also extended to his management and leadership of the Federal Ministry of Foreign Affairs. His domineering and abrasive style resulted in conflicts with those who, at various periods, served as his deputies (*Theweek* 21 April 1997, 10–14; *Theweek* 7 September 1998, 14).

Baba Gana Kingibe, who was the first person to hold the position of the minister of Foreign Affairs in the Abacha Government, was also active in articulating and expressing his views on foreign policy issues. Though President Sani Abacha, while meeting with media executives in early 1994 in Abuja, had expressed the view that "Africa still remains the centre-piece of Nigeria's foreign policy" (*Nigeria News Update* 14–27 April 1994, 14), in late 1994 Kingibe was suggesting that, since the Soviet Union was no longer in existence, international and regional dynamics may mean the need to place "Nigeria and Nigeria's interests at the center of" Nigeria's foreign policy (*West Africa* 14–20 November 1994, 1953). Kingibe also strongly advocated that Nigeria be made a permanent member of the Security Council of the United Nations (*West Africa* 14–20 November 1994, 1952). On the same subject, Professor Ibrahim Gambari, the

Nigerian permanent representative to the United Nations, was of the view that the democratization of the Nigerian political system would help the country to become a permanent member of the Security Council (*West Africa* 30 January–5 February 1995, 147). On another occasion, Gambari also implored Nigeria to improve its political, social, and economic systems in order not to be left behind by a new and virile South Africa in the African scene (*West Africa* 23–29 May 1994, 906–7).

On the whole, as shown above by the activities of the ministry and its senior officials and diplomats, the Ministry of Foreign Affairs was the hub and fulcrum of the country's foreign policy decision-making system, especially in the political dimension of foreign policy.

It is important to note that during the Abacha Government the title of the position director-general reverted back to permanent secretary (*Theweek* 25 August 1997, 5), which was the title used before the Babangida Government. Also, permanent secretaries were to be appointed from among the career officers who were serving senior officials (*Newswatch* 12 October 1998, 25–26), as was also the tradition before the Babangida Government. Thus for the Ministry of Foreign Affairs and all other ministries, the position of the director-general reverted back to the permanent secretary. Another change made by the Abacha Government was that the Office of the Head of the Civil Service was restored (*Theweek* 25 August 1997, 5). All these changes were applicable at the federal level and not the state level. According to Momodu Yusuf, an official of the Presidency, "In the spirit of true federation, the states civil service are not obliged to adopt all these measures" (Yusuf, quoted in *Theweek* 25 August 1997, 5).

In the security, cultural, and economic dimensions of the country's foreign policy, the Ministry of Foreign Affairs mainly cooperated with other ministries and agencies (as had always been the situation in previous governments), which in many instances were the major ministries or agencies primarily in charge of these other various dimensions of the country's foreign policy. For an example, the Ministry of Defense was the major ministry primarily in charge of managing the security components of the country's foreign relations.

Issues like the Nigeria-Cameroun border conflict (which had occurred during almost all previous governmental eras) made the security components of the country's foreign policy significant. The fact that the border conflict was tense enough to result in a large deployment of the armed forces of Nigeria (in various operational activities) in the border area in dispute, though mostly in a defensive posture (*West Africa* 7–13 March 1994, 397–401), meant that the Ministry of Defense played a very prominent role, with the help of other security-related organs, to manage and minimize this border conflict. This border problem also included Cameroun filing applications in the International Court of Justice at The

Hague to lay claims to the Bakasi Peninsula of Nigeria (which ignited the dispute in 1994) and the Adamawa and Bornu States of Nigeria (*West Africa* 12–18 September 1994, 1594). However (as in all previous governments in Nigeria), during the Abacha Government diplomatic efforts (which involved the Presidency, the Ministry of Foreign Affairs, the Ministry of Justice, the Ministry of Defense, and other security related agencies actively working together to handle the border problems), some military activities, and international legal involvements were used to contain or minimize Nigeria-Cameroun border conflicts (*Newswatch* 23 March 1998, 25; *Theweek* 19 August 1996, 8–11; *West Africa* 7–13 March 1994, 402; *West Africa* 14–20 March 1994, 459; *West Africa* 28 March–6 April 1994, 540–42; *West Africa* 26 December 1994–8 January 1995, 2209; *West Africa* 27 February–5 March 1995, 309).

The 1994 Bakasi Peninsula conflict between Nigeria and Cameroun also had the added dimension of reemphasizing the thinking of Nigerian political leaders, military officials, other security-related officials, and international security scholars that French military and security activities and roles in Africa (and the west Africa subregion in particular) posed continuous, serious threats to the national security interests of Nigeria. The fact that France backed the secession of Biafra (the secession did not succeed and Biafra again became part of Nigeria) during the Nigerian Civil War, which lasted from 1967 to 1970, plays a significant role in the development of the Nigerian perception of France as posing a serious threat to Nigeria's national security interests (*Theweek* 19 August 1996, 11). Nigeria believed that French military forces were in the Cameroun border area to help the Cameroun military forces in the Nigeria-Cameroun conflict over the Bakasi Peninsula, though France denied this, claiming that it only sent in technical military assistance to nonborder areas of Cameroun to comply with a prior Cameroun-French defense pact. Nigeria also believed that military maneuvers the French military forces carried out with the Republic of Benin military forces in the Republic of Benin, and twice with the military forces of Cote d'Ivoire in Cote d'Ivoire, were timed and organized in such a way as to prepare the French forces to be ready to intervene in support of Cameroun in the Nigeria-Cameroun conflict over the Bakasi Peninsula and that France prodded and assisted Cameroun to raise the issue of the Nigerian-Cameroun conflict over the Bakasi Peninsula before the International Court of Justice at The Hague and before the Security Council of the United Nations, thereby delaying a peaceful solution to the conflict, which Nigeria had preferred to quickly contain through direct bilateral Nigeria-Cameroun talks and negotiations (*West Africa* 28 March–3 April 1994, 541–42). With reference to the French military maneuvers with (and in) the Republic of Benin, specifically, which was watched by Nigerian military observers at the invitation (and insistence) of the Republic of Benin (*West Africa* 28 March–3 April 1994, 542; *West Africa* 11–17 April 1994, 648), the director of Nigerian Army Public Relations stated that "the level of participation and the manner in which the week-long exercise was conducted showed that it was a preparation by France to eventually intervene on the side of Cameroun should the Bakassi dispute escalate" (*West Africa* 11–17 April 1994, 648).

Though Nigeria was eventually able to contain the Nigeria-Cameroun conflict through mostly diplomatic, military, and legal means, as noted earlier, Nigeria's traditional perception of French military and security activities in Africa (and the west African subregion in particular) as posing continuous, serious threats to the national security interests of Nigeria increased, rather than decreased. Logically, also, the neighboring countries (which are former French colonies) were perceived as similarly posing serious threats to the national security interests of Nigeria. According to Air Vice Marshal Babatunde Osibo, the air officer commanding of the Logistics Command of the Nigerian air force, "Nigeria has to consider all the French-speaking neighboring states as one potential threat, whose capabilities and intentions must be assessed and countered" (Air Vice Marshal Osibo, quoted in *Newswatch* 15 May 1995, 7). This statement by Osibo strongly indicated that the military planners and strategists in the Ministry of Defense, in performing their functions, often gave very high priority to the security problems posed by all the French-speaking countries neighboring Nigeria.

Another security dimension of Nigeria's foreign relations was the involvement of the Nigerian military in many international security management operations and the United Nations peacekeeping operations. In Liberia and Sierra Leone, the Nigerian military continued its international security management operations, which had started during the Babangida Government; in 1994 Angola, Rwanda, Somalia, and the former Yugoslavia were some of the countries in which the Nigerian military was involved in United Nations peace-keeping operations (*West Africa* 7–13 November 1994, 1911; *West Africa* 17–23 April 1995, 586). In 1994 it was also announced that Nigeria had agreed to send a police contingent to the United Nations peacekeeping mission in Mozambique with one of its functions slated to be the training and reorganization of the Mozambican police, particularly the Mobile Police Force (*West Africa* 21–27 February 1994, 312).

The prominent role of the Nigerian armed forces in the ECOMOG forces in Liberia, which started during the Babangida Government, also continued during the Abacha Government (*West Africa* 7–13 March 1994, 390–93). There was even a report in May 1994 that the Nigerian military peacekeeping force in Liberia was arming one of the rebel groups in Liberia (*Tallahassee Democrat* 15 May 1994, 15A).

Toward the end 1994 the government of Nigeria was very displeased with the continuing intransigence of Liberian factional groups refusing to end the conflict, and was ordering a reduction of Nigerian military forces in Liberia and also considering further actions (*West Africa* 12–18 December 1994, 2127); however, it seems that the Nigerian government quickly changed its mind and recommitted itself very strongly to continue in helping to bring stability to Liberia. For an example, in mid-1995, Nigeria was hosting a Liberian peace talk, and even Charles Taylor (who was then a leader of one of the warring factions in Liberia), "who had launched Liberia's civil war in 1989" and who had also "previously accused Nigeria of plotting against him," was planning to attend this conference in Nigeria (*The Wall Street Journal* 31 May 1995, A1). Taylor did, in fact, attend that conference (*Africa Today* November/December 1996, 42). And even though many Nigerian newspapers had been calling for the total withdrawal or the reduction of Nigerian military forces in Liberia (due to the expense Nigerial was incurring), the Nigerian government recommitted strongly defended its role in Liberia (*West Africa* 17–23 April 1995, 586). Brigadier-General Fred Chijuka, the director of Nigerian Defense Information, for example, was very busy telling the Nigerian media that stability in the west African region was in the economic interests of Nigeria, since such stability opens the regional market to Nigerian products (*West Africa* 17–23 April 1995, 586). Expressing the same line of thinking, President Sani Abacha, while swearing in a new Nigerian ambassador to Liberia, stated that "the issue of peace in the west African sub-region should supersede the economic interest of individual states as there cannot be economic progress without peace in the sub-region" (Abacha, quoted in *West Africa* 17–23 April 1995, 586).

Heading the ECOMOG military forces in Liberia in 1994 was Major-General John Inienger of the Nigerian army, an infantry officer with about 27 years in the military, who was also "both an experienced officer in combat and peace-keeping" (*West Africa* 7–13 March 1994, 393). According to Inienger, "in peacekeeping, one is sometimes humiliated, harassed, and so it requires a lot of patience," and on Liberia he added that "the situation is not as hopeless as some think," since "the parties are talking and there is relative peace," and that, due to "the fact that the people are talking," he was "optimistic that sooner or later peace will come to Liberia" (Major-General John Inienger, quoted in *West Africa* 17–23 April 1995, 587). (Inienger commanded an ECOMOG military force of 9,000 military personnel, later reduced to 6,000, with other Economic Community of West African States countries Ghana, Guinea, Sierra Leone, and The Gambia as well as east African countries contributing the rest [*West Africa* 17–23 April 1995, 586, 587].) Inienger's optimism about the future of Liberia seems to have been correct. In August 1995, the Abuja Peace

Accord was signed by the Liberian warring groups in a meeting held in Abuja, Nigeria, and chaired by President Sani Abacha of Nigeria (*Africa Today* November/December 1996, 42–43). This Abuja Peace Accord laid the foundations for the end of the conflict in Liberia and for the transition to democracy in that country. The Liberian warring groups agreed to end the civil war in their country and also agreed to forge together a new Liberian government (*The New York Times* 2 September 1995, 4). Thus "Liberia's three principal militia leaders were formally seated on a new six-member Council of State," which was given the mandate "to govern the country and lead it to democratic elections in the coming year" (*The New York Times* 2 September 1995, 4).

The foundations for stability in Liberia were laid by west African countries. When Liberia was gripped by severe instability, "a Nigerian-led West African Peacekeeping force intervened to" stop one of the Liberian warring groups from overrunning Monrovia, the capital of Liberia (*The New York Times* 2 September 1995, 4). It was this military role of the ECOMOG force (which endured for years the frustrations of peacekeeping duties in Liberia) and the diplomatic efforts of the ECOWAS countries (which also endured for years the numerous failures of the Liberian warring groups to implement peace agreements) that finally led to the successful implementation of the peace agreement and the installation of a new government. in Liberia, in 1995. As noted by a newspaper report, the happy occasion of the formal installation of the Council of State of the new government of Liberia "represented a major victory for a regional diplomatic and military effort led by Nigeria and Ghana, which persisted even after the United Nations, the United States and many other would-be peacebrokers seemingly threw up their hands in frustration over what only recently appeared to be a hopeless conflict" (*The New York Times* 2 September 1995, 4). Thus, in 1995, Nigeria and other ECOWAS countries provided the world with a successful and positive lesson on how a regional group can restore peace and stability to an area of conflict in its region. Possibly, such a lesson was relevant to Bosnia and Herzegovina, Chechenya, Rwanda, Somalia, and other similar areas where conflicts were still brewing in 1995.

In 1996 and 1997, Nigeria and other ECOWAS countries made even more dramatic achievements in bringing stability to Liberia. In 1996 Major-General Victor Malu became the new commander of ECOMOG (*Africa Today* November/December 1996, 43). General Malu, a Nigerian army officer, was seriously determined to fully implement the Abuja Peace Accord of 1995, bringing stability and peaceful conditions that would allow free and fair elections in Liberia. By March 1997, Malu was able to note that Liberia "was completely cleared of land mines" and that "Liberian refugees had returned from neighboring countries" (*The New York Times* 27 March 1997, A4). Also, Malu ensured that ECOMOG was able to disarm all the warring groups in Liberia in order to provide peaceful conditions for elections and for the future stability of the country (*Theweek* 17 March 1997, 13; *Theweek* 31 March 1997, 5). Thus by March 1997, it was noted that the disarming of all the warring Liberian groups "was said to have been concluded by January 31 as scheduled" (*Theweek* 17 March 1997, 13).

The Liberian Independent Electoral Commission was created to conduct elections and this electoral body also received logistical support from ECOMOG and positive policy inputs from ECOWAS (*Africa Today* May/June 1997, 36; *The New York Times* 22 July 1997, A6; *Theweek* 14 April 1997, 26; *Theweek* 2 June 1997, 5).

It was also observed that Charles Taylor (who was then the leader of one of the warring groups), who, as noted earlier, strongly opposed Nigeria's dominating role in Liberia, seemed to have established a more friendly relationship with Nigeria after the Abuja Peace Accord (*Africa Today* May/June 1997, 36; *Theweek* 17 March 1997, 8–13). It can be surmised that the rapprochement between Nigeria and Charles Taylor was due to the fact that Taylor reasoned that it was a good idea not to be antagonistic with the most powerful formal authority then in Liberia and that Nigeria also recognized that Taylor had the most powerful support in Liberia (and was thus sure to win the election) (*Africa Today* May/June 1997, 5; *Theweek* 17 March 1997, 8–13). As expected, Charles Taylor, in an election that was internationally seen as being free and fair, comfortably won the election and became the president of Liberia in 1997 (*The New York Times* 22 July 1997, A6; *The New York Times* Thursday, 24 July 1997, A14; *Theweek* 4 August 1997, 22–23; *Theweek* 18 August 1997, 21). Former United States President Jimmy Carter and former United States Senator Paul Simon, who were observers of the Liberian election, "said that the Liberian election was run better than ones they had seen in Bosnia, Croatia and Haiti," and the two also "particularly praised the Nigerian military commander, Maj. Gen. Victor Malu" (*The New York Times* 22 July 1997, A6). In a newspaper editorial, Major General Malu was seen as "the Nigerian general . . . that imposed enough stability on Liberia for the elections to take place" (*The New York Times* 24 July 1997, A14). Thus, ECOMOG also "won virtually universal praise" for bringing peace and stability to Liberia (*The New York Times* 22 July 1997, A6). The fact that Nigeria provided most of the forces for ECOMOG meant that peace and stability in Liberia was also mostly due to the effort of Nigeria. Nigeria also spent a lot of its resources for the Liberian peacekeeping operations; from 1990 to 1997, Nigeria spent U.S. $3.5 billion (*The New York Times* 22 July 1997, A6).

The paradox was that it was the undemocratic and repressive government of President Sani Abacha in Nigeria that worked so hard and gave so much to reestablish democracy in Liberia.

After becoming the president of Liberia, Charles Taylor was initially grateful to Nigeria for its role in bringing stability to his country (*Theweek* 11 August 1997, 24). However, it did not take long before President Taylor, rightly or wrongly, reverted to being mistrustful, suspicious, and uncomfortable with Nigeria's roles and goals in Liberia, and this resulted in a lot of disagreements between President Taylor and ECOMOG (*Africa Today* April 1998, 14–15; *Newswatch* 8 December 1997, 23; *Theweek* 24 November 1997, 26; *Theweek* 1 June 1998, 33). One of the major issues between Taylor and ECOMOG was over Taylor not allowing ECOMOG (as mandated by the Abuja Peace Accord of 1995) to independently create, train, and equip a military force for Liberia that was not dominated by members of particular Liberian ethnic groups or particular former Liberian warring groups, in order to avoid future instability in Liberia (*Africa Today* April 1998, 14–15; *The New York Times* Tuesday, 22 July 1998, A6). Taylor seems to have also perceived ECOMOG as encroaching on his powers as the president and on the sovereignty of Liberia. Thus, President Taylor vented anger at "ECOMOG commander, Major-General Victor Malu, a Nigerian, accusing him of encroaching on his executive powers and trying to run a parallel government in Liberia" (*Africa Today* April 1998, 14). According to Taylor, "there will not be a parallel authority in this Republic," and he further added that "[n]o officer of any nation or any force will share power with the President of this Republic or challenge the sovereignty of the Republic of Liberia" (President Taylor, quoted in *Africa Today* April 1998, 14). This rift between Malu and Taylor led to Nigeria recalling Malu and posting him to Ibadan, Nigeria, as the general officer commanding of the Second Mechanized Division of the Nigerian army; Malu was replaced by Major-General Timothy Shelpidi of Nigeria, whose prior position was that of chief of Defense Training, Operations, and Planning in Nigeria (*Newswatch* 19 January 1998, 24). (Major-General Malu was later reposted from Ibadan to Lagos as the general officer commanding of the Lagos Garrison.) The conflict between President Taylor and ECOMOG also resulted in the reduction of ECOMOG forces in Liberia (*Theweek* 15 December 1997, 22). Though the relationship between President Taylor and Major-General Shelpidi was not as tense as that between Taylor and Malu, there were still some uneasy issues between Taylor and ECOMOG (*West Africa* 2–15 March 1998, 296; *West Africa* 16–29 March 1998, 340).

As noted earlier, the Abacha Government also played a very prominent and pivotal role in Sierra Leone. In 1994 a 32-member team of Nigerian military officials, led by Brigadier-General Seidu Zubeiru, arrived in Sierra Leone to help "train and reorganize the Sierra Leonean armed forces" (*West Africa* 23–29 May 1994, 917). However, it seems that the roles of the Nigerian military in Sierra Leone were not limited to the training and reorganization of the Sierra Leonean armed forces. In 1995, it was reported that the Nigerian military, with other forces, had been helping the government of Sierra Leone to "ward off rebel incursions, especially in Freetown and its surrounding districts" (*Newswatch* 29 May 1995, 33). Thus, the Nigerian military forces seem to have been also involved in helping the government of Sierra Leone in its civil war against rebel forces.

A close analysis also shows that the roles of Nigerian military forces in Liberia and Sierra Leone, though they appeared to have been two separate military operations, were actually very closely related. According to Brigadier-General Fred Chijuka, the Director of the Nigerian Defense Information, "Nigeria went to Sierra Leone to protect Lungi Airport which is vital to overall ECOMOG operations" (*West Africa* 17–23 April 1995, 587). He also added that "we are there to protect our aircraft, equipment and troops. We are not pulling out yet. We were already in Sierra Leone when the present government toppled the Joseph Momoh government. Did we protect Momoh? We were there on a different mission" (Brigadier-General Fred Chijuka, quoted in *West Africa* 17–23 April 1995, 587). The envoy of Sierra Leone to Nigeria also added that "until the Liberian crisis was solved, it would be unwise of Nigeria to pull its forces out of Sierra Leone because the crises were linked" (*West Africa* 17–23 April 1995, 587). Therefore, it can be said that the Nigerian military forces in Sierra Leone were in that country to help bring stability to Sierra Leone and to also assist the Nigerian military forces in Liberia (which shares its western border with Sierra Leone).

In November 1996 the Abidjan Peace Accord was signed between the government of Sierra Leone and the rebels (*Theweek* 21 April 1997, 30), but it seems this accord was not implemented, for it did not lead to peace in Sierra Leone.

In March 1997, Foday Sankoh, the leader of the Revolutionary United Front (RUF), the Sierra Leonean rebel group, "was reportedly arrested at the Murtala Muhammed Airport, Lagos on March 15 for allegedly being in possession of some ammunition" (*Theweek* 21 April 1997, 30). However, the rebels were of the opinion that President Ahmed Tejan Kabbah of Sierra "not only tricked Sankoh into his . . . ordeal in Nigeria, given his [Kabbah's] closeness to Sani Abacha, the Nigerian head of state, but also instigated the revolt within the rebel group shortly after Sankoh was apprehended." Though some rebels defected after Sankoh's arrest, most remained loyal to him. In reaction to their perception of Kabbah's role in Sankoh's arrest, the rebels kidnapped Mohammed Diaby (the ambassador of Sierra Leone to Guinea), who went to negotiate with the RUF in the eastern part of Sierra Leone (*Theweek* 21 April 1997, 30). In reaction to the kidnapping of Diaby, President Kabbah noted that he was "prepared to beg Nigeria to free Sankoh in the interest of peace in the country" (President Kabbah, quoted in *Theweek* 21 April 1997, 30). Kabbah's statement was "viewed as a surreptitious admission of the Nigerian government's involvement in Sankoh's ordeal as alleged by the rebels" (*Theweek* 21 April 1997, 30). The involvement of Nigeria in Sankoh's problem was seen as being further indicated by the fact that "Sankoh reportedly said that he was in the country to see Abacha and that the government was aware of his trip" (*Theweek* 21 April 1997, 30). It was also noted that "experts are of the view that such connivance is fast becoming the norm" (*Theweek* 21 April 1997, 30) in Nigeria's foreign policy and diplomatic practice. For an example, during "the Liberian crisis, Yormie Johnson, leader of one of the warring factions, came to Nigeria in a similar manner and was subsequently offered political asylum by the government of Ibrahim Babangida" (*Theweek* 21 April 1997, 30) of Nigeria.

The fact that Sankoh was encouraged to visit Nigeria and arrested upon his arrival shows that Nigeria's role in Sierra Leone during the Abacha Government was expansive, deep, and complex. The additional fact that the Nigerian armed forces based in Sierra Leone were training the armed forces of Sierra Leone, and also helping the government of Sierra Leone to fight the rebels, further shows the enormous involvement of Nigeria in Sierra Leone. Therefore, Nigeria's foreign policy decision-making structures and processes were also enormous, expansive, deep, and complex. The stationing of Nigerian armed forces in Sierra Leone and the luring of Sankoh to visit the Nigerian president and upon his arrival arrest and detain him, show that numerous governmental organs and ministries were involved in Nigeria's policy toward this country. The major governmental organs and ministries that had to be significantly involved were the Presidency, the Federal Ministry of Defense, the Federal Ministry of Foreign Affairs, the National Intelligence Agency, the Federal Ministry of Planning, the Federal Ministry of Finance, and the Federal Ministry of Information, with the Presidency obviously directly coordinating and supervising the other governmental organs and ministries.

As a further indication of strong Nigerian involvement even in the internal affairs of Sierra Leone, the government of Sierra Leone charged "three journalists in that country" for treason, due to their publication of "an article critical of Sani Abacha, the Nigerian leader" (*Theweek* 7 April 1997, 27). "The journalists had in the article accused the Nigerian government of involvement in the removal of Foday Sankoh as leader of the Sierra Leonian Revolutionary United Front" (*Theweek* 7 April 1997, 27).

Sankoh was in detention in Nigeria until the end of the Abacha Government. (In 1998, the Abubakar Government of Nigeria sent Sankoh to

Sierra Leone, where the Kabbah Government of Sierra Leone put him on trial.)

May 1997 to June 1998 witnessed even more involvement of the Abacha Government in Sierra Leone. In May 1997, some members of the armed forces of Sierra Leone ousted President Kabbah from power (*The Atlanta Journal/The Atlanta Constitution* 26 May 1997, A10; *The New York Times* 26 May 1997, A5; *Theweek* 9 June 1997, 24). The State of Forces Agreement (SOFA), the bilateral agreement between Sierra Leone and Nigeria "under which Nigeria specifically undertook to provide Sierra Leone with military and security support" (*Africa Today* July/August 1997, 24), was used by President Kabbah to entitle the Nigerian armed forces based in Sierra Leone to fight the Sierra Leonean armed forces and restore him to power. Also, through "the terms of SOFA, President Kabbah and the rump of his government had given an official invitation to ECOWAS (in effect, Nigeria) to intervene militarily to oust" the Sierra Leonean military from power (*Africa Today* July/August 1997, 25). This action "earned the instant support of the OAU (the Organization of African Unity)" and the United Nations (*Africa Today* July/August 1997, 25). Thus, the role Nigeria was to play in restoring Kabbah to power had strong legal backing as well as the solid backing of the international community. In order to enjoy such sound bases for involvement in Sierra Leone, the Nigerian Federal Ministry of Foreign Affairs and the Presidency obviously worked hard and in adequate coordination of their activities. According to Major-General Victor Malu (the force commander of ECOMOG at the time Kabbah was ousted), troops from Ghana and Guinea, before and after the ouster of Kabbah, had also been helping Nigeria to play its role in Sierra Leone (*Newswatch* 27 October 1997, 37). After his ouster, President Kabbah lived in neighboring Guinea (*Africa Today* July/August 1997, 24).

Interestingly, Sankoh, from his detention in a hotel room in Abuja, the capital of Nigeria, asked his RUF rebels to join forces with the Sierra Leonean military (*The Atlanta Journal/The Atlanta Constitution* 29 May 1997, A6; *Theweek* 9 June 1997, 24) (the Sierra Leonean military had earlier invited the RUF to join them in taking power from President Kabbah) (*Theweek* 9 June 1997, 24). However, when Nigeria decided to restore Kabbah to power, "the Nigerian authorities ordered the tightening of security around Corporal Foday Sankoh, the RUF (Revolutionary United Front) leader who had been held under house arrest since March 2 in a suite of an Abuja five-star hotel" (*Africa Today* July/August 1997, 24). Obviously, with this action Sankoh could no longer freely communicate with his RUF rebels or others.

The Nigerian government used three simultaneous policy instruments to remove the Sierra Leonean military and rebels and return President Kabbah to power: of land, air, and sea blockades of Sierra Leone; military force to remove the Sierra Leonean military and rebels from power; and diplomatic efforts to negotiate with the Sierra Leonean military and rebels to facilitate the return of President Kabbah to power. The fact is that after the military and rebels took over the government in Sierra Leone, the Nigerian armed forces (which had been based in Sierra Leone for a long time), continued to control major positions and parts of the country. Nigerian army units were still stationed in some towns and on the outskirts of Freetown, the capital. The Nigerian air force and army units completely controlled the Lungi International Airport (the most important airport for Freetown and, in fact, for the whole of Sierra Leone). Additionally, Nigerian navy ships were stationed off the coast. All these army, air force, and navy units in Sierra Leone were thus adequately positioned to enforce the blockade Leone and also use force to flush out the Sierra Leonean military and rebels from power. In fact, after President Kabbah was ousted, from power, Nigeria increased its troops strength in Sierra Leone. For an example, in May 1997, it was noted that

> several hundred Nigerian troops docked in Freetown ports . . . to support the ousted government in its battle to regain control from mutinous soldiers.
>
> The arrival of the troops in this impoverished West African nation signaled that Nigeria—the region's biggest military power—was reserving a military option to try to restore President Ahmed Tejan Kabbah to power if diplomatic pressure failed.
>
> Mutineers standing on shore taunted the troops sent by Nigeria's leader, Gen. Sani Abacha, as they disembarked from their ships and headed for barracks outside the capital, where they were to bolster other Nigerians stationed here since 1994. (*The Atlanta Journal/The Atlanta Constitution* 29 May 1997, A6)

Nigeria used its increased military presence in Sierra Leone to launch many military actions against the military and rebels, who refused to relinquish power. For an example, it was reported that "Nigerian warplanes bombed a television and radio station near the capital today, knocking out broadcasts" (*The New York Times* 17 October 1997, A7). At one point air attacks by the Nigerian air force were almost a daily affair. "Hundreds of youths angered by near-daily air attacks took to the streets . . . in a protest, saying Nigeria was trying to colonize Sierra Leone" (*The New York Times* 17 October 1997, A7).

Nigeria also used some of its armed forces that were stationed in neighboring Liberia to bolster its military actions in Sierra Leone. Air force planes based in Liberia were used to attack Sierra Leone and army units in Liberia were used to control the situation in border areas between Sierra Leone and Liberia. President Charles Taylor of Liberia, who was seen as being sympathetic to the rebels in Sierra Leone, was not particularly happy with how ECOMOG forces in Liberia were being used to handle the situation in Sierra Leone (*Newswatch* 10 November 1997, 26; *Theweek* 24 November 1997, 26).

Simultaneously with its military attacks on Sierra Leone, Nigeria continued to negotiate with the Sierra Leonean military and rebels (as it had from the beginning) to seek a diplomatic solution to the problem. The Federal Ministry of Foreign Affairs and the Presidency tried in many forums to negotiate a diplomatic solution (*Theweek* 28 July 1997, 27; *Theweek* 8 September 1997, 22). These diplomatic efforts resulted in the Conakry Peace Plan, in October 1997. The peace plan which was signed in Conakry, Guinea, between the ECOWAS Ministerial Committee of Five (consisting of the foreign ministers of Nigeria, Ghana, Guinea, Cote d'Ivoire, and Liberia) and the Sierra Leonean military and rebels, provided for power to be handed back to President Kabbah in April 1998 (*Newswatch* 10 November 1997, 26; *The New York Times* 24 October 1997, A6). it is possible this peace plan was viewed by the Sierra Leonean military and rebels "as a ploy to gain time" (*Newswatch* 10 November 1997, 26). It seems Nigeria did not take the peace plan seriously, either. During the period leading up to the peace plan, Nigeria "stepped up its policing of the sanctions . . . launching air and artillery attacks in which some civilians have been killed" (*The New York Times* 24 October 1997, A6). After the peace plan was agreed, military attacks by Nigeria continued. In fact it seems that the peace plan was also used as a ploy by Nigeria to hide its true intention to use military force to restore President Kabbah to power. In February 1998, two months before the April 1998 deadline, Nigerians attacked and removed the Sierra Leonean military and rebels from power (*The Atlanta Journal/The Atlanta Constitution,* 15 February 1998, A18; *The New York Times* 14 February 1998, A3; *The New York Times* 15 February 1998, 3; *The New York Times* 17 February 1998, A9; *The New York Times* 18 February 1998, A4; *The New York Times* 19 February 1998, A6; *St. 4 Petersburg Times* 14 February 1998, 11A; *St. Petersburg Times* 16 February 1998, 2A; *Tallahassee Democrat* 16 February 1998, 7A). The Kamajors (a peasant based militia force supporting the government of President Kabbah) also joined the Nigerian forces in militarily removing the Sierra Leonean military and rebels from power (*Newswatch* 23 February 1998, 23; *St. Petersburg Times* 19 February 1998, 14A). The military actions of Nigeria were well coordinated and very successful (*Newswatch* 30 March 1998, 27–29).

The return of President Kabbah was well planned and the formal ceremony of his return was attended by President Sani Abacha of Nigeria, President Oumar Konare of Mali, President Lansana Conte of Guinea, and President Ibrahim Mainasara of Niger (*Africa Today* March 1998, 43–44; *Africa Today* April 1998, 12–14; *Africa Today* May 1998, 14–16; *The Atlanta Journal/The Atlanta Constitution* 11 March 1998, A4; *Newswatch*

2 March 1998, 25; *Newswatch,* 23 March 1998, 29–30; *St. Petersburg Times* 11 March 1998, 15A; *Tallahassee Democrat,* Wednesday, 11 March 1998, 5A; *Theweek* 16 March 1998, 24; *Theweek* 23 March 1998, 29–30; *West Africa* 2–15 March 1998, 296; *West Africa* 16–29 March 1998, 340).

The reinstatement of President Kabbah was seen as an event of historical significance—for which success the Abacha Government of Nigeria was responsible. The return of Kabbah to power was seen as "first in the continent where a regional group would eject an unconstitutional ruler to reinstate the constitutional one" (*Theweek* 23 March 1998, 29). Also, Salim Ahmed Salim, the secretary-general of the Organization of African Unity, was full of praise for Abacha and ECOMOG. He described the performance of ECOMOG during the operation as "professional." Salim said that "ECOMOG's role in Liberia and Sierra Leone had given Africa a role of honour. It was also an indication that Africa can chart its own history" (*Newswatch* 23 March 1998, 30). In recognition of the pivotal role of President Sani Abacha, Kabbah also highly honored him. "Kabbah extolled Abacha for the role he played in the resolution of the crisis. After seeking the opinion of Sierra Leonians present at the reinstatement ceremony, Kabbah renamed Kissy Street, one of the longest streets in Freetown, General Sani Abacha Street" (*Newswatch* 23 March 1998, 30).

As this study has shown, the success of the Abacha Government in Sierra Leone was the product of the roles of various organs, agencies, and ministries of the Nigerian government: the Federal Ministry of Defense, the National Intelligence Agency, the Federal Ministry of Planning, the Federal Ministry of Finance, the Federal Ministry of Information, the federal Ministry of Foreign Affairs, and the Presidency. Of all these, the Federal Ministry of Defense, the Federal Ministry of Foreign Affairs, and the Presidency were the most vital.

The fact that the Sierra Leonean military and rebels were military removed from power makes the role of the Federal Ministry of Defense very significant. The Nigerian army, through their units based in Sierra Leone and Liberia, enforced the sanctions against Sierra Leone and militarily confronted the Sierra Leonean military and rebels unceasingly from the beginning, culminating in the use of these Nigerian military forces to remove that illegal government. In order to accomplish this task, the armed forces of Nigeria in Sierra Leone probably had to utilize the intelligence outputs of their own intelligence units as well as those of the National Intelligence Agency (NIA). The Federal Ministry of Planning is the ministry that formally handled Nigerian ties with ECOWAS, while the Federal Ministry of Foreign Affairs is more active in ECOWAS matters (*West Africa* 16–22 February 1998, 225). The fact that Nigeria played its prominent role in the Sierra Leonean crisis through the formal auspices of ECOMOG (an ECOWAS body) meant that the Federal Ministry of Planning had something to do with Sierra Leone, though mostly in terms of formality and with minimum impact. The fact that the Nigerian role in the Sierra Leone crisis cost Nigeria a significant amount of money also meant that the Federal Ministry of Finance had to help to channel enough funds for Nigerian military and diplomatic operations. The Federal Ministry of Information helped to handle the information the Nigerian government gave about its role in the Sierra Leonean crisis.

The Federal Ministry of Foreign Affairs was continually active in arranging and managing the diplomatic efforts that seem to have paralleled the military actions of Nigeria in Sierra Leone. The role of the Federal Ministry of Foreign Affairs was increased by the fact that the Nigerian minister of Foreign Affairs (Tom Ikimi) was the "Chairman of ECOWAS Committee of Five on the Sierra Leonean situation" (*West Africa* 16–22 February 1998, 224). The personality of Tom Ikimi and the confidence President Abacha had in his ability to lead the Federal Ministry of Foreign Affairs, further expanded that ministry's role in the Sierra Leonean situation. Ikimi's background was that of "an architect with a flourishing private practice," who was also "a chairman of one of the political parties during" the incomplete civilian transition period of the Babangida Government (*West Africa* 16–21 February (1998, 225). "If his boss," President Abacha, had

> a laid-back attitude and lets his actions speak for him, Ikimi is an aggressive personality who believes firmly in his avowed opinions. He has used his diplomacy skills successfully, first in Liberia and now in Sierra Leone.
> One of the reasons that Ikimi was retained in the last reshuffle of Nigeria's executive council was the Sierra Leonean impasse. (*West Africa* 16–22 February 1998, 225)

As Abacha reasoned, Ikimi was the person who had the ability to lead the Federal Ministry of Foreign Affairs to achieve Nigerian goals in Sierra Leone. And indeed Ikimi performed as expected.

At the apex of the Nigerian foreign policy decision-making system was the Presidency. The Presidency coordinated and supervised all the organs, agencies, and ministries that were involved in the Sierra Leonean situation. The fact that the Federal Ministry of Defense (which carried out sanctions enforcements and military operations in Sierra Leone) and the Federal Ministry of Foreign Affairs (which handled diplomatic matters and general political issues) were able to operate efficiently and coordinate their roles was due to the excellent coordinating framework and close supervision provided by the Presidency. The fact that President Abacha was the chairman of ECOWAS made this strong coordination and supervision by the Presidency necessary. However, it was the strong and genuine interest that Abacha had in solving the problem in Sierra Leone that made the role of the Presidency very effective, efficient, and successful. The personal interest that President Abacha had in solving the Sierra Leonean problem was indicated by the extraordinary amount of time he spent studying the issues and problems in Sierra Leone. After a visit of President Kabbah to Abacha in 1996 (almost a year before the military and rebels took over power from Kabbah in 1997) Kabbah said that "he was surprised at the Nigerian leader's indepth knowledge of the problems in Sierra Leone" (*Theweek* 9 June 1997, 25). Abundantly armed with knowledge of the issues and problems in Sierra Leone, President Abacha was able to lead Nigeria to achieve its goals.

Thus, on the whole, just as in the Babangida Government period, the military role of Nigeria in the west African sub-region was very prominent during the Abacha Government. These roles of the Nigerian military in Sierra Leone and Liberia, in the United Nations' peacekeeping missions in other parts of Africa and in other continents, and in the management and containment of border conflicts which Nigeria had with some neighboring countries, made the security dimensions of Nigerian foreign policy very significant. As noted earlier, this also meant that the Ministry of Defense, in the course of planning, implementing, and managing these various Nigerian involvements in international security management operations, had a prominent role in the management of the security components of the country's foreign policy. In order to continue to perform these international security management operations well (and, at the same time, also adequately provide for the defense needs of the country), the Ministry of Defense also had to increasingly improve the strength of the Nigerian armed forces, both in terms of their personnel training and readiness and the quality of the military hardware. For example, according to Air Commodore Idi Musa, the air officer commanding of the 301 Air Force training school (located in Kaduna) of the Nigerian air force (NAF), some NAF instructor pilots, in 1994, were involved in a conversion training program in Kaduna for the flying of NAF 040 Air Beetle aircrafts, which are made in Nigeria (*Nigeria News Update* 22 March-4 April 1994, 3). Air Commodore Idi Musa added that "the Air Beetle was conceptualised by the research and development unit of the NAF headquarters which is attached to the Aeronautical Industrial Engineering Project, which built the aircraft" (*Nigeria News Update* 22 March–4 April 1994, 3). The development of the Nigerian-made training aircrafts for the NAF is part of the drive to produce more military weapon systems in Nigeria (which started with previous governments), and thereby strengthen the security capability of the country.

Training and readiness were also important for all the armed forces. For example, according to Rear Admiral Jibril Ayinla, the flag officer commanding of the Western Naval Command of the Nigerian navy, a navy ship, NNS Aradu, was to visit some countries in the Caribbean and possibly also Brazil, later in 1994 (*Nigeria News Update* 14–27 April 1994, 14). During such naval vessel voyages across the oceans of other parts of the world, such as those of the Americas, the officers and other personnel of the Nigerian navy are able to gain valuable military training and readiness experience. As noted in an earlier section, during the Babangida Government Nigeria established the Nigerian War College for the educational needs of senior military officers. This war college has since been growing in strength, as evidenced by the quality of its educational programs for Nigerian senior military officers and even senior military officers from other countries. For example, while exchanging views with visiting Brazilian naval officers, Rear Admiral Ayinla announced that some senior Brazilian military officers had been reserved vacancies to study at the Nigerian War College; and, according to the Brazilian ambassador to Nigeria, the Brazilian National War College had also reserved places for some senior Nigerian military officers (*Nigeria News Update* 14–27 April 1994, 14). Rear Admiral Ayinla also used the occasion to call "for greater co-operation between Brazil and other countries in the Southern Hemisphere" (*Nigeria News Update* 14–27 April 1994, 14). Interestingly, Rear Admiral Ayinla was to later hold the position of the commandant of the Nigerian War College (*West Africa* 28 November–4 December 1994, 2034).

The Nigerian air force also did a lot to boost the national security capability of Nigeria. According to Air Marshall Nsikak Eduok, the chief of staff of the Nigerian air force, the NAF "has successfully demonstrated that air power is not only a major factor in safe-guarding our national unity, but also a great tool for furthering Nigeria's offshore obligations" (Eduok, quoted in *Newswatch* 11 May 1998, 27). Also, in a speech at the Air Weapons School in Kainji, Niger State, Eduok was "full of praises for the officers and men of NAF for their contribution in global peace keeping efforts especially in Liberia (*Newswatch* 8 December 1997, 15).

Yormie Johnson (a leader of one of the political groups in Liberia who was in political asylum in Nigeria) notes that, while during the Babangida Government a political officer from the Presidency was attached to him, during the Abacha Government he was "being taken care of . . . by the Defence Intelligence" (*Theweek* 20 July 1998, 28). The fact that an important Liberian political leader who was in political asylum in Nigeria was under the direct control of the Defense Intelligence of Nigeria shows that the Federal Ministry of Defense was an organ of the government playing an increasing vital role in the management of foreign security relations.

The expanding role Nigeria was playing in terms of international security operations and relations, especially in west Africa, along with changing defense realities and needs in the west African subregion, necessitated that the Abacha Government review and adapt the defense policy of Nigeria (*Theweek* 3 March 1997, 6; *Theweek* 5 May 1997, 5).

This increasing profile of the security dimensions of Nigeria's foreign relations might have also increased awareness of national security needs among the foreign policy elite. For example, Baba Gana Kingibe, the first minister of Foreign Affairs during the Abacha era, giving an address at the end of the 1993/1994 session of the Nigerian Foreign Service Academy in Lagos, "charged those entrusted with classified information to ensure that these are protected" (*West Africa* 14–20 March 1994, 460). The heightened awareness of national security also resulted in normal diplomatic matters sometimes being handled as a serious national security matter. For an example, it has been noted that Ismaila Gwarzo, the national security adviser "in a memorandum reference number NSA/A/320/S, addressed to the Head of State, Commander-in-Chief of the Armed Forces of the Federation, Presidential Villa, Abuja and titled Request for Funds requested Abacha to approve release of . . . amounts for the prosecution of a campaign to cultivate the friendship of the East African countries with a view to using them, alongside ECOWAS countries and the entire Organization of African Unity for a permanent seat in the Security Council of the United Nations in the near future (*Theweek* 13 July 1998, 16). The fact that the national security adviser, an official of the Presidency, handled the above matter instead of the diplomats in the Federal Ministry of Foreign Affairs, shows how the Abacha Government sometimes viewed a normal diplomatic matter (Nigeria's desire to have a permanent seat in the Security Council of the United Nations in the future) as being a national security matter. The increased national security consciousness during the Abacha Government also resulted in the heads of the State Security Service (SSS) (which handled domestic intelligence), the National Intelligence Agency (NIA) (which handled foreign intelligence), the Directorate of Military Intelligence (DMI), the Military Intelligence Service (MIS), and the Nigerian Army Intelligence Corps (NAIC) being more directly coordinated by officials in the Presidency (*Newswatch* 31 August 1998, 8–12). This sort of situation, expectedly, resulted in these intelligence organs having increasing impacts on domestic and foreign policies.

As during most previous governments, during the Abacha Government the Federal Ministry of Information continued the tradition of being in charge of the management and operation of Nigeria's external publicity and information activities and other aspects of international cultural relations (while also working with the Ministry of External Affairs to carry out these functions). The relationship between the Federal Ministry of Information and the Ministry of Foreign Affairs, in terms of their working together to handle these external publicity and information and other international cultural relations matters, has sometimes been less than cordial due to bureaucratic turf battles.

Specifically, it is the External Publicity Department of the Federal Ministry of Information that is often primarily in charge of these external publicity and information and other international cultural relations matters. For example, in early 1994 it was reported that a chief information officer in the External Publicity Department of the ministry had assumed the post of the information attaché at the Nigerian foreign mission in the United Kingdom (*West Africa* 17–23 January 1994, 84).

The adverse international publicity caused by the Abacha Government's failure to complete Nigeria's transition to democracy meant that the Federal Ministry of Information had the unenviable task of attempting to minimize or counter international disapproval. Thus, it was not surprising that it was the federal minister for Information, Professor Jerry Gana (incidentally, the first person to hold this ministerial portfolio during the Abacha Government), who, while meeting reporters in Aba in Abia State, announced that "the Federal government" was "to take steps to counter adverse reports emanating from foreign media" (*West Africa* 19–25 September 1994, 1634). For the Federal Ministry of Information to be able to lead in carrying out that task adequately, it seemed that it needed to effectively cooperate with other agencies and ministries. As a case in point, when the Federal Ministry of Information earlier invited two journalists from the Cable Network News (CNN) of the United States to tour Nigeria for four weeks to gain a firsthand understanding of the country, these journalists were forced to leave the country before they had completed their visit (*West Africa* 5–11 September 1994, 1554). Although Professor Gana said that the federal government had the right to send the two CNN journalists out of the country, he admitted that the expulsions were "most unfortunate," and also added "that by the time his attention was drawn to the fate of the journalists and before he could do something about it, the CNN team had already left the country on the orders of the State Security Service (SSS)" (*West Africa* 5–11 September 1994, 1554). This incident shows that either the Federal Ministry of Information did not adequately relate with other agencies or ministries of carrying out its functions, or that the Federal Ministry of Information could be outmaneuvered by other agencies or ministries if they did not like the policies or actions of the Federal Ministry of Information.

In order to minimize the negative perceptions that many important countries had about the Abacha Government, Nigeria engaged in vigorous international public relations campaigns. Those that Nigeria launched in the United States were particularly elaborate (*Theweek* 17 March 1997, 28–29; *The Washington Post National Weekly Edition* 2–8 December

1996, 22–23). For an example, it was reported that the Nigerian government "employed the services of nine U.S. public relations and lobbying firms spanning the American political spectrum" (*The Washington Post National Weekly Edition* 2–8 December 1996, 22).

On the whole, the Federal Ministry of Information seems to have been doing its best in performing its functions. For example, in 1994 the federal minister for Information assured Lev Parshin, the Russian ambassador to Nigeria, that the Nigeria-Russia Cultural Agreement, which had expired in 1991, would be revived. He also called for the continued support of Russia for the completion of the Ajaokuta Steel Complex (*West Africa* 28 February–6 March 1994, 358), which was being constructed with the help of the technical assistance of a Russian organization.

The effort to push for the completion of the Ajaokuta Steel Complex reflected the continued importance of the economic components of foreign relations, which had been much emphasized during the prior Babangida Government. As with previous governments, during the Abacha Government many various ministries and agencies were involved in the handling of the economic components of foreign relations. For example, the federal minister of Industries, Bamanga Tukur, was interested in finding ways to complete the construction of the Ajaokuta Steel Complex and other industrial projects (*West Africa* 12–18 December 1994, 2129), while the federal minister of Power and Steel, Bashir Dalhatu (while hosting Oleg Davydov, the Russian deputy prime minister), also reiterated the desire of the federal government of Nigeria to complete and commission the Ajaokuta Steel Complex soon (*West Africa* 26 December 1994–8 January 1995, 2217).

The Abacha Government, like previous governments, also paid significant attention to international economic bodies. For example, the Federal Ministry of Finance continued to work with the World Bank to deal with Nigeria's international debt situation (*West Africa* 19–25 December 1994, 2170). However, in some other circumstances Nigeria seems to have held different views from those of the industrialized countries. For example, at a meeting of the African Development Bank (located in Abidjan, Cote d'Ivoire), which was held in 1995 in Abuja, Nigeria, to elect a new president for the bank, Nigeria tried to stop efforts of the industrialized western countries to increase their influence and role in the bank (*The New York Times* Friday, 26 May 1995, A3).

There was also interest among the policy elites, through conferences and workshops, to explore more ways for enabling the Economic Community of West African States (ECOWAS) to reach its full potential, so as to improve economic conditions for Nigeria and other ECOWAS member countries through increased regional economic integration (*West Africa* 17–23 April 1995, 592).

A highlight of Nigeria's role in international organizations was its role in the Organization of Petroleum Exporting Countries (OPEC) in 1994. From June to November 1994, OPEC's position of secretary-general, or chief administrator, was left vacant, due to a deadlock in the selection of a new secretary-general. Iran, stating that it was its turn to provide the person to fill the position, presented a candidate to block the candidate from Venezuela, who would otherwise have won the post. During this period of deadlock, Nigeria was able to mount a very effective diplomatic lobby among OPEC member countries, which resulted in Rilwanu Lukman (a former Nigerian minister of Petroleum) being presented at the November 1994 OPEC meeting at Bali, Indonesia, as a compromise candidate. He was selected as the secretary-general of OPEC (*The New York Times* 23 November 1994, C2; *The Wall Street Journal* 23 November 1994, A2–A10; *West Africa* 16–22 January 1995, 53).

There were also a lot of activities in terms of Nigeria's bilateral international economic relations. For example, the Federal Ministry of Transport and Aviation continued to foster cooperation between Nigeria and Poland in the field of transportation. Nigerdock (a Nigerian ship repair company completed in 1986 with the technical assistance of Navimore, a Polish ship repair and shipbuilding company), for instance, was planning to move into shipbuilding in its next development phase (*West Africa* 4–10 July 1994, 1184). The Federal Ministry of Transport and Aviation was also working to create a Nigerian-Namibian pact that would enable Nigeria to extend its role in African maritime trade (*West Africa* 21–27 March 1994, 508).

Nigeria's international economic activities during the Abacha Government continued to be very pronounced in the west African subregion, both in terms of the actions of the Nigerian government and the initiatives of Nigerian private investors. For example, Banque Internationale du Benin (BIBE) (a bank in the Republic of Benin owned by Nigerian investors), which was founded in 1990, had by 1995 become the third largest bank in the Republic of Benin and also had control of over 19 percent of the banking market in that country (*Newswatch* 10 April 1995, 28–29). This sort of progress by private Nigerian businessmen in west African countries often helps to speed up the economic integration of the west African subregion (thus helping to realize the goals of the Economic Community of West African States [ECOWAS]) and, in particular, helps Nigerian exporters and other businessmen to gain more access to the west African market.

In another development, it was reported that Nigeria saw a future politically stable Liberia as a source of supply of iron ore for the steel industry in Nigeria, and it was also announced that Liberia had requested "the assistance of Nigeria's National Electric Power Authority (NEPA) in providing Liberia's power supply" (*West Africa* 28 February–6 March 1994, 366). It was also reported that Nigeria was soon to extend gas pipelines to the west African countries of Ghana, Togo, and the Republic of Benin, for the purpose of supplying Nigerian gas to these three countries in a project that could fetch Nigeria about $500 million dollars (*West Africa* 16–22 January 1995, 75; *West Africa* 10–16 April 1995, 537).

Efforts to reduce the importation of raw materials for industrial plants in Nigeria, through increased domestic production, also continued during the Abacha Government. Addressing the Manufacturers' Association of Nigeria (MAN), the federal minister of Industries urged Nigerian industrial plants to buy more raw materials in Nigeria (*Nigerian Record* May 1995, 1). An example of efforts to produce more raw materials in Nigeria was the 1995 commissioning of the Talc Processing Company in Niger State (a joint enterprise owned by the Raw Materials Research and Development Council of Nigeria, the government of Niger State, and some private businessmen), which was expected to meet all the talc needs of industrial plants in Nigeria; prior to the establishment of this company, Nigeria used to import more than 3,000 metric tons of talc annually (*West Africa* 27 February–5 March 1995, 305).

Increase in the export of Nigeria's products, especially manufactured products, continued to be a high-priority policy during the Abacha Government. Even the Presidency was keenly interested in concrete improvements in this area. The Presidency seems to have held the view that the improvement of the quality of Nigerian products was one good way to increase exports. At the occasion of the commissioning of the first phase of the Iwopin Pulp and Paper Project in Ogun State, President Sani Abacha, in a speech that was read by Major-General Abdulsalam Abubukar, the chief of defense staff, who represented Abacha at the occasion, urged that Nigerian "industries should strive for the production of good quality products in order to compete in international markets" (*West Africa* 19–25 December 1994, 2163).

The Export Processing Zone (EPZ) in Calabar was seen as another instrument to increase the export of products manufactured in Nigeria. The federal minister of Commerce and Tourism, while grappling with the completion of the EPZ in Calabar, also announced that there were plans for more EPZs in the future (*West Africa* 26 September–2 October 1994, 1675).

During the Abacha Government there were also efforts to harmonize the functions of the Nigerian Export Promotion Council (NEPC) and the Nigerian Export Import Bank (NEXIM) so as to increase the export of Nigerian goods, by making the NEPC concentrate on the education of "exporters on export procedures and markets and the administration of export incentives," while NEXIM focused on "the provision of export credit guarantee and insurance cover" (*Nigeria News Update* 28 April–11 May 1994, 9).

Even Nigerian embassies in foreign countries seem to have been more involved in the task of helping to promote Nigerian economic interests abroad. For example, the Nigerian foreign mission in Harare, Zimbabwe, was very active in helping Nigerian entrepreneurs, arranging for them to be organized and registered, relating on their behalf with the officials of Zimbabwe, and holding weekly meetings with the Nigerian Businessmen's Association in Zimbabwe. For this help the Nigerian entrepreneurs in Zimbabwe were very grateful. (*Nigeria News Update* 4–17 June 1994, 8). This sort of help greatly helps to promote Nigeria's economic interests in the host country—for example, it can lead to an increase in the export of Nigerian products to that host country.

The grand economic policy and plan of the Abacha Government was the program called the Vision 2010. The Vision 2010 aimed at transforming Nigeria into an economically industrialized and robust country and a sociopolitically stable nation by the year 2010 (*Newswatch* 15 December 1997, 8–14). It was also perceived that the Abacha Government aimed at using the Vision 2010 to improve its international image (*The New York Times* 29 November 1996, A10).

However, throughout its duration, the Abacha Government did not enjoy a generally favorable international image. It had most of its problems with Western countries. For example, Nigerian-United States relations were very rocky during this period. Walter C. Carrington, the United States ambassador to Nigeria for most of the Abacha Government, constantly had problems with the Nigerian government. For an example, the Nigerian police force wanted Carrington's diplomatic immunity, and that of some of his staff, to be waived so that Carrington and his staff could be interrogated by the police about some bombing incidents in Nigeria (*Theweek* 28 July 1997, 21; *The New York Times* 17 July 1997, A5). Even when Carrington was finally leaving Nigeria, a farewell party for him was disallowed by the Nigerian police force (*The New York Times* 26 September 1997, A6).

The tensions in Nigerian-United States relations were also reflected by the fact that, after New York City officials renamed a street corner near the Nigerian United Nations Mission as Kudirat Abiola Corner (in honor of the slain wife of M. K. O. Abiola, who was jailed in Nigeria after the cancellation of the presidential election that he apparently won), the Eti-Osa local government in Lagos State renamed the street on which stood the embassies of the United States, Britain, Finland, Germany, Italy, the Russian Federation, and Sweden as Louis Farrakhan Crescent (in honor of an African-American Muslim leader unfriendly to the U.S. government) (*International Herald Tribune* 7–8 February 1998, 5; *West Africa* 23 February–1 March 1998, 254).

Also, when President Clinton of the United States visited some African countries in 1998, Nigeria was not one of them because of the unsatisfactory relations between the two countries (*Africa Today* May 1998, 27). The United States and some European countries also maintained some measures of economic and military sanctions against Nigeria.

The poor relations between Canada and Nigeria resulted in Nigeria closing its foreign mission in Canada in 1996 and Canada closing its foreign mission in Nigeria in 1997 (*Africa Today* May/June 1997, 11). Relations between Nigeria and the Commonwealth also remained poor. The suspension of Nigerian membership in the Commonwealth that was imposed due to the execution of Ken Saro Wiwa (the Nigerian human rights activist) remained till the end of the Abacha Government, though Nigeria was able to weaken some of the further actions that the Commonwealth was supposed to carry out against Nigeria (*Newswatch* 10 November 1997, 17–19).

One of the few diplomatic respites from the West was the visit of Pope John Paul II to Nigeria to beatify the late Father Iwene Tansi (Nigeria's first candidate for Catholic sainthood), although the Pope's visit also meant strong pressure on the Abacha Government to improve its human rights record (*The New York Times* 23 March 1998, A3; *The New York Times* 24 March 1998, A11).

The unsatisfactory diplomatic relations the Abacha Government had with the Western countries that had been traditionally friendly to Nigeria resulted in that government cultivating increased ties with France, China, and other countries; and in the case of France encouraging the teaching of the French language in Nigeria (*Newswatch* 24 November 1997, 41–45; *Newswatch* 23 March 1998, 26; *Theweek* 23 September 1996, 26–27; *Theweek* 26 May 1997, 14–18). Nigeria also increased its links with Islamic countries. For examples, Nigeria joined an organization comprised of countries with predominantly Islamic populations: Bangladesh, Egypt, Indonesia, Iran, Malaysia, Pakistan, and Turkey) (*Theweek* 27 January 1997, 26–27), and in 1998 it was again announced that Nigeria was a full member of the Organization of Islamic Conference (OIC) (*Newswatch* 4 May 1998, 25).

One continent in which Nigeria was able to retain significant influence was Africa, especially west Africa. With the successes of its interventions in Liberia and Sierra Leone to help restore political stability to those countries, Nigeria was able to extend its security and economic ties with the countries of the Economic Community of West African States (ECOWAS) (*Newswatch* 10 November 1997, 27; *Theweek* 7 April 1997, 22; *West Africa* 23 February–1 March 1998 278; *West Africa* 16–29 March 1998, 339). The fact that Oluyemi Adeniji, a Nigerian diplomat, was appointed in early 1998 as the special representative of the secretary-general of the United Nations to Central African Republic to supervise the United Nations' Peacekeeping force and other United Nations' activities in that country (*Africa Today* June 1998, 36), shows that Nigeria's influence in Africa was significant. The paradox of President Abacha was that while important Western countries did not like him, African leaders seem to have seen the roles his government played in Liberia and Sierra Leone as being very important. For an example, soon after Abacha's sudden death in 1998, President Yahaya Jameh of Gambia, President Baare Mainasara of Niger, President Idris Deby of Chad, and President Ange-Felix Batassee of the Central African Republic paid condolence visits to Nigeria; and later some other African leaders also paid condolence visits to Nigeria (*Newswatch* 22 June 1998, 12). It was also reported that African leaders paid glowing tributes to Abacha, describing him as a man who dedicated his "body and soul to his country," and as "Africa's most illustrious son" (African leaders quoted by *The New York Times* 14 June 1998, 6). *The New York Times* also added that "and as could be expected upon the death of an American President, General Abacha's death unleashed a flood of eulogies praising his immense qualities as a statesman. Fittingly, after the death of the leader of a great country, no fewer than seven African heads of state rushed to pay their respects" (*The New York Times* 14 June 1998, 6).

In terms of foreign policy decision-making coordination structures and processes, the profile and dynamics that were in place since the Babangida Government, and through the brief interlude of the Shonekan Government, continued during the Abacha Government. Though the foreign policy coordination machinery seems to have generally functioned adequately during the Abacha Government, it performed very inadequately at least in one particular instance. The shocking actions of executing Ken Saro-Wiwa (a human rights and environmental leader) and eight other leaders from the Ogoni area of the Rivers State, in 1995, presented a situation where there seems to have been a problem of foreign policy coordination. The fact that the Abacha Government carried out these executions of Saro-Wiwa and the others baffled many Nigerians (*Newswatch* 11 December 1995, 16). They happened despite "local and international pleas for clemency for the nine people" (*Newswatch* 20 November 1995, 24). International pleas came from many world leaders, including President Nelson Mandela of South Africa, President Bill Clinton of the United States, and Prime Minister John Major of the United Kingdom (*Africa Today* January/February 1996, 6). Additionally, these executions took place during the period of the Commonwealth Summit in New Zealand; many had long expected that at this summit the Commonwealth would seriously consider economic sanctions against Nigeria—even, perhaps, its suspension or expulsion from the Commonwealth—because of the lack of democracy and adequate human rights protection in Nigeria) (*Newswatch* 20 November 1995, 24). That these executions took place, and that they did so during the 1995 Commonwealth Summit, meant either that the Abacha Government was showing its contempt for the opinions and positions of many prominent world leaders, or that it experienced a significant problem of policy coordination among the relevant government decision-making structures: the Provisional Ruling Council, the Presidency, the Ministry of Foreign Affairs and the Federal Ministry of Information. Possibly it was a combination of contempt and inadequate policy coordination.

Certain facts are clear. For example, on the eve of the Commonwealth Summit, the Provisional Ruling Council (Nigeria's highest decision-making body), "at the end of a five-hour meeting . . . upheld judgement of the Ogoni Civil Disturbance Special Tribunal which found Ken Saro-Wiwa and eight others guilty of the murder of four Ogoni leaders in May 1994" (*Newswatch* 20 November 1995, 24). After this meeting of the Provisional Ruling Council, "Victor Malu, a major-general and general officer commanding the 82 airborne division of the Nigerian Army" addressed media correspondents (*Newswatch* 20 November 1995, 24). Malu stated that the Provisional Ruling Council "unanimously accepted the verdict of the tribunal," and also added that "we went through all the papers in detail and we were completely satisfied with both the constitution, outcome and the verdict of the tribunal," that "those who were convicted should die" (Malu, quoted in *Newswatch* 20 November 1995, 24). The cavalier manner in which the Provisional Ruling Council handled the decisions shows that this body might not have adequately considered the serious negative foreign policy implications that the executions of Saro-Wiwa and the others were bound to generate. Considering the fact that many world leaders had pleaded with the Abacha Government to rescind the verdict of the tribunal, the Provisional Ruling Council should have elaborately sought the inputs of the officials of the Ministry of Foreign Affairs and the Federal Ministry of Information before deciding on the Saro-Wiwa issue. The fact that the Provisional Ruling Council did not do so, treating the Saro-Wiwa issue as a mere homicide trial rather than as an international incident, shows that it might not have adequately sought and/or utilized inputs from the officials of the Ministry of Foreign Affairs and the Federal Ministry of Information. Also, the fact that Tom Ikimi, the minister of Foreign Affairs, was attending the Commonwealth Summit in New Zealand but was not immediately contacted by Abuja when Saro-Wiwa and the others were executed (Ikimi, indeed, "initially treated the story of the killings as a rumour") (*Newswatch* 27 November 1995, 15) further demonstrates the lack of policy coordination by the Abacha Government. Additionally, the fact that Walter Ofonagoro, the federal minister of Information, held the view that "the time of execution was wrong" (*Newswatch* 11 December 1995, 16), shows that the Federal Ministry of Information might not have been adequately involved in deciding the issue.

The executions of Saro-Wiwa and the eight others resulted in swift and massive negative reactions by many countries of the world. The media in many countries decried the executions, Nigeria was suspended from the Commonwealth (and was informed that it would be expelled from that organization if a democratic polity was not created in Nigeria within two years), many world leaders condemned the executions, many important countries (including South Africa, the United States, and several European countries) curtailed their diplomatic, economic, military, and cultural contacts with Nigeria, and there were also threats of further international actions against Nigeria (for example, an embargo on petroleum) if the country did not soon achieve transition to a democratic polity (*Africa Today* January/February 1996, 5–9; *Newswatch* 27 November 1995, 14–23; *Newswatch* 4 December 1995, 8–14).

While there was a problem of inadequate policy coordination within the Abacha Government in relation to the executions, there was an efficient and effective coordination in terms of how the government handled and managed the consequent adverse international reactions. The actions of the Provisional Ruling Council, the Presidency, the Ministry of Foreign Affairs, the Federal Ministry of Information, and other relevant ministries and agencies were carefully coordinated. For example, the Presidency put in place a policy "to coordinate" Nigeria's "responses in the diplomatic face-off" so as to prevent Nigerian officials "speaking at cross-purposes" (*Newswatch* 11 December 1995, 17). The policies of the Abacha Government involved "talking tough," while also making efforts "to reach out to friends of Nigeria to explain the issues" (*Newswatch* 11 December 1995, 17) and mobilize support, both domestically and internationally, for Nigeria's actions (*Africa Today* January/February 1996, 5–7; *Newswatch* 4 December 1995, 8–14; *Newswatch* 11 December 1995, 16–18). The Provisional Ruling Council, the Presidency, the Federal Ministry of Information, the Ministry of Foreign Affairs, and other relevant ministries, agencies and organs were involved in formulating, implementing and evaluating the above policies in a coordinated manner. It was therefore not surprising that Walter Ofonagoro, the federal minister of Information, while attending "a week-long exhibition of contemporary arts in Owerri," the capital of Imo State, stated that "Nigeria will not be stampeded into changing its transition programme due to pressure from the international community," and, thus, was "reinforcing the position of the head of state at the chief of army staff conference" during the previous week (*Newswatch* 18 December 1995, 16). In this instance, the Presidency and the Federal Ministry of Information were acting in a coordinated fashion.

In addition, in keeping with the policy of talking tough while being conciliatory, in the same speech to the Chief of Army Staff Conference, Sani Abacha noted that "The armed forces have to adjust to the democratic changes now taking place around the world. What is even more significant is the need for the Nigerian army to readjust itself to the negative signals emerging from the strategic global environment, especially seen against the backdrop of the current wave of international community to castigate Nigeria" (Abacha, quoted in *Newswatch* 18 December 1995, 16).

The Provisional Ruling Council, in some of its views, also sounded a conciliatory note. After a meeting of the council held after the execution of Saro-Wiwa and the eight others, a member of that body, "Victor Ombu, a rear-admiral and flag officer commanding the Eastern Naval Command," told newsmen "that the federal government would educate those Commonwealth member-nations friendly to Nigeria but who were hoodwinked into taking their present stance against the country" (*Newswatch* 4 December 1995, 9).

The policy of mobilizing support both domestically and internationally was launched as a campaign with the catchy theme, "Not in Our Character" (*Africa Today* January/February 1996, 6). This campaign theme and the components of the campaign showed that the Federal Ministry of Information was utilizing its expert and savvy public relations and media specialists. Ademola Adebo, a leader of a citizens' group called All Nigeria Congress, was given prominent airtime on the television network to drum up public support for the federal government through a solidarity march (*Newswatch* 4 December 1995, 8). Also, the country's elite print media reporters elaborately documented that the solidarity march was mostly organized and/or promoted by organs of the local, state, and federal governments (*Newswatch* 4 December 1995, 8–14). In terms of the international aspects of this campaign, it seems that the Ministry of Foreign Affairs (through Nigerian embassies abroad) and the Federal Ministry of Information worked closely together. For example, about seven United States' public relations firms were hired by the Nigerian government to help in the public relations campaign in the United States, videos prepared by the Nigerian Television Authority were sent to Nigerian embassies abroad for use by nationals of the host countries, and the Nigerian government also placed advertisements in the press of such countries as South Africa and Zimbabwe (*Africa Today* January/February 1996, 6).

The Abacha Government also enlisted many former Nigerian presidents to help in the international aspects of the public relations campaign. "Former President Shehu Shagari was to exploit his contact with the German and French governments to influence their attitude," former President Ernest Shonekan "was to do the same with the British authorities," Yakubu Gowon "was to tap his relationship with some African leaders and Commonwealth members to turn the tide in favour of Nigeria," and other delegations were sent "to various regions of the world armed with the same mandate" (*Newswatch* 11 December 1995, 17). Additionally, Chukwuemeka Odumegwu Ojukwu (the leader of the defunct Biafra) also spent two months in Europe and the United States to help improve the image of the federal government (*Newswatch* 18 December 1995, 17). These foreign trips of former Nigerian presidents and other prominent Nigerians obviously involved close policy coordination among the Presidency, the Ministry of Foreign Affairs, and the Federal Ministry of Information.

On the whole, the nature and functioning of foreign policy decision-making structures during the Abacha Government were not much different from those of the Babangida Government and the brief Shonekan Government. As shown in this study, during the Abacha Government some Nigerian foreign policy actions and activities were aimed at minimizing the pressures the government was receiving from important industrialized countries because of these countries' displeasure with the non-democratization of the Nigerian political system. As also shown in this study, the Presidency, the Ministry of Foreign Affairs, and the Federal Ministry of Information, in particular, focused on these actions and activities to minimize or contain these external pressures from other countries. The unity of purpose among these ministries and agencies, and the intensity of their actions, most probably resulted from close coordination of these ministries and agencies by the Presidency. Thus, on the whole, the profile and dynamics of foreign policy decision-making associated with the efforts to minimize or contain the external pressures mostly reflected the rational-actor model of foreign policy decision-making.

In terms of Nigeria's role in international security management operations in the west African subregion, the Abacha Government, as shown earlier, after initial hesitations about Nigeria's role in Liberia quickly recommitted itself to the prominent role of Nigeria in the ECOMOG forces in Liberia, and, later, also in Sierra Leone. The Presidency and the Ministry of Defense issued almost exact statements, as noted in this study, regarding the rationale for Nigeria's role in these countries. According to the Presidency and the Ministry of Defense, the stability of the west African subregion helps the economic growth of all countries in the region (including Nigeria); thus, the economic cost of using Nigerian military forces to help maintain stability in the subregion is a good investment for Nigeria. This similarity of views, unity of purpose, and intense commitment to international security management operations in the west African subregion by the Presidency and the Ministry of Defense in this area also mostly reflected the rational-actor model.

As also shown in this study, many ministries and agencies continued the tradition of being involved in the economic and cultural components of foreign policy. As in previous governments, the routine and mundane aspects of foreign economic or cultural policy decision-making within ministries or agencies often involved the dynamics of following standard operating rules and procedures of each ministry or agency, thus reflecting the organizational process model of decision-making. However, as was also the case during previous governments, the involvement of two or more ministries and/or agencies in shaping a particular foreign economic or cultural policy continued to result in each of these various ministries and agencies seeking to advance their particular interests, instead of focusing on policies and actions to advance the interests of the country as a whole. Also, as in previous governments, sometimes the competing divergent interests resulted in bargaining and then a compromise among these ministries and agencies—thus reflecting the bureaucratic politics model of foreign policy making—but because in most instances there was an effective primary or leading ministry or agency in charge of particular foreign economic or cultural policy areas, and because units of the Presidency did also easily step in to effect coordination when and where necessary, the other ministries or agencies were often influenced to focus on the general interests and goals of the government—thus reflecting the rational-actor model of foreign policy decision-making.

11
Opening a New Chapter: The Abubakar Era

THE ABUBAKAR GOVERNMENT CAME INTO BEING SUDDENLY. THE UNEXpected death of President Abacha resulted in General Abdulsalami Abubakar being appointed the president of Nigeria by the Provisional Ruling Council (the country's highest decision-making body). The Abubakar Government, which came into being in early June 1998, decided to return the country to democratic civilian polity in May 1999. Thus, the Abubakar Government was short and transitional. In the history of modern Nigeria, only the Ironsi Government and the Shonekan had similarly short durations. But unlike those governments (which started with political crises, operated through political crises, and were succeeded by governments that witnessed more political crises), the Abubakar Government came into being with a legacy of political crisis left by preceding governments, then calmed the political system: giving Nigerians hope that succeeding governments will bring even calmer, more stable, and more prosperous dynamics to the country. Thus, the Abubakar Government seems to have been opening a new chapter for the country. History will note whether that government succeeded or failed in such an endeavor.

Being a short and transitional government, the Abubakar Government used mostly the same major national domestic and foreign policy decision-making bodies that the Abacha Government had used, with the obvious difference being that there were some key personnel changes in these decision-making bodies.

The Provisional Ruling Council continued as the highest policy-making body for the country, and the National Council of States and the Federal Executive Council also continued to perform the same functions that they had during the previous governments.

Expectedly, Abubakar, who had a pleasant and open personality, also ushered in a government that was more open, more stable, and more humane. Thus, this government was quite different from the tough, rigid, and authoritarian Abacha Government. The Abubakar Government, therefore, had more support domestically and internationally.

During the Abubakar Government, the key officials were Vice Admiral Okhai Akhigbe, the chief of general staff (who was next to the president in terms of power and protocol); Air Marshall Al-Amin Daggash, the chief of defense staff; Lieutenant General Ishaya Bamaiyi, the chief of army staff; Vice Admiral Jubril Ayinla, the chief of naval staff; and Air Marshall Nsikak Eduok, the chief of the air staff (*Newswatch* 4 January 1999, 22). The Presidency also continued as the nerve center of national policy-making. In order to have his imprint on the government, Abubakar changed some of the key special advisers and presidential assistants in the Presidency (*Newswatch* 19 October 1998, 27). Abubakar also appointed new members to the Cabinet. In terms of foreign policy matters, the major change was the replacement of the combative Ikimi as the minister of Foreign Affairs with Ignatius Olisemeka (*Newswatch* 7 September 1998, 20) who, as a career diplomat, was more cautious and diplomatic in character.

Early in the life of the Abubakar Government, M. K. O. Abiola (who was the apparent presidential winner of the election that was annulled by the Babangida Government, and who had been in detention since the Abacha Government), died in detention (*Tallahassee Democrat* 9 July 1998, 1A, 7A). The calm and stable nature of the Abubakar Government enabled it to soothe domestic tension and also to reassure the international community of its intention to lead Nigeria successfully through a transition period.

During the Abubakar Government, the Petroleum Trust Fund (PTF), headed by Muhammed Buhari (a former head of state), continued to be a major source of funds for the building and maintenance of economic and social infrastructures in the country. The PTF, which was established by the Abacha Government, was seen as a positive force in the economic transformation of the country.

During his visits to both the United States and Britain, Abubakar was warmly received by the leaders of those countries (*Newswatch* 5 October 1998; *The New York Times* 25 September 1998, A7). These visits show that during the Abubakar Government diplomatic relations between Nigeria and Western countries greatly improved, which also resulted in improved economic relations with these countries and the international economic bodies they controlled (*Newswatch* 10 August 1998, 32; *Newswatch* 5 October 1998, 15; and *Newswatch* 28 December 1998, 35). Nigeria and France also continued to have good relations (*Newswatch* 28 December 1998, 29).

Like previous Nigerian governments, the Abubakar Government saw Africa, particularly west Africa, as the centerpiece of Nigerian foreign policy. President Abubakar, therefore, made most of his diplomatic visits to the Economic Community of West African States (ECOWAS) countries, and most of his government's foreign policy initiatives and actions focused on these countries. For an example, during the ECOWAS summit in

Nigeria in 1998, a Peace Accord for the peaceful resolution of the internal conflict that erupted in Guinea Bissau in the middle of 1998 was signed (*Newswatch* 16 November 1998, 28).

The continued influence of Nigeria in west Africa was shown by the fact that Brigadier-General Maxwell Khobe (the Nigerian army officer who led the ECOMOG troops that had restored President Kabbah of Sierra Leone to power) was made the chief of staff of Sierra Leonean military forces and the minister of Internal Security for Sierra Leone (*Theweek* 10 August 1998, 33). Also, when there was a tense stand-off between Liberia and the United States, due to the fact that Roosevelt Johnson (a leader of a Liberian political group) took refuge in the American Embassy in Monrovia, Liberia, helicopters from Nigerian-led ECOMOG forces flew Johnson and some of his family members and supporters to Nigeria, thus helping to defuse international tensions (*Africa Today* November 1998, 47; *The New York Times* 26 September 1998, A3).

When Sierra Leonean rebel forces attacked Freetown again, the Nigerian-led ECOMOG forces were able to get them again out of that city in early 1999. Air Marshall Al-Amin Daggash, the chief of defense staff of Nigeria, and Ignatius Olisemeka, the Nigerian foreign minister, also visited President Kabbah in early 1999 to evaluate the military and political situations in Sierra Leone soon after ECOMOG drove the rebels out of Freetown (*Newswatch* 8 February 1999, 28). The fact that Daggash and Olisemeka visited Kabbah together shows that the close foreign policy coordination between the ministries of Foreign Affairs and Defense continued during the Abubakar Government.

During the Abubakar Government, increased planning and cooperation among the military and security officials of ECOWAS countries also continued (*Theweek* 9 November 1998, 29; *West Africa* 3–16 August 1998, 606). Economic cooperation and integration among ECOWAS countries also was progressing, with the highlight being the introduction of ECOWAS traveler's checks for the ECOWAS countries (*Newswatch* 8 February 1999, 36; *Theweek* 23 November 1998, 27). The ECOWAS travelers' checks, which were printed by the Nigerian Security Printing and Minting Company, were seen as instruments that would increase business links between and among ECOWAS countries (*Newswatch* 8 February 1999, 36).

To show the continuing excellent bilateral links between Niger and Nigeria, President Bare Mainasara of Niger awarded President Abubakar with the highest honor in Niger (*Theweek* 28 September 1998, 33). Nigeria's relations with South Africa, which had soured during the Abacha Government, also returned to normal during the Abubakar Government (*Newswatch* 7 September 1998, 26–27).

On the whole, although its tenure was brief, the Abubakar Government, using the same foreign policy decision-making structures and processes of the Abacha Government (but with some new sets of officials and with more openness and goodwill) was able to vastly improve Nigeria's relations with Western countries, while still strengthening Nigeria's role in west Africa.

12
The Obasanjo Government: The Second Episode

THIS CHAPTER COVERS THE EARLY PHASE OF THE OBASANJO GOVERNment. Twenty years after Olusegun Obasanjo (a former military head of state) handed over power to an elected civilian government in 1979, he was elected the president in 1999. Thus, Obasanjo, who once headed a military government, also had an opportunity to serve as an elected president in a democratic polity. In the 1970s, he had headed the second phase of the Muhammed/Obasanjo Government, which was known for its dynamic and assertive foreign policy. The Nigeria that Obasanjo headed in 1999 had far less economic strength, compared to the economically strong Nigeria of the oil-boom years of the 1970s. This reality affected the foreign policy goals and actions of the Obasanjo Government, at least in its early phase. Additionally, the foreign policy decision-making structures and processes of the democratic polity of the early phase of the Obasanjo Government were different from those of the Muhammed/Obasanjo Government, and consequently foreign policy decision-making structures and processes also made the foreign policy goals and actions were correspondingly different.

The Obasanjo Government inherited a polity that not only had significant internal sociopolitical and economic problems, but that was also experiencing an inhospitable international environment. As elaborated in these preceding chapters, the annulment of the presidential election that was won by M. K. O. Abiola by the Babangida Government set in motion the dynamics of political crises. The Shonekan Government and the Abacha Government were consumed by these political crises. The rigidity, bad human rights record, and other political excesses of the Abacha Government greatly escalated and compounded the political crises in the country. The execution of Saro-Wiwa by the Abacha Government clearly underlined the political excesses of that government. The sudden death of President Abacha ushered in the more humane Abubakar Government. Abacha's death was soon followed by the equally sudden death of Abiola. Some of the earlier chapters of this book have shown that President Abacha was bent on preventing Abiola from becoming president of the country, and Abiola was a man who wanted to fulfill his electoral mandate by becoming the president. Thus, the sudden deaths of both Abacha and

Abiola resulted in new political dynamics in the country, leading to the peaceful election of Obasanjo as the President.

Thus, the Obasanjo Government presented the country with a great opportunity to make sociopolitical and economic progress and the opportunity also to foster a more hospitable international environment. It was therefore not surprising that starting in its early phase, the Obasanjo Government eagerly laid some foundations for political, social, and economic transformations, and also strove to gain more international friends and allies.

In terms of foreign policy decision-making systems, the Obasanjo Government had to work with foreign policy decision-making structures and processes that are applicable in a democracy. The National Assembly (consisting of the Senate and the House of Representatives) is the highest legislative body. The committees of both the Senate and the House that focus on foreign relations, defense, and intelligence matters help the National Assembly to play its role in foreign affairs. Even in the early phase of the Obasanjo Government, federal legislators displayed a strong desire to play the roles that are expected of them in terms of foreign relations. For an example, the Senate Foreign Relations Committee was very assertive during the confirmation process of new Nigerian ambassadors.

The Presidency (with its complex substructures of ministers within the Presidency, special presidential advisers, and presidential assistants) was well organized and staffed right from the early phase of the Obasanjo Government. Thus, the Presidency was adequately equipped and positioned to assist the president in the shaping and coordination of foreign policy matters. The chief of staff of the Presidency directly managed and administered the functioning of the Presidency. Thus, that person was in the vantage position to manage the flow of policy papers and officials that directly reached the president. Therefore, the chief of staff of the Presidency was able to manage the structures and processes of the highest level of policy formulation (including foreign policy formulation). The secretary to the Federal Government coordinated the federal ministries and other federal units and also served as secretary to national policy bodies such as the Federal Executive Council and the National Council of States. The secretary to the Federal Government of Nigeria was, therefore, also in the vantage position to help shape and coordinate policies (including foreign policies). The minister (within the Presidency) for Cooperation and Integration in Africa (*Newswatch* 12 July 1999, 10) was another important official within the Presidency who played a prominent role in foreign policy decision-making. The Obasanjo Government was the first Nigerian government to establish this ministerial position. This action signaled the desire of the Obasanjo Government to make increased political and security cooperation and accelerated economic integration in Africa some of the cardinal goals of the Nigerian foreign policy. Other important officials within the Presidency who were significantly involved in foreign policy decision-making (even though most of their duties involved domestic matters) were the chief economic adviser to the president, the adviser on Petroleum Resources, the adviser on Political Matters, and the National Security adviser (who cooridnated the various intelligence organizations). A very important official within the Presidency, in terms of foreign policy matters, was the special adviser to the president on International Relations. This official was in a central position to help shape and coordinate foreign policies.

As shown above, the Presidency was adequately organized and staffed to assist the president in the shaping and coordination of foreign policy decision-making. The high number of officials who were involved in foreign relations matters shows that, even in its early phase, the Obasanjo Government) was equipping the Presidency to take away some foreign policy formulation functions from the Federal Ministry of Foreign Affairs.

Despite this, during the early phase of the Obasanjo Government (just as during the Muhammed/Obasanjo Government), the Federal Ministry of Foreign Affairs still had a significant foreign policy formulation role and also continued as the hub for foreign policy implementation and management. The Federal Ministry of Foreign Affairs was headed by the minister of Foreign Affairs, who was assisted by a minister of state for Foreign Affairs. (As noted in some earlier chapters of this book, during some governmental eras this ministry had both a minister of Foreign Affairs and a minister of state for Foreign Affairs—frictions between the two sometimes affected the smooth functioning of the ministry). During the early phase of the Obasanjo Government, these two leaders of the ministry were functioning adequately.

As in other governmental eras, Presidency and the Federal Ministry of Foreign Affairs, other ministries and agencies continued to play significant roles in the country's international relations. The Ministry of Defense and the intelligence organizations continued their prominent roles as the important organs in the foreign security relations of the country. The Obasanjo Government appointed Uche Okeke, a diplomat, to serve as the director-general of the National Intelligence Agency (which focuses on international intelligence) (*Newswatch* 28 June 1999, 50). A diplomat heading this organization underlined the long tradition of the Federal Ministry of Foreign Affairs also having a significant role in the country's foreign security relations.

In the area of the country's foreign cultural relations, the Federal Ministry of Foreign Affairs worked with the Federal Ministry of Culture and Tourism, the Federal Ministry of Information, and the Federal Ministry of Sports and Social Development. Likewise, the Federal Ministry of Foreign

Affairs worked with the Federal Ministry of Finance, the Federal Ministry of Commerce, and the Central Bank of Nigeria to help shape the country's foreign economic relations.

The democratic nature of the Obasanjo Government enabled political parties and interest groups to have more impact on how the executive and legislative organs shaped foreign policies. Also, state and local governments (especially those that share borders with foreign countries) were more able to work through federal legislative and executive organs to have some impact on foreign policies.

The foreign policy outputs of the early phase of the Obasanjo Government, therefore, were the results of how the national foreign policy decision-making structures functioned, and the sort of impact and feedback that they received from political parties, interest groups, state and local governments, and even individuals.

13
An Overview of Nigeria's Foreign Policy Decision-Making System

THE NATURE AND FUNCTIONING OF THE FOREIGN POLICY DECISION-making structures during the Balewa, Ironsi, Gowon, Muhammed/ Obasanjo, Shagari, Buhari, Babangida, Shonekan, Abacha, Abubakar and Obasanjo Governments manifested both changes and continuities.

As shown in this study, various organs, ministries, and agencies were involved in the country's foreign policy decision-making, in all its facets: political, security, cultural, and economic. Additionally, some foreign policy decision-making structures, like the Federal Ministry of External Affairs (which at some periods has also been named the Federal Ministry of Foreign Affairs), have been shown to focus all their activities fully on foreign policy issues, while many other structures involved in foreign policy decision-making, like the Federal Ministry of Trade (which at some periods has also been named the Federal Ministry of Commerce) and the Federal Ministry of Information, have been shown to partially focus on foreign policy issues. This study has also shown that organizations such as the Federal Ministries of External Affairs, Trade, and Information are continuously and consistently involved in the shaping of the country's foreign relations, since their activities must occur on a continuous and consistent basis in the international system. On the other hand, some organs, ministries, or agencies, like the Federal Ministry of Works (which has the main duties of building, managing, and maintaining federal roads, buildings, and other public works), are only involved in international relations activities on an intermittent basis—for example, if a civil engineer employed by the ministry is sent to a neighboring country to assist in road design and construction.

All organs, ministries and agencies can be classified into one or more of the following three categories: foreign policy formulation structures, foreign policy implementation structures, and foreign policy advisory structures. An example of a structure that can be classified as a mostly foreign policy formulation body is the Federal Executive Council (the federal cabinet body). Structures like the Federal Ministries of External Affairs,

Finance, Trade, National Planning, Defense, and Information can be classified as being both foreign policy formulation structures and foreign policy implementation structures, since apart from their major roles in helping to implement important aspects of the country's foreign policy, these structures also supply the information and analyses for decision-making and also work with national leadership organs to formulate foreign policies in various dimensions of foreign relations. On the other hand, structures like the Nigerian Institute of International Affairs (NIIA), the National Institute for Policy Studies and Strategy (NIPSS), and the Nigerian Institute for Social and Economic Research (NISER) (which are semi-autonomous think tanks funded and owned by the federal government) are primarily foreign policy advisory structures, since they mainly provide rigorous intellectual inputs into the foreign policy decision-making system in the form of foreign policy analyses, generation of foreign policy options and alternatives, and general foreign policy advice.

This study has also shown that from the Balewa Government to the Obasanjo Government, the Federal Ministry of External Affairs remained the hub of the foreign policy decision-making system in terms of the political/diplomatic dimensions of the country's foreign policy (though, during the Balewa Government, the Office of the Prime Minister handled a good portion of the foreign policy formulation activities that the Federal Ministry of External Affairs should have handled; during the Muhammed/Obasanjo Government, the Supreme Military Council and the Supreme Military Headquarters—especially as represented by the powerful "Committee of Five"—handled a very significant portion of foreign policy formulation activities that the Federal Ministry of External Affairs used to handle; and during the Obasanjo Government, the Presidency handled some foreign policy formulation activities).

The important role that the Federal Ministry of External Affairs played does not mean that national leadership bodies (for example, the Federal Executive Council of the Balewa Government to the Obasanjo Government; the Supreme Military Council and the Supreme Military Headquarters of the Gowon, Muhammed/Obasanjo, and Buhari Governments; the Presidency of the Babangida, Abacha, Abubakar, and Obasanjo Governments; the Armed Forces Ruling Council of the Babangida Government; and the Provisional Ruling Council of the Abacha and Abubakar Governments) did not play very important foreign policy roles. As this study has shown, these national leadership bodies played a very important role as continuous foreign policy decision-making coordinating structures. Even more importantly, in cases of vital and sensitive foreign policy issues, the final decisions were made by these bodies: for examples, the decision of Nigeria to recognize the MPLA Government (during the Muhammed/Obasanjo Government), the decision to nationalize the British Petroleum

Company in Nigeria (during the Muhammed/Obasanjo Government), the decision to boycott the 1986 Edinburgh Commonwealth of Nations Games (during the Babangida Government), the decision regarding Nigeria's relationship with the Organization of Islamic Conference (during the Babangida Government), and the decision to lay the foundations for the formation of the African Petroleum Producers' Association (during the Babangida Government).

Though the Federal Ministry of External Affairs was the hub of foreign policy decision-making in terms of the political/diplomatic components of foreign policy, this study has shown that other ministries and agencies were more important in the handling of the security, cultural, and economic components of foreign policy. The Federal Ministry of Defense was the leading structure in the handling of the security components of foreign policy, with other security-related agencies and ministries also participating. The Federal Ministry of External Affairs mainly works with the Federal Ministry of Defense and other security-related agencies and ministries to help manage the security components of foreign policy—for example, the Federal Ministry of External Affairs (through the Nigerian embassies in some foreign countries) houses Nigerian defense attachés, who play very important roles in the security relations Nigeria has with other countries.

The Federal Ministry of Information was in charge of external publicity, external information, and other aspects of international cultural relations. In this arena, the Federal Ministry of External Affairs had to cooperate to help manage these cultural components of foreign policy. The Federal Ministry of External Affairs (through the Nigerian embassies) also houses the information attachés. The relationship between the Federal Ministry of External Affairs and the Federal Ministry of Information has continually been mostly conflictual, due to the bureaucratic turf battles.

The economic components of the country's foreign policy, from the Balewa Government to the Obasanjo Government, have also been shown in this study to be primarily and continuously in the hands of the Federal Ministry of Finance, the Federal Ministry of Trade, the Federal Ministry of National Planning (which at some periods had been named the Federal Ministry of Economic Development), the Federal Ministry of Petroleum Resources, the Nigerian National Petroleum Corporation, the Central Bank of Nigeria, the Nigerian Export Promotion Council and the Nigeria Export and Import Bank. The Federal Ministry of External Affairs work with these other ministries and agencies to help manage the economic components of foreign relations.

This study has also shown that since the formation of the Economic Community of West African States (ECOWAS), the Federal Ministry of National Planning has been formally and primarily in charge of Nigeria's relations with this regional body. Thus, this ministry handles one of the most important foreign policy goals of Nigeria since the Gowon Government—the economic integration of the west African subregion through ECOWAS, with the attendant increase in Nigeria's economic and political role in this subregion. Thus, the Federal Ministry of External Affairs plays a subsidiary role in terms of handling ECOWAS affairs. This means that the Federal Ministry of National Planning is primarily in charge of Nigeria's multilateral international relations in the west African subregion with the Federal Ministry of External Affairs handling bilateral international relations. However, this study has also shown that in reality, when ECOWAS is involved in peacekeeping operations, military interventions, and other international security management operations (for example, the ECOMOG operations in Liberia and Sierra Leone), the Federal Ministry of External Affairs doe in fact become the leading ministry handling Nigeria's relations with ECOWAS. Thus, during the ECOMOG operations in Sierra Leone, the Nigerian minister of External Affairs headed the ECOWAS Committee of Five that handled the ECOWAS role in Sierra Leone. This study has, therefore, shown that the Federal Ministry of National Planning plays a leading role in handling Nigeria's relations with ECOWAS in economic matters, while the Federal Ministry of External Affairs takes the lead in military and political matters.

From the Balewa Government to the Obasanjo Government, the foreign policy decision-making dynamics mostly reflected the rational-actor model. In the areas of the economic and cultural components of foreign policy, where the Federal Ministry of External Affairs had to work with other ministries and agencies, some tendencies of the bureaucratic politics model of foreign policy decision-making did often crop up. However, because the ministry or agency that was primarily in charge of a particular foreign policy issue, or a national policy coordinating body like the Supreme Military Headquarters, the Federal Executive Council, or the Presidency, did often step in during the later phases of contentious foreign policy decision-making situations to play a leading and decisive role, the bureaucratic politics model was often superseded by the rational-actor model of foreign policy decision-making at the later and final phases of foreign policy decision-making. In the aspects of political, security, cultural, and economic components of foreign relations that dealt with routine and mundane activities, the foreign policy decision-making dynamics mostly reflected the organizational process model, since the ministries or agencies involved often simply followed the standard operating rules and procedures of decision-making used in such ministries or agencies.

This study has also shown that the governments and political leaders of some states in the country did sometimes get involved in helping to shape the country's foreign relations. The leaders of states that share some of their borders with a foreign country were particularly, likely to wish to be involved in this sort of role in foreign relations, by helping the relevant federal organs, ministries, and agencies to manage or minimize border conflicts and to promote economic and cultural contacts with bordering countries. Because some of the border states suffer from a lack of an adequate sense of security does encourage such states to help the federal government to manage, contain, or solve border conflicts. The cultural heritage that some of the border states share with neighboring countries also prompts them to desire the promotion of cultural and economic links with neighboring countries. The nature and dynamics of the federal system of government in Nigeria do sometimes provide state governments the political ability (though not necessarily the constitutional ability) to help the federal government to promote positive relations with neighboring countries. In fact, in most instances, the federal government often perceives shared cultural heritage as a positive factor that should be utilized to promote good relations with neighboring countries. However, there are some federal ministries or agencies involved in foreign relations that are not pleased to be assisted by the states, since they often perceive the governments and leaders of the states as not having the foreign policy and diplomatic skills and knowledge to truly help, and thus they believe these states encumber rather than facilitate the diplomatic process. A foreign policy role for the states works best when the state governments and leaders know their limitations and realize when and where they are (and are not) needed in the diplomatic process. However, this is not really a major problem, because the federal government often makes that decision.

From the Balewa Government to the Obasanjo Government, the political, security, cultural, and economic components of foreign policy have been shown to manifest themselves differently, due to which of these components was most emphasized by the particular government. The Balewa Government seems to have emphasized the political components, perhaps because it was the first government for an independent Nigeria. The need to build up diplomatic relations with other countries and with international organizations, and the fact that major foreign policy issues were the 1960s issues of decolonization (in many African countries that were not yet independent) and the lack of black majority rule in Namibia, Zimbabwe, and South Africa, accounted for the emphasis on political dimensions of foreign policy. The Ironsi Government and the later Shonekan Government were very brief, and also had very unstable domestic political systems; thus, they had no opportunity to make bold foreign policy initiatives that would have indicated the components of foreign policy they favored. The Gowon Government, during the Civil War, gave a lot of attention to the security components of foreign policy due to the need to buy adequate arms to handle the conflict. After the Civil War it devoted a great deal of attention to the economic components of foreign policy because the Gowon Government led and championed the creation of ECOWAS and also because of the tremendous increase in petroleum export revenues. The political components of foreign relations were alos emphasized by this government because after the Civil War Nigeria played a more active role in African affairs and the nonaligned movement. The Muhammed/Obasanjo Government had a more assertive foreign policy profile and a stronger role in Africa—thus focusing more on the political components of foreign policy. During the Shagari Government, the political, security, cultural, and economic components of foreign policy were all handled in a mostly routine way since a nonassertive foreign policy posture was in place during this period; however, the country's negative international debt situation forced the government to pay closer attention to the economic components of foreign policy. The Buhari Government's strong stand on handling the problem of undocumented aliens from neighboring countries, its general determination to stop the smuggling of goods through the borders, and its desire to extradite former Nigerian politicians to Nigeria to stand trial for corruption charges, led to an emphasis on the security dimension of foreign policy. The continuing external debt problem also meant some emphasis on the economic components of foreign policy. However, during the Babangida Government, the economic facet of foreign policy was formally adopted as the primary focus of the country's policy. Nigeria's very active, elaborate, and expansive role in international security management operations and peacekeeping role in Liberia and Sierra Leone, as well as in the United Nations peacekeeping missions in various parts of the world, meant that the security aspects of foreign policy was also very important during the Babangida Government. These emphases on economic and security facets of foreign policy also continued during the Abacha, Abubakar, and Obasanjo Governments. (Note must be taken of the fact that from the Balewa Government to the Obasanjo Government, all the governments paid adequate attention to the political, security, cultural, and economic components of foreign policy; emphasis on one or more components simply meant extra focus on a particular aspect or aspects.)

Such varying emphases during different governmental eras meant that the focus of human and material diplomatic resources also varied to fit in with the focus of each particular government. Thus, for example, during a governmental era that emphasized the economic components of foreign policy, the ministries and agencies that were involved in foreign economic policy decision-making had more human and material resources, organizational efficiency, and overall enhanced visibility in the foreign policy decision-making milieu.

The Muhammed/Obasanjo Government, as noted earlier, formally placed Africa as the centerpiece of Nigeria's foreign policy and many succeeding governments have continued to see Africa in this way. This has meant the strengthening of Nigeria's foreign missions in Africa, both in terms of staffing and material resources. Overall, to a very high degree the political, security, economic, and cultural aspects of Nigeria's foreign relations have been focused on Africa.

On the whole, this study is a look at the profile and functioning of foreign policy decision-making structures in Nigeria. The foreign policy decision-making system has been shown to be both elaborate and complex, and, from the Balewa Government to the Obasanjo Government, both changes and continuities have been shown in the country's foreign policy decision-making system.

Bibliography

Adefuye, Ade. 1992. "Nigeria and the Black World." *West Africa,* 17–23 February, pp. 276–77.

Adeniji, Olu. 1990. "Implementation and Administration of Foreign Policy: A Note on the Relationship between the Ministry of External Affairs and the Nigerian Missions Abroad." In Gabriel O. Olusanya and R. A. Akindele, editors, *The Structure and Processes of Foreign Policy Making and Implementation in Nigeria, 1960–1990.* Lagos: Nigerian Institute of International Affairs, pp. 143–58.

African Concord, 30 October 1986.

———. 15 May 1989.

———. 6 August 1990.

———. 10 September 1990.

———. 17 September 1990.

———. 10 June 1991.

———. 1 July 1991.

———. 28 October 1991.

———. 23 March 1992.

———. 18 May 1992.

———. 26 October 1992.

———. 9 November 1992.

———. 24 May 1993.

African Events, October 1989.

The African Guardian, 17 July 1986.

———. 16 April 1990.

Africa Today, January/February 1996.

———. November/December 1996.

———. May/June 1997.

———. July/August 1997.

———. March 1998.

———. April 1998.

———. May 1998.

———. June 1998.

———. November 1998.

Agbakoba, C. N. O. 1982. "The OAU Forces in Chad." *Nigerian Journal of International Affairs,* vol. 8, no. 2, pp. 31–56.

Ajala, Adekunle. 1986. "Nigeria and Southern Africa." in G. O. Olusanya and R. A. Akindele, editors, *Nigeria's External Relations: The First Twenty-Five Years.* Ibadan, University Press Limited, pp. 196–210.

Akindele, R. A. 1981. "President Shehu Shagari on Nigerian Foreign Policy Objectives." *Nigerian Forum,* vol. 1, no. 1, pp. 29–35.

―――. "African States and the Middle East Conflict: OAU's 1971 Peace Offensive Revisited." *Nigerian Journal of International Affairs,* vol. 11, no. 2, pp. 50–61.

―――. 1986 "Prescriptive Signals for Nigeria's Foreign Policy in the 1970s: The View from the Second National Development Plan; 1970–74." In G. O. Olusanya and R. A. Akindele, editors, *Nigeria's External Relations: The First Twenty-Five Years.* Ibadan: University Press Limited, pp. 59–70.

―――. 1990a. "Constitutional Structure for Nigeria's Foreign Policy." In Gabriel O. Olusanya and R. A. Akindele, editors, *The Structure and Processes of Foreign Policy Making and Implementation in Nigeria, 1960–1990.* Lagos: Nigerian Institute of International Affairs, pp. 55–71.

―――. 1990b. "Coordination of Domestic and Foreign Policies: Reflections on Institutional Structures and Political Processes." In Gabriel O. Olusanya and R. A. Akindele, editors, *The Structure and Processes of Foreign Policy Making and Implementation in Nigeria, 1960–1990.* Lagos: Nigerian Institute of International Affairs, pp. 243–51.

―――. 1990c. "The Formulation and Implementation of Nigeria's External Economic Policy: Institutional Structure and Process." In Gabriel O. Olusanya and R. A. Akindele, editors, *The Structure and Processes of Foreign Policy Making and Implementation in Nigeria, 1960–1990.* Lagos: Nigerian Institute of International Affairs, pp. 106–23.

―――. 1990d. "Nigerian Parliament and Foreign Policy, 1960–1966." In Gabriel O. Olusanya and R. A. Akindele, editors, *The Structure and Processes of Foreign Policy Making and Implementation in Nigeria, 1960–1990,* Lagos: Nigerian Institute of International Affairs, pp. 159–73.

―――. 1990e. "The Operation and Management of Nigeria's Foreign Policy System: Reflections on the Experience of the First Thirty Years." In Gabriel O. Olusanya and R. A. Akindele, editors, *The Structure and Processes of Foreign Policy Making and Implementation in Nigeria, 1960–1990,* Lagos: Nigerian Institute of International Affairs, pp. 531–47.

Akindele, R. A., and Bassey E., Ate. 1986. "Nigeria's Foreign Policy, 1986–2000 A.D.: Background to the Reflections on the Views from Kuru." *Nigerian Journal of International Affairs,* vol. 12, nos. 1 and 2, pp. 12–22.

Akindele, R. A., and Segun, Johnson. 1990. "Public Involvement and Participation in the Shaping of Nigeria's Foreign Policy: Reflections on the All-Nigeria (Peoples') Conferences of 1961 and 1986." In Gabriel O. Olusanya and R. A. Akindele, editors, *The Structure and Processes of Foreign Policy Making and Implementation in Nigeria, 1960–1990.* Lagos: Nigerian Institute of International Affairs, pp. 212–32.

Akindele, R. A., and Segun, Olusola. 1990. "Embassy of Nigeria in Ethiopia: Structure and Processes for Foreign Service Role Performance." In Gabriel O. Olusanya and R. A. Akindele, editors, *The Structure and Processes of Foreign Policy Making and Implementation in Nigeria, 1960–1990.* Lagos: Nigerian Institute of International Affairs, pp. 124–42.

Akindele, R. A., and M. A. Vogt, editors. 1983. *Smuggling and Coastal Piracy in Nigeria: Proceedings on a Workshop.* Lagos: Nigerian Institute of International Affairs/Nigerian Navy.

Akinsanya, Adeoye A. 1986. "Nigeria and the Multinationals." In G. O. Olusanya and R. A. Akindele, editors, *Nigeria's External Relations: The First Twenty-Five Years.* Ibadan: University Press Limited, pp. 211–32.

Akinterinwa, Bola A. 1989. "French Military Posture in Africa: Implications and Options for Nigeria." *Nigerian Journal of Policy and Strategy,* vol. 4, no. 2, pp. 91–122.

———. 1990. "The Termination and Re-establishment of Diplomatic Relations with France: A Study in Nigeria's Foreign Policy Decision-Making." In Gabriel O. Olusanya and R. A. Akindele, editors, *The Structure and Processes of Foreign Policy Making and Implementation in Nigeria, 1960–1990.* Lagos: Nigerian Institute of International Affairs, pp. 275–93.

Akinyemi, A. B. 1974. *Foreign Policy and Federalism: The Nigerian Experience.* Ibadan: Ibadan University Press.

———. 1979a. "Federalism and Foreign Policy." In A. B. Akinyemi, P. D. Cole, and Walter Ofonagoro, editors, *Readings in Federalism.* Lagos: Nigerian Institute of International Affairs, pp. 36–43.

———. 1979b"Muhammed/Obasanjo Foreign Policy." In Oyeleye Oyediran, editor, *Nigerian Government and Politics Under Military Rule, 1966–1979.* New York: St. Martin's Press, pp. 150–68.

———. 1981. "Chad: The Lessons for Nigeria." *Nigerian Forum,* vol. 1, no. 1, pp. 7–13.

———. Circa 1983. *A Farewell to Policy.* Lagos: Nigerian Institute of International Affairs.

Alli-Balogun, Gbolahan. 1986. "Nigeria and Eastern Europe." In G. O. Olusanya and R. A. Akindele, editors, *Nigeria's External Relations: The First Twenty-Five Years.* Ibadan: University Press Limited, pp. 337–59.

———. 1988. "Soviet Technical Assistance and Nigeria's Steel Complex." *The Journal of Modern African Studies,* vol. 26, no. 4, pp. 623–37.

Allison, Graham T. 1971. *Essence of Decision: Explaining the Cuban Missile Crisis,* Boston: Little, Brown.

Aluko, Olajide, 1976. "The 'New' Nigerian Foreign Policy: Developments since the Downfall of General Gowon." *The Round Table,* no. 264, pp. 405–14.

———. 1983. "Bureaucratic Politics and Foreign Policy Decision-Making in Nigeria." In Timothy M. Shaw and Olajide Aluko, editors, *Nigerian Foreign Policy: Alternative Perceptions and Projections.* New York: St. Martin's Press, pp. 77–92.

———. 1985. "The Expulsion of Illegal Aliens from Nigeria: A Study in Nigeria's Decision-Making." *African Affairs,* vol. 48, no. 337, pp. 539–60.

———. 1986. "Nigeria and the Organization of African Unity." In G. O. Olusanya and R. A. Akindele, editors, *Nigeria's External Relations: The First Twenty-Five Years.* Ibadan: University Press Limited, pp. 89–97.

———. 1990a. "The Nationalization of the Assets of the British Petroleum." In Gabriel O. Olusanya and R. A. Akindele, editors, *The Structure and Processes of Foreign Policy Making and Implementation in Nigeria, 1960–1990.* Lagos: Nigerian Institute of International Affairs, pp. 375–97.

———. 1990b. "Public Opinion and Nigerian Foreign Policy Under the Military." In Gabriel O. Olusanya and R. A. Akindele, editors, *The Structure and Processes of Foreign Policy Making and Implementation in Nigeria, 1960–1990.* Lagos: Nigerian Institute of International Affairs, pp. 194–211.

Aminu, A. L. 1986. "Nigeria's Defense Preparedness and Planning." *Nigerian Journal of International Affairs,* vol. 12, nos. 1 and 2, pp. 77–87.

Amuwo, Kunle. 1990. "Resumption of Diplomatic Relations with Gabon, Cote d'lvore, Zambia and Tanzania after the 1967–1970 Nigerian Civil War." In Gabriel O. Olusanya and R. A. Akindele, editors, *The Structure and Processes of Foreign Policy Making and Implementation in Nigeria, 1960–1990.* Lagos: Nigerian Institute of International Affairs, pp. 306–21.

Anderson, Paul A. 1987. "What Do Decision Makers Do When They Make a Foreign Policy Decision? The Implications for the Comparative Study of Foreign Policy." In Charles F. Hermann, Charles W. Kegley, Jr., and James N. Rosenau, editors, *New Directions in the Study of Foreign Policy.* Boston: Allen and Unwin, pp. 285–308.

Anglin, Douglis G. 1964. "Nigeria: Political Non-alignment and Economic Alignment." *Journal of Modern African Studies,* vol. 2, no. 2, 1964, pp. 247–64.

Arisbisala, Femi. 1986a. "Nigeria and West Germany." In G. O. Olusanya and R. A. Akindele, editors, *Nigeria's External Relations: The First Twenty-Five Years.* Ibadan: University Press Limited, pp. 308–18.

———. 1986b. "Nigeria in OPEC: The Weakest Link in the Cartel Chair." In G. O. Olusanya and R. A. Akindele, editors, *Nigeria's External Relations: The First Twenty-Five Years.* Ibadan: University Press Limited, pp. 110–25.

Asobie, H. Assisi. 1986. "Nigeria and the Non-Aligned Movement." In G. O. Olusanya and R. A. Akindele, editors, *Nigeria's External Relations: The First Twenty-Five Years.* Ibadan: University Press Limited, pp. 141–64.

———. 1990. Asobie, H. Assisi, "Decision-Making Models Revisited: An Analysis of the Application of Theories and Models of Foreign Policy Decision-Making to the Study of Nigeria's Foreign Policy." In Gabriel O. Olusanya and R. A. Akindele, editors, *The Structure and Processes of Foreign Policy Making and Implementation in Nigeria, 1960–1990.* Lagos: Nigerian Institute of International Affairs, pp. 3–52.

Ate, Bassey E. 1985. "A Note on the Superpower and African Security." *Nigerian Journal of International Affairs,* vol. 11, no. 2, pp. 62–67.

———. 1990. "Personality, the Role Theory, Structural Adjustment Programme and Policy-Making in Nigeria's Foreign Relations, 1985–1987: Focus on the 'Lagos Forum'" In Gabriel O. Olusanya and R. A. Akindele, editors, *The Structure and Processes of Foreign Policy Making and Implementation in Nigeria, 1960–1990.* Lagos: Nigerian Institute of International Affairs, 1990, pp. 446–65.

The Atlanta Journal/The Atlanta Constitution, 26 May 1997.

———. 29 May 1997.

———. 15 February 1998.

———. 11 March 1998.

Ayeni, Victor. 1986. "Nigeria's Ombudsman System: A Literature Review." *ODU: A Journal of West African Studies,* new series, no. 29, pp. 138–53.

Ayodele, A. Sesan. 1989. "International Economic Security." *Nigerian Journal of Policy and Strategy,* vol. 4, no. 2, pp. 140–57.

Balogun, Ola. 1986. *Cultural Policies as an Instrument of External Image-Building: A Blueprint for Nigeria.* Lagos: Nigerian Institute of International Affairs.

Banjo, A. O. 1986. *Nigerian Institute of International Affairs, 1961–1986: The Story So Far.* Lagos: Nigerian Institute of International Affairs.

Biersteker, Thomas J. 1989. *Reaching Agreement with the IMF: The Nigerian Negotiations, 1983–1986 (Pew Case Studies in International Affairs: Case 205).* Washington, D.C.: Pew Case Studies Center, Institute for the Study of Diplomacy, Georgetown University.

Chilaka, Uche, and George, Imanyi. 1989. "The Use of Educational Technology in Management Training in Nigeria." *Nigerian Management Review: A Journal of the Centre for Management Development.* vol. 4, no. 204, pp. 213–17.

Diplomat. January/February 1995.

Dlakwa, Haruna Dantaro. 1992. "Salient Features of the 1988 Civil Service Reforms in Nigeria." *Public Administration and Development.* vol. 12, no. 3, pp. 297–311.

Dougherty, James E., and Robert L. Pfaltzgrarff, Jr. 1981. *Contending Theories of International Relations: A Comprehensive Survey.* New York: Harper and Row Publishers.

East, Maurice A., Stephen A. Salmore, and Charles F. Hermann editors. 1978. *Why Nations Act: Theoretical Perspectives for Comparative Foreign Policy Studies.* Beverly Hills, Sage Publications.

Ebo, C. 1989. "The Structure of Local Government in Nigeria: A Brief Historical Review." *The Nigerian Journal of Local Government Studies.* vol. 3, no. 1, pp. 127–38.

Ebony. February 1990.

Ede, Oscar O. B.1986. "Nigeria and Francophone Africa." In G. O. Olusanya and R. A. Akindele, editors, *Nigeria's External Relations: The First Twenty-Five Years.* Ibadan: University Press Limited, pp. 176–95.

Eleazu, Uma O. circa 1979. *Think Tanks and National Development.* Lagos: Nigerian Institute of International Affairs.

The Europa World Year Book 1982: A World Survey, Volume Two. 1982. London: Europa Publications.

The Europa World Year Book 1983: A World Survey, Volume 2. 1983. London: Europa Publications.

Eze, Osita C. 1986. "Nigeria and South-South Cooperation." In G. O. Olusanya and R. A. Akindele, editors, *Nigeria's External Relations: The First Twenty-Five Years.* Ibadan: University Press Limited, pp. 165–75.

Ezenwe, Uka 1981. "Reflections on the Economic Community of West African States." *The Nigerian Journal of Economic and Social Studies.* vol. 23, no. 2, pp. 187–208.

Falola, Toyin, and Julius Ihonvbere. 1985. *The Rise and Fall of Nigeria's Second Republic 1979–84.* London: Zed Books.

Fawole, W. Alade. 1981–1983. "Regional Interference and the Internationalisation of the Chadian Civil War." *Nigerian Journal of International Studies.* Vols. 5–7, pp. 94–102.

Gambari, Ibrahim Agboola. 1975. "Nigeria and the World: A Growing Internal Stability, Wealth, and External Influence." *Journal of International Affairs.* vol. 29, no. 2, pp. 155–69.

———. 1989. *Theory and Reality in Foreign Policy Making: Nigeria after the Second Republic.* Atlantic Highlands, N.J.: Humanities Press International.

Garba, Joe. 1987. *Diplomatic Soldiering: Nigerian Foreign Policy, 1975–1979.* Ibadan: Spectrum.

Gboyega, Alex. 1985. "The Notion of Viability in Nigerian Local Government Study: A Comment." *Nigerian Journal of Administrative Science.* vol. 2, no. 1, pp. 41–50.

Haley, P. Edward. 1984. *Quaddafi and the United States since 1969.* New York: Praeger.

Halliru, Suleiman, "Some Observations on Nigeria-Japan Economic Relations." *The Farfaru Journal of Multi-Disciplinary Studies.* vol. 2, nos. 1 and 2, pp. 101–10.

Halperin, M. H. 1974. *Bureaucratic Politics and Foreign Policy.* Washington, D.C.: Brookings.

Henderson, Robert D'A. 1981. "Nigeria: A Future Nuclear Power?" *Orbis.* vol. 25, no. 2, pp. 409–23.

Hermann, Charles F. 1978. "Decision Structure and Process Influences on Foreign Policy." In Maurice A. East, Stephen A. Salmore, and Charles F. Hermann, editors, *Why Nations Act: Theoretical Perspectives for Comparative Foreign Policy Studies*. Beverly Hills, California: Sage Publications, pp. 69–102.

Hermann, Charles F., Charles W. Kegley, Jr., and James N. Rosenau, editors. 1987. *New Directions in the Study of Foreign Policy*. Boston: Allen and Unwin.

Hermann, Margaret G., Charles F. Hermann, and Joe D. Hagan. 1987. "How Decision Units Shape Foreign Policy Behavior." In Charles F. Hermann, Charles W. Kegley, Jr., and James N. Rosenau, editors, *New Directions in the Study of Foreign Policy*. Boston: Allen and Unwin, pp. 309–36.

Hilsman, Roger. 1987. *The Politics of Policy Making in Defense and Foreign Affairs: Conceptual Models and Bureaucratic Politics*. Englewood Cliffs, N.J.: 1987.

Idang, Gordon J. 1973. *Nigeria: Internal Politics and Foreign Policy 1960–1966*. Ibadan: Ibadan University Press.

Igweonwu, C. I. 1985. "The Economic Component of the Nation's Foreign Policy Formulation: A Neglected Issue?" *Nigerian Forum*. vol. 5, nos. 5 and 6, pp. 106–15.

Ikporukpo, C. O. 1984. "Politics and Regional Planning: A Niger Delta Case Study." *AMAN: Journal of Society, Culture and Environment*. vol. 4, no. 1, pp. 29–38.

Inamete, Ufot B. 1990. "Nigeria's IMF Loan Arrangement Decision-Making (Shagari to Babangida Administrations) and Decision-Making Theories." *The Australian Journal of Politics and History*. vol. 36, no. 1, pp. 39–50.

———. 1993. "The Conceptual Framework of Nigerian Foreign Policy." *The Australian Journal of Politics and History*. vol. 39, no. 1, pp. 72–87.

International Herald Tribune, 7–8 February 1998.

International Research Centers Directory, 1994–1995. 1994. Detroit: Gale Research Inc.

The Jamaican Weekly Gleaner. 23 January 1989.

———. 7 August 1989.

———. 14 August 1989.

———. 9 October 1989.

Janis, I. L. 1972. *Victims of Group Think*. Boston: Houghton Mifflin.

Johnson, Segun. 1990. "Wanted: Democratization of Foreign Policy-Making Processes in Nigeria." In Gabriel O. Olusanya and R. A. Akindele, editors, *The Structure and Processes of Foreign Policy Making and Implementation in Nigeria, 1960–1990*. Lagos: Nigerian Institute of International Affairs, pp. 507–23.

Kegley, Charles W., Jr. 1987. "Decision Regimes and the Comparative Study of Foreign Policy." In Charles F. Hermann, Charles W. Kegley, Jr., and James N. Rosenau, editors, *New Directions in the Study of Foreign Policy*. Boston: Allen and Unwin, pp. 247–68.

Macebuh, Stanley. 1979. "Minimum Government by Shagari." *West Africa*. 12 November, p. 2077.

Newswatch. 13 October 1986.

———. 20 October 1986.

———. 1 December 1986.

———. 12 January 1987.

———. 27 November 1989.

———. 9 April 1990.

———. 16 July 1990.

———. 24 May 1993.

———. 23 August 1993.
———. 15 November 1993.
———. 6 December 1993.
———. 28 March 1994.
———. 3 April 1995.
———. 10 April 1995.
———. 24 April 1995.
———. 1 May 1995.
———. 15 May 1995.
———. 29 May 1995.
———. 14 August 1995.
———. 25 September 1995.
———. 2 October 1995.
———. 30 October 1995.
———. 20 November 1995.
———. 27 November 1995.
———. 4 December 1995.
———. 11 December 1995.
———. 18 December 1995.
———. 27 October 1997.
———. 10 November 1997.
———. 24 November 1997.
———. 8 December 1997.
———. 15 December 1997.
———. 19 January 1998.
———. 23 February 1998.
———. 2 March 1998.
———. 9 March 1998.
———. 23 March 1998.
———. 30 March 1998.
———. 4 May 1998.
———. 11 May 1998.
———. 22 June 1998.
———. 13 July 1998.
———. 10 August 1998.
———. 31 August 1998.
———. 7 September 1998.
———. 5 October 1998.
———. 12 October 1998.
———. 19 October 1998.
———. 16 November 1998.
———. 28 December 1998.
———. 4 January 1999.
———. 1 February 1999.

———. 8 February 1999.
———. 28 June 1999.
———. 12 July 1999.
Newswatch Who's Who in Nigeria. 1990. Lagos: Newswatch Communications Limited.
Newsweek (Washington, D.C., edition), 2 September 1991.
The New York Times. 23 November 1994.
———. 26 May 1995.
———. 2 September 1995.
———. 29 November 1996.
———. 27 March 1997.
———. 26 May 1997.
———. 17 July 1997.
———. 26 September 1997.
———. 22 July 1997.
———. 24 July 1997.
———. 26 September 1997.
———. 17 October 1997.
———. 24 October 1997.
———. 14 February 1998.
———. 15 February 1998.
———. 16 February 1998.
———. 17 February 1998.
———. 18 February 1998.
———. 19 February 1998.
———. 23 March 1998.
———. 24 March 1998.
———. 14 June 1998.
———. 25 September 1998.
———. 26 September 1998.
Nigeria: A Country Study. 1992. Washington, D.C.: Headquarters, Department of the Army.
Nigeria News Update. 22 March–4 April 1994.
———. 14–27 April 1994.
———. 28 April–11 May 1994.
———. 20 May–3 June 1994.
———. 4–17 June 1994.
Nigerian Journal of International Affairs. 1984. Vol. 10, no. 2, 1984.
Nigerian Record. May 1995.
Nweke, G. Aforka. 1983. "Reciprocity in African International Economic Relations." *Nigerian Journal of International Affairs.* vol. 9, no. 1, pp. 18–41.
Nweke, G. Aforka. 1986. "The Domestic Structure and Processes of Nigeria's Foreign Policy." In G. O. Olusanya and R. A. Akindele, editors, *Nigeria's External Relations: The First Twenty-Five Years.* Ibadan: University Press Limited, pp. 33–58.
———. 1990. "Policy Response to the May 1981 Nigeria-Cameroun Border Crisis." In Gabriel O. Olusanya and R. A. Akindele, editors, *The Structure and Processes of Foreign*

Policy Making and Implementation in Nigeria, 1960–1990. Lagos: Nigerian Institute of International Affairs, 1990, pp. 398–420.

Nwoke, Chibuzo N. 1990. "Nigeria's Decision to Initiate the Formation of the African Petroleum Producers' Association (APPA)." In Gabriel O. Olusanya and R. A. Akindele, editors, *The Structure and Processes of Foreign Policy Making and Implementation in Nigeria, 1960–1990.* Lagos: Nigerian Institute of International Affairs, pp. 479–87.

Nwokedi, Emeka. 1985. "Sub-Regional Security and Nigerian Foreign Policy." *African Affairs.* vol. 84, no. 335, pp. 195–209.

———. 1986. "Nigeria and France." In G. O. Olusanya and R. A. Akindele, editors, *Nigeria's External Relations: The First Twenty-Five Years.* Ibadan: University Press Limited, pp. 284–93.

Ofoegbu, Ray. 1979. "Foreign Policy and Military Rule." In Oyeleye Oyediran, editor, *Nigerian Government and Politics under Military Rule, 1966–1979.* New York: St. Martin's Press, pp. 124–49.

———. 1990. Ofoegbu, Ray, "The Structure and Process of Foreign Policy Formulation and Implementation in Nigeria: A Study of the Ministry of External Affairs." In Gabriel O. Olusanya and R. A. Akindele, editors, *The Structure and Processes of Foreign Policy Making and Implementation in Nigeria, 1960–1990.* Lagos: Nigerian Institute of International Affairs, pp. 72–105.

Ogunbadejo, Oye. 1978. "Ideology and Pragmatism: The Soviet Role in Nigeria, 1960–1977." *Orbis.* vol. 25, no. 4, pp. 803–30.

———. 1980. "Foreign Policy Under Nigeria's Presidential System." *The Round Table.* no. 280, pp. 401–8.

———. 1984. "Africa's Nuclear Capability." *The Journal of Modern African Studies.* vol. 22, no. 1, pp. 19–43.

———. 1986. "Nigeria and the Soviet Union, 1960–1985." In G. O. Olusanya and R. A. Akindele, editors, *Nigeria's External Relations: The First Twenty-Five Years.* Ibadan: University Limited, pp. 249–73.

———. 1988. "Nigerian-Soviet Relations, 1960–87." *African Affairs.* vol. 87, no. 346, pp. 83–104.

———. 1986. "Foreign Service: The Nigerian Ambassador and His Tasks." *Nigerian Journal of International Affairs.* vol. 12, nos. 1 and 2, pp. 162–72.

Ogunbambi, R. O. 1981. "Nigerian-Soviet Dialogue: The Soviet in Perspective." *Nigerian Forum.* vol. 1, no. 5, pp. 173–78.

Ogundowole, E. Kola. 1989. "National Ideological Orientation: A Methodological Approach." *The Nigerian Journal of Philosophy.* vol. 9, nos. 1 and 2, pp. 87–95.

Ogwu, U. Joy. 1981. "Nigeria and Brazil: Perspectives on a Dialogue." *Nigerian Forum.* vol. 1, no. 5, pp. 167–72.

———. 1986. "New Dimensions in Nigeria's Foreign Policy Towards Latin America." *Nigerian Journal of International Affairs.* vol. 12, nos. 1 and 2, pp. 108–22.

Ojo, Olatunde J. B. 1976. "Commercial Representation in Nigeria's Overseas Missions: Its Nature, Functions and Problems." *Nigerian Journal of International Affairs.* vol. 2, nos. 1 and 2, pp. 50–66.

———. 1980. "Nigeria and the Formation of ECOWAS." *International Organization.* vol. 34, no. 4, pp. 571–604.

———. 1981. "Continuity and Change in Nigeria's Non-Aligned Foreign Policy." *Nigerian Journal of International Affairs.* vol. 7, nos. 1 and 2, pp. 31–53.

———. 1990a. "The Making and Termination of the Anglo-Nigerian Defense Pact." In Gabriel O. Olusanya and R. A. Akindele, editors, *The Structure and Processes of Foreign*

Policy Making and Implementation in Nigeria, 1960–1990. Lagos: Nigerian Institute of International Affairs, pp. 255–74.

———. 1990b. "Sponsorship and Membership of the Economic Community of West African States (ECOWAS)." In Gabriel O. Olusanya and R. A. Akindele, editors, *The Structure and Processes of Foreign Policy Making and Implementation in Nigeria, 1960–1990.* Lagos: Nigerian Institute of International Affairs, pp. 346–63.

Ojo, Olusola. 1986. "Nigeria and Israel." In G. O. Olusanya and R. A. Akindele, editors, *Nigeria's External Relations: The First Twenty-Five Years.* Ibadan: University Press Limited, pp. 436–50.

Olowu, Dele. 1988. "Local Government and Grassroot Democracy in Nigeria's Third Republic." *Nigerian Journal of Policy and Strategy.* vol. 3, no. 2, pp. 78–97.

Olukoshi, Adebayo O. 1990a. "The Long Road to Fez: An Examination of Nigeria's Decision to Become a Full Member of the Organization of Islamic Conference (OIC)." In Gabriel O. Olusanya and R. A. Akindele, editors, *The Structure and Processes of Foreign Policy Making and Implementation in Nigeria, 1960–1990.* Lagos: Nigerian Institute of International Affairs, pp. 488–504.

———. 1990b. Olukoshi, Adebayo O., "Sports and Foreign Policy: Nigeria's Decision to Boycott the 1986 Edinburgh Commonwealth Games Revisited." In Gabriel O. Olusanya and R. A. Akindele, editors, *The Structure and Processes of Foreign Policy Making and Implementation in Nigeria, 1960–1990.* Lagos: Nigerian Institute of International Affairs, pp. 466–78.

Olusanya, G. O. 1984. "Nigeria and the World Economy." *Nigerian Journal of International Affairs.* vol. 10, no. 2, pp. 55–66.

———. 1990. "Research and Public Policy: An Explanatory Note on the Contribution of the Nigerian Institute of International Affairs to the Making of Nigeria's Foreign Policy." In Gabriel O. Olusanya and R. A. Akindele, editors, *The Structure and Processes of Foreign Policy Making and Implementation in Nigeria, 1960–1990.* Lagos: Nigerian Institute of International Affairs, pp. 233–42.

Olusanya, G. O., and R. A. Akindele. 1986a. "The Fundamentals of Nigeria's Foreign Policy and External Economic Relations." In G. O. Olusanya and R. A. Akindele, editors, *Nigeria's External Relations: The First Twenty-Five Years.* Ibadan: University Press Limited, pp. 1–32.

———. editors. 1986b. *Nigeria's External Relations: The First Twenty-Five Years.* Ibadan: University Press Limited.

———. editors. 1990. *The Structure and Processes of Foreign Policy Making and Implementation in Nigeria, 1960–1990.* Lagos: Nigerian Institute of International Affairs.

Onajide, M. O. 1989. "Budgetary and Financial Management in Local Government." *Nigerian Journal of Local Government Studies.* vol. 3, no. 1, pp. 33–38.

Orobator, S. E. 1983. "The Nigerian Civil War and the Invasion of Czechoslovakia." *African Affairs.* vol. 82, no. 329, pp. 201–14.

Owoeye, Jide. 1986. "Nigeria and China." In G. O. Olusanya and R. A. Akindele, editors, *Nigeria's External Relations: The First Twenty-Five Years.* Ibadan: University Press Limited, pp. 294–307.

Peters, Jimi. 1986. "Intelligence: Its Role and Future in Nigeria's External Relations." *Nigerian Journal of International Affairs.* vol. 12, nos. 1 and 2, pp. 151–61.

Peters, Jimi, and A. L. Aminu. 1986. "The Armed Forces and Nigeria's Foreign Policy: Reflections on Past Experiences and a Note on the Future." *Nigerian Journal of International Affairs.* vol. 12, nos. 1 and 2, pp. 88–99.

Powell, Charles A., Helen E. Purkitt, and James W. Dyson. 1987. "Opening the Black Box: Cognitive Processing and Optimal Choice in Foreign Policy Decision Making." In

Charles F. Hermann, Charles W. Kegley, Jr., and James N. Rosenau, editors, *New Directions in the Study of Foreign Policy.* Boston: Allen and Unwin, pp. 203–20.

Soremekun, Kayode. 1990. "Nigeria's Membership in the Organization of Petroleum Exporting Countries (OPEC)." In Gabriel O. Olusanya and R. A. Akindele, editors, *The Structure and Process of Foreign Policy Making and Implementation in Nigeria, 1960–1990.* Lagos: Nigerian Institute of International Affairs, pp. 294–305.

Sotunmbi, Abiodun Olufemi. 1981 *Nigeria's Recognition of the MPLA Government in Angola: A Case Study in Decision-Making and Implementation.* Lagos: Nigerian Institute of International Affairs.

———. 1990. "From Support to a Government of National Unity to a Pro-MPLA Policy in Angola in 1975." In Gabriel O. Olusanya and R. A. Akindele, editors, *The Structure and Processes of Foreign Policy Making and Implementation in Nigeria, 1960–1990.* Lagos: Nigerian Institute of International Affairs, pp. 364–74.

St. Petersburg Times. 14 February 1998.

———. 16 February 1998.

———. 19 February 1998.

———. 11 March 1998.

Sunday Times. 23 April 1989.

Tallahassee Democrat. 15 May 1994.

———. 16 February 1998.

———. 11 March 1998.

———. 9 July 1998.

Tawari, O. C. 1985. "An Analysis of the Organizational Structure and the Decision-Making Process in Nigerian Universities." *Nigerian Journal of Administrative Science.* vol. 2, no. 1, pp. 62–76.

Theweek. 19 August 1996.

———. 23 September 1996.

———. 27 January 1997.

———. 3 March 1997.

———. 10 March 1997.

———. 17 March 1997.

———. 31 March 1997.

———. 7 April 1997.

———. 14 April 1997.

———. 21 April 1997.

———. 5 May 1997.

———. 26 May 1997.

———. 2 June 1997.

———. 9 June 1997.

———. 7 July 1997.

———. 28 July 1997.

———. 4 August 1997.

———. 11 August 1997.

———. 18 August 1997.

———. 25 August 1997.

———. 8 September 1997.
———. 24 November 1997.
———. 15 December 1997.
———. 16 March 1998.
———. 23 March 1998.
———. 1 June 1998.
———. 15 June 1998.
———. 13 July 1998.
———. 20 July 1998.
———. 10 August 1998.
———. 7 September 1998.
———. 28 September 1998.
———. 9 November 1998.
———. 23 November 1998.
Thisweek, 20 October 1986.
Udoidem, S. I. 1989. "Prudence, Law and Morality." *Ogele: Journal of the Social Sciences and Humanities.* vol. 4, no. 1, pp. 109–17.
Viotti, Paul R., and Mark V. Kauppi. 1987. *International Relations Theory: Realism, Pluralism, Globalism.* New York: Macmillan Publishing Company.
Vogt, M. A. 1981. "Dialogue with the Scandinavians." *Nigerian Forum.* vol. 1, no. 5, pp. 179–83.
The Wall Street Journal. 23 November 1994.
———. 31 May 1995.
The Washington Post National Weekly Edition. 2–8 December 1996.
West Africa. 15 October 1979.
———. 22 October 1979.
———. 12 November 1979.
———. 26 September 1983.
———. 10 October 1983.
———. 5 December 1983.
———. 9 January 1984.
———. 6 February 1984.
———. 27 February 1984.
———. 26 March 1984.
———. 9 April 1984.
———. 16 July 1984.
———. 15 October 1984.
———. 22 October 1984.
———. 10 December 1984.
———. 17 December 1984.
———. 7 January 1985.
———. 4 February 1985.
———. 11 March 1985.
———. 15 April 1985.

———. 22 April 1985.
———. 27 May 1985.
———. 3 June 1985.
———. 29 July 1985.
———. 5 August 1985.
———. 5–11 September 1988.
———. 17–23 October 1988.
———. 22–28 May 1989.
———. 5–11 June 1989.
———. 3–9 July 1989.
———. 18–24 September 1989.
———. 9–15 October 1989.
———. 4–10 December 1989.
———. 22–28 January 1990.
———. 18–24 June 1990.
———. 2–8 July 1990.
———. 10–16 September 1990.
———. 8–14 October 1990.
———. 24 December 1990–6 January 1991.
———. 8–14 April 1991.
———. 20–26 May 1991.
———. 3–9 June 1991.
———. 10–16 June 1991.
———. 26 August–1 September 1991.
———. 23–29 September 1991.
———. 2–8 December 1991.
———. 23 December 1991–5 January 1992.
———. 6–12 January 1992.
———. 17–23 February 1992.
———. 2–8 March 1992.
———. 9–15 March 1992.
———. 23–29 March 1992.
———. 6–12 April 1992.
———. 20–26 April 1992.
———. 4–10 May 1992.
———. 25–31 May 1992.
———. 22–28 June 1992.
———. 17–23 August 1992.
———. 31 August–6 September 1992.
———. 7–13 December 1992.
———. 21–27 December 1992.
———. 28 December 1992–10 January 1993.
———. 25–31 January 1993.
———. 1–7 February 1993.

———. 15–21 February 1993.
———. 22–28 February 1993.
———. 8–14 March 1993.
———. 15–21 March 1993.
———. 29 March–4 April 1993.
———. 24–30 May 1993.
———. 31 May–6 June 1993.
———. 6–12 September 1993
———. 22–28 November 1993.
———. 29 November–5 December 1993.
———. 6–12 December 1993.
———. 17–23 January 1994.
———. 21–27 February 1994.
———. 28 February–6 March 1994.
———. 7–13 March 1994.
———. 14–20 March 1994.
———. 21–27 March 1994.
———. 28 March–3 April 1994.
———. 11–17 April 1994.
———. 23–29 May 1994.
———. 4–10 July 1994.
———. 18–24 July 1994.
———. 22–28 August 1994.
———. 5–11 September 1994.
———. 12–18 September 1994.
———. 19–25 September 1994.
———. 26 September–2 October 1994.
———. 7–13 November 1994.
———. 14–20 November 1994.
———. 28 November–4 December 1994.
———. 12–18 December 1994.
———. 19–25 December 1994.
———. 26 December 1994–8 January 1995.
———. 16–22 January 1995.
———. 24–29 January 1995.
———. 30 January–5 February 1995.
———. 27 February–5 March 1995.
———. 20–26 March 1995.
———. 27 March–2 April 1995.
———. 3–9 April 1995.
———. 10–16 April 1995.
———. 17–23 April 1995.
———. 26 January–1 February 1998.
———. 16–22 February 1998.

———. 23 February–1 March 1998.
———. 2–15 March 1998.
———. 16–29 March 1998.
———. 4–17 May 1998.
———. 3–16 August 1998.
Wiarda, Howard J. 1990. *Foreign Policy without Illusions: How Foreign Policy Works and Fails to Work in the United States.* Glenview, Ill.: Scott Foresman/Little Brown Higher Education.

Index

Abacha, Sani, 133, 209–10, 237, 240–80
Abiola, M. K. O., 273, 282, 285
Abubakar, Abdusalami, 272, 281–84
Abubakar, Iya, 96–97
Adedeji, Adbayo, 66
Adefuye, Adebowale, 190–91, 197–99
Ahmed, Kabir, 239
Ahmed, Tijani, 239
Aikhomu, Augustus, 136, 137, 161–67
Akhigbe, Okhai, 281–82
Akinyemi, Bolaji, 94–96, 173, 177, 181–83, 192–93, 207, 209
Alhaji, Alhaji Abubakar, 249
Anglo-Nigerian Defense Pact, 23, 37
Angola, 66–68
Ani, Anthony, 422
Anyaoku, Emeka, 166, 185
Arikpo, Okoi, 53, 55
Armed Forces Ruling Council (AFRC), 139–46
Asiodu, Phillip Chinedo, 60
Audu, Ishaya, 112, 113
Ayinla, Jibril, 266–67, 282

Babangida, Ibrahim, 65, 136–236, 237
Balewa, Tafawa, 20–41
Bali, Domkat, 209, 210
Bamaiyi, Ishaya, 282
Bamali, Nuhu, 27
Bello, Ahmadu, 23–24, 38, 39
Biafra, 44–45, 54
Bokolor, Patrick, 112, 113
Britain, 54
Buhari, Muhammadu, 122–35

Cabinet, the, 24, 33–34, 35
Cabinet Office, the, 51, 80–81, 111–12, 125–26
Cameroun, 204, 246, 248, 256–54

Central Bank of Nigeria (CBN), 57, 116
Chad, Republic of, 77
China, 54
Civil War, 44–45, 48, 53, 54–56
Commerce, Ministry of, 116
Congo, Democratic Republic of (or Zaire), 29, 32
Czechoslovakia, 55

Daggash, Al-Amin, 282, 283
Dalhatu, Bashir, 239
Danjuma, Theophilus, 65
Defense, Ministry of, 28–30, 40, 55–56, 88–92, 114–15, 129, 209–20
Defense Intelligence Agency (DIA), 101–2, 221
Dikko, Umaru, 131–32
Directorate of Air Intelligence (DAI), 102, 221, 222
Directorate of Military Intelligence (DMI), 102, 221, 222
Directorate of Naval Intelligence (DAI), 102, 221, 222
Diya, Oladipo, 244–45
Dodan Barracks, 45–49, 51, 53, 69

Ebor, Okotie, 23
Economic Community of West African States (ECOWAS), 49, 55, 60–61, 98–99
ECOWAS Monitoring Group (ECOMOG), 159, 217–20, 238, 254–66
Economic Development, Ministry of, 56–57
Eduok, Nsikak, 267, 282
Ekwueme, Alex, 106
Elias, Taslim Olawale, 32
Equatorial Guinea, 204–5

Etete, Dan, 242
External Affairs, Ministry of (MEA), 21, 24–28, 36, 40–41, 47–61, 81–88, 112–14, 122–23, 175–209

Federal Executive Council (FEC), 49–50, 52–53, 79, 109, 124–25, 241
Finance, Ministry of, 30, 40, 56–57, 126
Foreign Affairs, Ministry of, 176, 239, 248–53
France, 39, 218–19, 253–54

Gambari, Ibrahim, 122, 133, 248–49, 251–52
Gana, Jerry, 269
Garba, Joseph, 68, 80–81, 87, 185
Germany, 54
Gowon, Yakubu, 44–61, 64
Gwarzo, Ismaila, 238–39, 247, 268

Hamma, Sule, 246

Ibrahim, Waziri, 23
Idiagbon, Tunde, 124, 131–35
Idris, Gidado, 246
Ikimi, Tom, 248, 249–51, 265, 276
Industries, Ministry of, 56–57
Information, Ministry of, 30, 32, 40–41, 58, 98
Inienger, John, 255
Internal Affairs, Ministry of, 117
Internal Affairs, Ministry of, 30, 130
Ironsi, J. T. U., 42–43
Iyalla, Joe, 52–53

Jamaica, 166–67

Kabbah, Tejan, 259–64, 266
Khobe, Maxwell, 283
Kingibe, Baba Gana, 251
Kouna, Ja'affa, 239

Liberia, 205, 217–18, 240, 248, 254–58
Lukman Rilwanu, 177, 181, 184, 185, 271

Malu, Victor, 256–58, 261
Marwa, Mohammed, 242
Mbadiwe, K. O., 21–22
Mbu, M. T., 28, 177, 181, 184–85
MPLA, 66–68
Muhammed, Murtala, 62–103

National Council of Nigerian Citizens (NCNC), 36, 38, 39
National Council of Ministers (NCM), 147–49
National Council of States (NCS), 62–65, 78–79, 109–11, 125, 149–53
National Defense Council (NDC), 109–11, 146–47
National Intelligence Agency (NIA), 101–2, 221, 239
National Security Council (NSC), 109–11, 146–47
Niger, Republic of, 239
Nigerian Institute for Policy and Strategic Studies (NIPSS), 96 117, 130, 154–56, 229
Nigerian Institute of International Affairs (NIIA), 40, 58–59, 92–97, 117–18, 130, 229–31
Nigerian Institute of Social and Economic Research (NISER), 96, 229
Nigerian National Democratic party (NNDP), 36
Nigerian National Petroleum Corporation (NNPC), 47–58, 60, 100, 116
Nigerian Security Organization (NSO), 101, 117, 220–21
Nkrumah, Kwame, 22
Northern Peoples' Congress (NPC), 24, 36, 38, 39
Northern Elements Progressive Union (NEPU), 36, 39
Nwachukwu, Ike, 177, 181, 183–84
Nyerere, Julius, 29

Obasanjo, Olusegun, 62–103, 185, 285–88
Ojukwu, Chukwemeka Odumegwu, 278–79
Okadigbo, Chuba, 108
Ombu, Victor, 278
Organization of African Unity (OAU), 33, 45, 49, 54–55
Organization of Islamic Conference (OIC), 140–45, 174, 187, 194–95
Organization of Petroleum Exporting Countries (OPEC), 44, 57–58, 60
Osibo, Babatunde, 254

Parliament, 35–38, 41, 42
Petroleum Resources, Ministry of, 57–58, 60

Presidency, the, 153–75, 241–48
Prime Minister, Office of the, 20–24, 38–41
Provisional Ruling Council (PRC), 240–41

Rafindadi, Mohammed, 133
Ribadu, Muhammadu, 23
Rimi, Abubakar, 242

Saleh, Aminu, 245–46
Sankoh, Foday, 259–61
Saro-Wiwa, Ken, 275–78
Shagari, Shehu, 104–21
Shelpidi, Timothy, 258
Shonekan, Ernest, 237–39, 240
Sierra Leone, 240, 248, 254, 258–66
South Africa, 33
Soviet Union, 54, 55–56
State Security Service (SSS), 102, 221
Sule, Maitama, 23
Supreme Military Council (SMC), 42, 45–46, 50, 62–68, 69, 70, 72, 123

Supreme Military Headquarters, 46–48, 123–24

Tanzania, 29
Taylor, Charles, 257–58
Technical Aid Corps (TAC), 173–74, 176–77, 182, 191–92

Ukiwe, Ebitu, 136, 161–63, 210
Umara, Mustapha, 239
United Nations, the, 45, 54
United States, the, 54, 71, 74, 273–74, 275
Usman, Abubakar, 112, 113

Wachuku, Jaja, 27, 38

Yadudu, Auwalu, 246
Yar'adua, Shehu, 65, 76
Yusuf, M. D., 66–67

Zimbabwe, 64, 73, 77